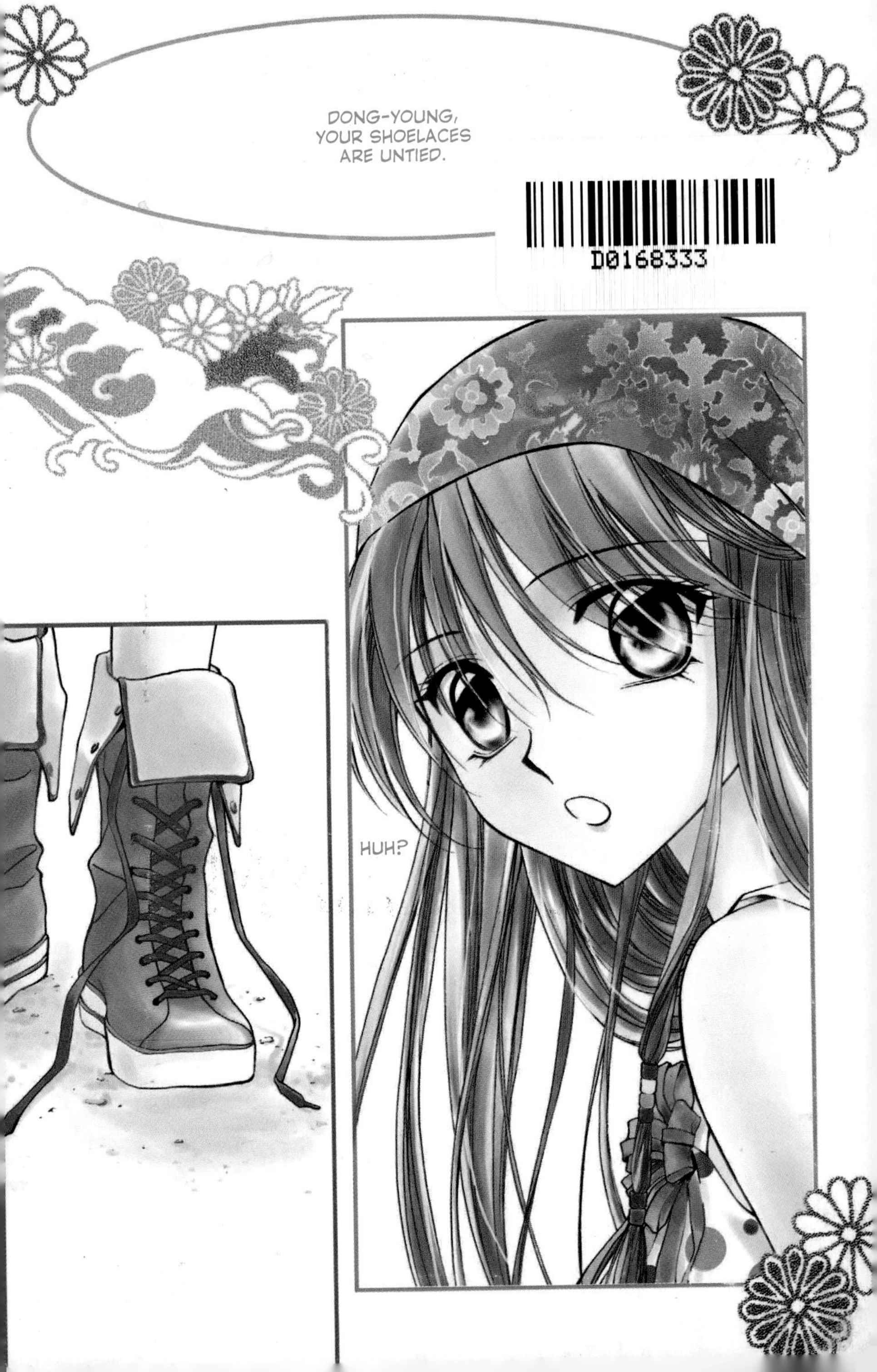
DONG-YOUNG, YOUR SHOELACES ARE UNTIED.
HUH?

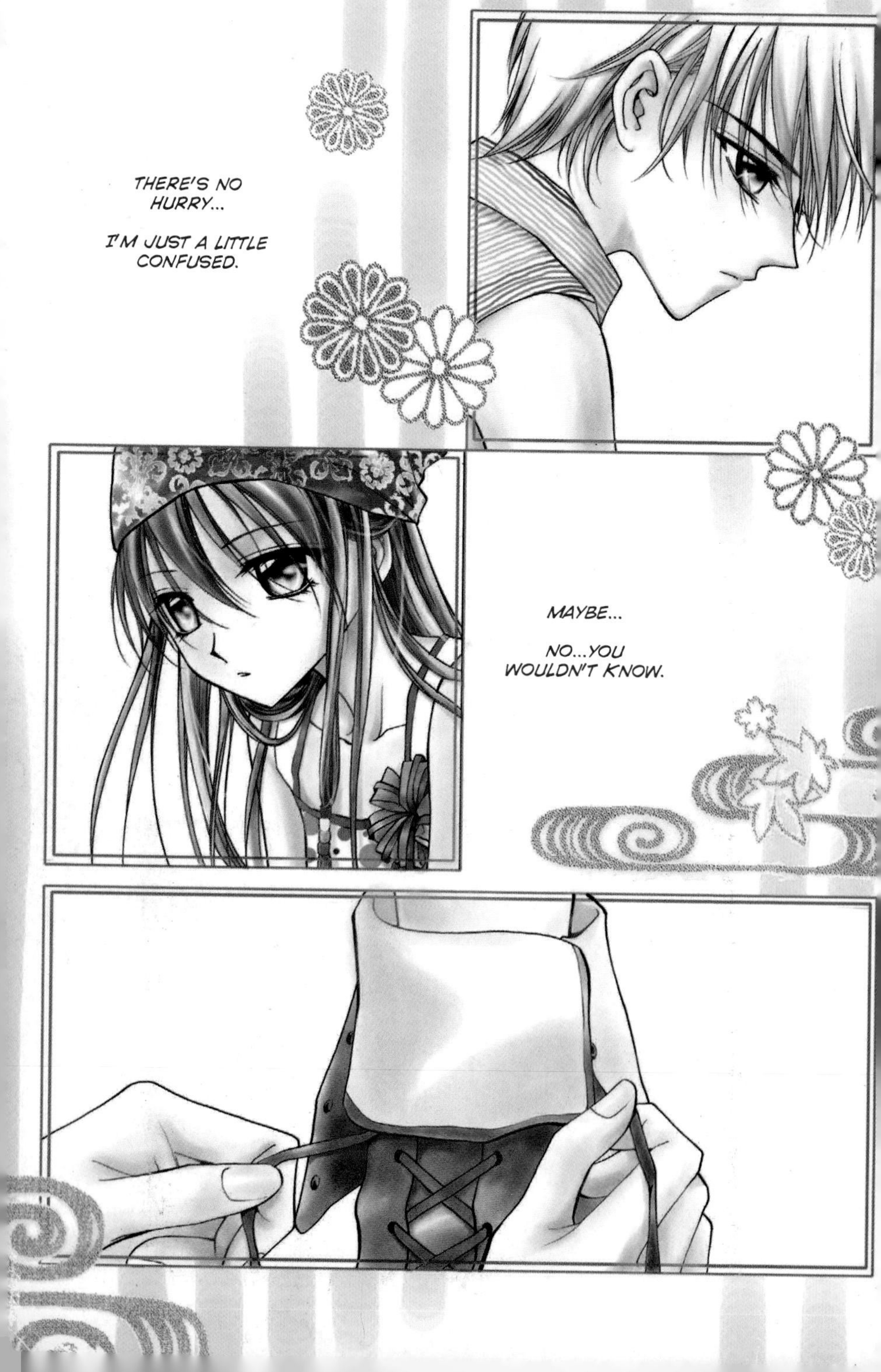
THERE'S NO HURRY...
I'M JUST A LITTLE CONFUSED.
MAYBE...
NO...YOU WOULDN'T KNOW.

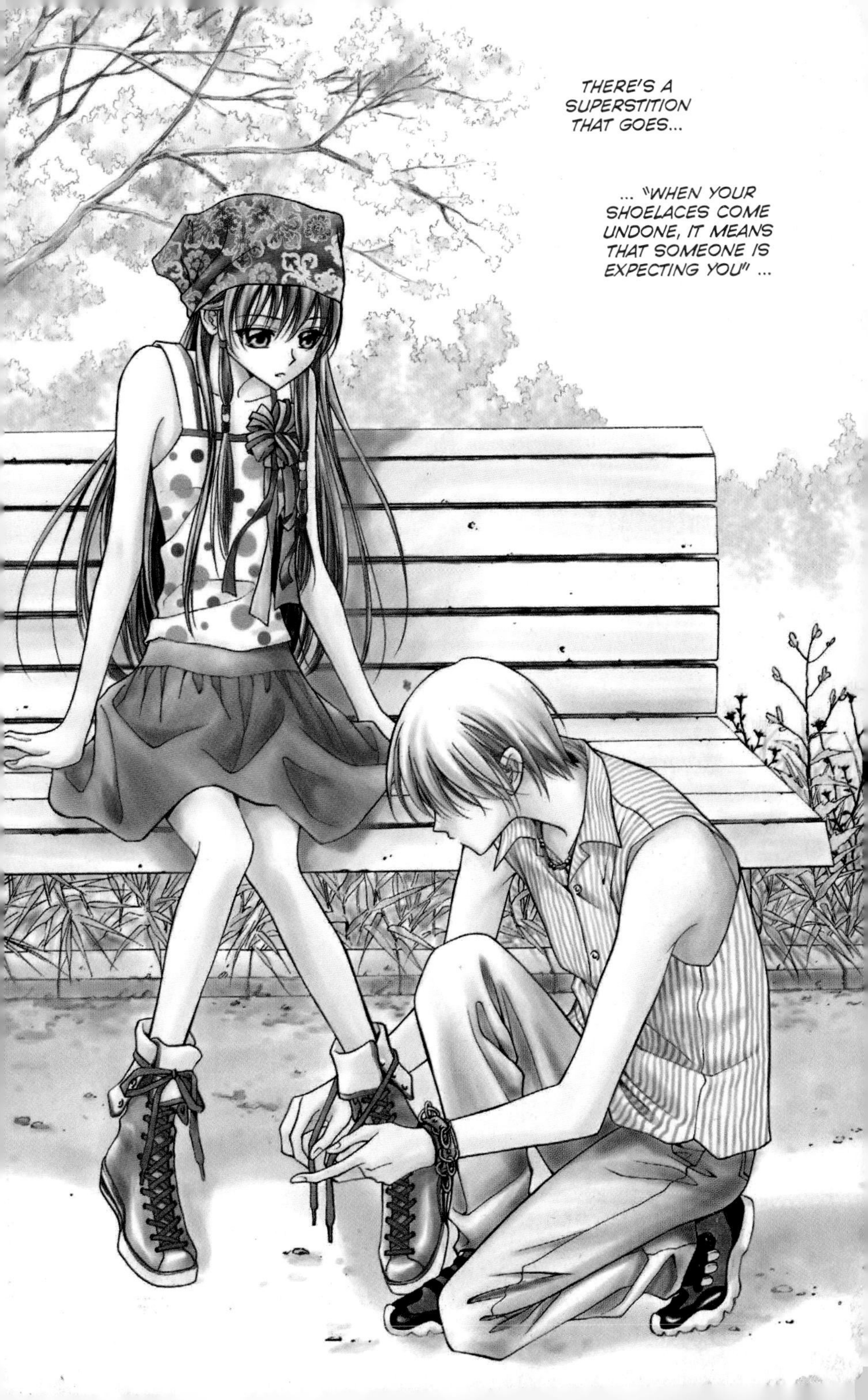
THERE'S A SUPERSTITION THAT GOES...
... "WHEN YOUR SHOELACES COME UNDONE, IT MEANS THAT SOMEONE IS EXPECTING YOU" ...

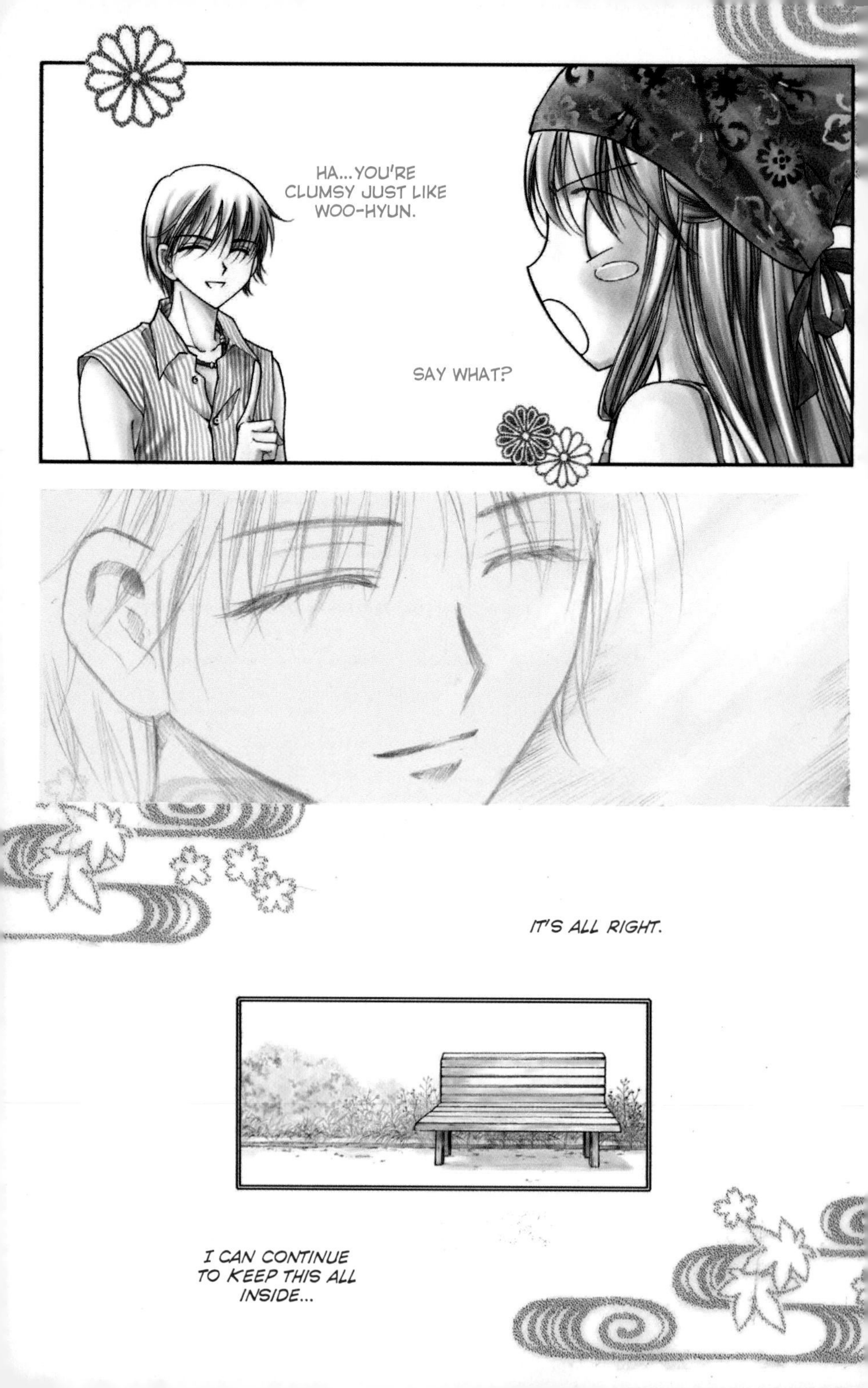
HA...YOU'RE CLUMSY JUST LIKE WOO-HYUN.
SAY WHAT?
IT'S ALL RIGHT.
I CAN CONTINUE TO KEEP THIS ALL INSIDE...

Angel Diary

vol.5

Kara · Lee YunHee

Yen Press

WORDS FROM THE CREATORS

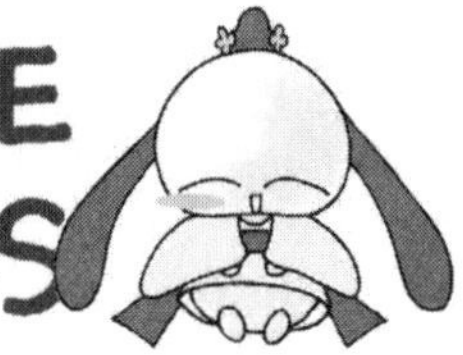

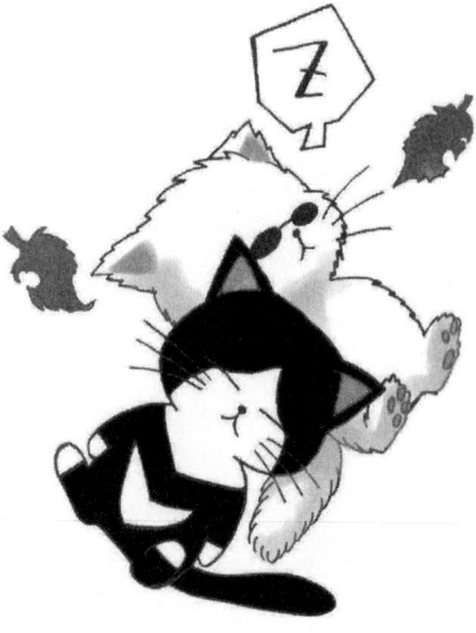
Z

Ah! We're at the midpoint of the story! It feels like we only started this yesterday... and even though it's the same amount of time from here until the end of the series, the future still feels so far away. -_-; Anyhow, we're done working on the first third of the next volume, so we'll see the end of this series soon if we keep it up. Then it's on to something new and exciting! ^^***

–Kara (Artists)

"Huh." I thought. "Volume 5 is here." Time really flies. There are lots of things that I want to do as well as have to do, but the days just fly by while I do nothing. Suddenly, a month passes. Someone please... hold back time~~~.

—Yun-Hee Lee (Writer)

CONTENTS

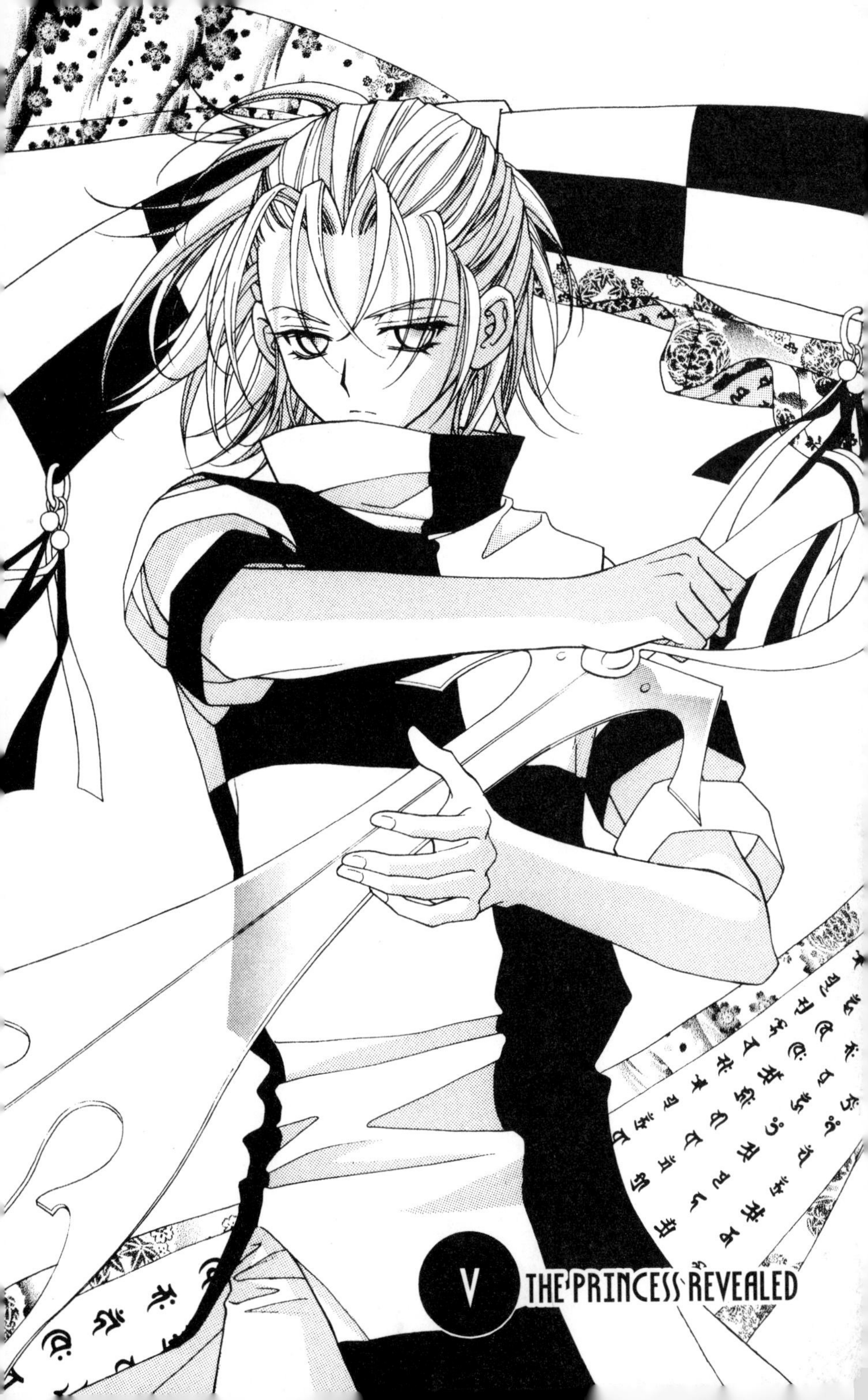
V
THE PRINCESS REVEALED

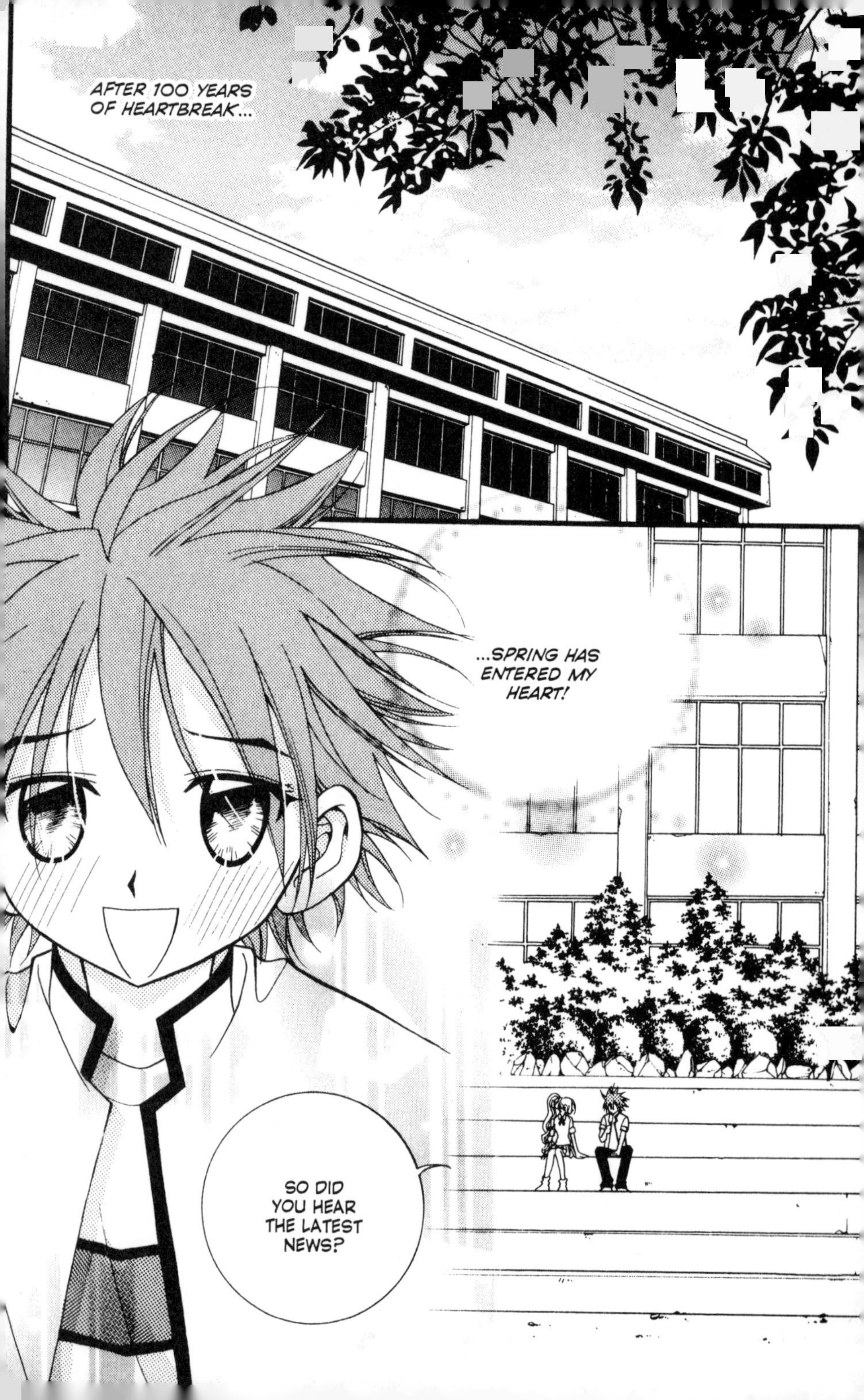
AFTER 100 YEARS OF HEARTBREAK...
...SPRING HAS ENTERED MY HEART!
SO DID YOU HEAR THE LATEST NEWS?

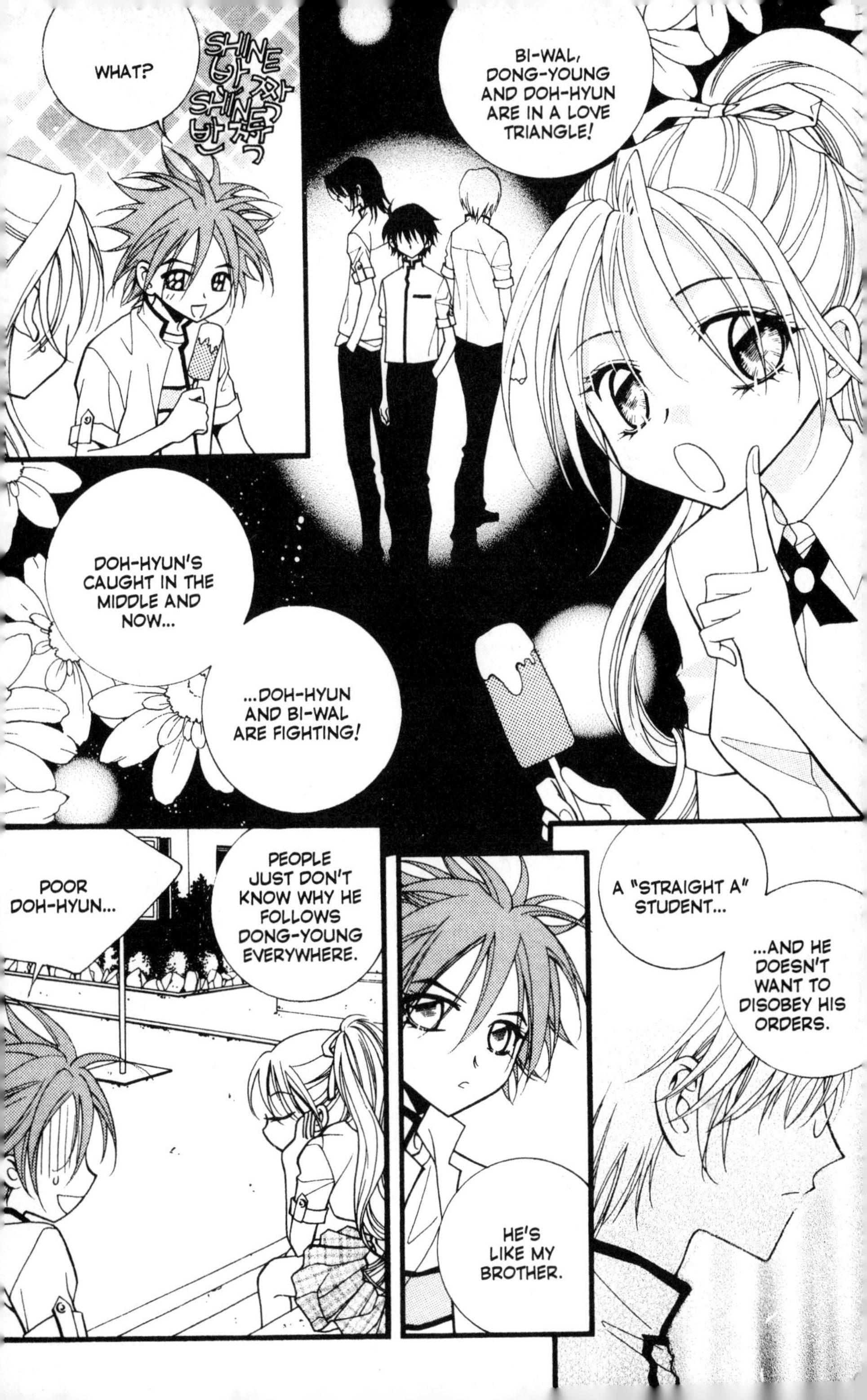
WHAT?
SHINE 반짝 SHINE 반짝
BI-WAL, DONG-YOUNG AND DOH-HYUN ARE IN A LOVE TRIANGLE!
DOH-HYUN'S CAUGHT IN THE MIDDLE AND NOW...
...DOH-HYUN AND BI-WAL ARE FIGHTING!
POOR DOH-HYUN...
PEOPLE JUST DON'T KNOW WHY HE FOLLOWS DONG-YOUNG EVERYWHERE.
HE'S LIKE MY BROTHER.
A "STRAIGHT A" STUDENT...
...AND HE DOESN'T WANT TO DISOBEY HIS ORDERS.

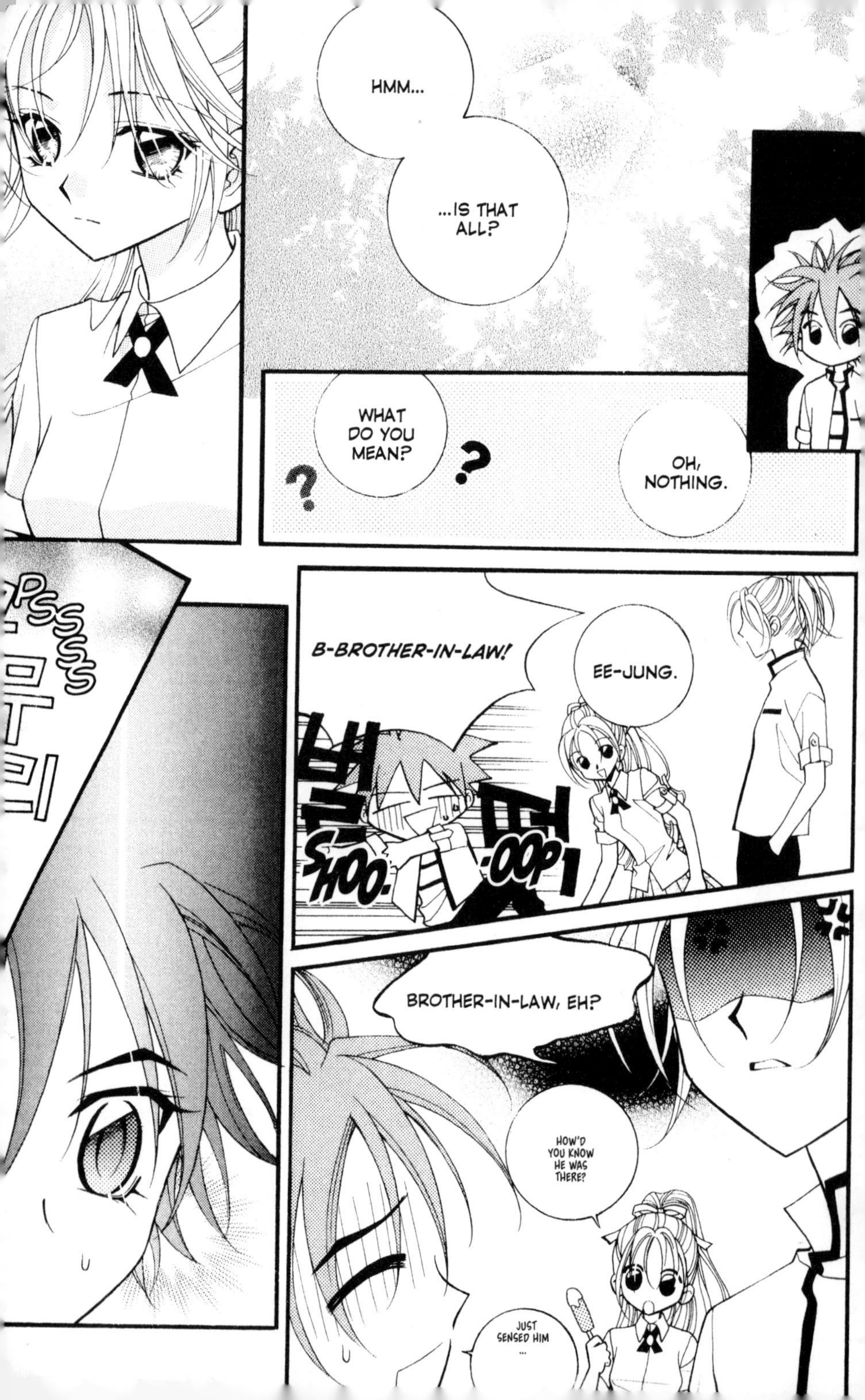
HMM...
...IS THAT ALL?
WHAT DO YOU MEAN?
? ?
OH, NOTHING.
PSSSSS
B-BROTHER-IN-LAW!
EE-JUNG.
SHOO- -OOP
BROTHER-IN-LAW, EH?
HOW'D YOU KNOW HE WAS THERE?
JUST SENSED HIM ...

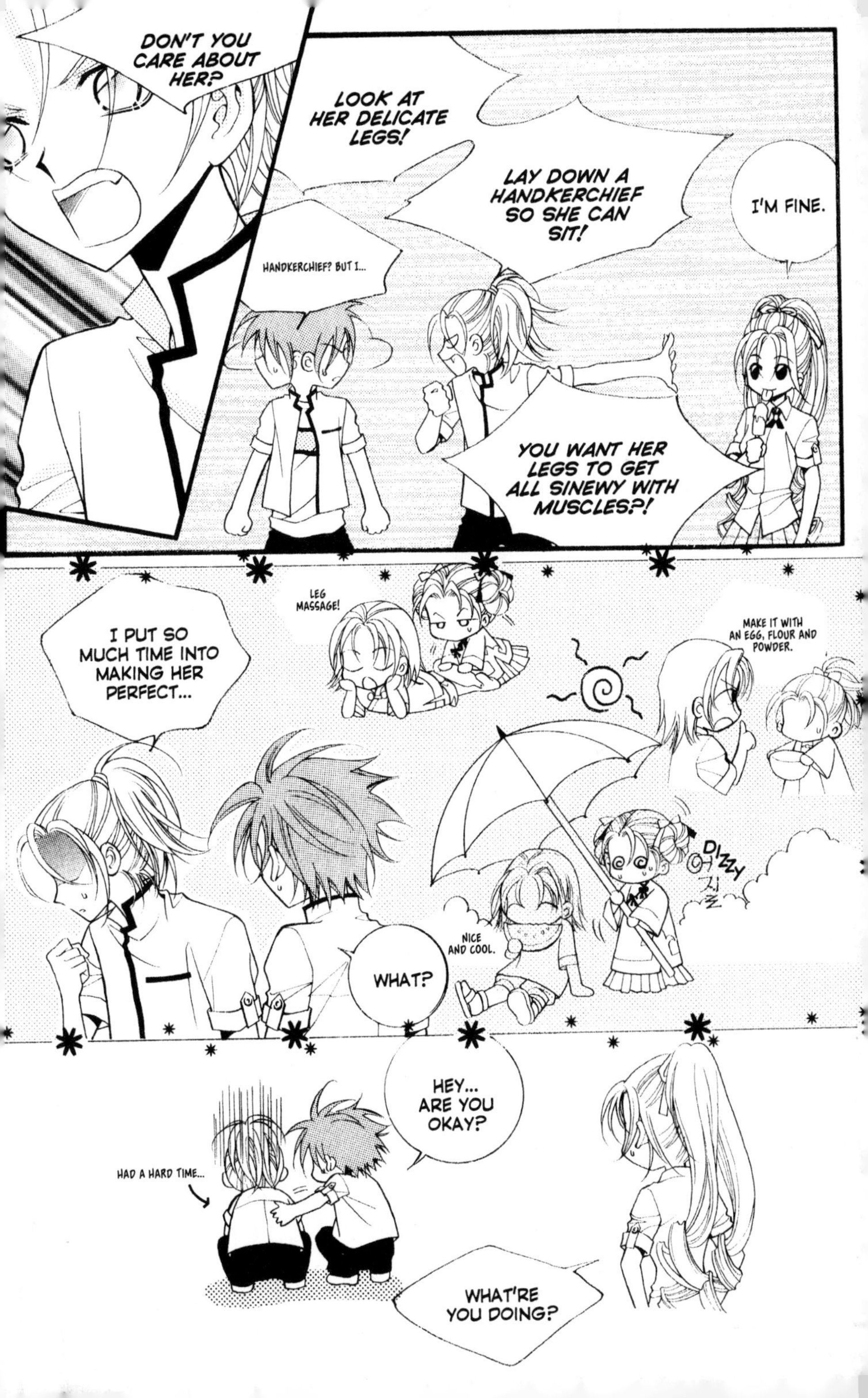
DON'T YOU CARE ABOUT HER?
LOOK AT HER DELICATE LEGS!
HANDKERCHIEF? BUT I...
LAY DOWN A HANDKERCHIEF SO SHE CAN SIT!
I'M FINE.
YOU WANT HER LEGS TO GET ALL SINEWY WITH MUSCLES?!
I PUT SO MUCH TIME INTO MAKING HER PERFECT...
LEG MASSAGE!
MAKE IT WITH AN EGG, FLOUR AND POWDER.
DIZZY
NICE AND COOL.
WHAT?
HAD A HARD TIME...
HEY... ARE YOU OKAY?
WHAT'RE YOU DOING?

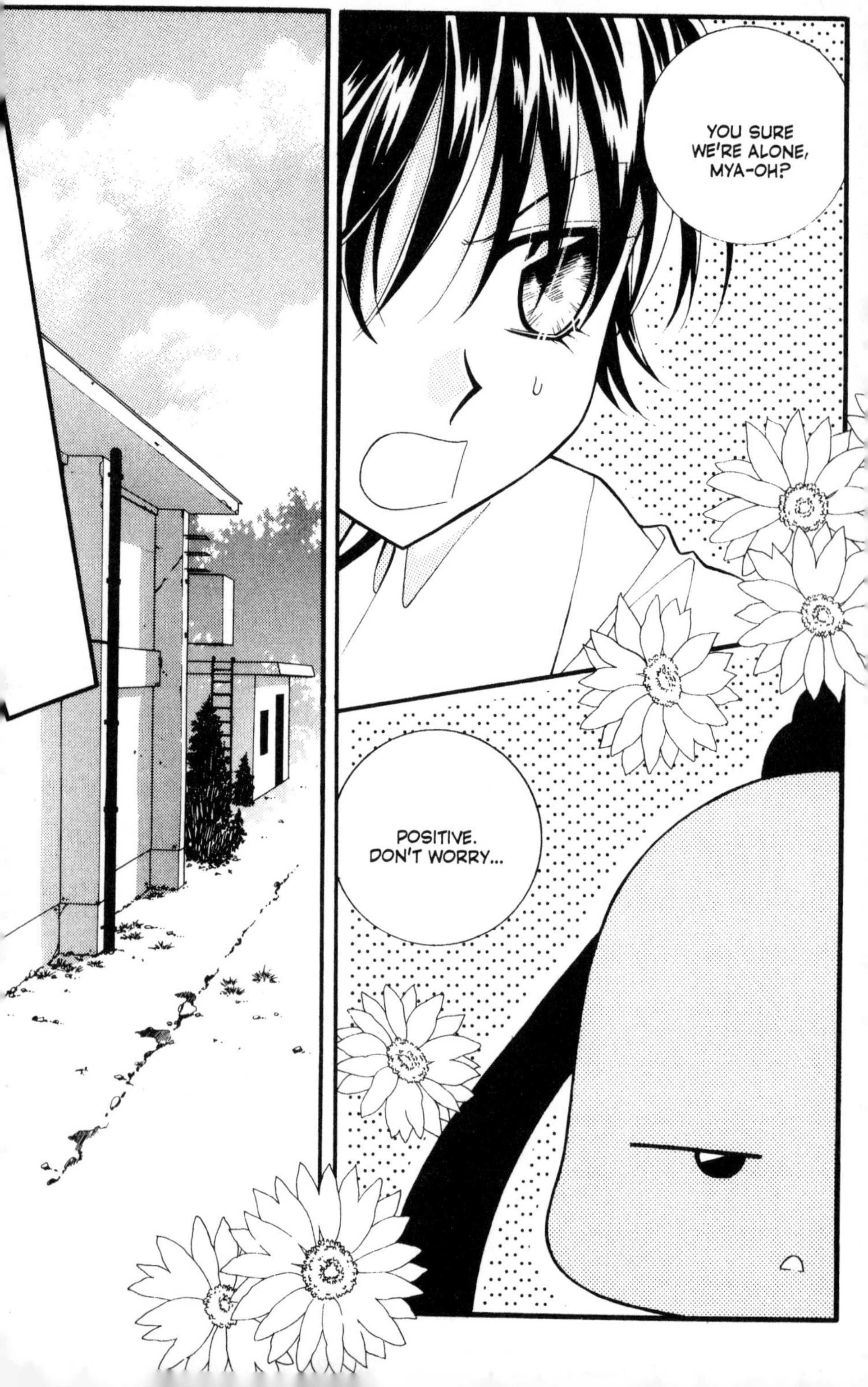
YOU SURE WE'RE ALONE, MYA-OH?
POSITIVE. DON'T WORRY...

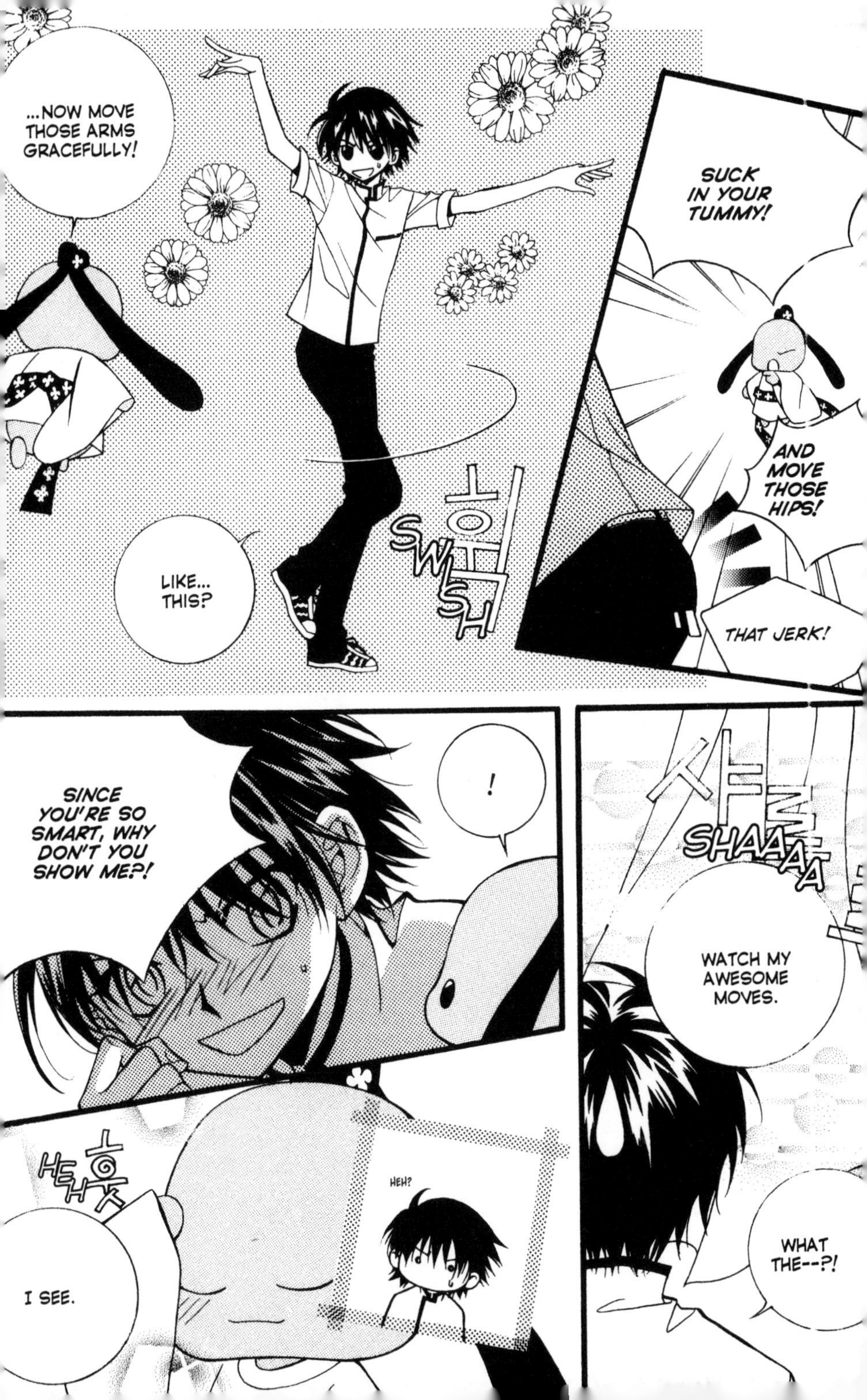

...NOW MOVE THOSE ARMS GRACEFULLY!
LIKE... THIS?
SWISH
SUCK IN YOUR TUMMY!
AND MOVE THOSE HIPS!
THAT JERK!
SINCE YOU'RE SO SMART, WHY DON'T YOU SHOW ME?!
!
HEH
I SEE.
HEH?
SHAAAAA
WATCH MY AWESOME MOVES.
WHAT THE--?!

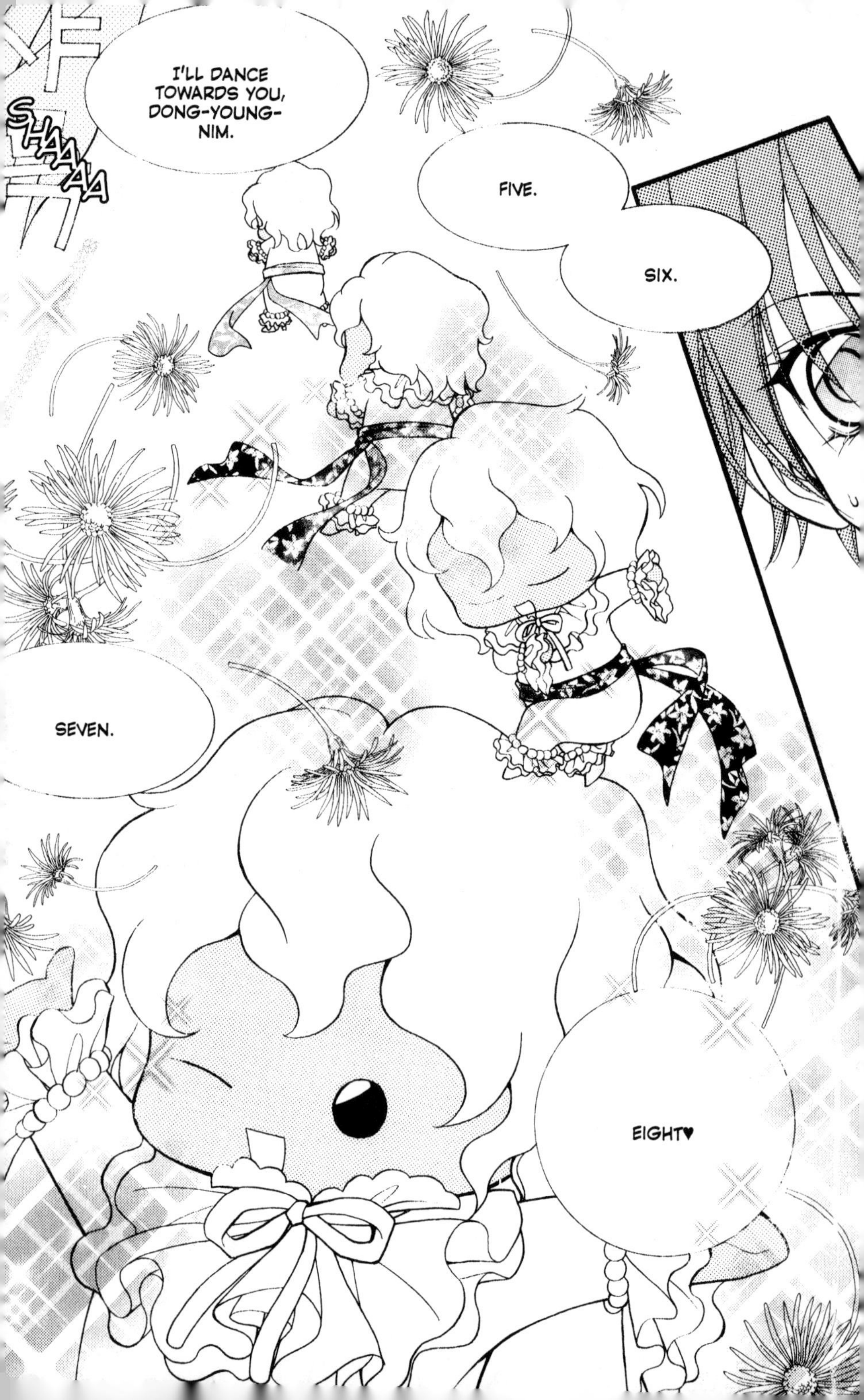
SHAAAAA
I'LL DANCE TOWARDS YOU, DONG-YOUNG-NIM.
FIVE.
SIX.
SEVEN.
EIGHT♥

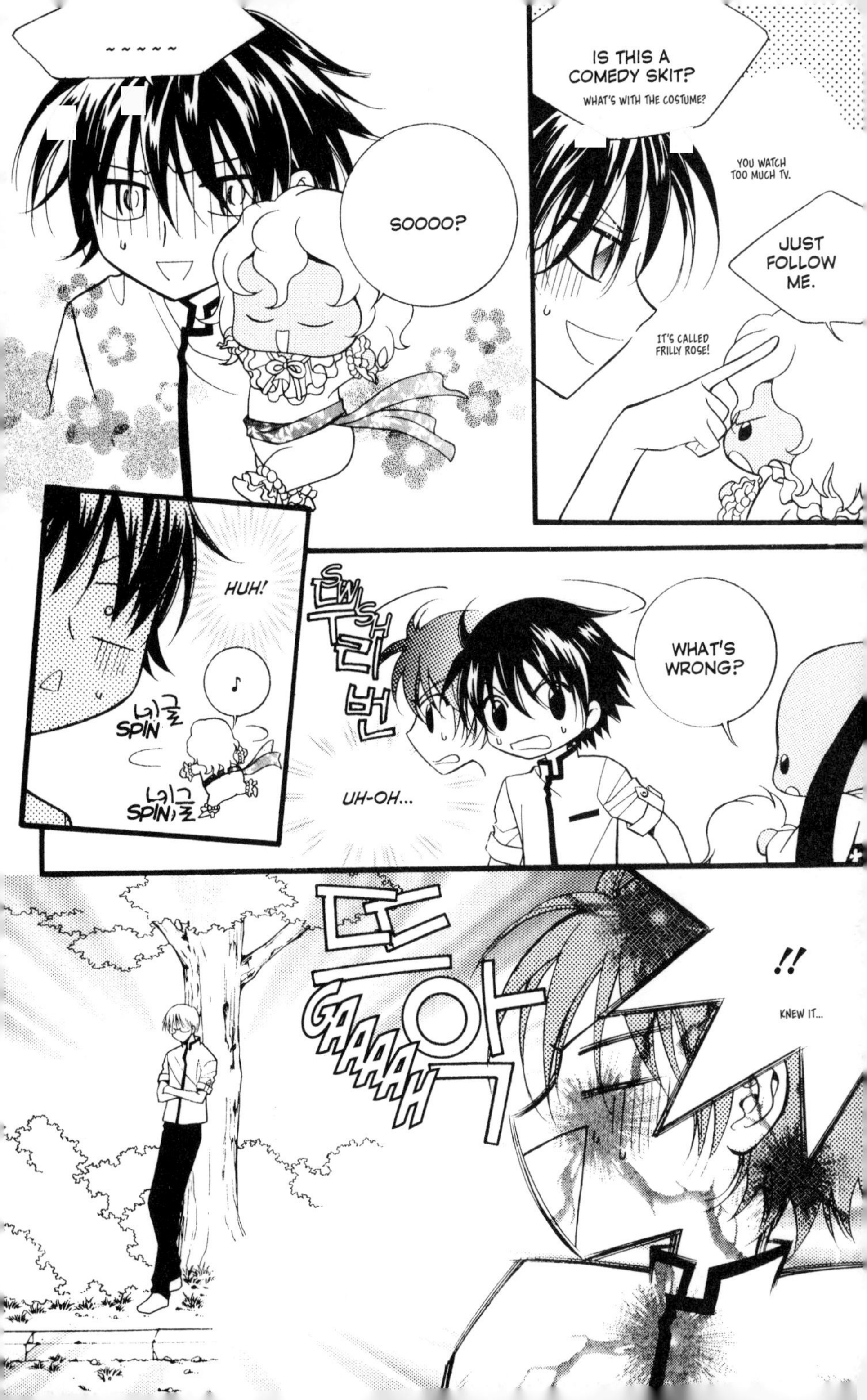

SOOOO?
IS THIS A COMEDY SKIT?
WHAT'S WITH THE COSTUME?
YOU WATCH TOO MUCH TV.
JUST FOLLOW ME.
IT'S CALLED FRILLY ROSE!
HUH!
♪
SPIN
SPIN
SWISH
UH-OH...
WHAT'S WRONG?
GAAAAH
!!
KNEW IT...

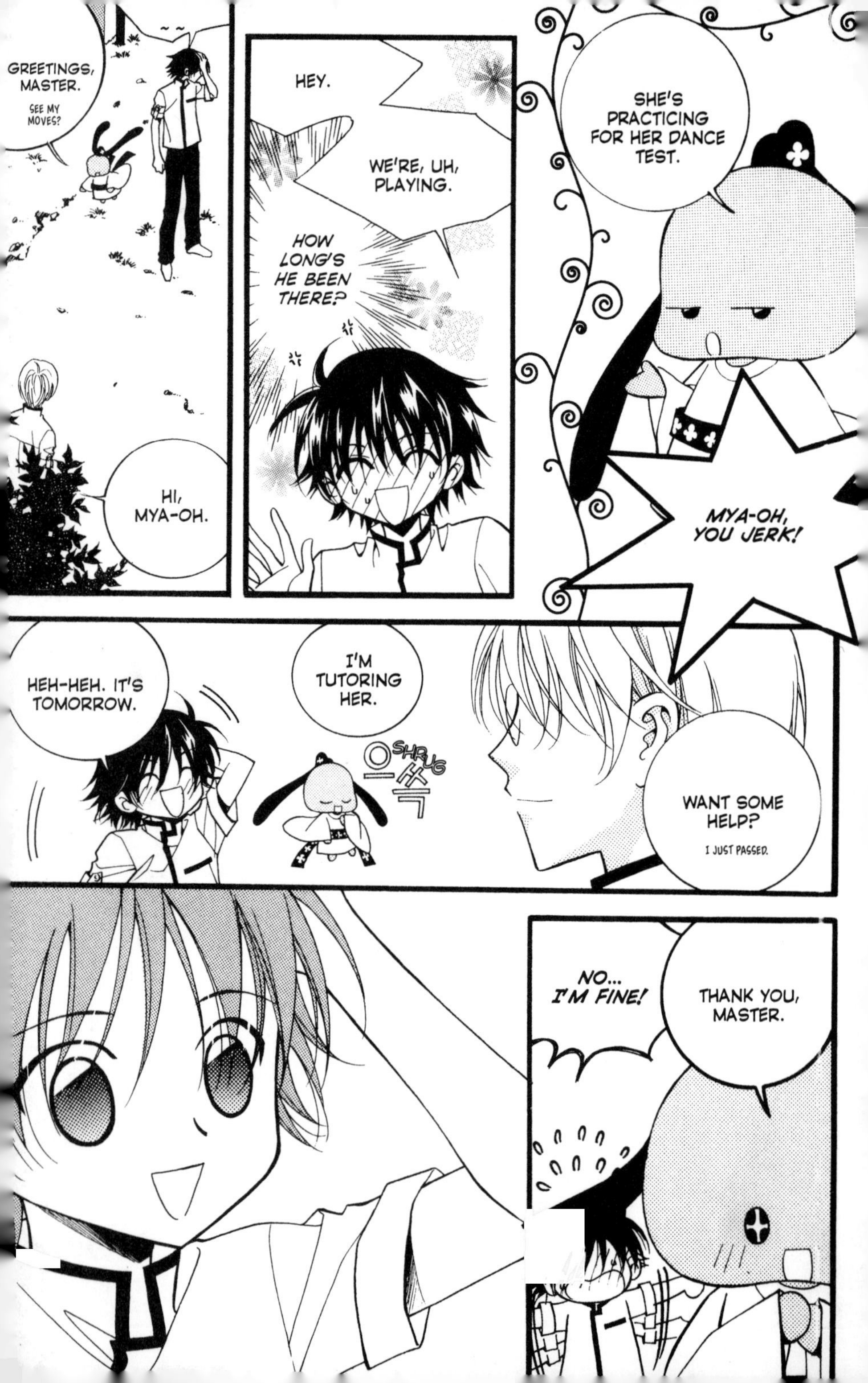
GREETINGS, MASTER.
SEE MY MOVES?
HI, MYA-OH.
HEY.
WE'RE, UH, PLAYING.
HOW LONG'S HE BEEN THERE?
SHE'S PRACTICING FOR HER DANCE TEST.
MYA-OH, YOU JERK!
HEH-HEH. IT'S TOMORROW.
I'M TUTORING HER.
으쓱 SHRUG
WANT SOME HELP?
I JUST PASSED.
NO... I'M FINE!
THANK YOU, MASTER.

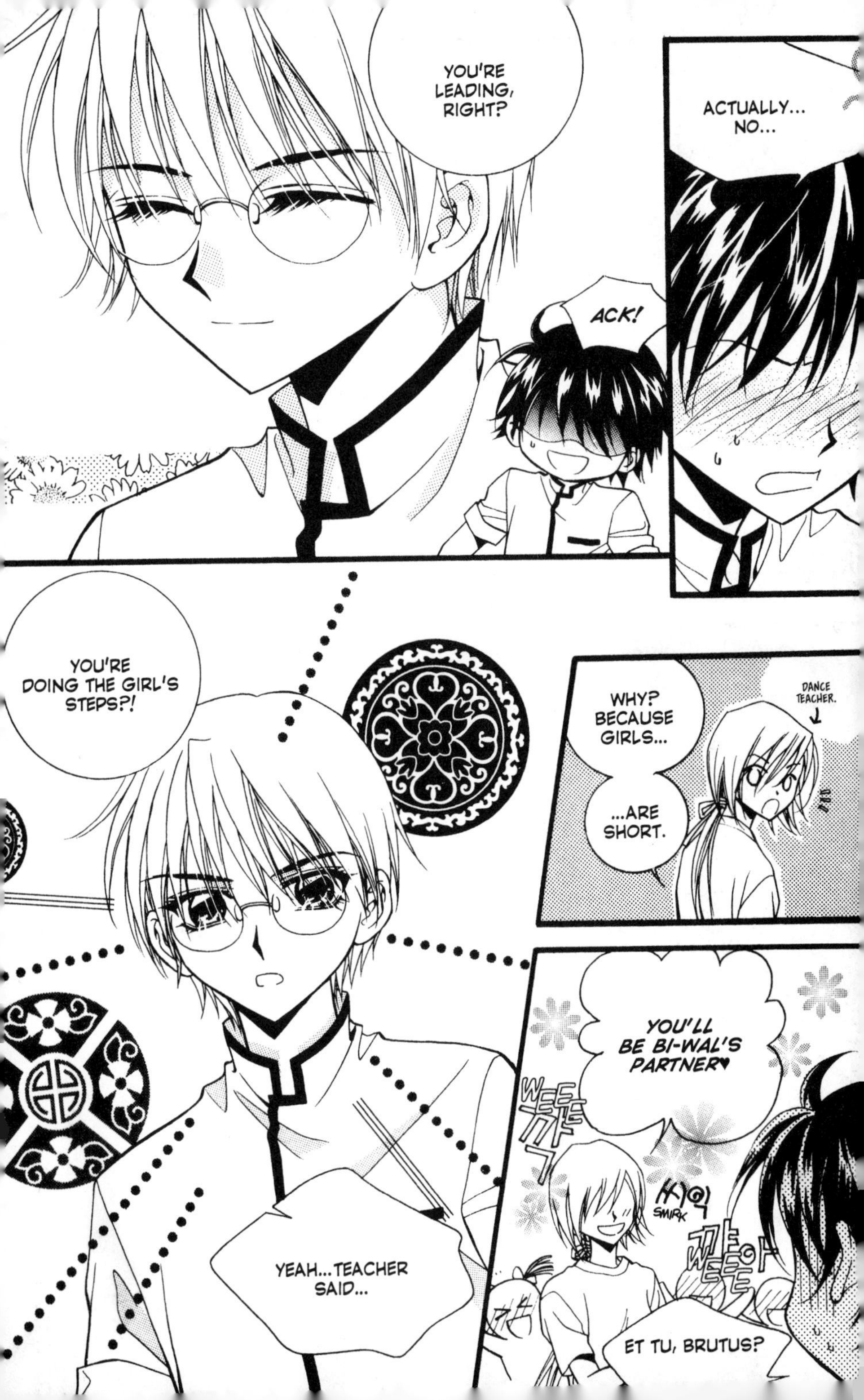

YOU'RE LEADING, RIGHT?
ACK!
ACTUALLY... NO...
YOU'RE DOING THE GIRL'S STEPS?!
YEAH...TEACHER SAID...
WHY? BECAUSE GIRLS...
...ARE SHORT.
DANCE TEACHER.
YOU'LL BE BI-WAL'S PARTNER♥
WEEE
SMIRK
WEEE
ET TU, BRUTUS?

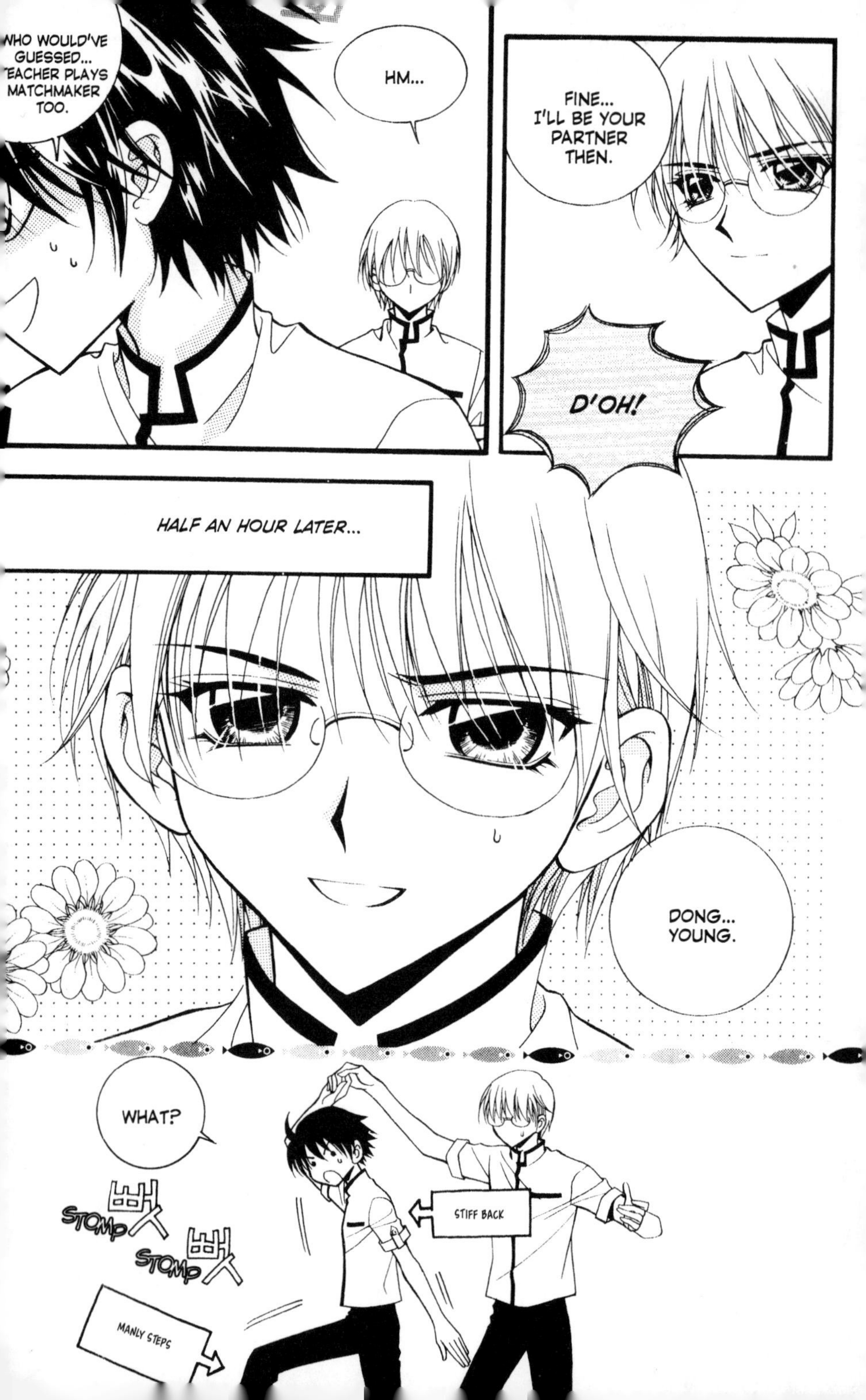
WHO WOULD'VE GUESSED... TEACHER PLAYS MATCHMAKER TOO.
HM...
FINE... I'LL BE YOUR PARTNER THEN.
D'OH!
HALF AN HOUR LATER...
DONG... YOUNG.
WHAT?
STOMP
STOMP
STIFF BACK
MANLY STEPS

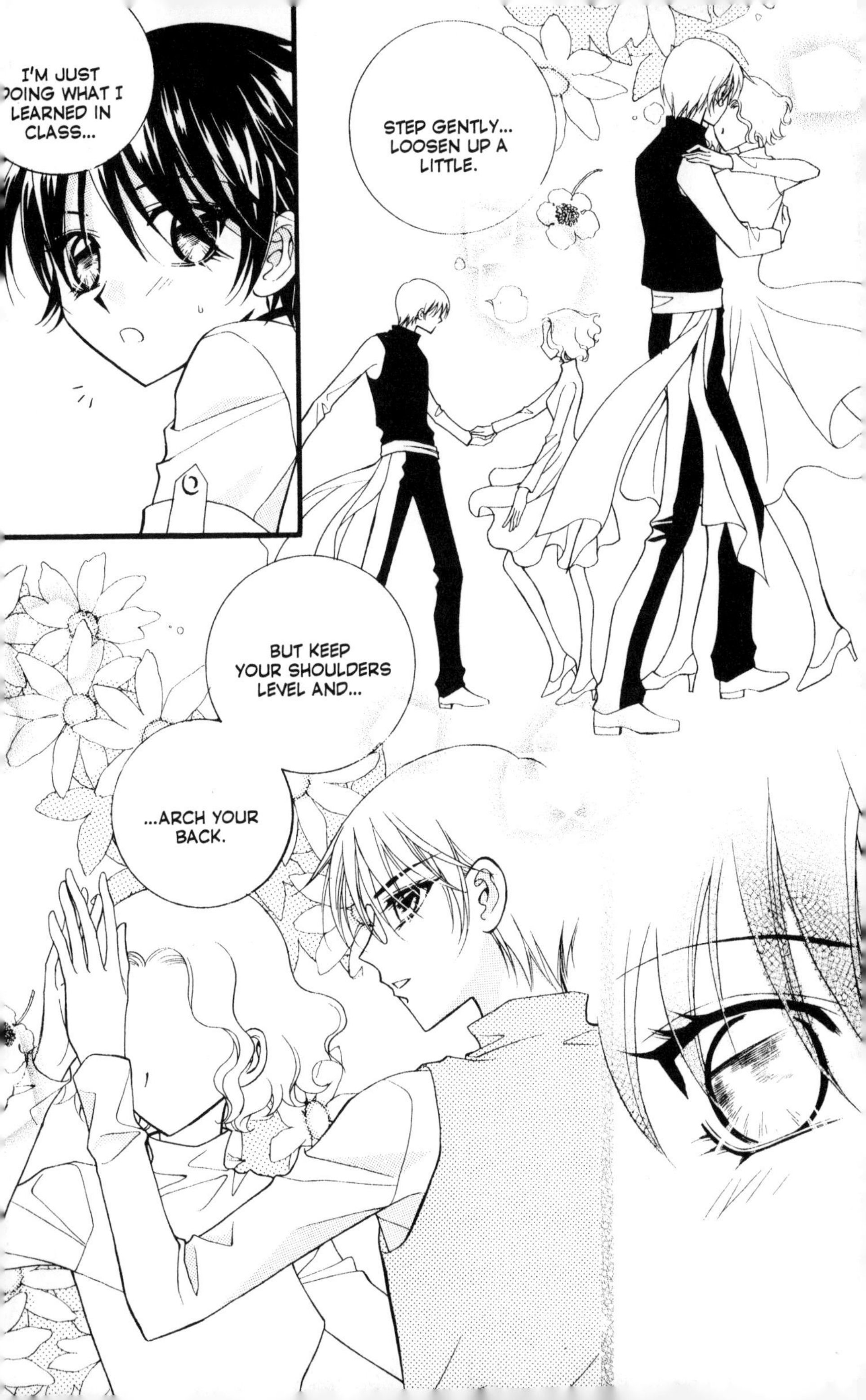
I'M JUST DOING WHAT I LEARNED IN CLASS...
STEP GENTLY... LOOSEN UP A LITTLE.
BUT KEEP YOUR SHOULDERS LEVEL AND...
...ARCH YOUR BACK.

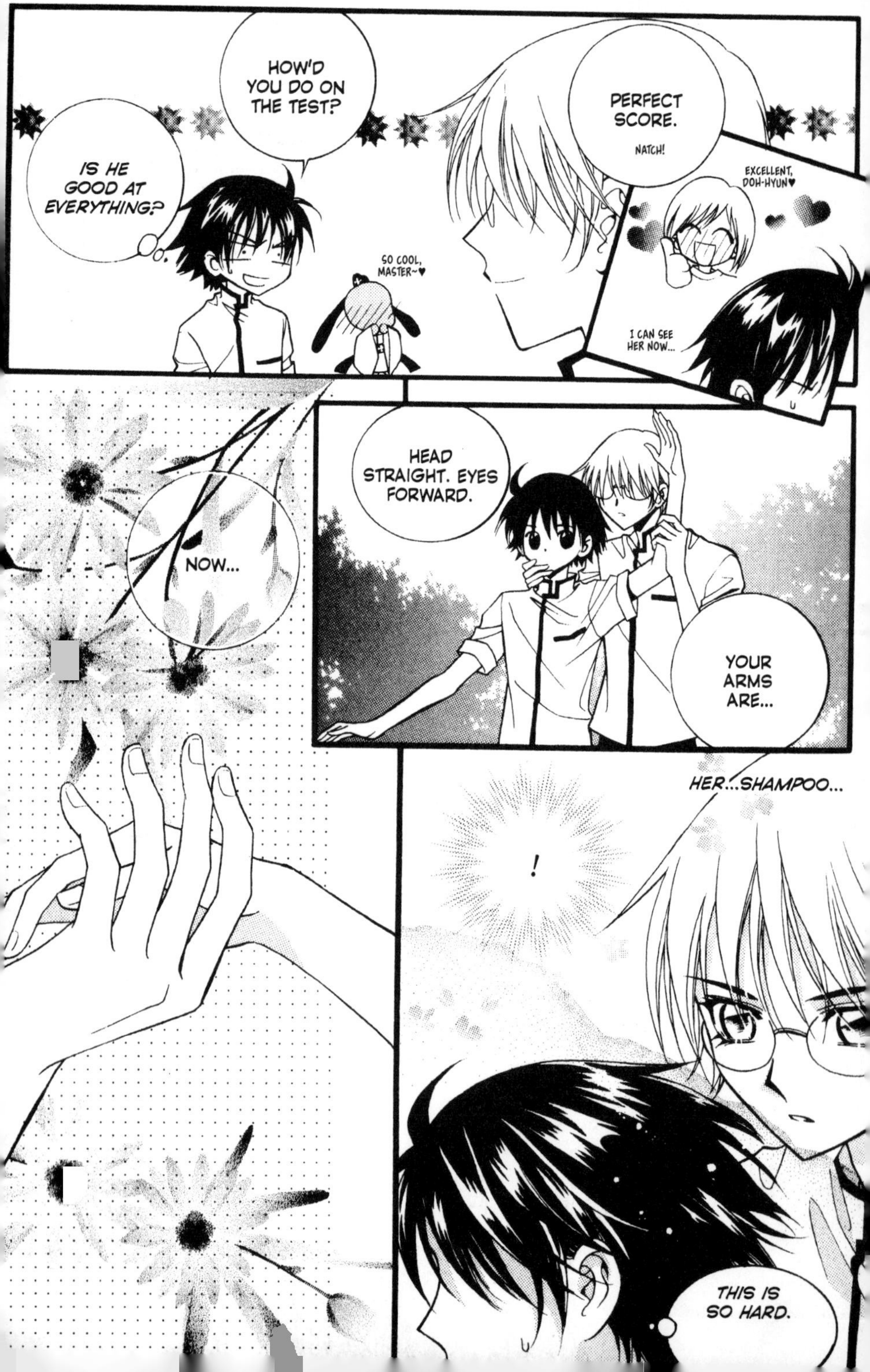
IS HE GOOD AT EVERYTHING?
HOW'D YOU DO ON THE TEST?
SO COOL, MASTER~♥
PERFECT SCORE.
NATCH!
EXCELLENT, DOH-HYUN♥
I CAN SEE HER NOW...
NOW...
HEAD STRAIGHT. EYES FORWARD.
YOUR ARMS ARE...
HER...SHAMPOO...
!
THIS IS SO HARD.

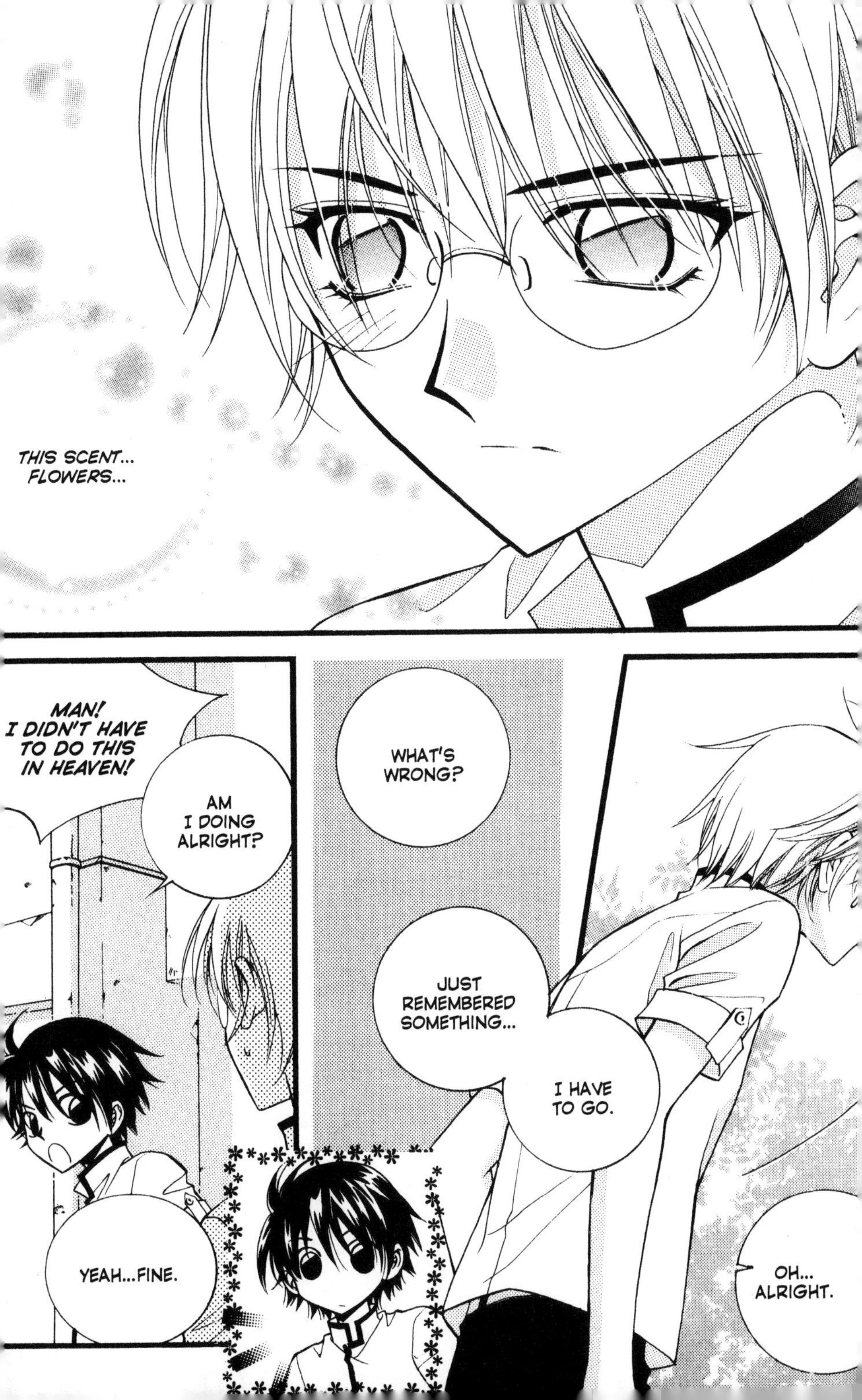
THIS SCENT... FLOWERS...
MAN! I DIDN'T HAVE TO DO THIS IN HEAVEN!
AM I DOING ALRIGHT?
YEAH...FINE.
WHAT'S WRONG?
JUST REMEMBERED SOMETHING...
I HAVE TO GO.
OH... ALRIGHT.

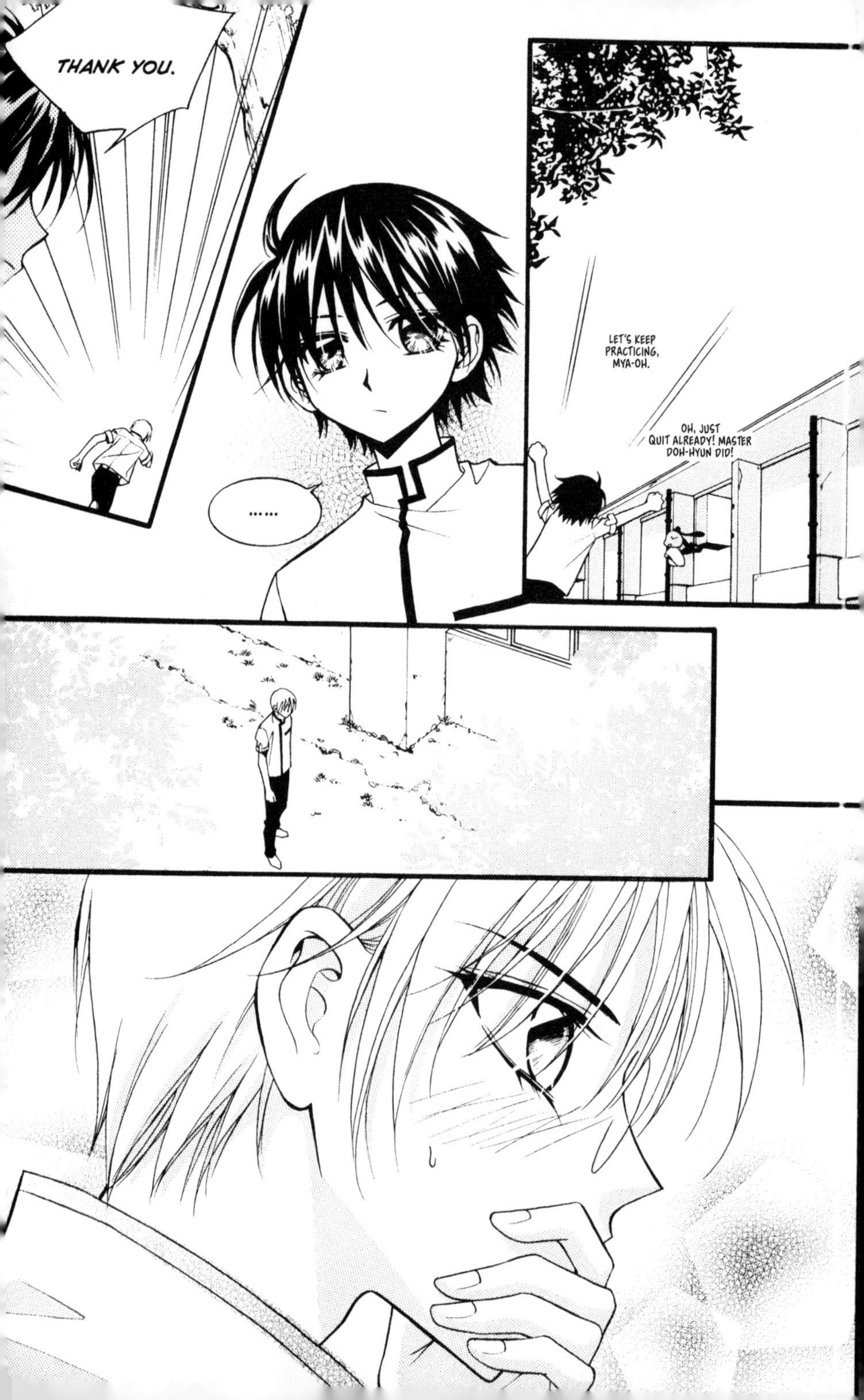
THANK YOU.
……
LET'S KEEP PRACTICING, MYA-OH.
OH, JUST QUIT ALREADY! MASTER DOH-HYUN DID!

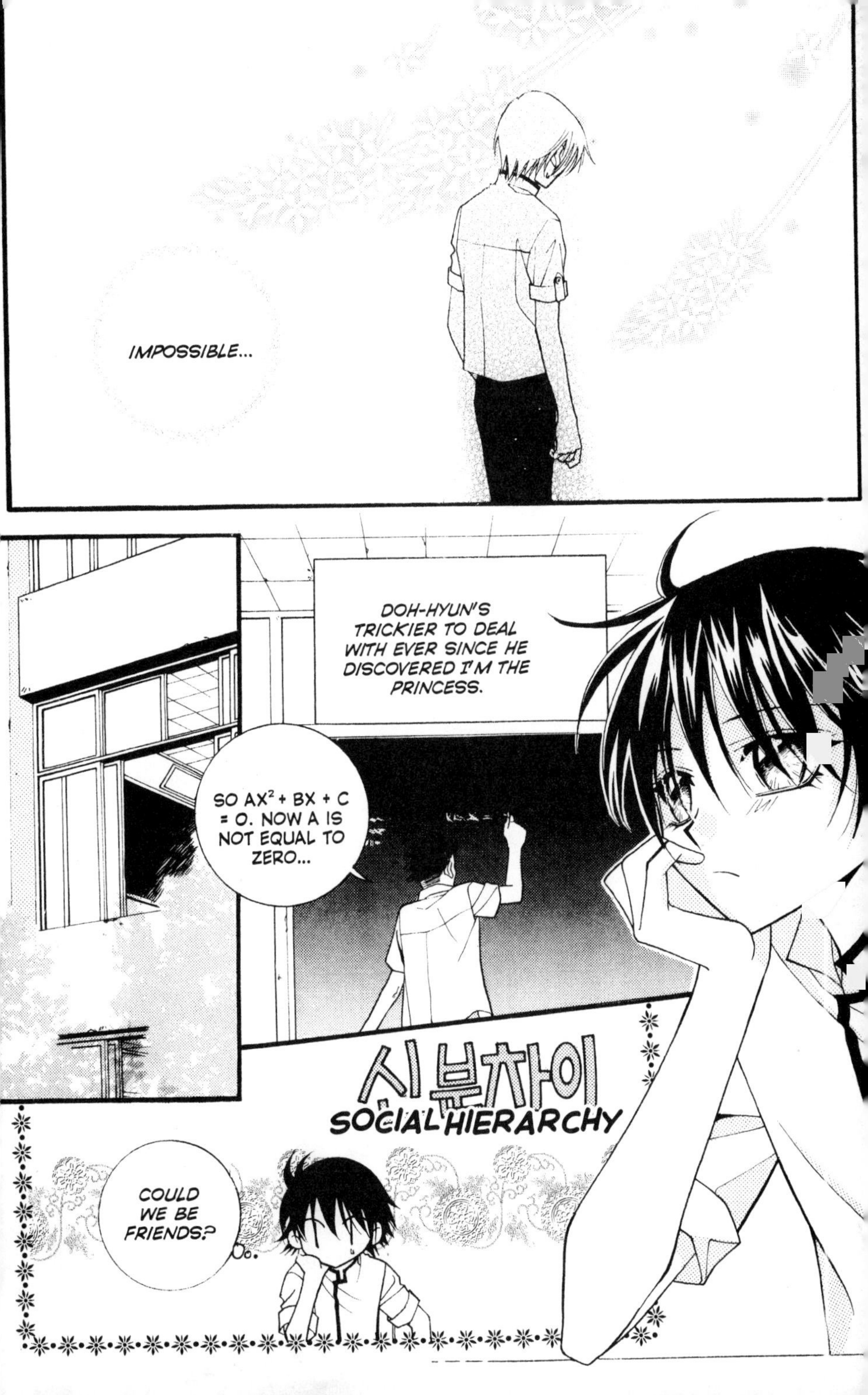
IMPOSSIBLE...
DOH-HYUN'S TRICKIER TO DEAL WITH EVER SINCE HE DISCOVERED I'M THE PRINCESS.
SO $AX^2 + BX + C = 0$. NOW A IS NOT EQUAL TO ZERO...
신분차이
SOCIAL HIERARCHY
COULD WE BE FRIENDS?

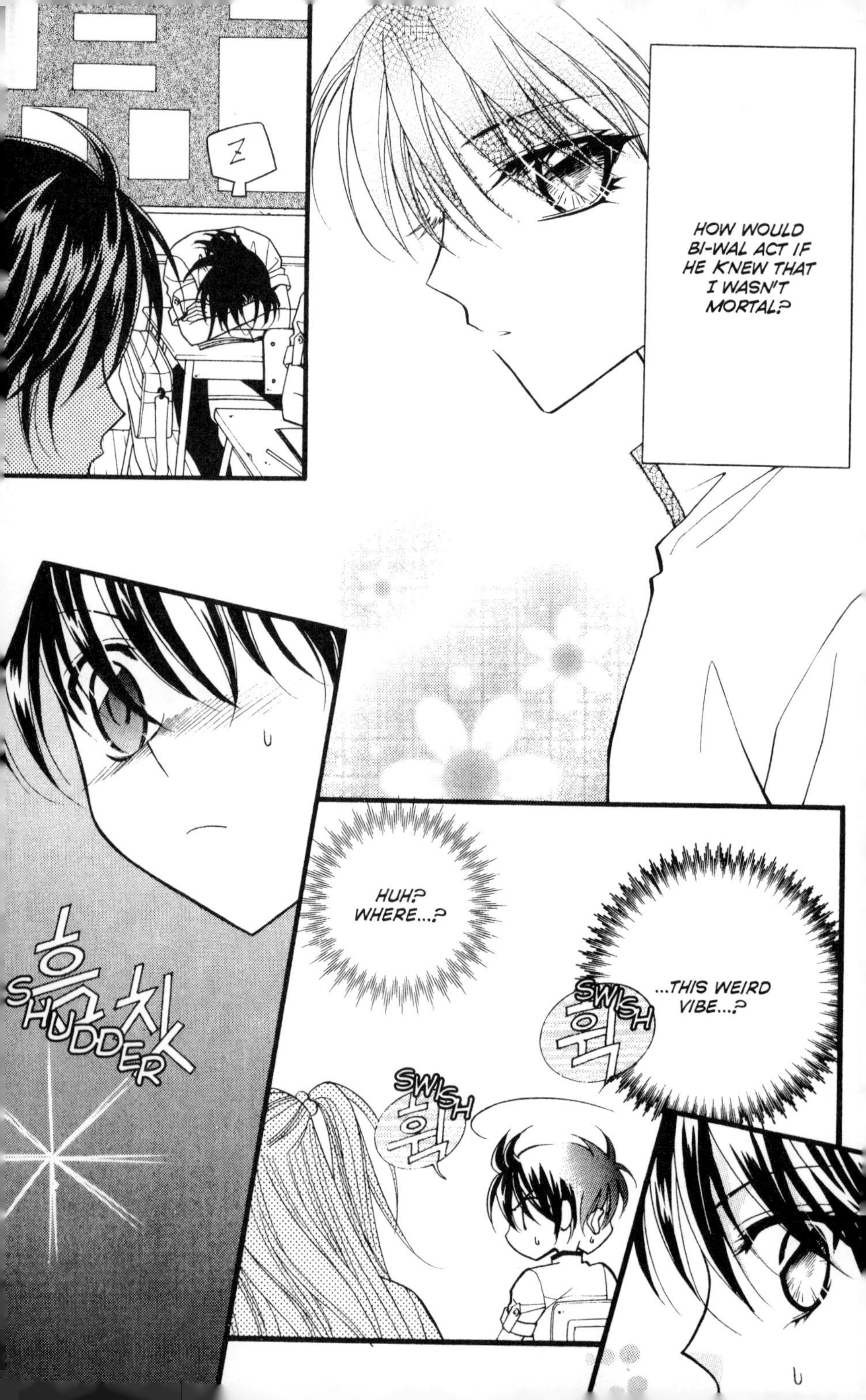
Z
HOW WOULD BI-WAL ACT IF HE KNEW THAT I WASN'T MORTAL?
흠칫
SHUDDER
HUH? WHERE...?
SWISH
휙
...THIS WEIRD VIBE...?
SWISH
휙

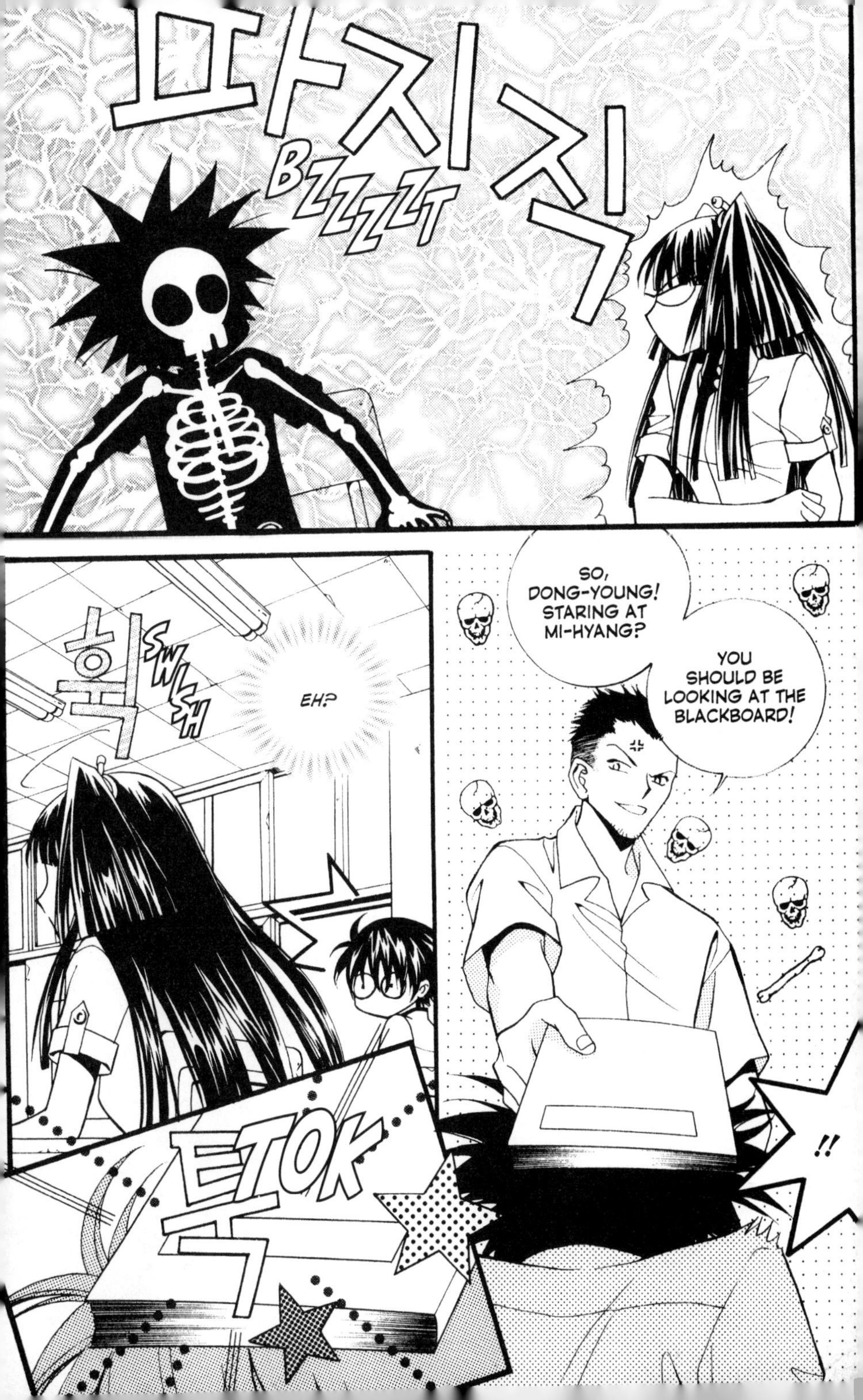
BZZZZZT
SWISH
EH?
SO, DONG-YOUNG! STARING AT MI-HYANG?
YOU SHOULD BE LOOKING AT THE BLACKBOARD!
ETOK
!!

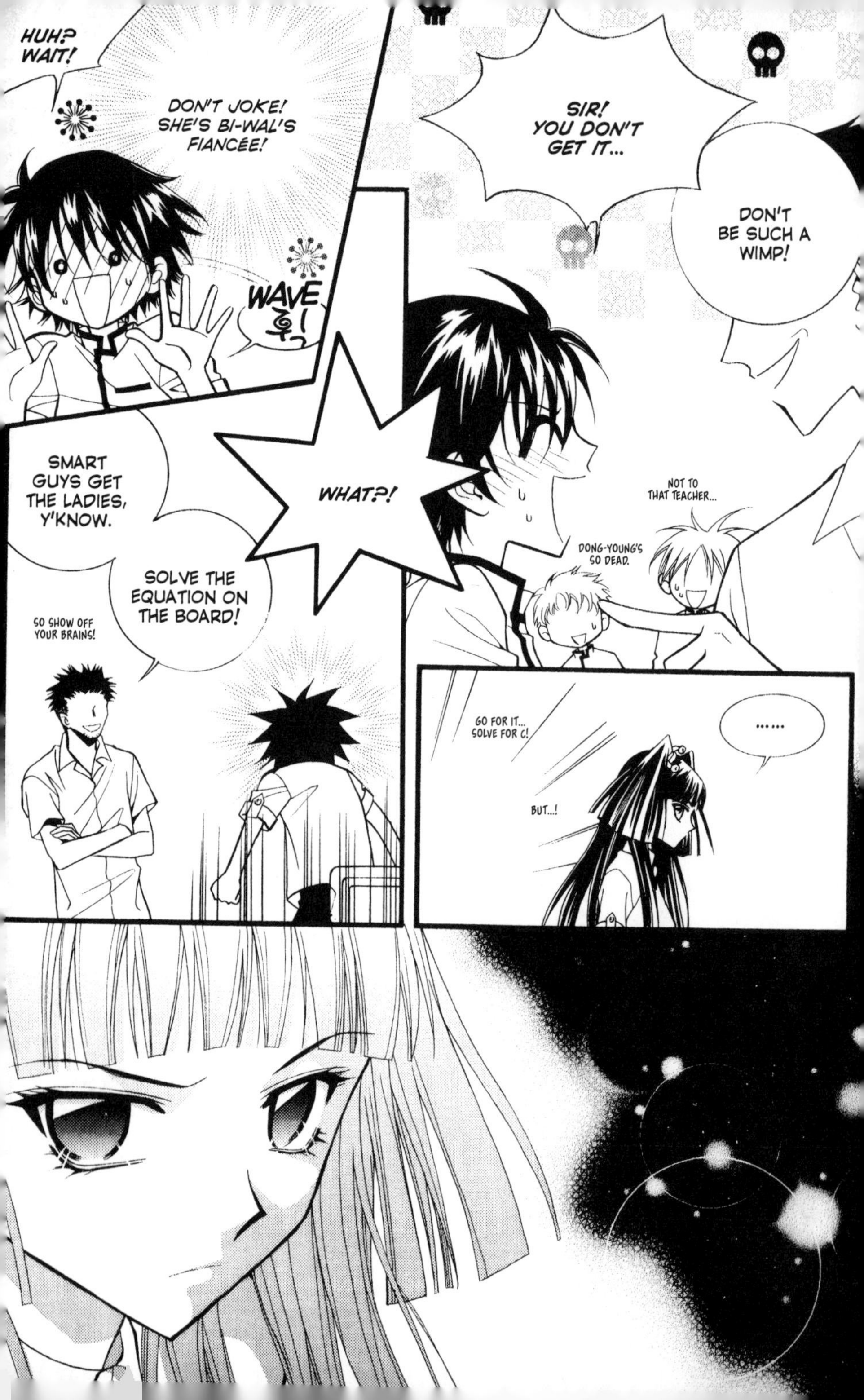
HUH? WAIT!
DON'T JOKE! SHE'S BI-WAL'S FIANCÉE!
WAVE
SMART GUYS GET THE LADIES, Y'KNOW.
SOLVE THE EQUATION ON THE BOARD!
SO SHOW OFF YOUR BRAINS!
WHAT?!
SIR! YOU DON'T GET IT...
DON'T BE SUCH A WIMP!
DONG-YOUNG'S SO DEAD.
NOT TO THAT TEACHER...
GO FOR IT... SOLVE FOR C!
......
BUT...!

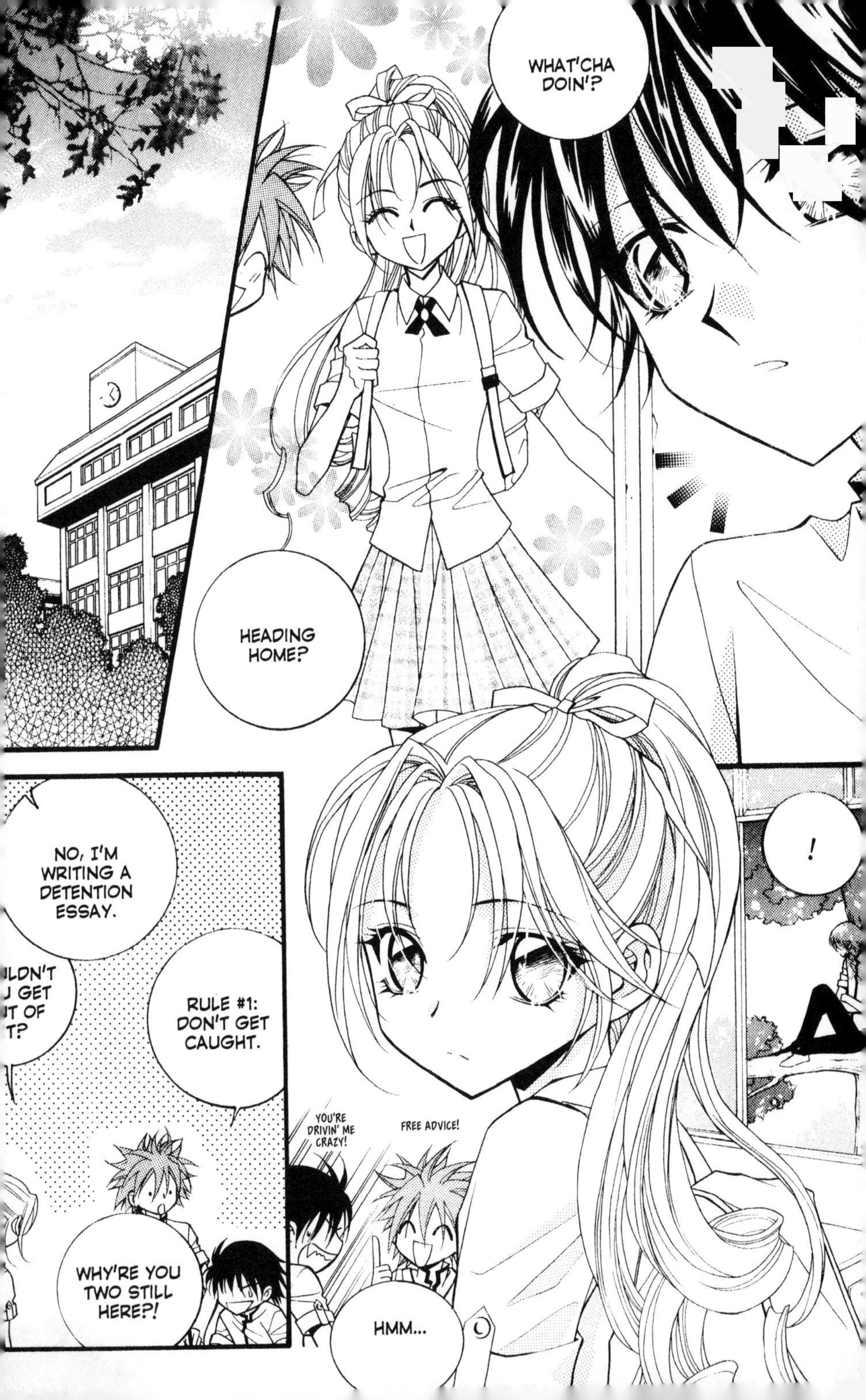
HEADING HOME?
WHAT'CHA DOIN'?
NO, I'M WRITING A DETENTION ESSAY.
RULE #1: DON'T GET CAUGHT.
WHY'RE YOU TWO STILL HERE?!
YOU'RE DRIVIN' ME CRAZY!
FREE ADVICE!
HMM...
!

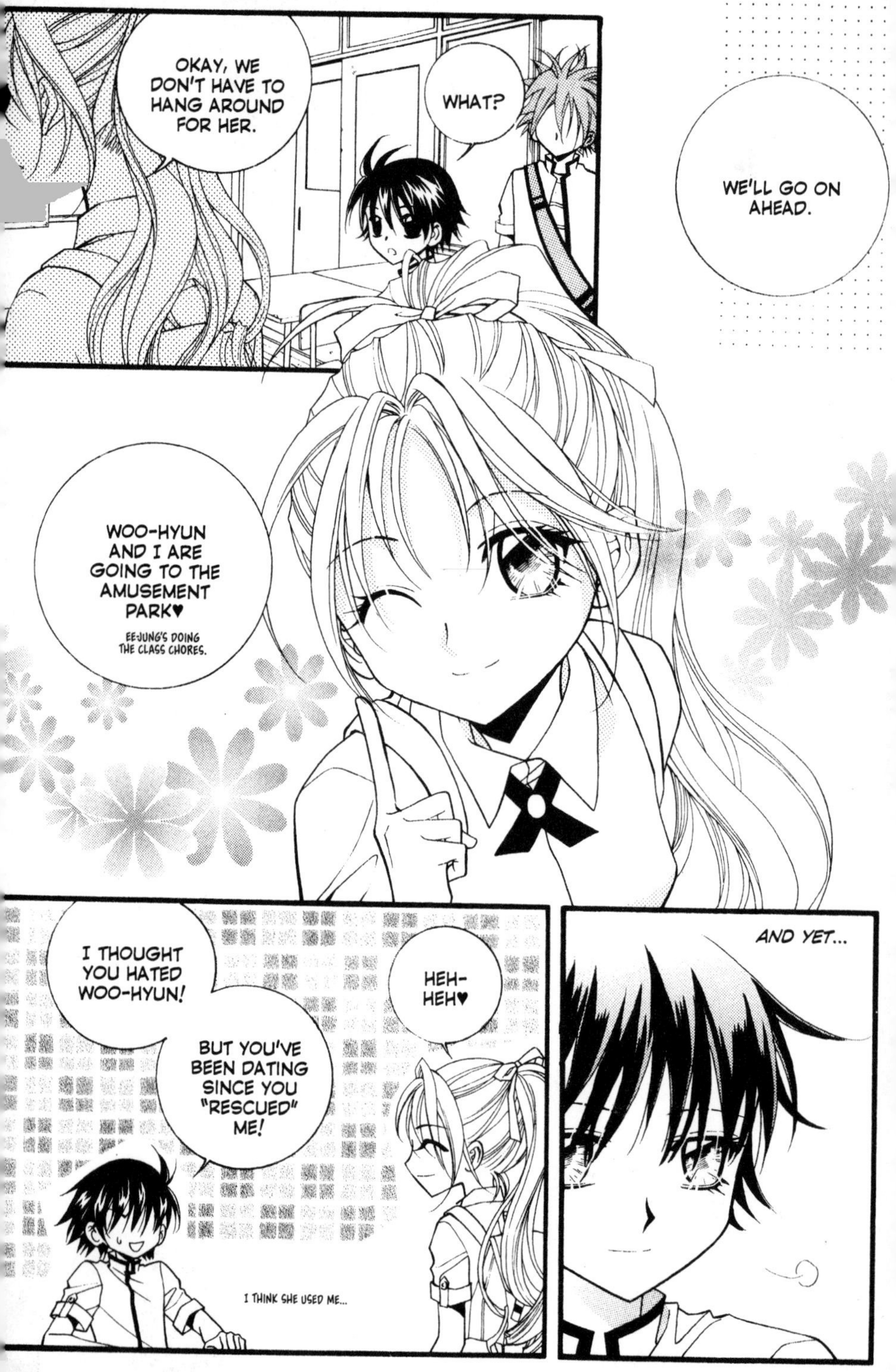
OKAY, WE DON'T HAVE TO HANG AROUND FOR HER.
WHAT?
WE'LL GO ON AHEAD.
WOO-HYUN AND I ARE GOING TO THE AMUSEMENT PARK♥
EE-JUNG'S DOING THE CLASS CHORES.
I THOUGHT YOU HATED WOO-HYUN!
BUT YOU'VE BEEN DATING SINCE YOU "RESCUED" ME!
HEH-HEH♥
I THINK SHE USED ME...
AND YET...

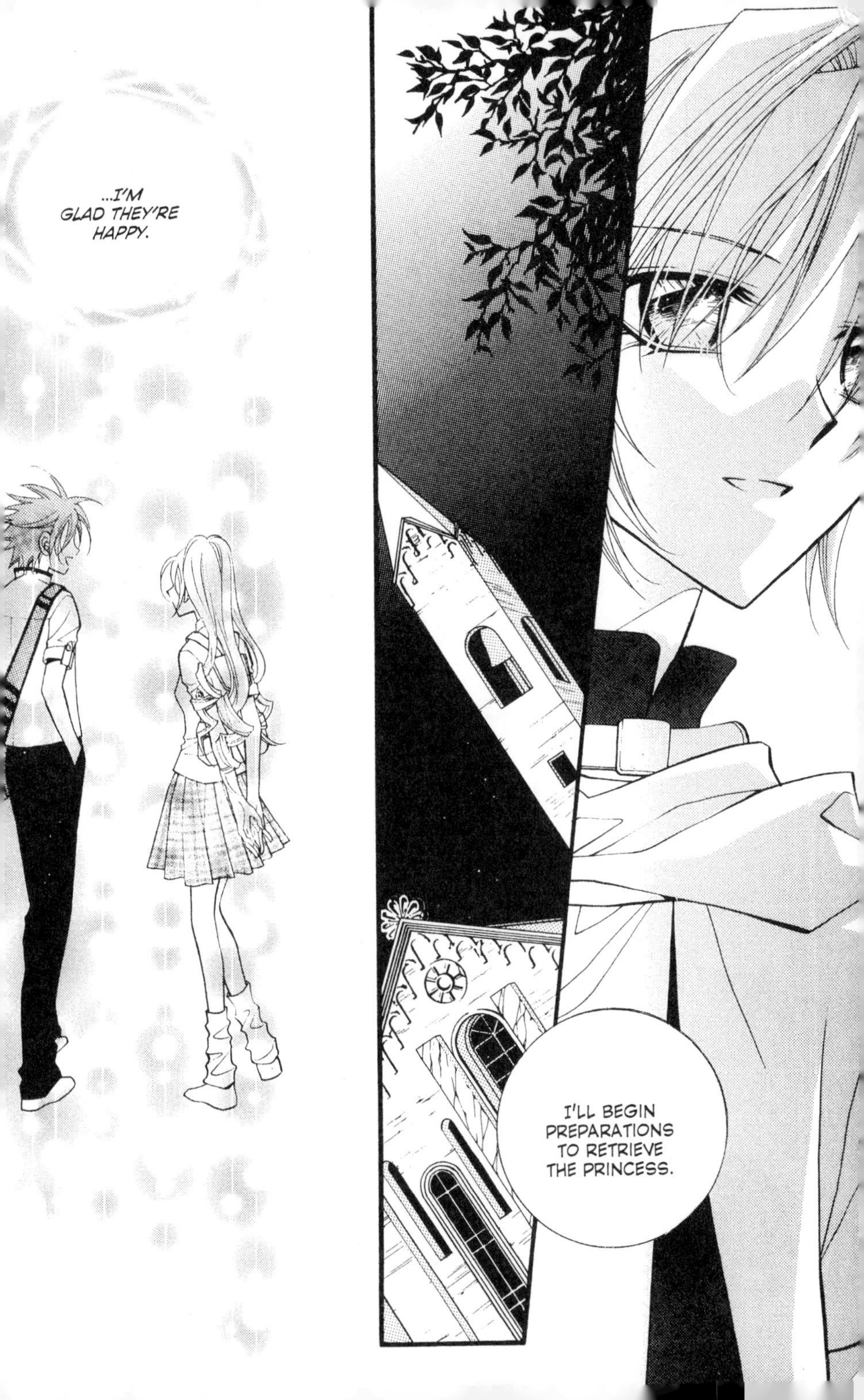
...I'M GLAD THEY'RE HAPPY.
I'LL BEGIN PREPARATIONS TO RETRIEVE THE PRINCESS.

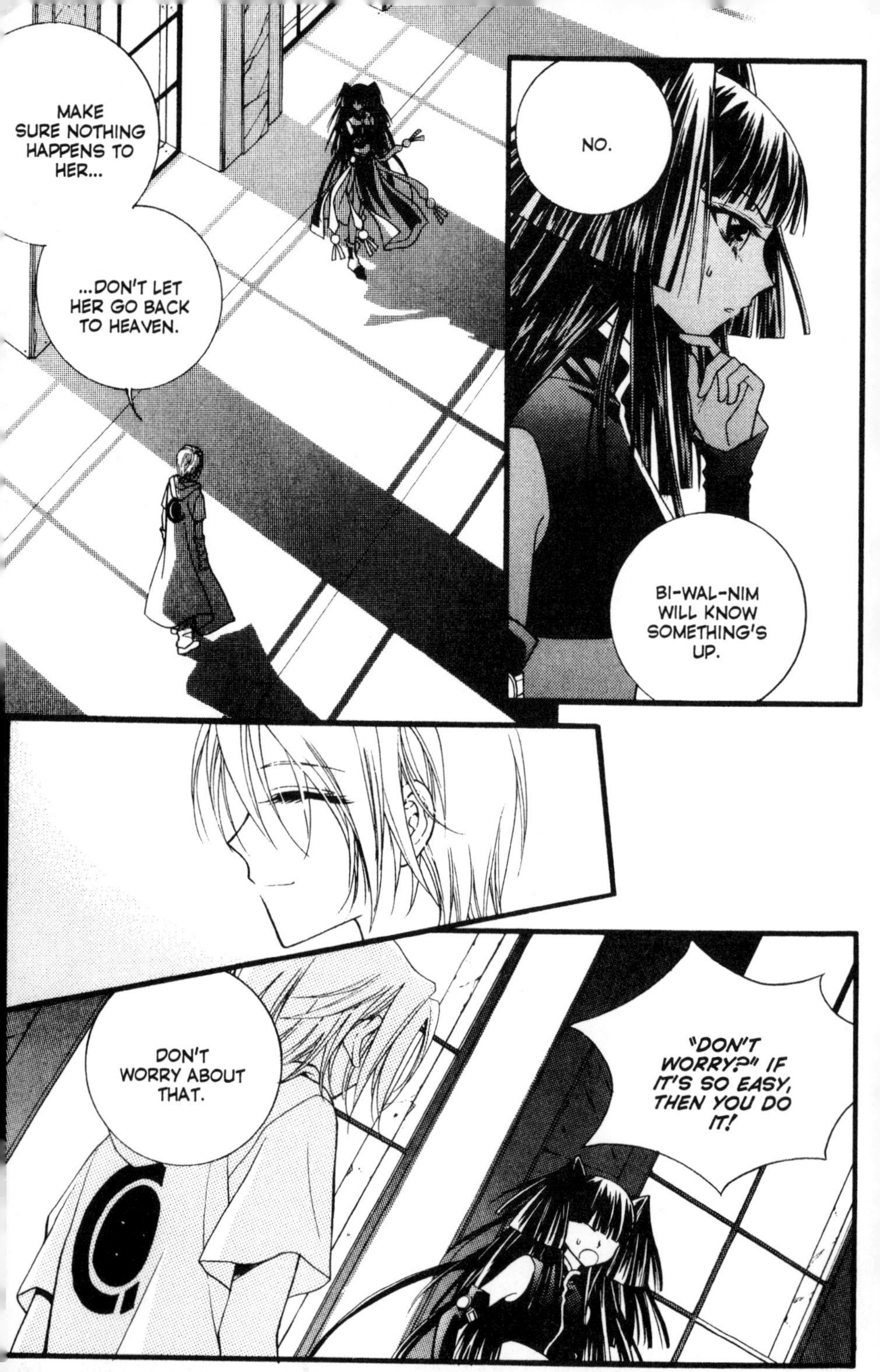
MAKE SURE NOTHING HAPPENS TO HER...
...DON'T LET HER GO BACK TO HEAVEN.
NO.
BI-WAL-NIM WILL KNOW SOMETHING'S UP.
DON'T WORRY ABOUT THAT.
"DON'T WORRY?" IF IT'S SO EASY, THEN YOU DO IT!

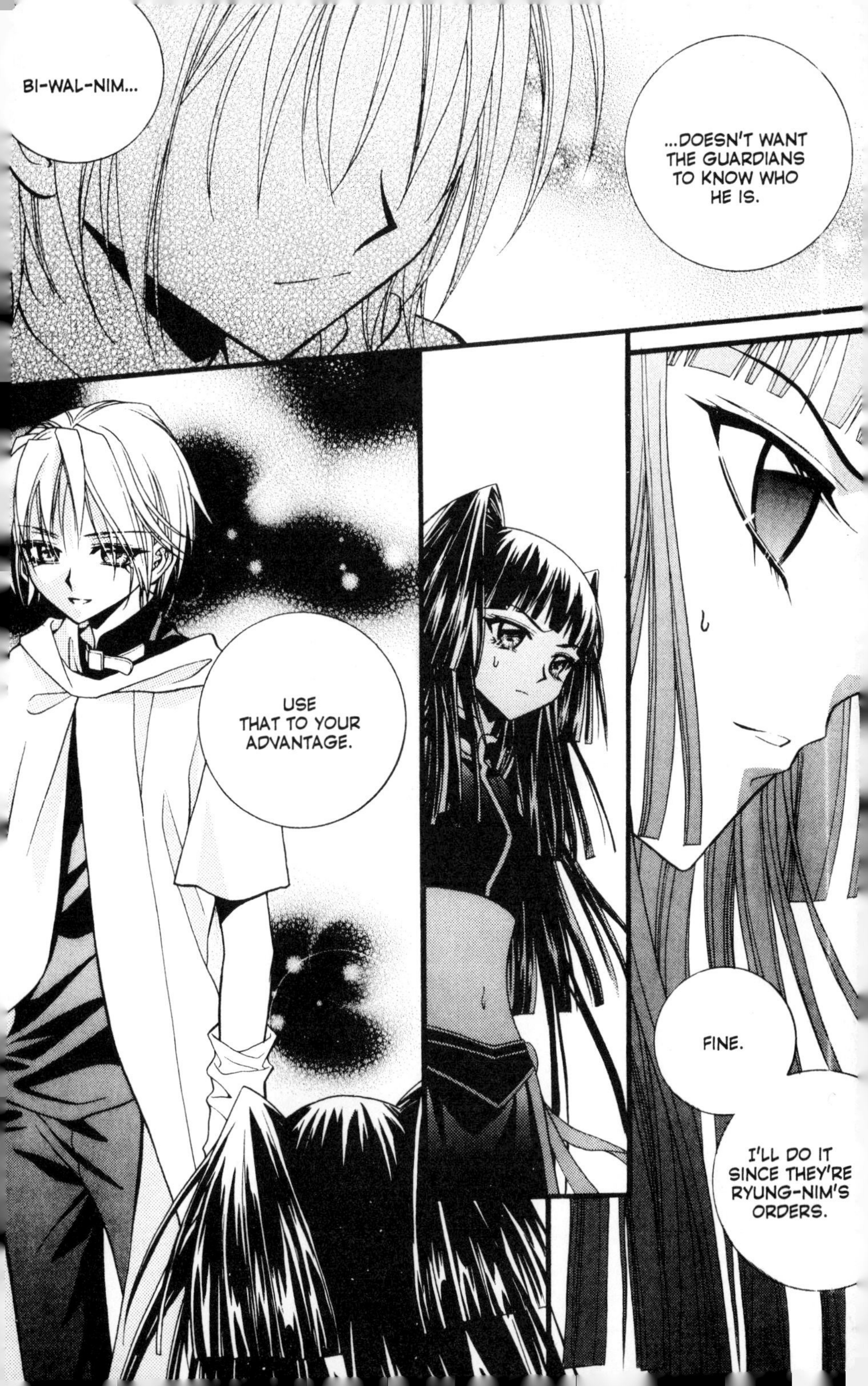
BI-WAL-NIM...
...DOESN'T WANT THE GUARDIANS TO KNOW WHO HE IS.
USE THAT TO YOUR ADVANTAGE.
FINE.
I'LL DO IT SINCE THEY'RE RYUNG-NIM'S ORDERS.

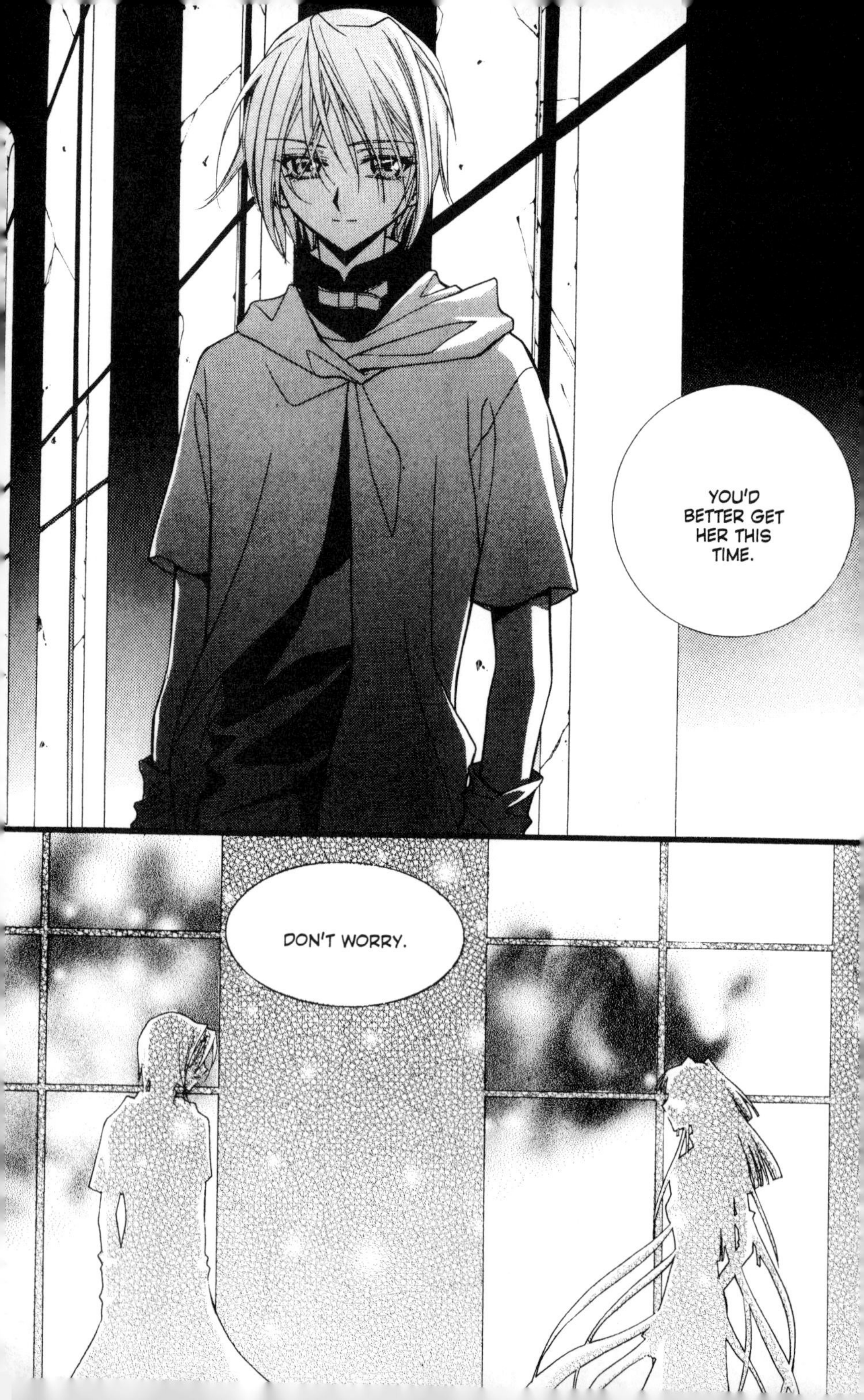
YOU'D BETTER GET HER THIS TIME.
DON'T WORRY.

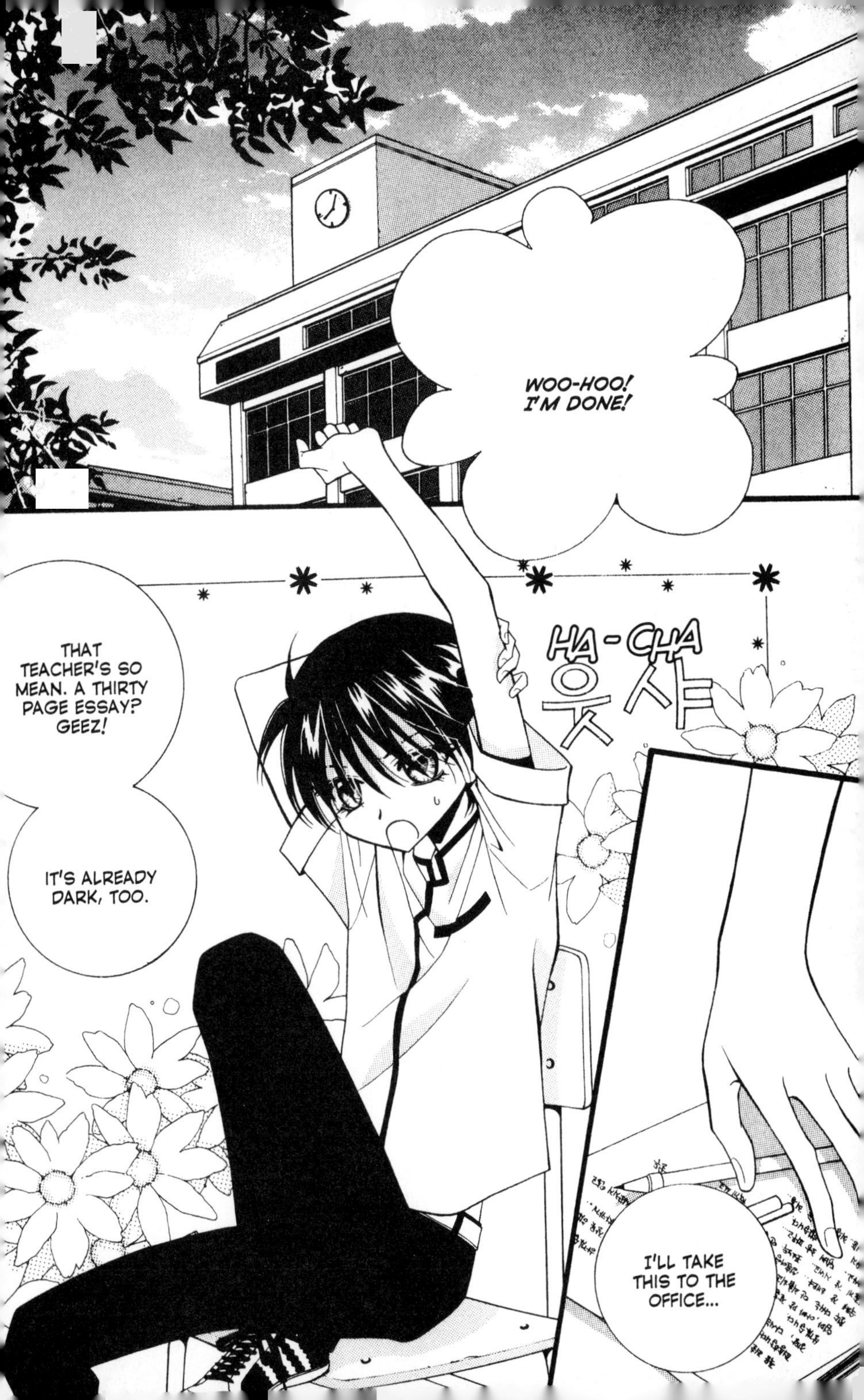
WOO-HOO! I'M DONE!
THAT TEACHER'S SO MEAN. A THIRTY PAGE ESSAY? GEEZ!
IT'S ALREADY DARK, TOO.
HA-CHA
읏샤
I'LL TAKE THIS TO THE OFFICE...

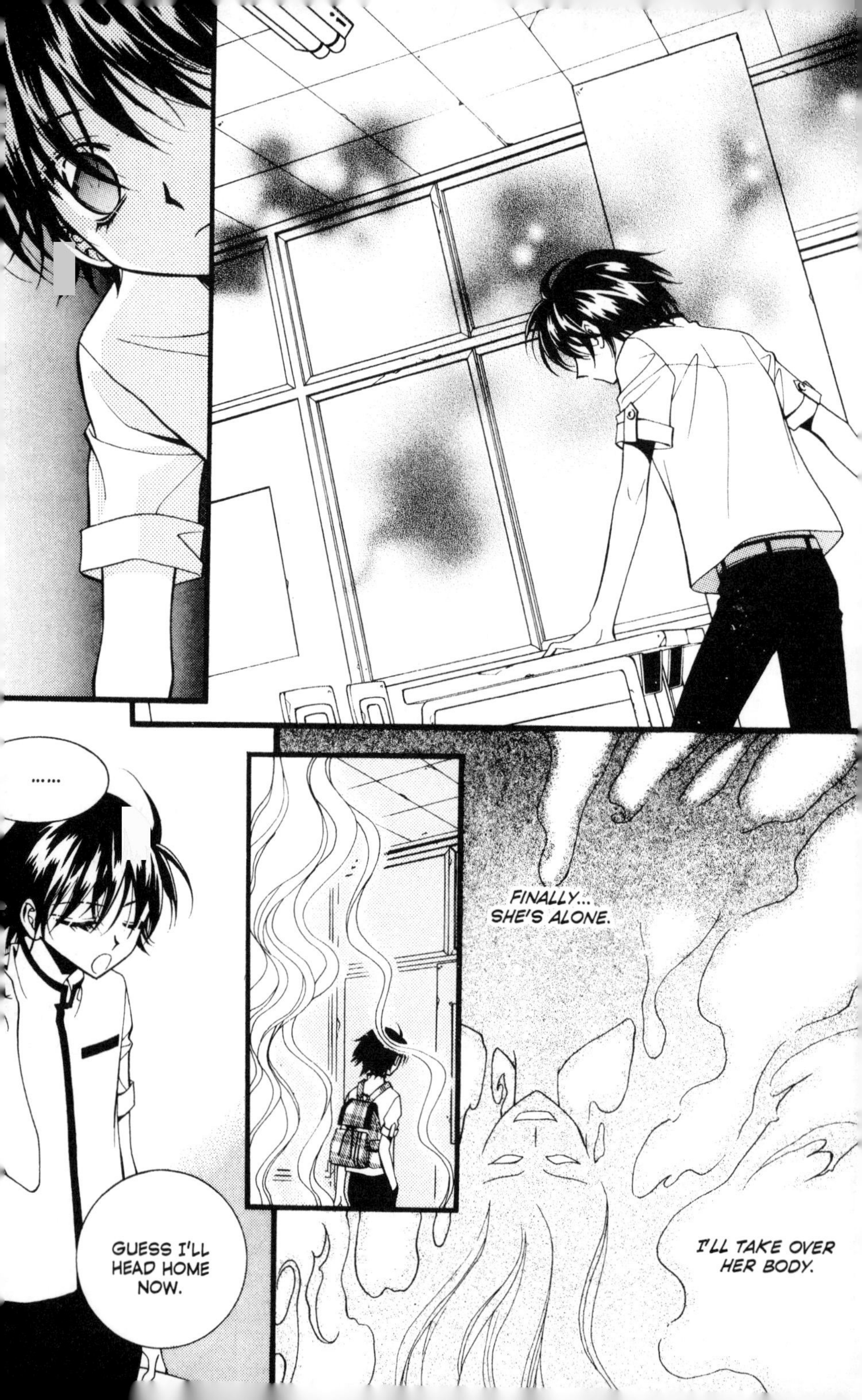
……
GUESS I'LL HEAD HOME NOW.
FINALLY... SHE'S ALONE.
I'LL TAKE OVER HER BODY.

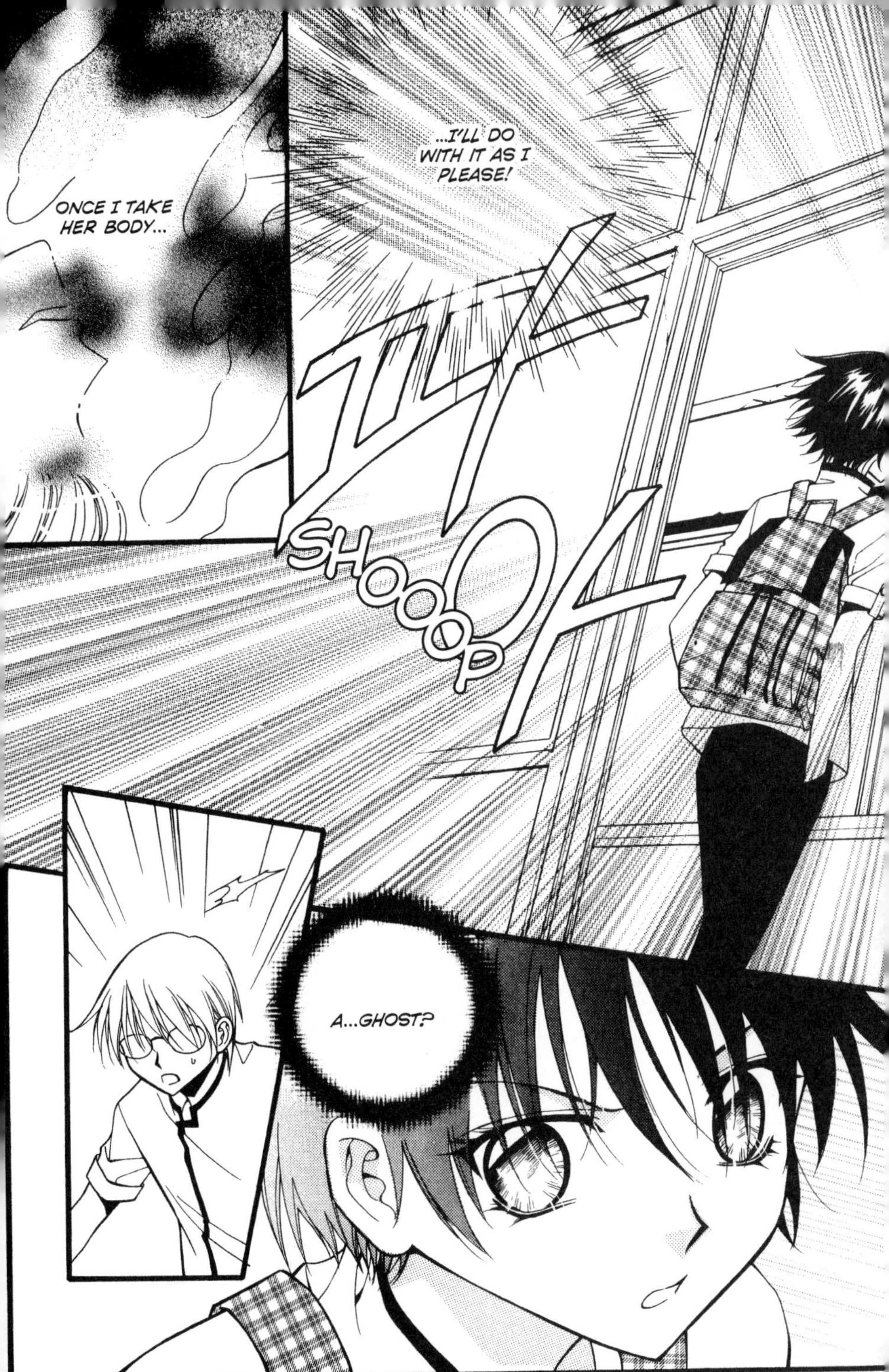
ONCE I TAKE HER BODY...
...I'LL DO WITH IT AS I PLEASE!
ZIP
SHOOOP
A...GHOST?

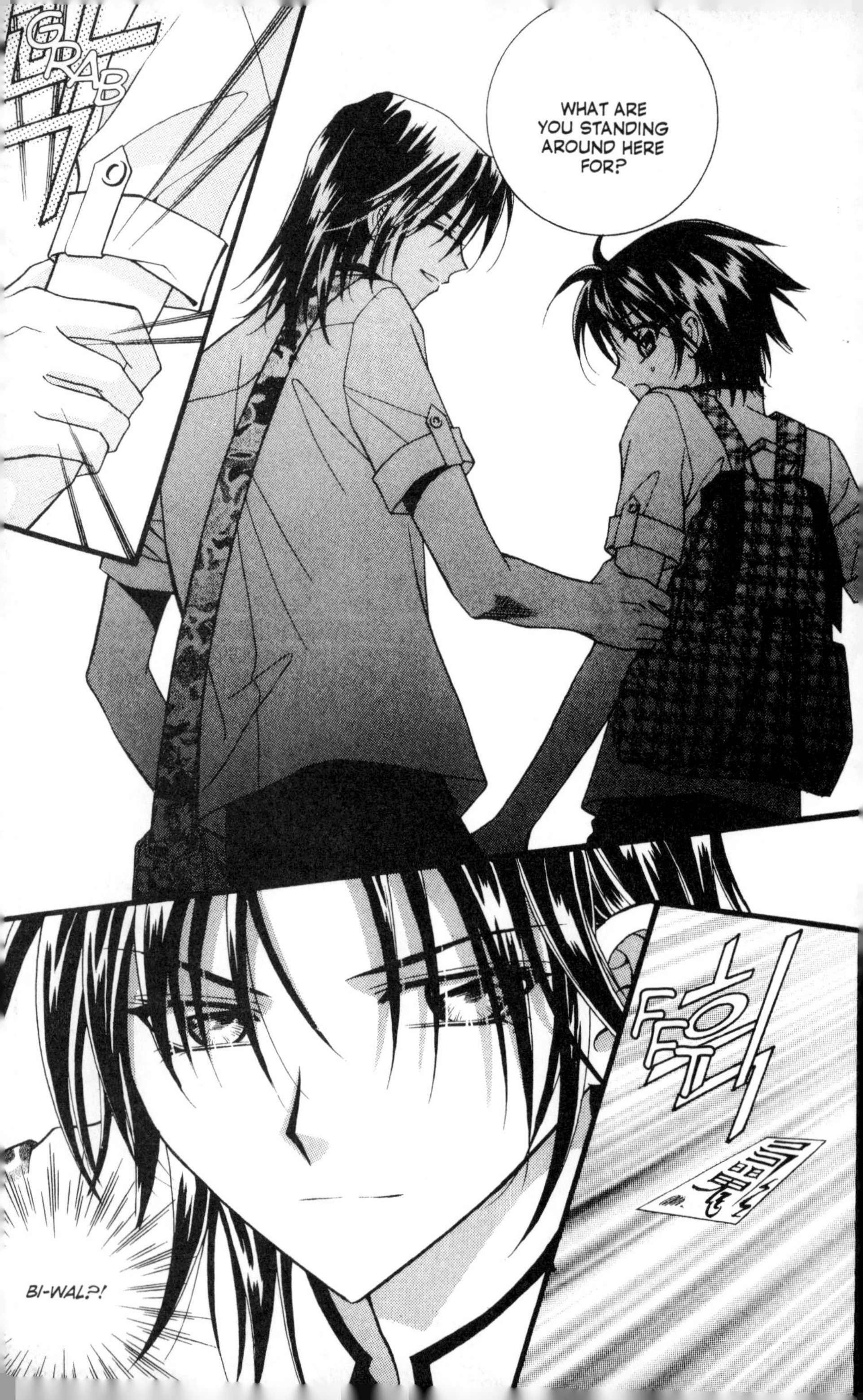
GRAB
WHAT ARE YOU STANDING AROUND HERE FOR?
BI-WAL?!
FFFT

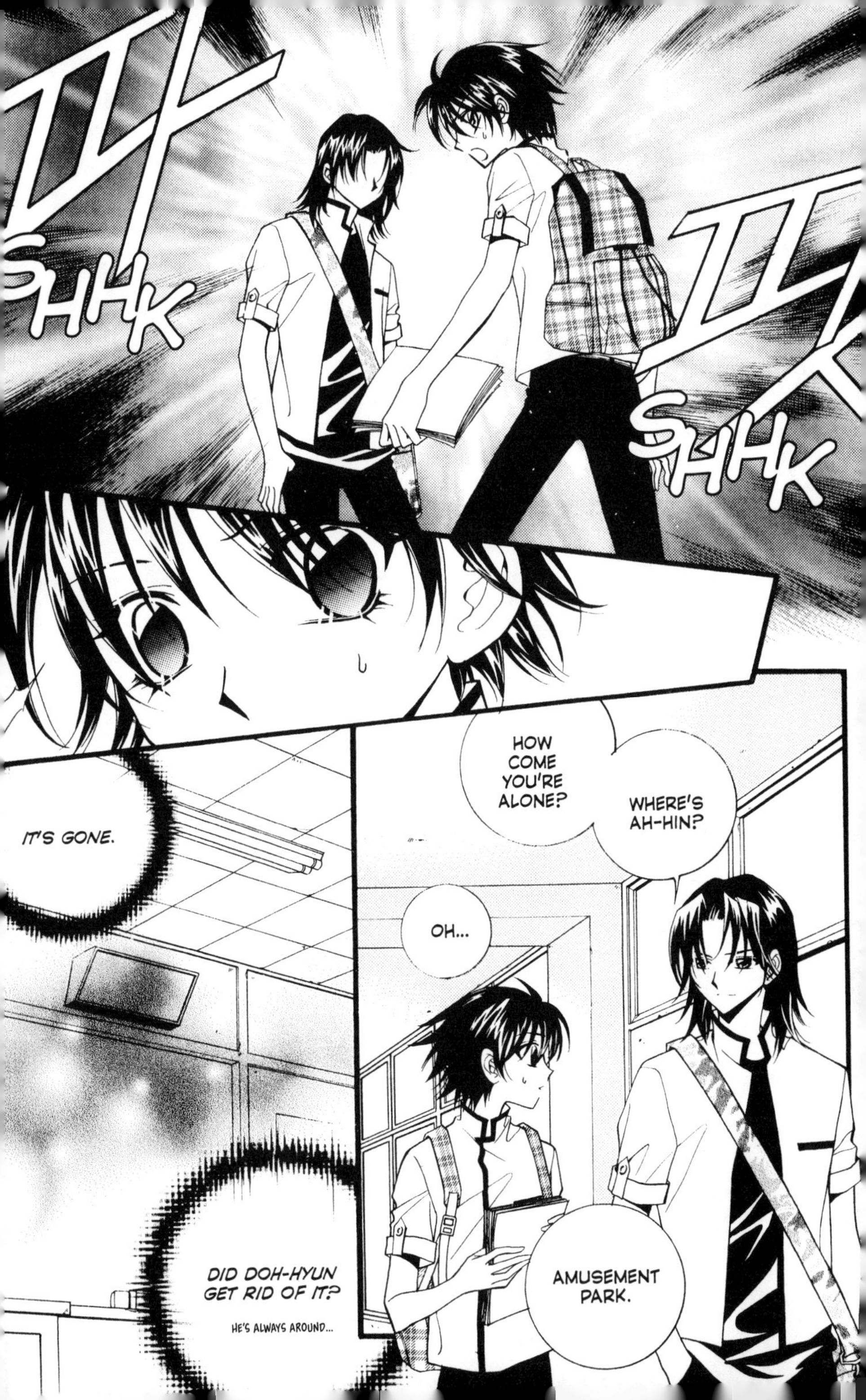
SHHK
SHHK
IT'S GONE.
DID DOH-HYUN GET RID OF IT?
HE'S ALWAYS AROUND...
HOW COME YOU'RE ALONE?
WHERE'S AH-HIN?
OH...
AMUSEMENT PARK.

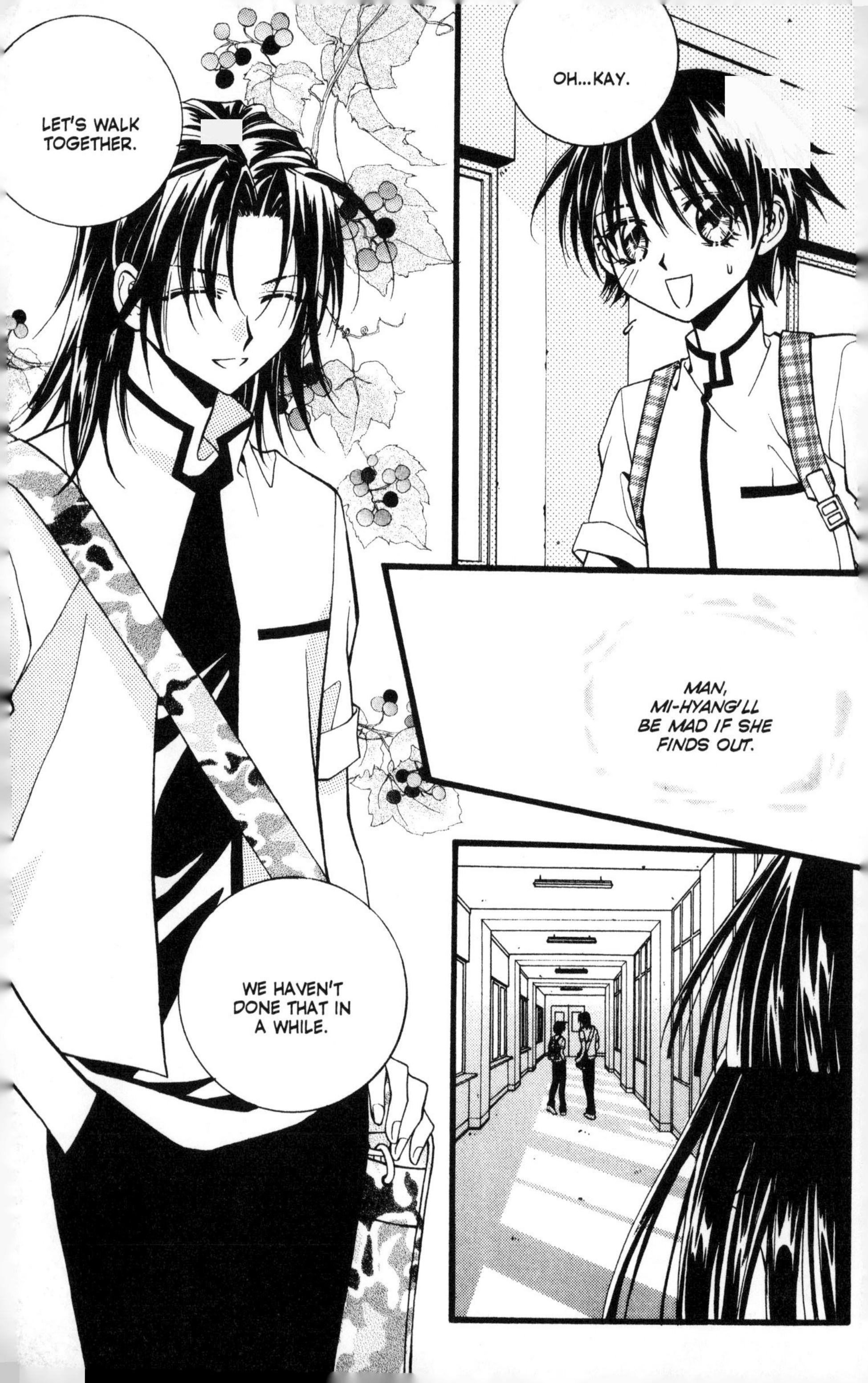
LET'S WALK TOGETHER.
WE HAVEN'T DONE THAT IN A WHILE.
OH...KAY.
MAN, MI-HYANG'LL BE MAD IF SHE FINDS OUT.

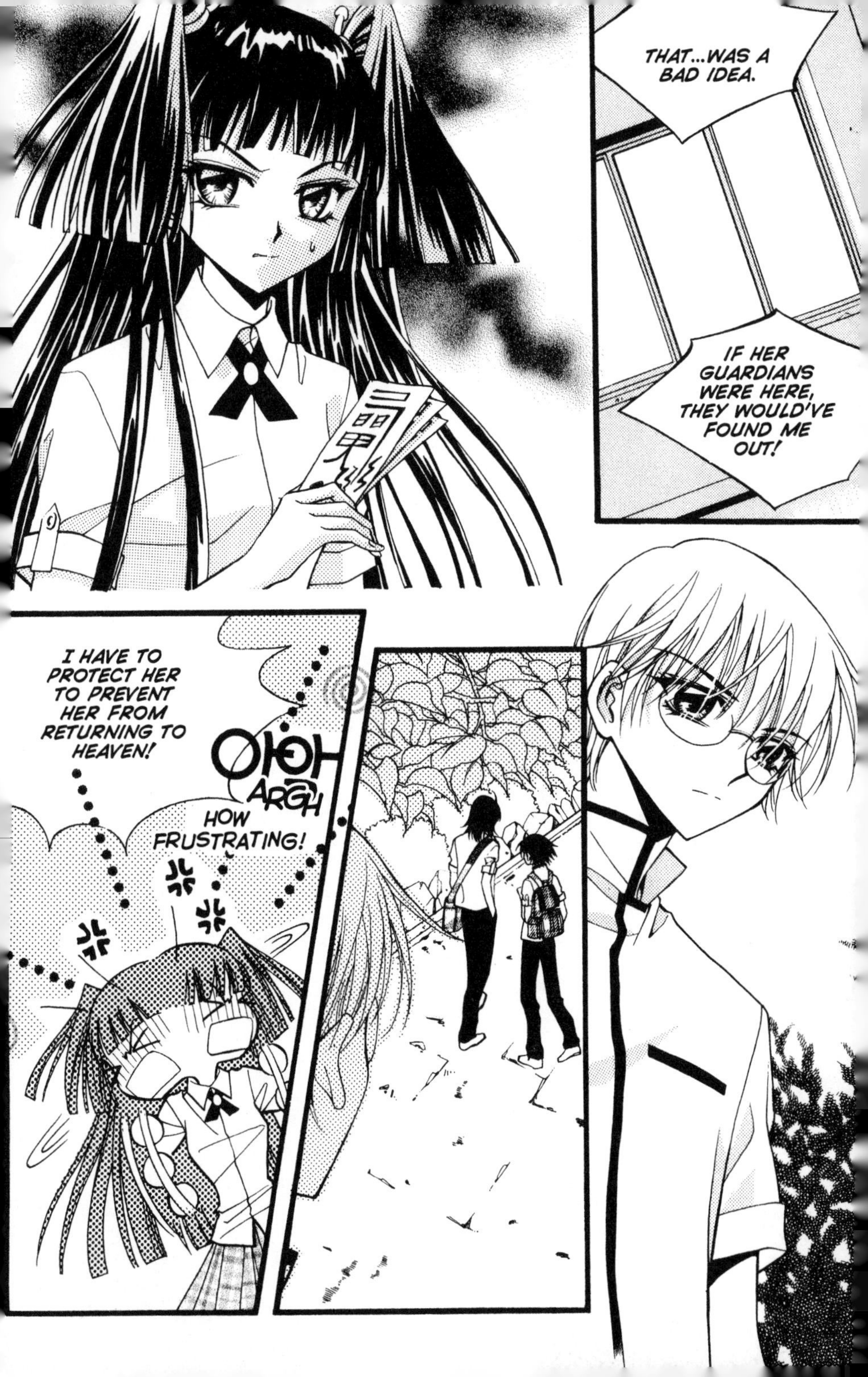
THAT...WAS A BAD IDEA.
IF HER GUARDIANS WERE HERE, THEY WOULD'VE FOUND ME OUT!
I HAVE TO PROTECT HER TO PREVENT HER FROM RETURNING TO HEAVEN!
ARGH
HOW FRUSTRATING!

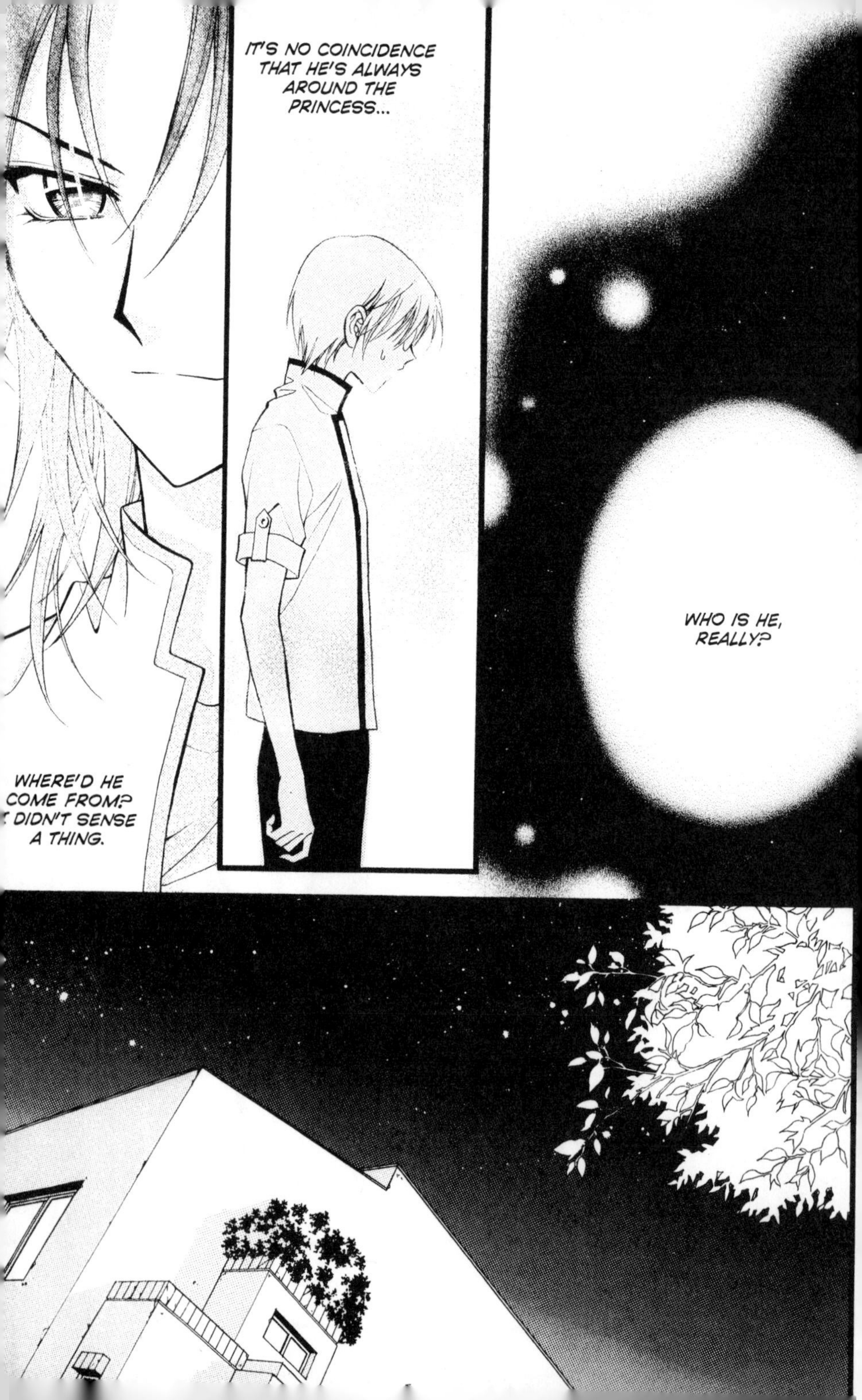
WHERE'D HE COME FROM? DIDN'T SENSE A THING.
IT'S NO COINCIDENCE THAT HE'S ALWAYS AROUND THE PRINCESS...
WHO IS HE, REALLY?

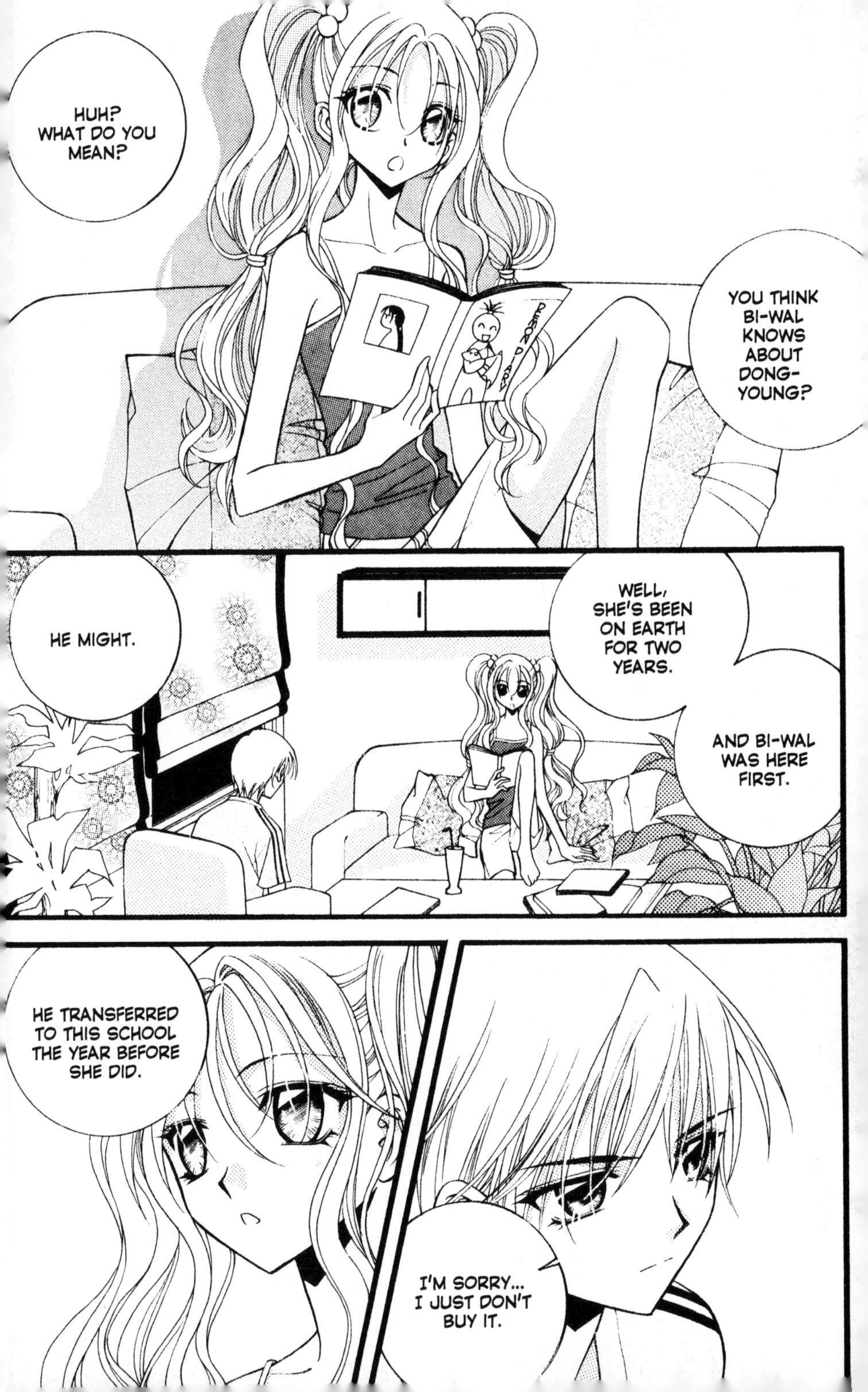
HUH? WHAT DO YOU MEAN?
YOU THINK BI-WAL KNOWS ABOUT DONG-YOUNG?
DEMON DIARY
HE MIGHT.
WELL, SHE'S BEEN ON EARTH FOR TWO YEARS.
AND BI-WAL WAS HERE FIRST.
HE TRANSFERRED TO THIS SCHOOL THE YEAR BEFORE SHE DID.
I'M SORRY... I JUST DON'T BUY IT.

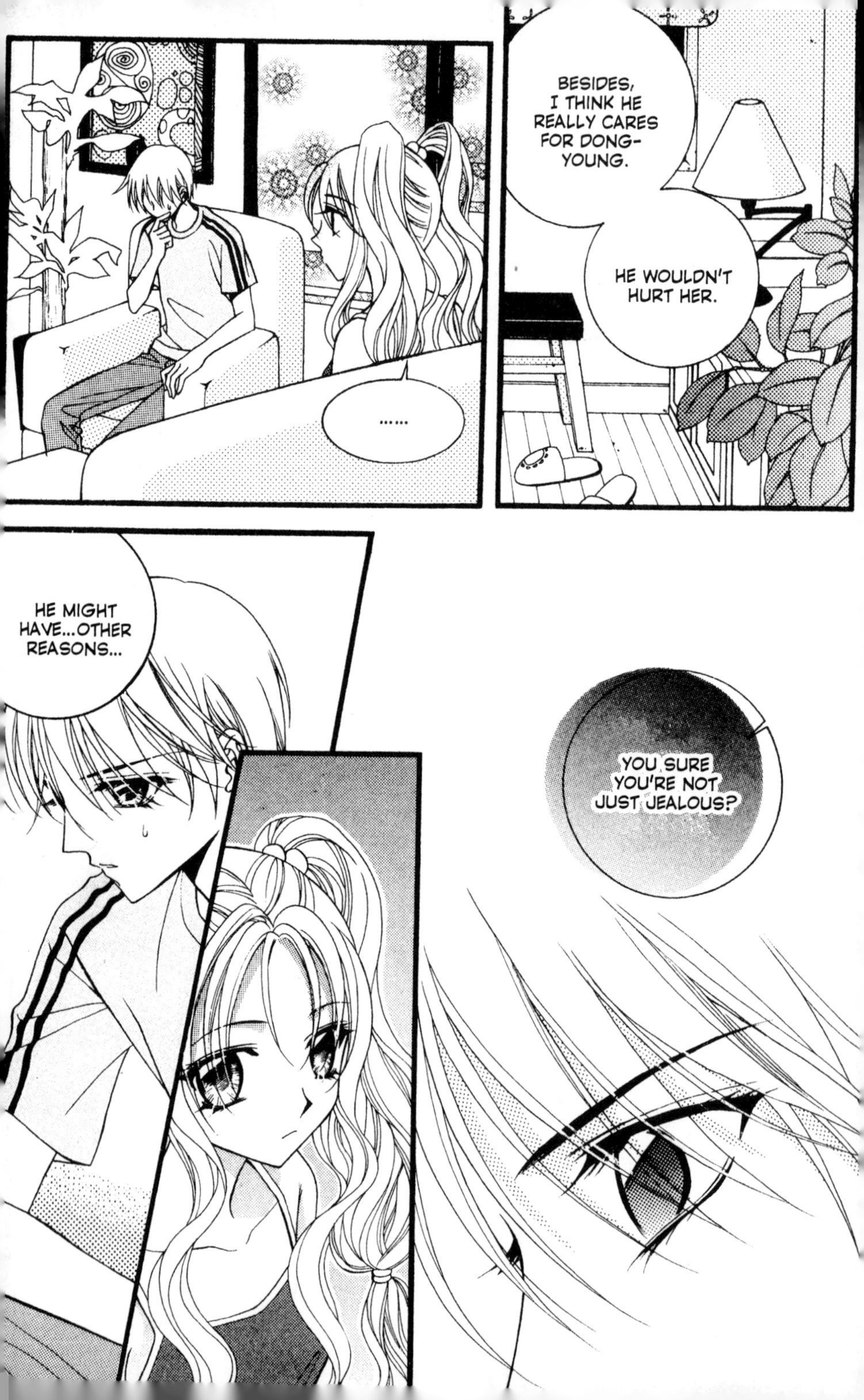
......
BESIDES, I THINK HE REALLY CARES FOR DONG-YOUNG.
HE WOULDN'T HURT HER.
HE MIGHT HAVE...OTHER REASONS...
YOU SURE YOU'RE NOT JUST JEALOUS?

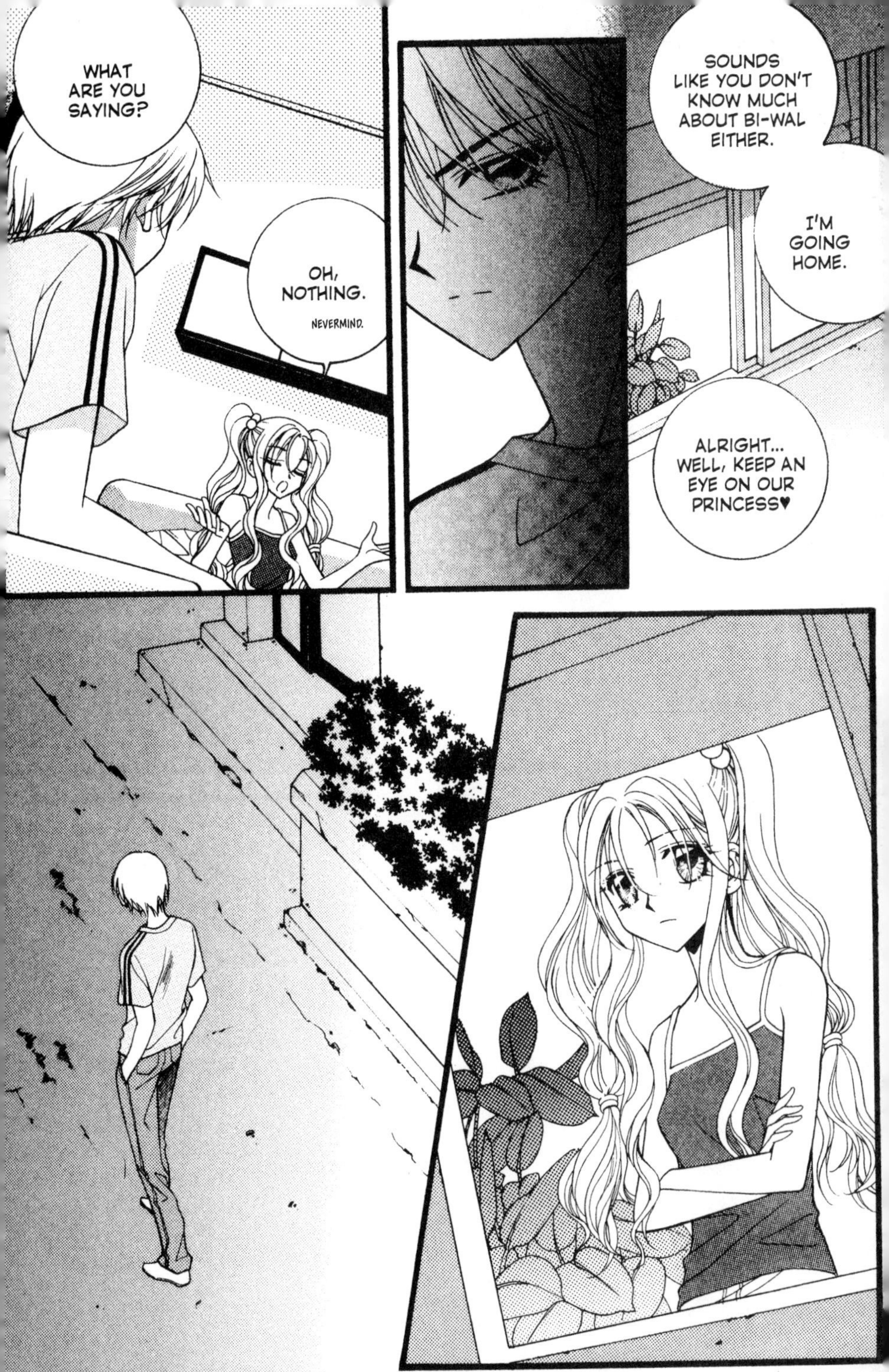
WHAT ARE YOU SAYING?
OH, NOTHING.
NEVERMIND.
SOUNDS LIKE YOU DON'T KNOW MUCH ABOUT BI-WAL EITHER.
I'M GOING HOME.
ALRIGHT... WELL, KEEP AN EYE ON OUR PRINCESS♥

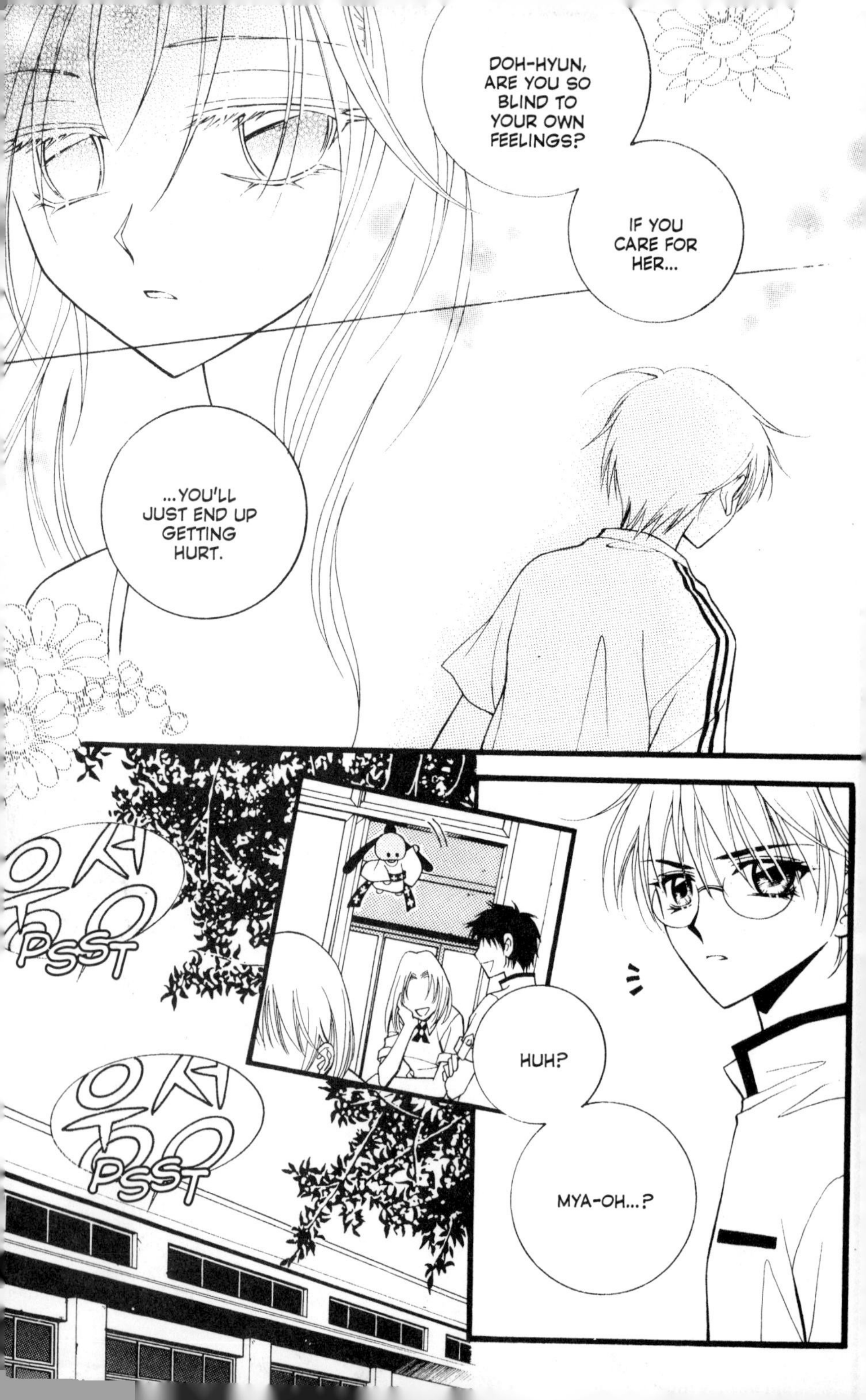
DOH-HYUN, ARE YOU SO BLIND TO YOUR OWN FEELINGS?
IF YOU CARE FOR HER...
...YOU'LL JUST END UP GETTING HURT.
PSST
PSST
HUH?
MYA-OH...?

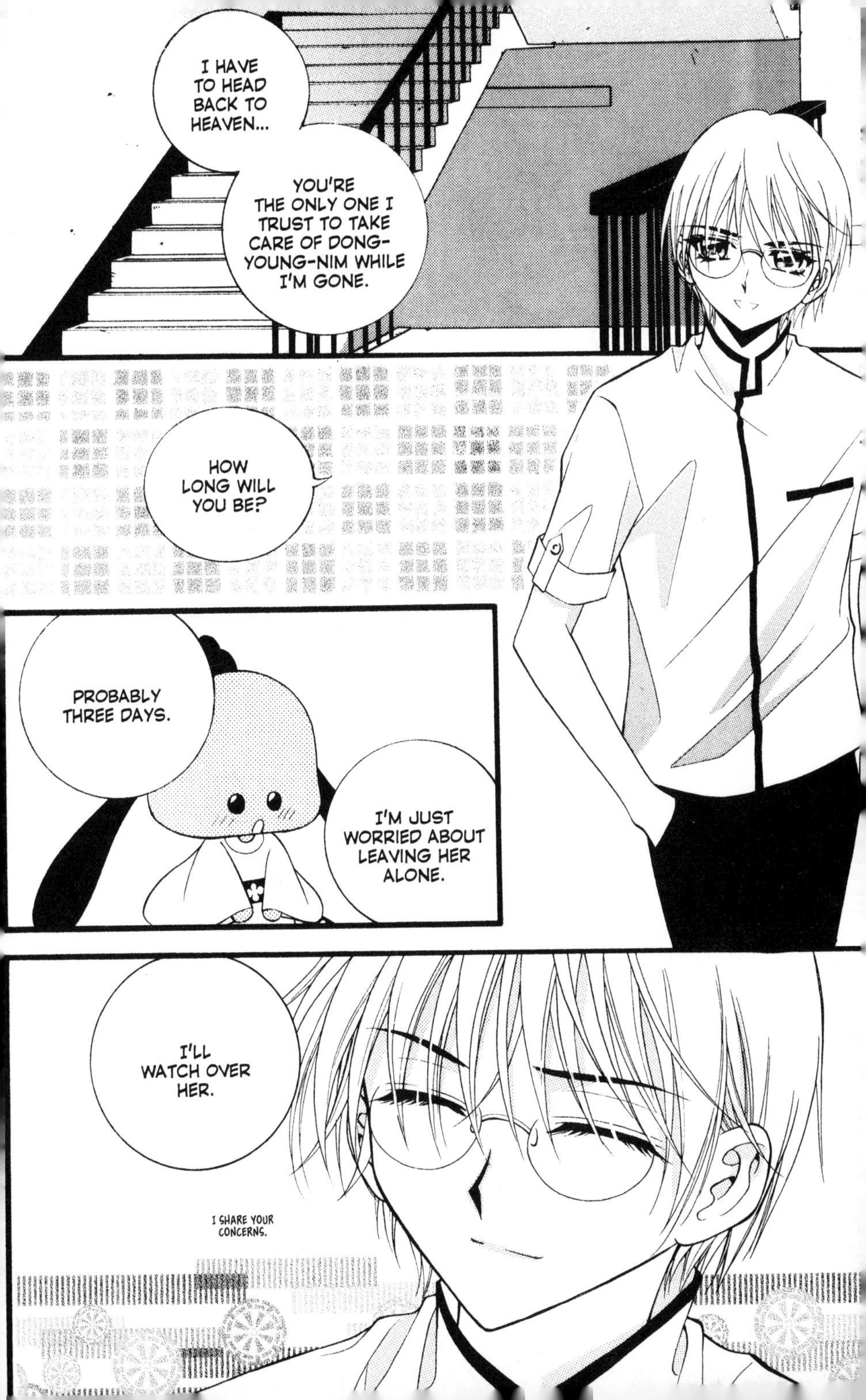
I HAVE TO HEAD BACK TO HEAVEN...
YOU'RE THE ONLY ONE I TRUST TO TAKE CARE OF DONG-YOUNG-NIM WHILE I'M GONE.
HOW LONG WILL YOU BE?
PROBABLY THREE DAYS.
I'M JUST WORRIED ABOUT LEAVING HER ALONE.
I'LL WATCH OVER HER.
I SHARE YOUR CONCERNS.

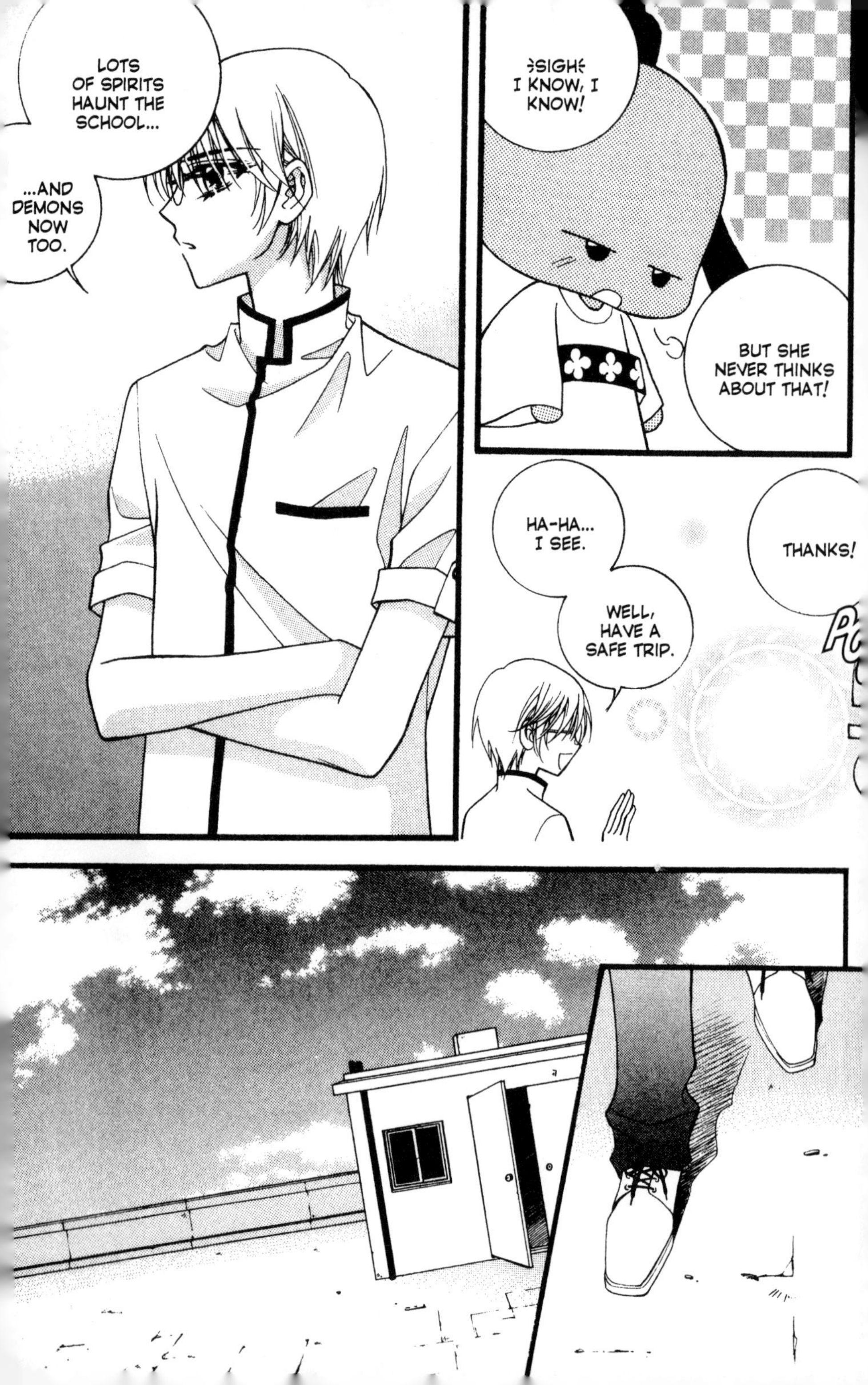
LOTS OF SPIRITS HAUNT THE SCHOOL...
...AND DEMONS NOW TOO.
SIGH I KNOW, I KNOW!
BUT SHE NEVER THINKS ABOUT THAT!
HA-HA... I SEE.
WELL, HAVE A SAFE TRIP.
THANKS!

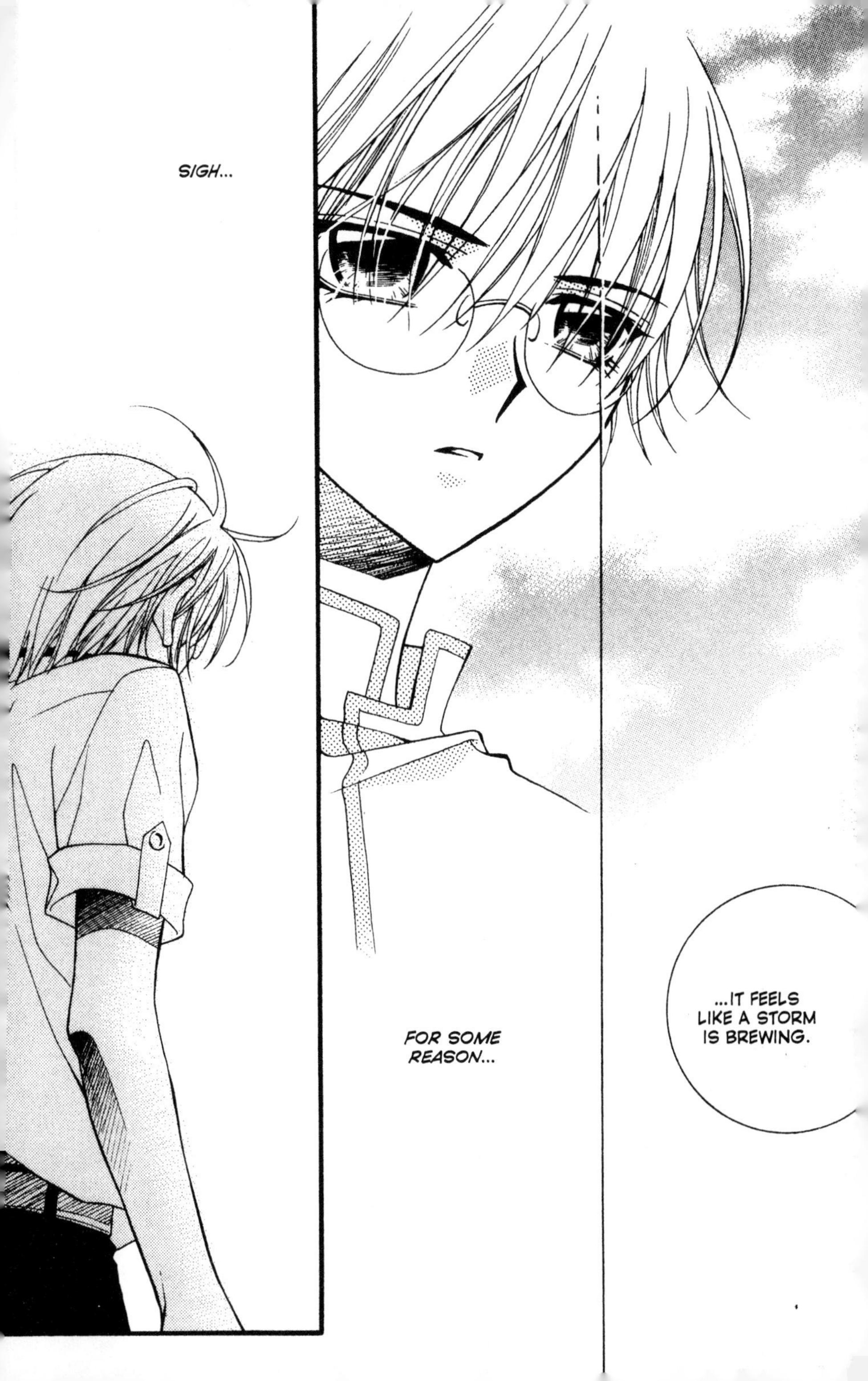
SIGH...
FOR SOME REASON...
...IT FEELS LIKE A STORM IS BREWING.

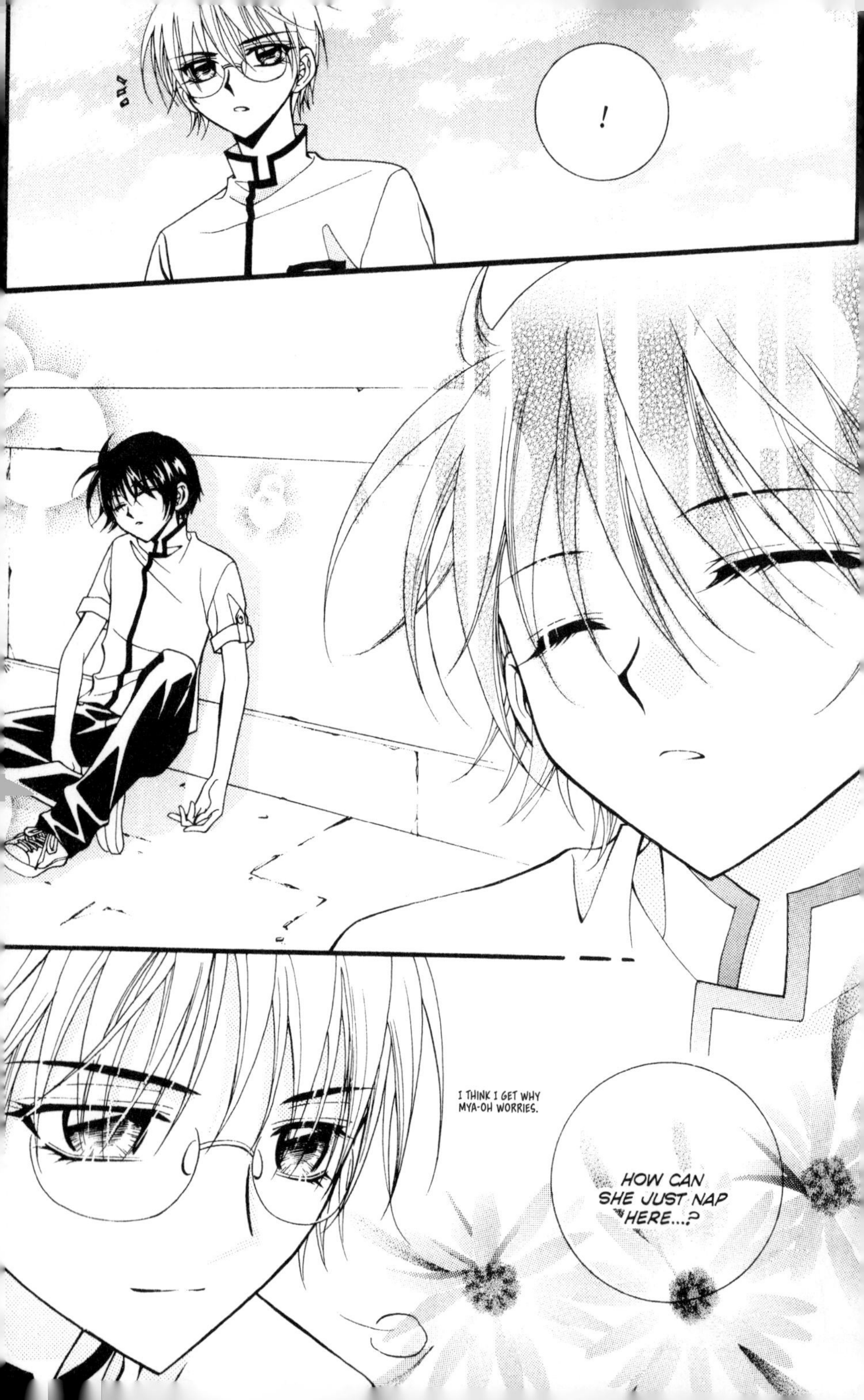
!
I THINK I GET WHY MYA-OH WORRIES.
HOW CAN SHE JUST NAP HERE...?

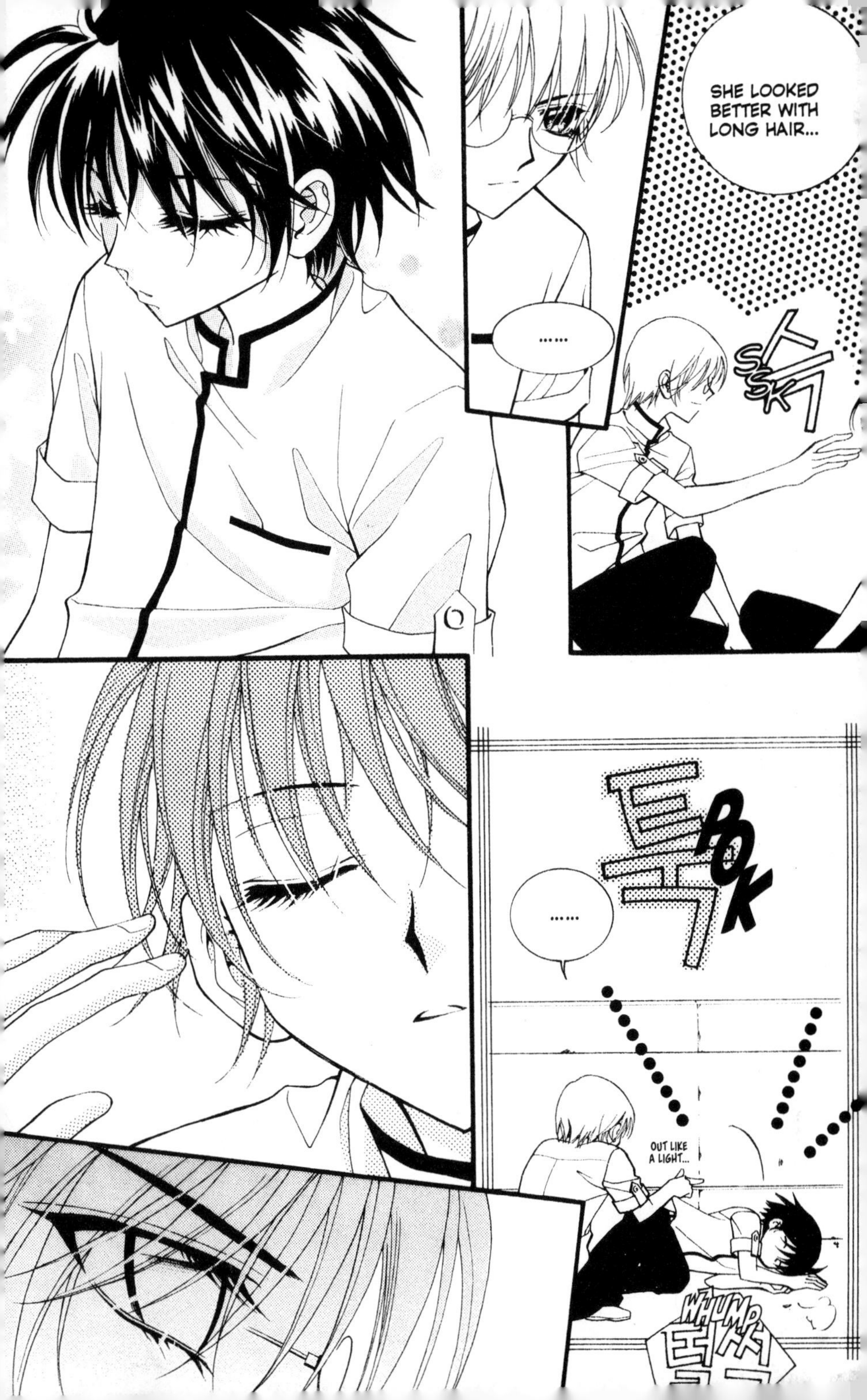

......
SHE LOOKED BETTER WITH LONG HAIR...
SSK
......
BOK
OUT LIKE A LIGHT...
WHUMP

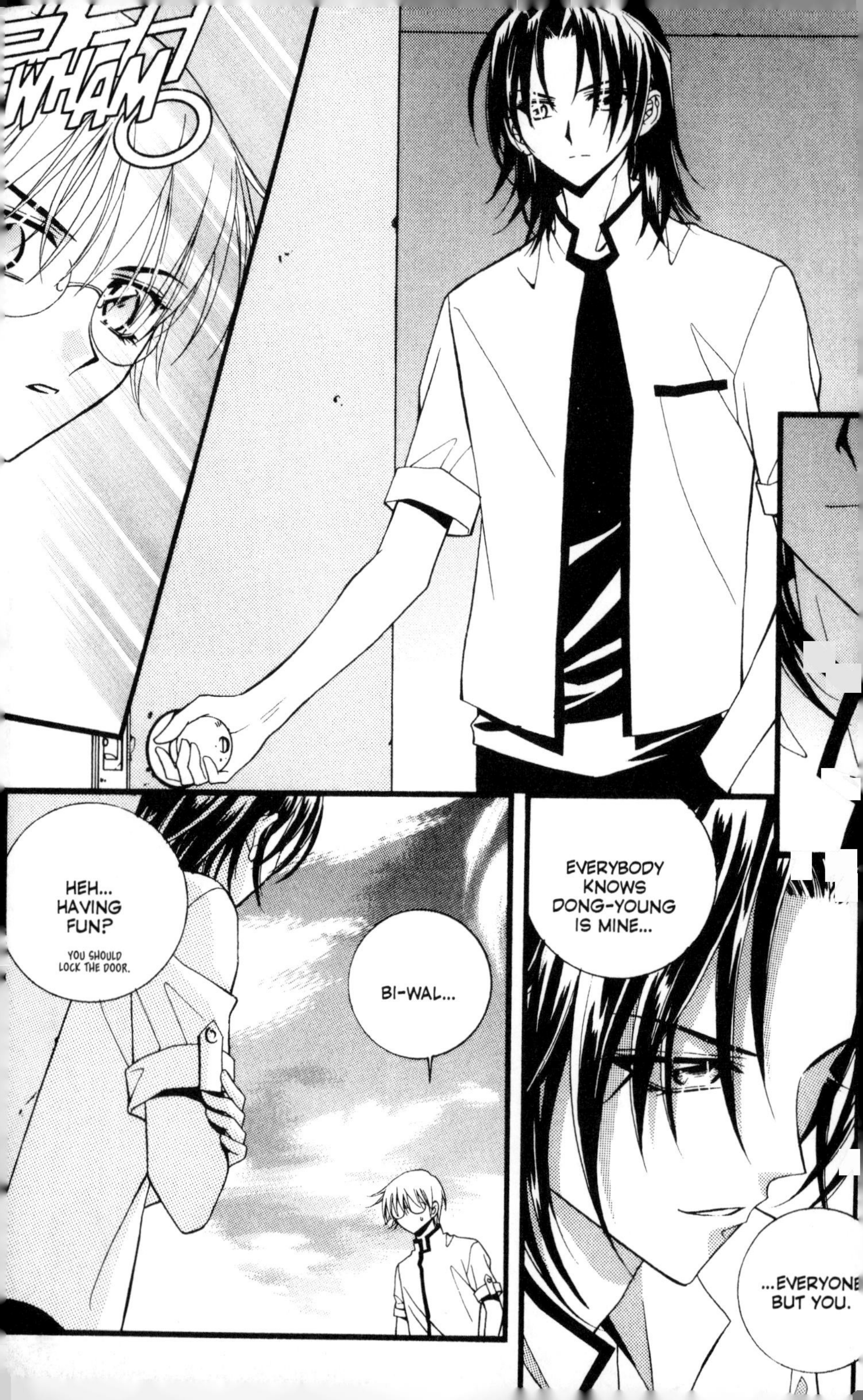
WHAM!
HEH... HAVING FUN?
YOU SHOULD LOCK THE DOOR.
BI-WAL...
EVERYBODY KNOWS DONG-YOUNG IS MINE...
...EVERYONE BUT YOU.

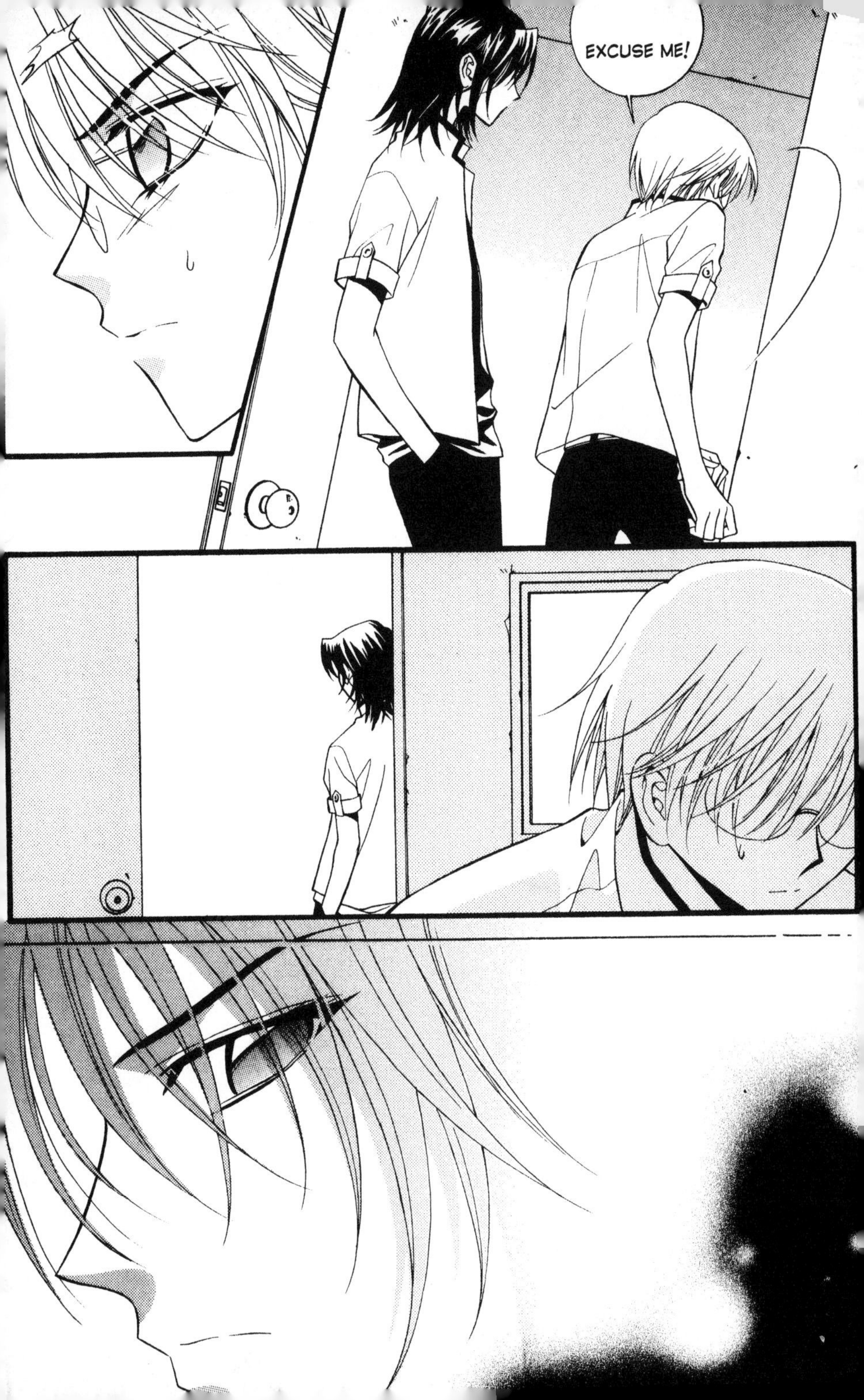
EXCUSE ME!

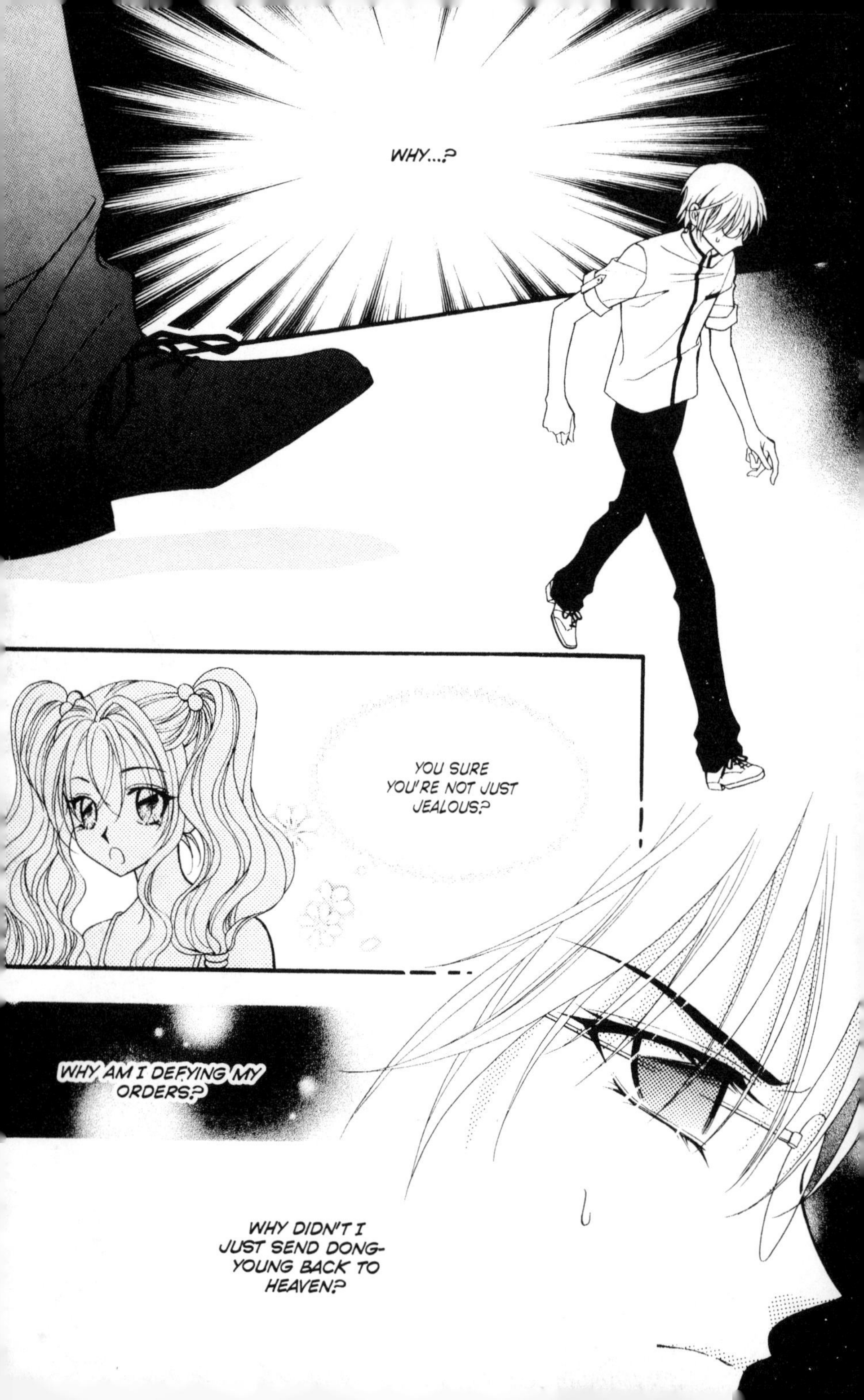
WHY...?
YOU SURE YOU'RE NOT JUST JEALOUS?
WHY AM I DEFYING MY ORDERS?
WHY DIDN'T I JUST SEND DONG-YOUNG BACK TO HEAVEN?

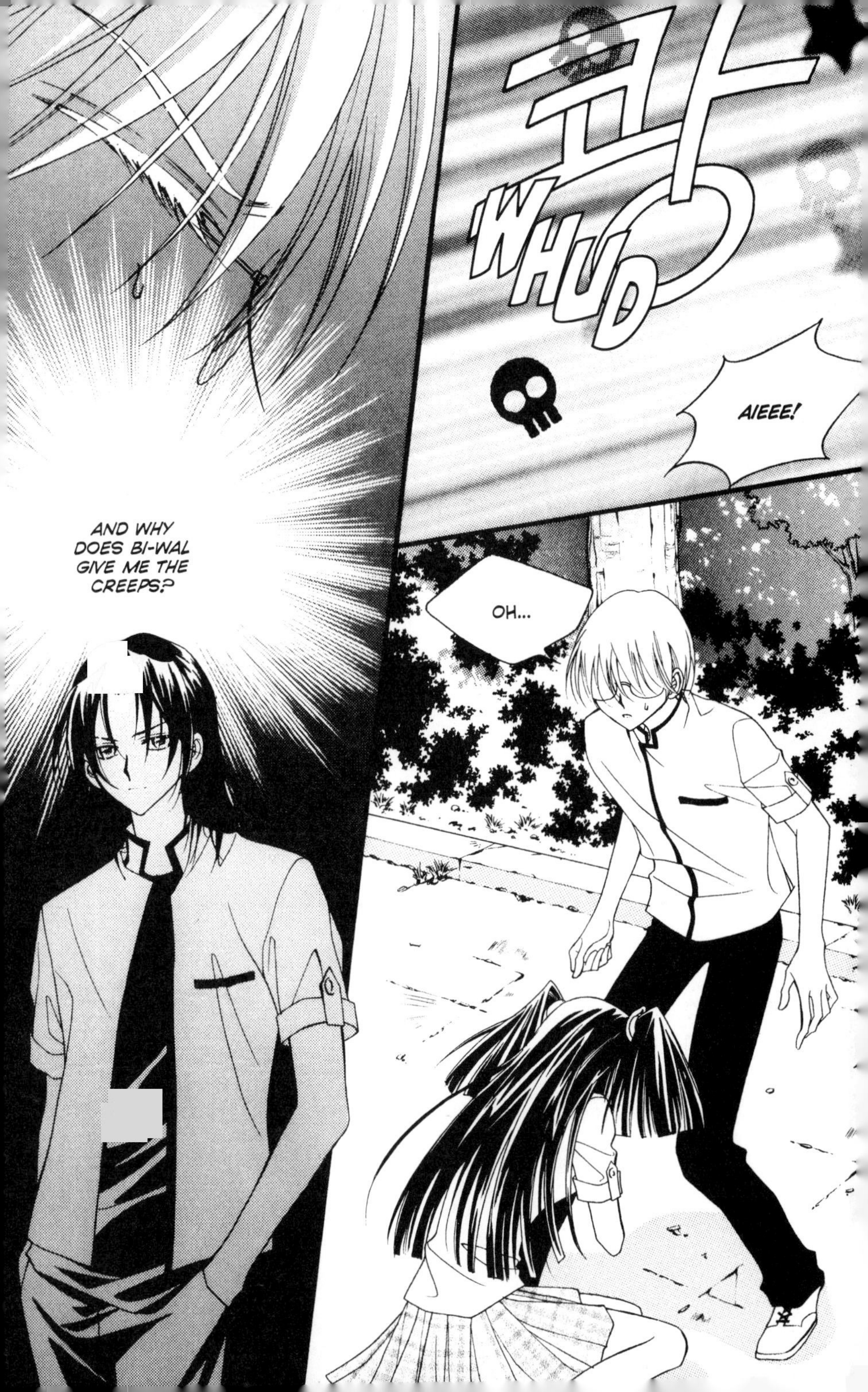
AND WHY DOES BI-WAL GIVE ME THE CREEPS?
WHUD
AIEEE!
OH...

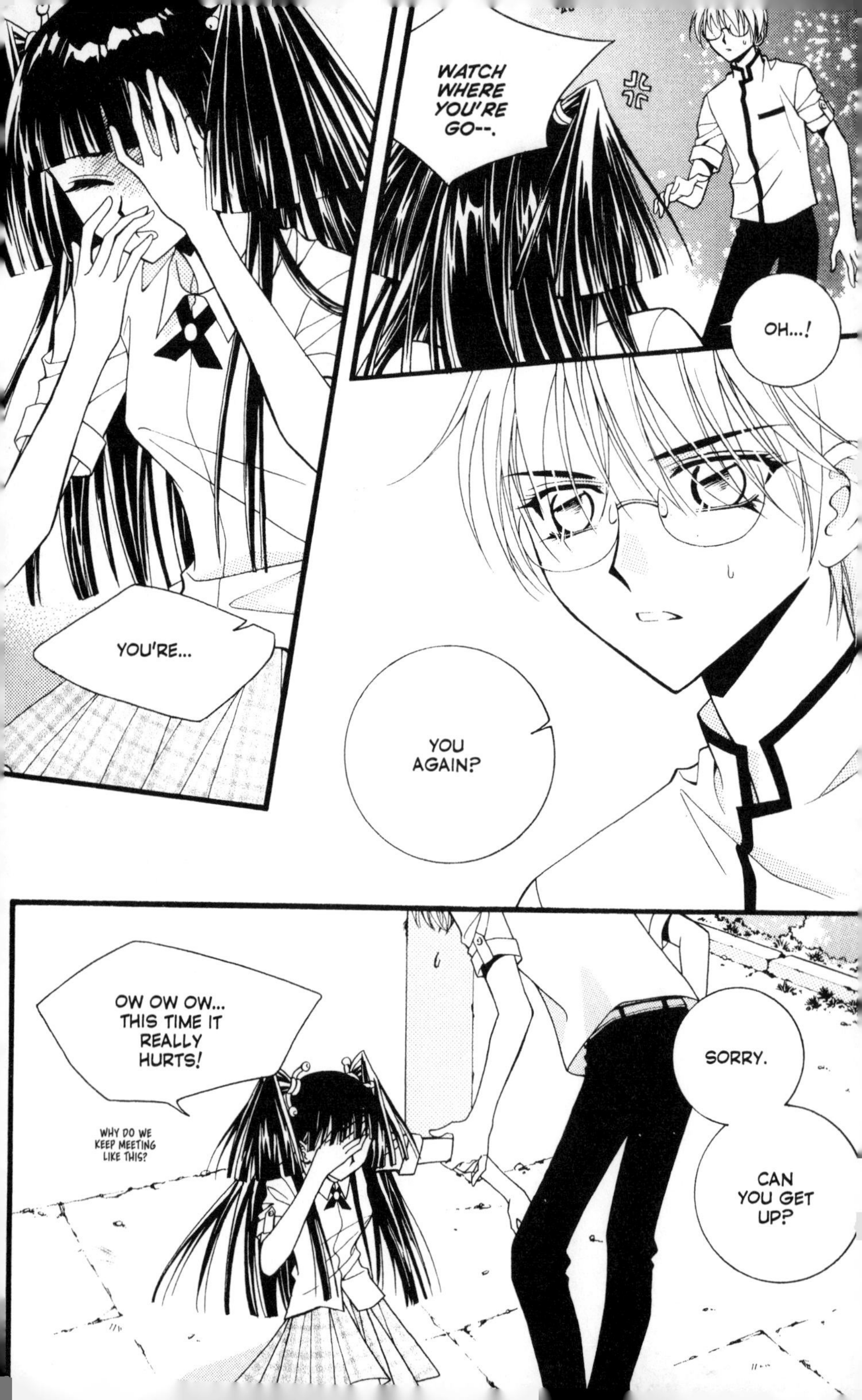
YOU'RE...
WATCH WHERE YOU'RE GO--.
OH...!
YOU AGAIN?
OW OW OW... THIS TIME IT REALLY HURTS!
WHY DO WE KEEP MEETING LIKE THIS?
SORRY.
CAN YOU GET UP?

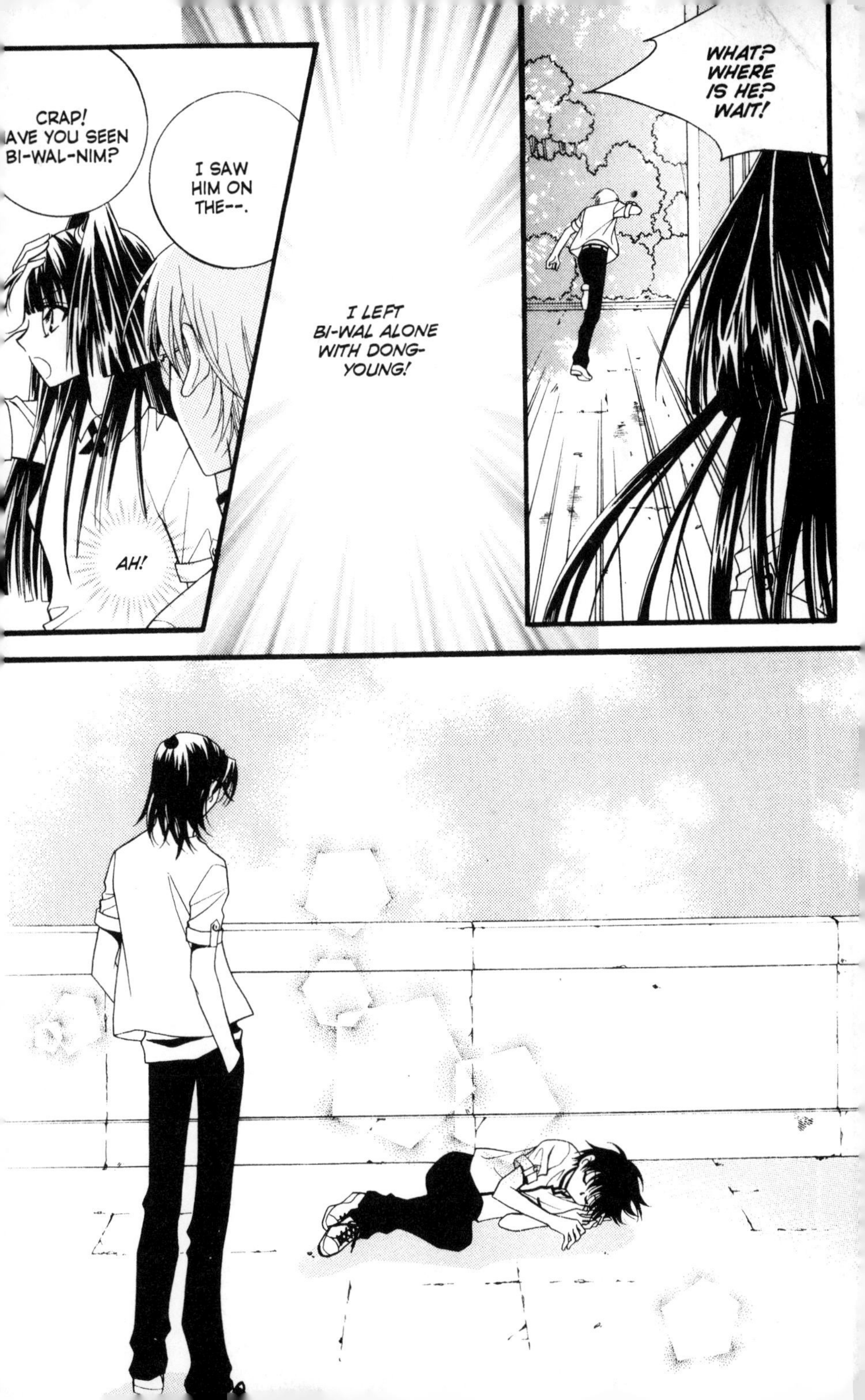
CRAP! AVE YOU SEEN BI-WAL-NIM?
I SAW HIM ON THE--.
AH!
I LEFT BI-WAL ALONE WITH DONG-YOUNG!
WHAT? WHERE IS HE? WAIT!

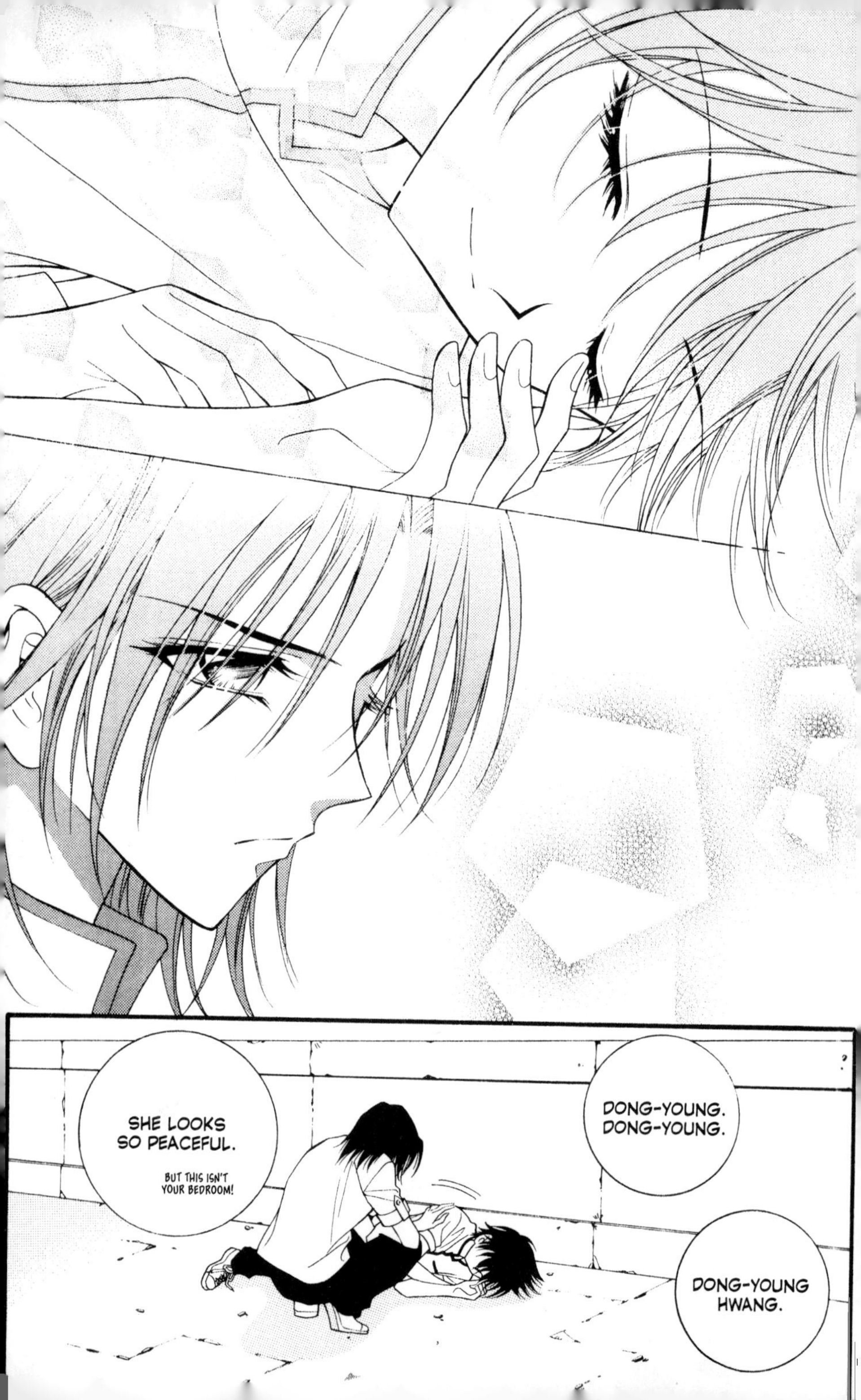
SHE LOOKS SO PEACEFUL.
BUT THIS ISN'T YOUR BEDROOM!
DONG-YOUNG. DONG-YOUNG.
DONG-YOUNG HWANG.

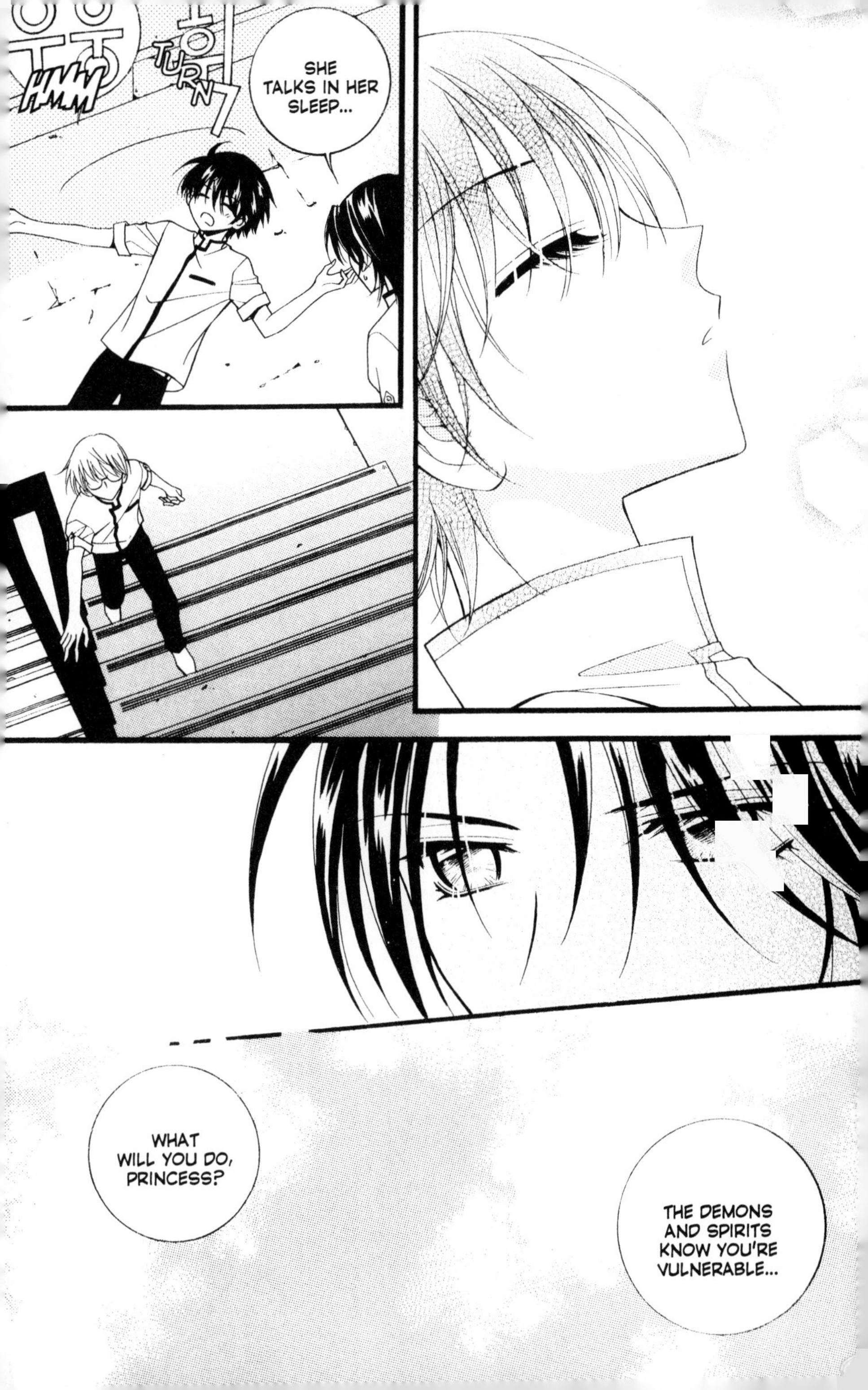
HMM
TURN
SHE TALKS IN HER SLEEP...
WHAT WILL YOU DO, PRINCESS?
THE DEMONS AND SPIRITS KNOW YOU'RE VULNERABLE...

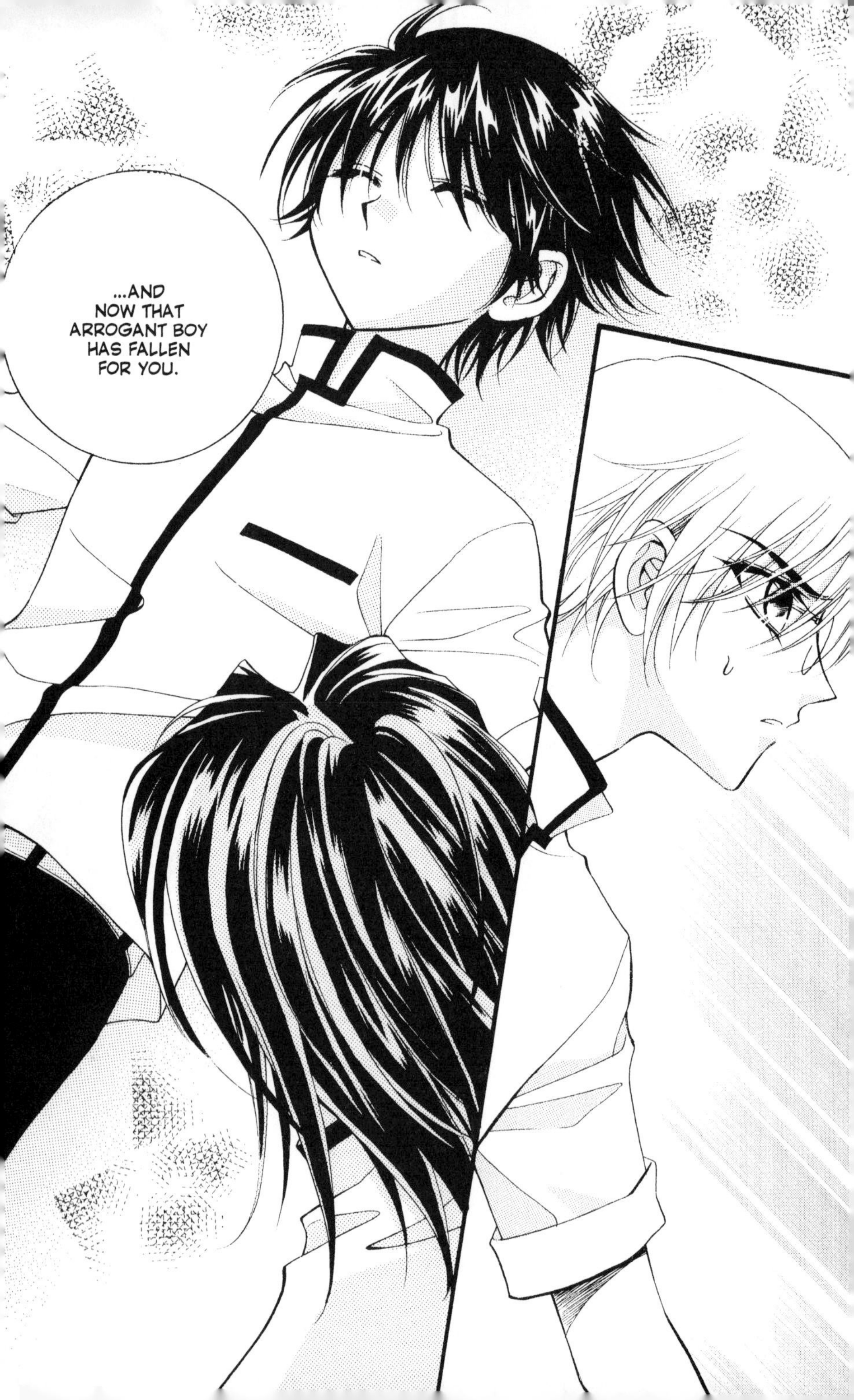
...AND NOW THAT ARROGANT BOY HAS FALLEN FOR YOU.

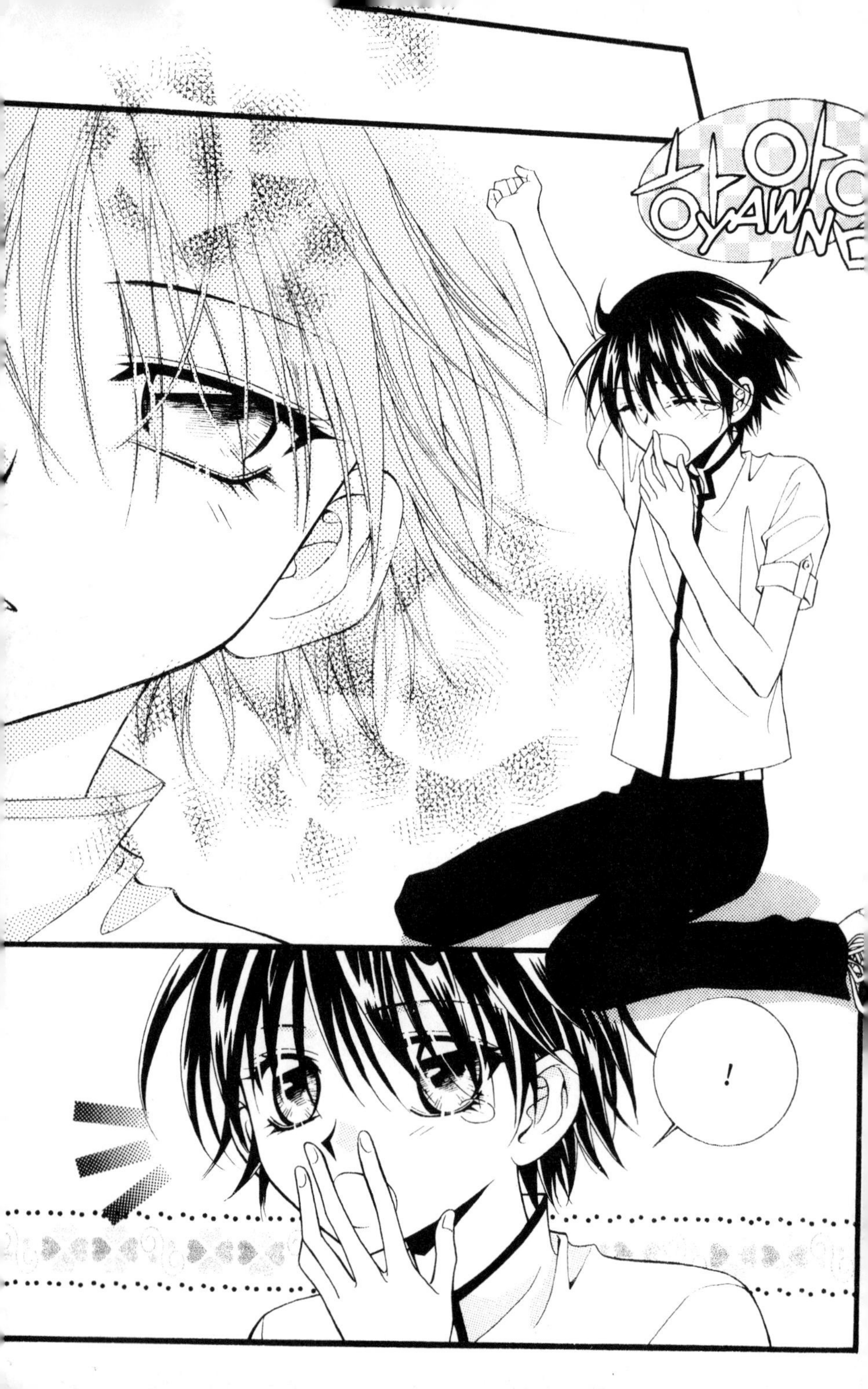
YAWN
!

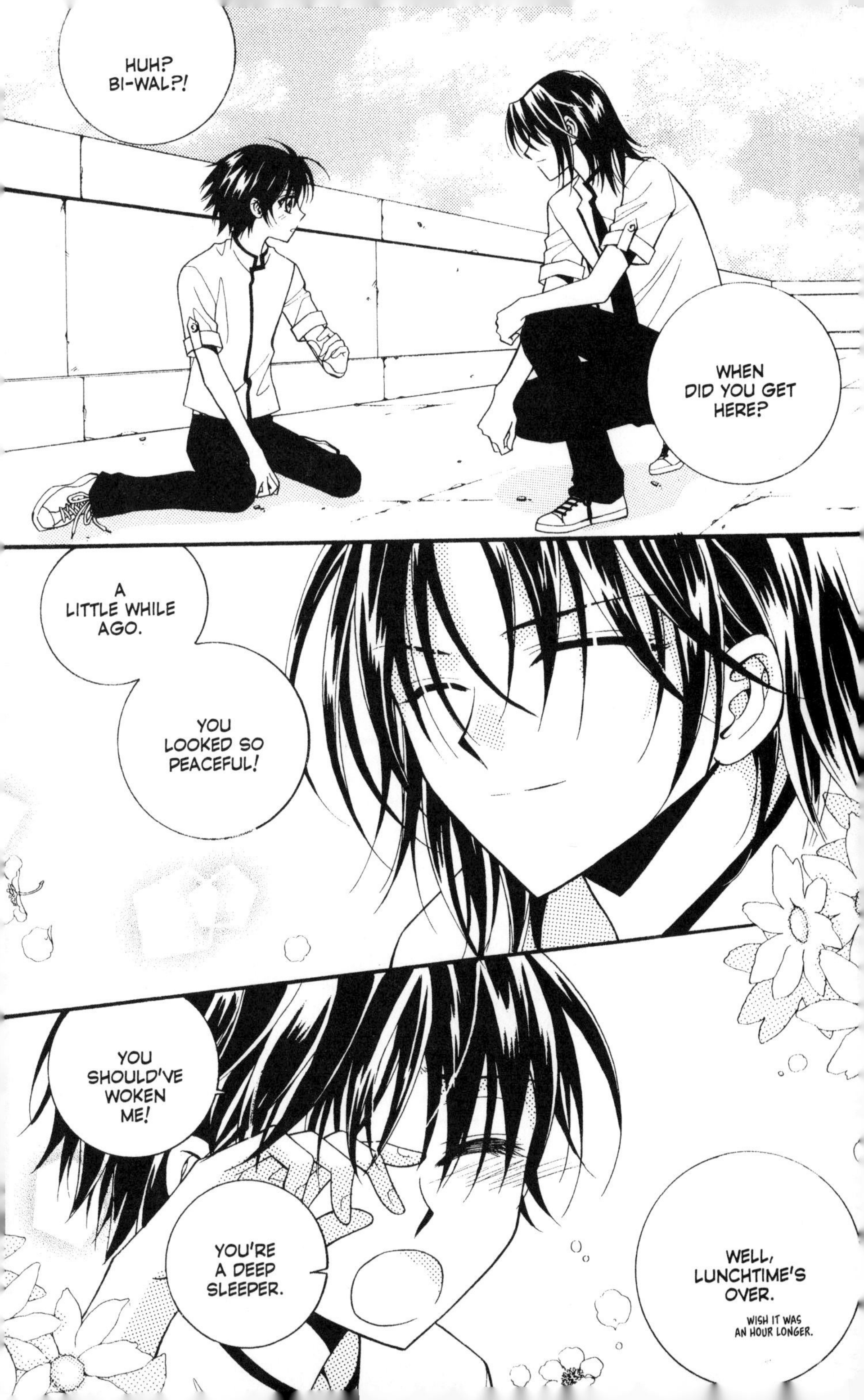
HUH? BI-WAL?!
WHEN DID YOU GET HERE?
A LITTLE WHILE AGO.
YOU LOOKED SO PEACEFUL!
YOU SHOULD'VE WOKEN ME!
YOU'RE A DEEP SLEEPER.
WELL, LUNCHTIME'S OVER.
WISH IT WAS AN HOUR LONGER.

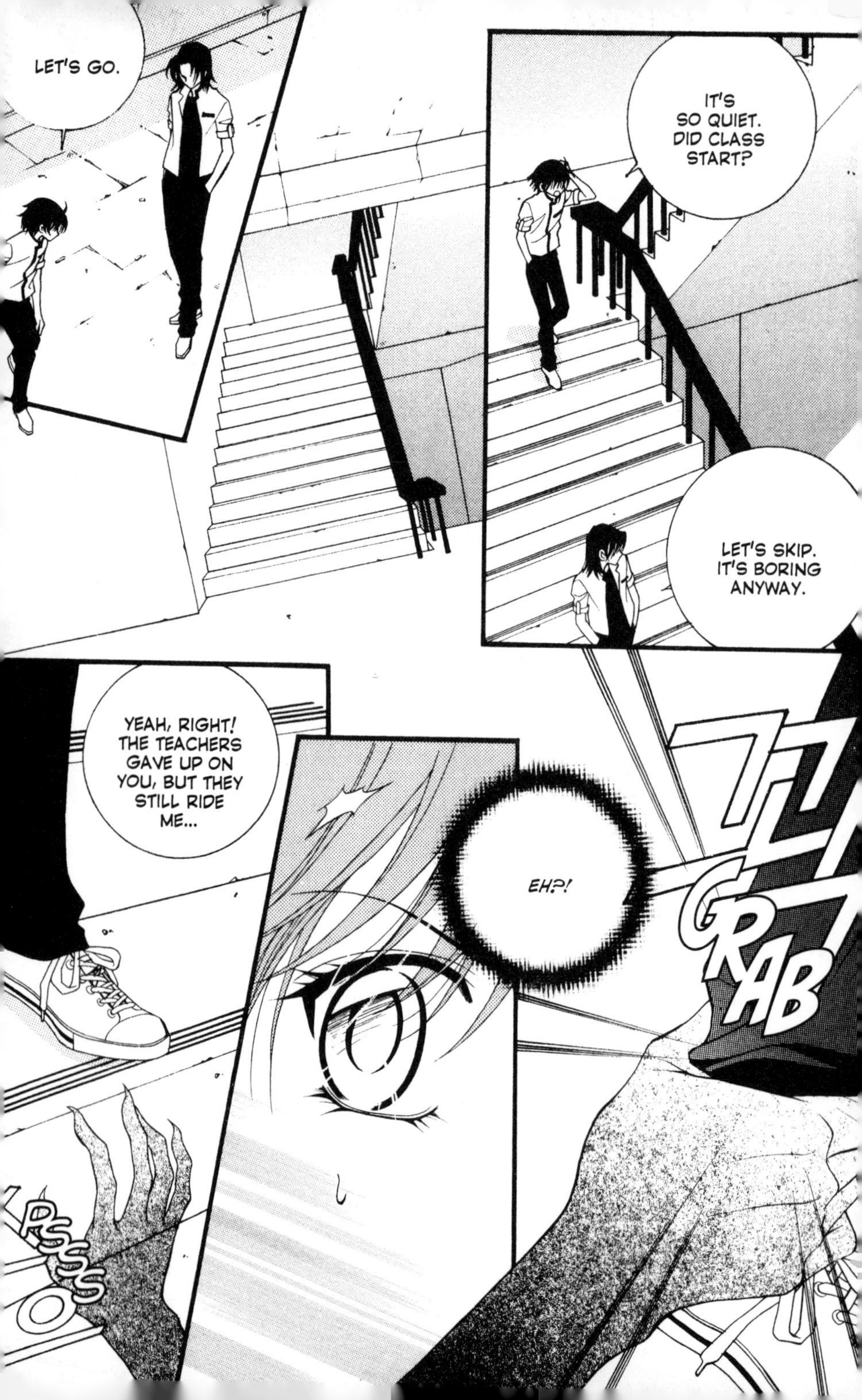
LET'S GO.
IT'S SO QUIET. DID CLASS START?
LET'S SKIP. IT'S BORING ANYWAY.
YEAH, RIGHT! THE TEACHERS GAVE UP ON YOU, BUT THEY STILL RIDE ME...
PSSSO
EH?!
GRAB

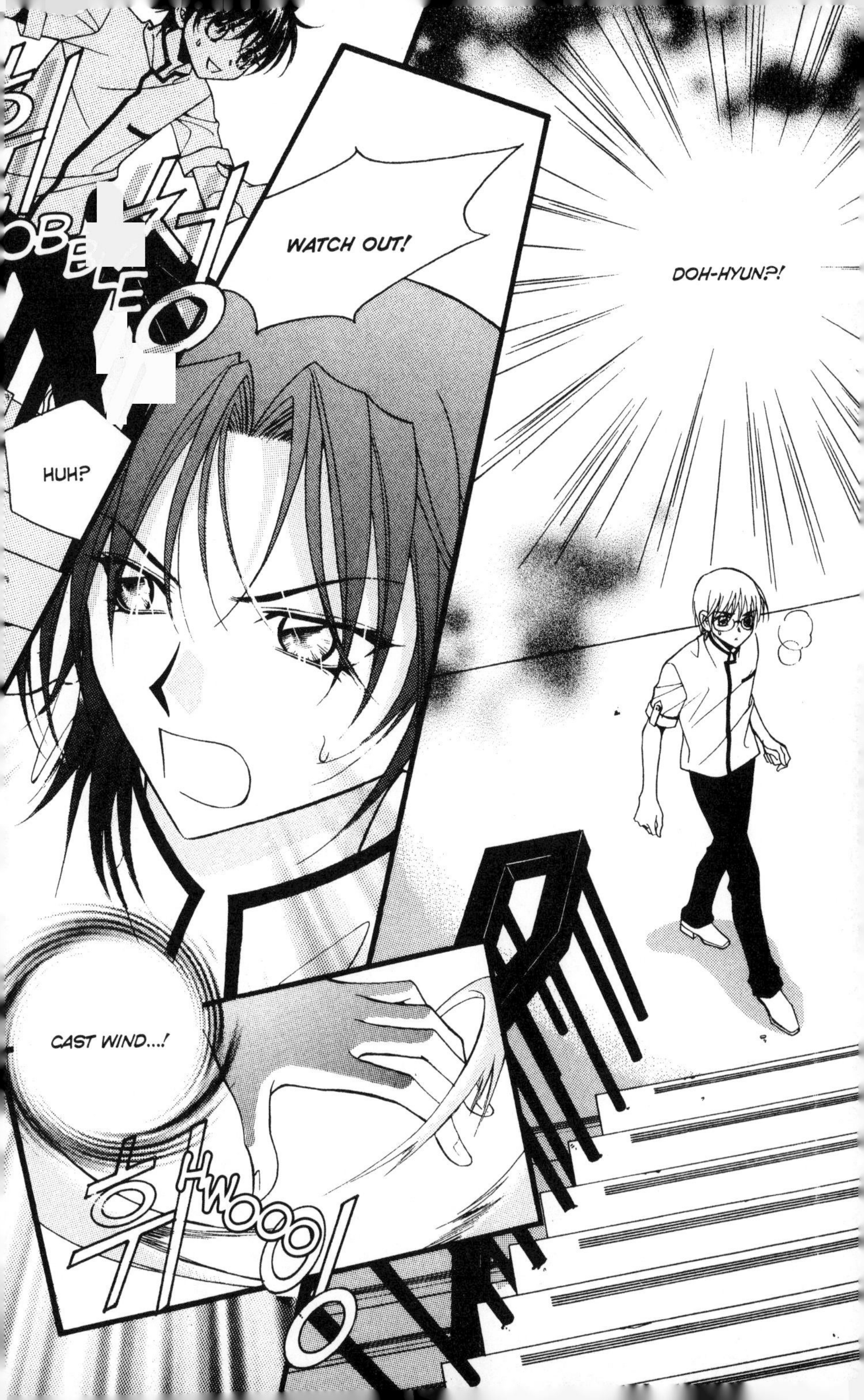

HUH?
WATCH OUT!
DOH-HYUN?!
CAST WIND...!
HWOOOO!

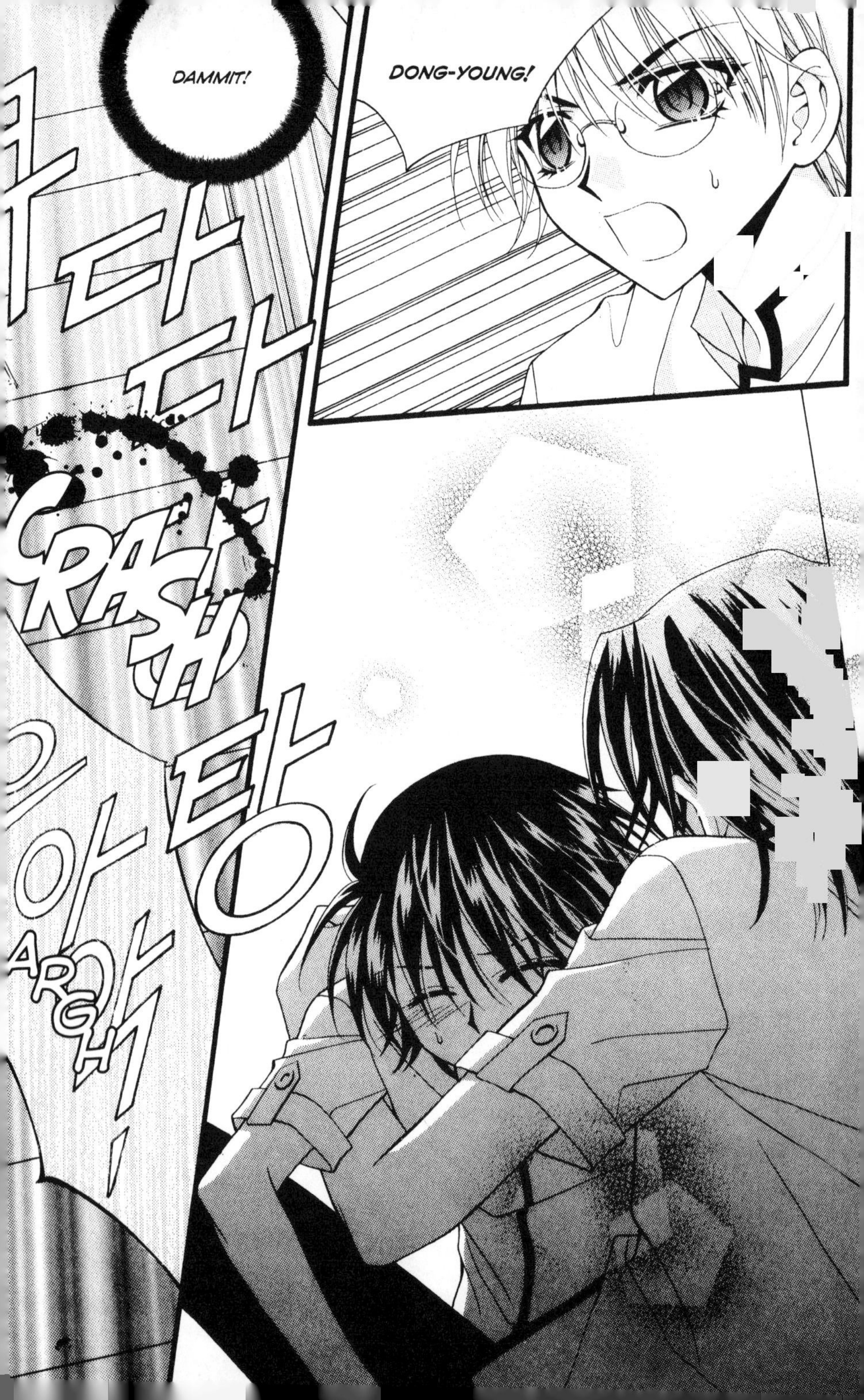
DAMMIT!
CRASH
ARGH!
DONG-YOUNG!

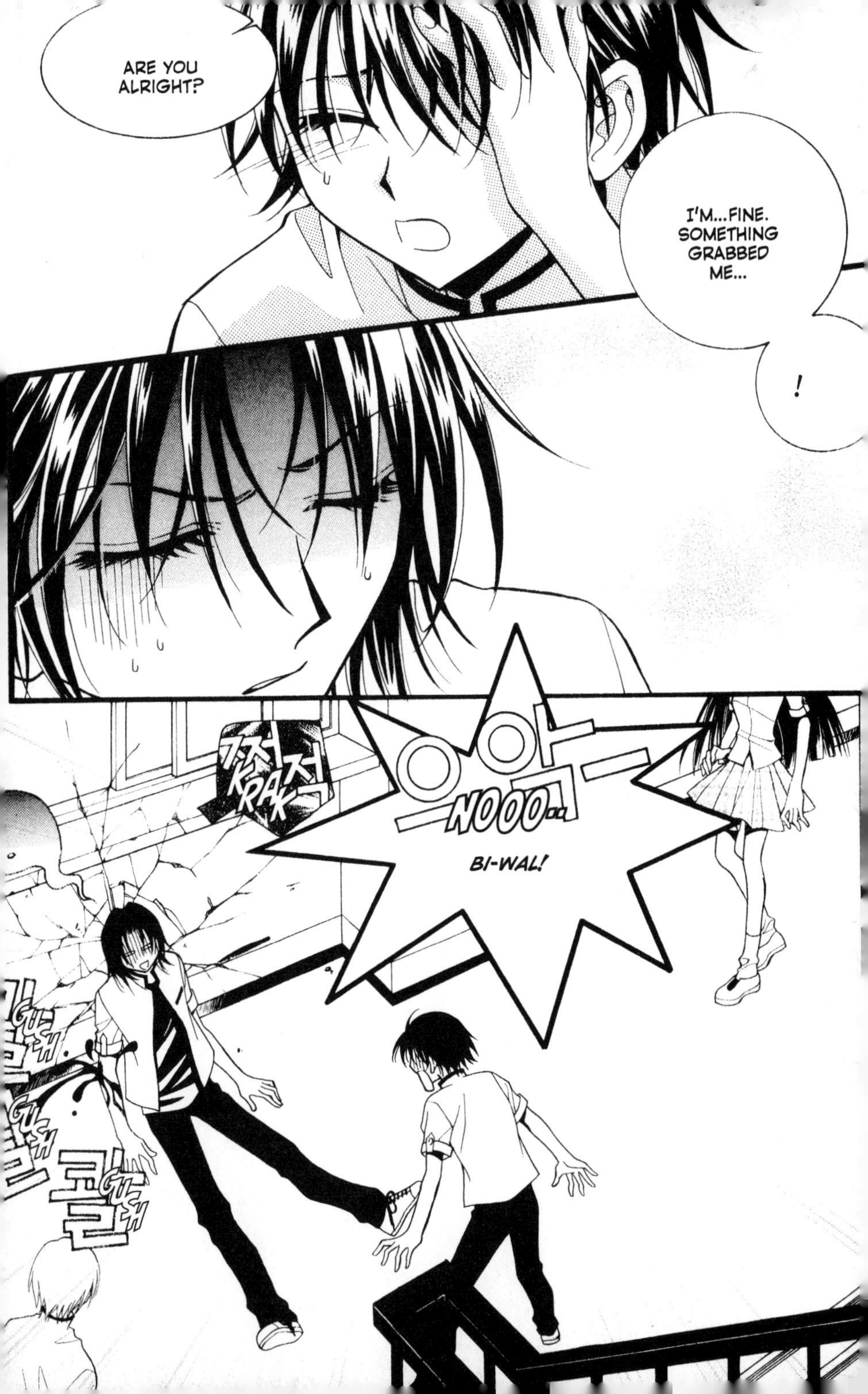
ARE YOU ALRIGHT?
I'M...FINE. SOMETHING GRABBED ME...
!
KRAK
NOOO..
BI-WAL!
GUSH
GUSH
GUSH

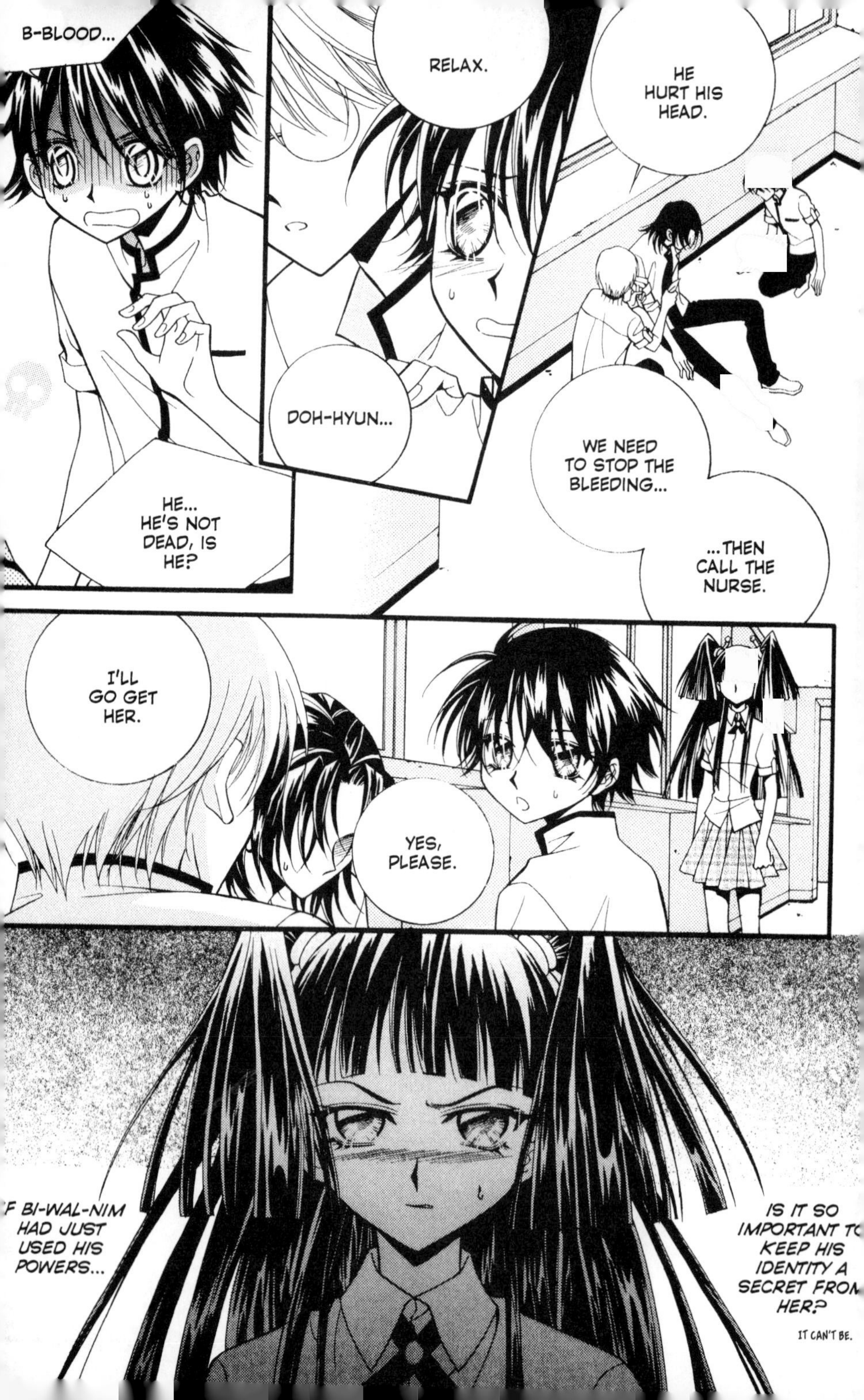
B-BLOOD...
HE... HE'S NOT DEAD, IS HE?
RELAX.
DOH-HYUN...
HE HURT HIS HEAD.
WE NEED TO STOP THE BLEEDING...
...THEN CALL THE NURSE.
I'LL GO GET HER.
YES, PLEASE.
F BI-WAL-NIM HAD JUST USED HIS POWERS...
IS IT SO IMPORTANT T KEEP HIS IDENTITY A SECRET FROM HER?
IT CAN'T BE.

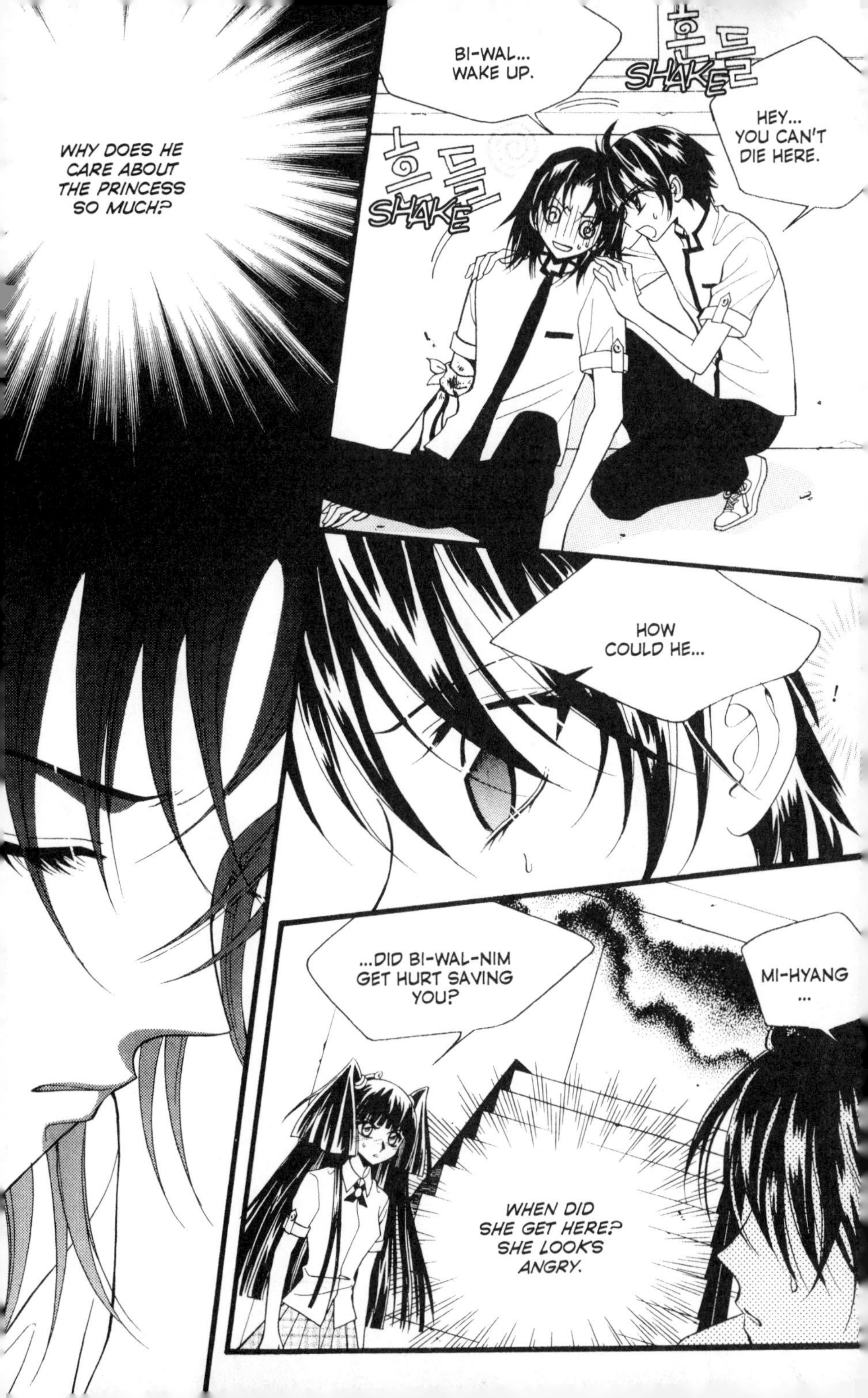
WHY DOES HE CARE ABOUT THE PRINCESS SO MUCH?
BI-WAL... WAKE UP.
SHAKE
SHAKE
HEY... YOU CAN'T DIE HERE.
HOW COULD HE...
!
...DID BI-WAL-NIM GET HURT SAVING YOU?
MI-HYANG ...
WHEN DID SHE GET HERE? SHE LOOKS ANGRY.

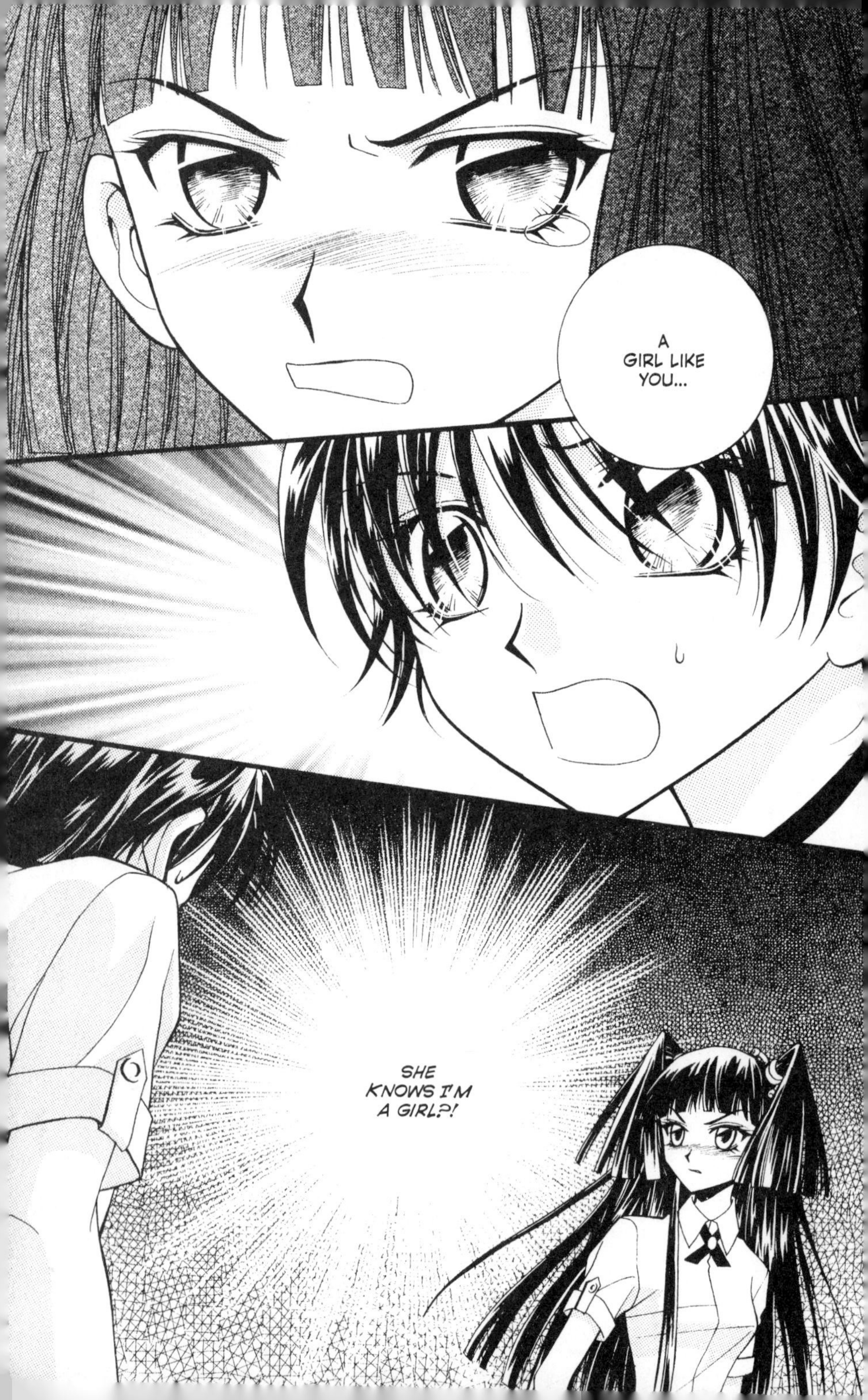
A GIRL LIKE YOU...
SHE KNOWS I'M A GIRL?!

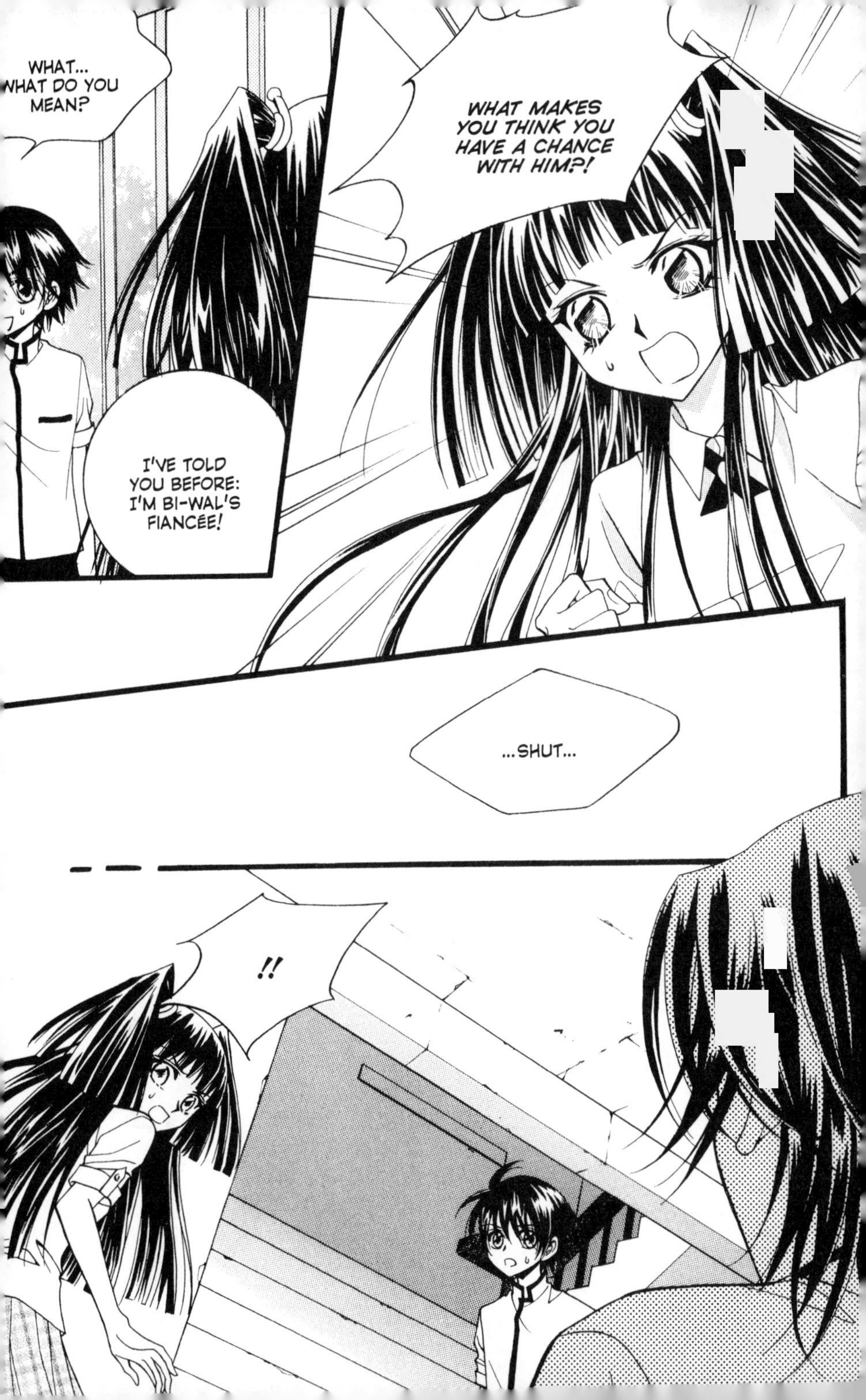
WHAT... WHAT DO YOU MEAN?
I'VE TOLD YOU BEFORE: I'M BI-WAL'S FIANCÉE!
WHAT MAKES YOU THINK YOU HAVE A CHANCE WITH HIM?!
...SHUT...
!!

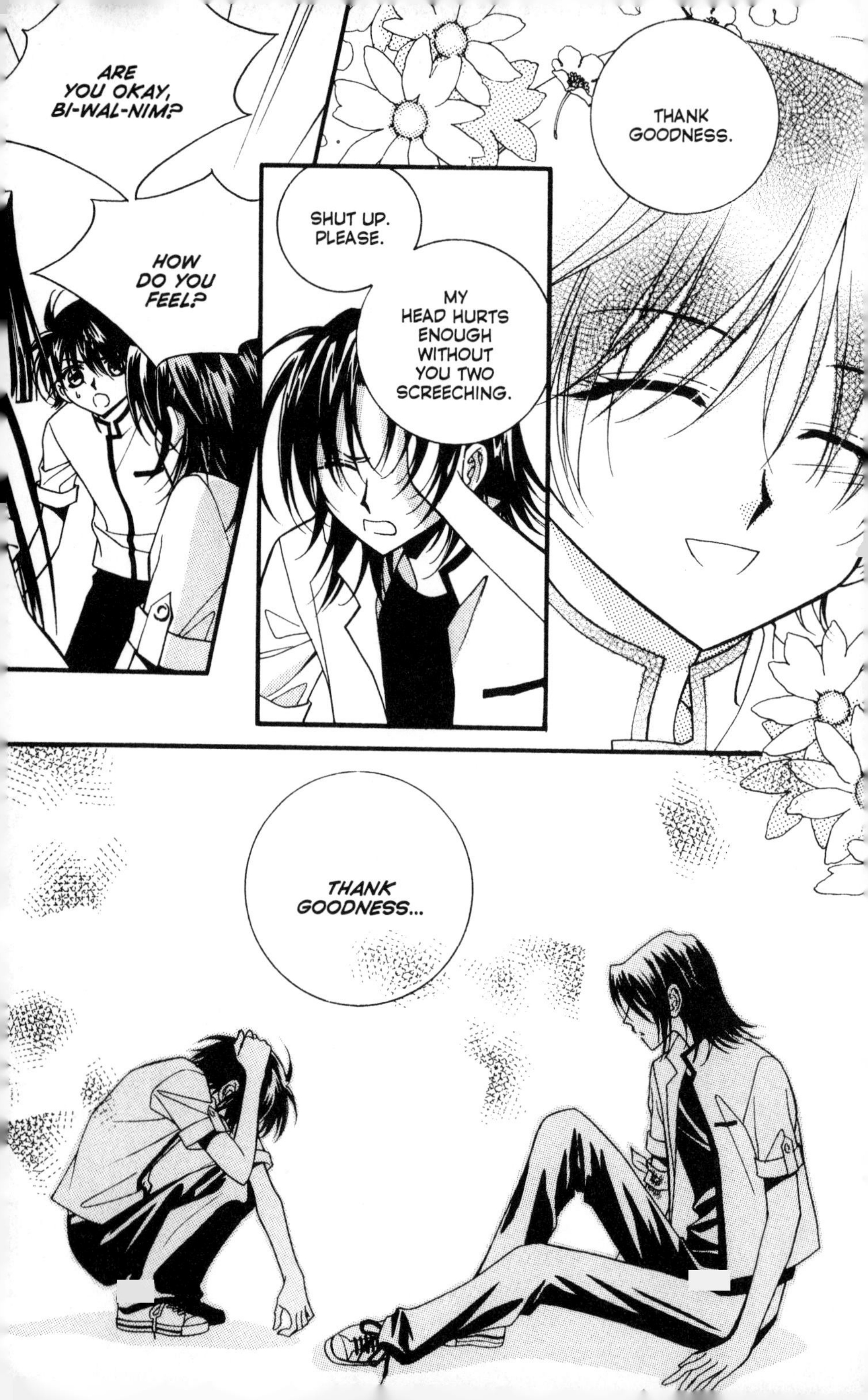
ARE YOU OKAY, BI-WAL-NIM?
HOW DO YOU FEEL?
SHUT UP. PLEASE.
MY HEAD HURTS ENOUGH WITHOUT YOU TWO SCREECHING.
THANK GOODNESS.
THANK GOODNESS...

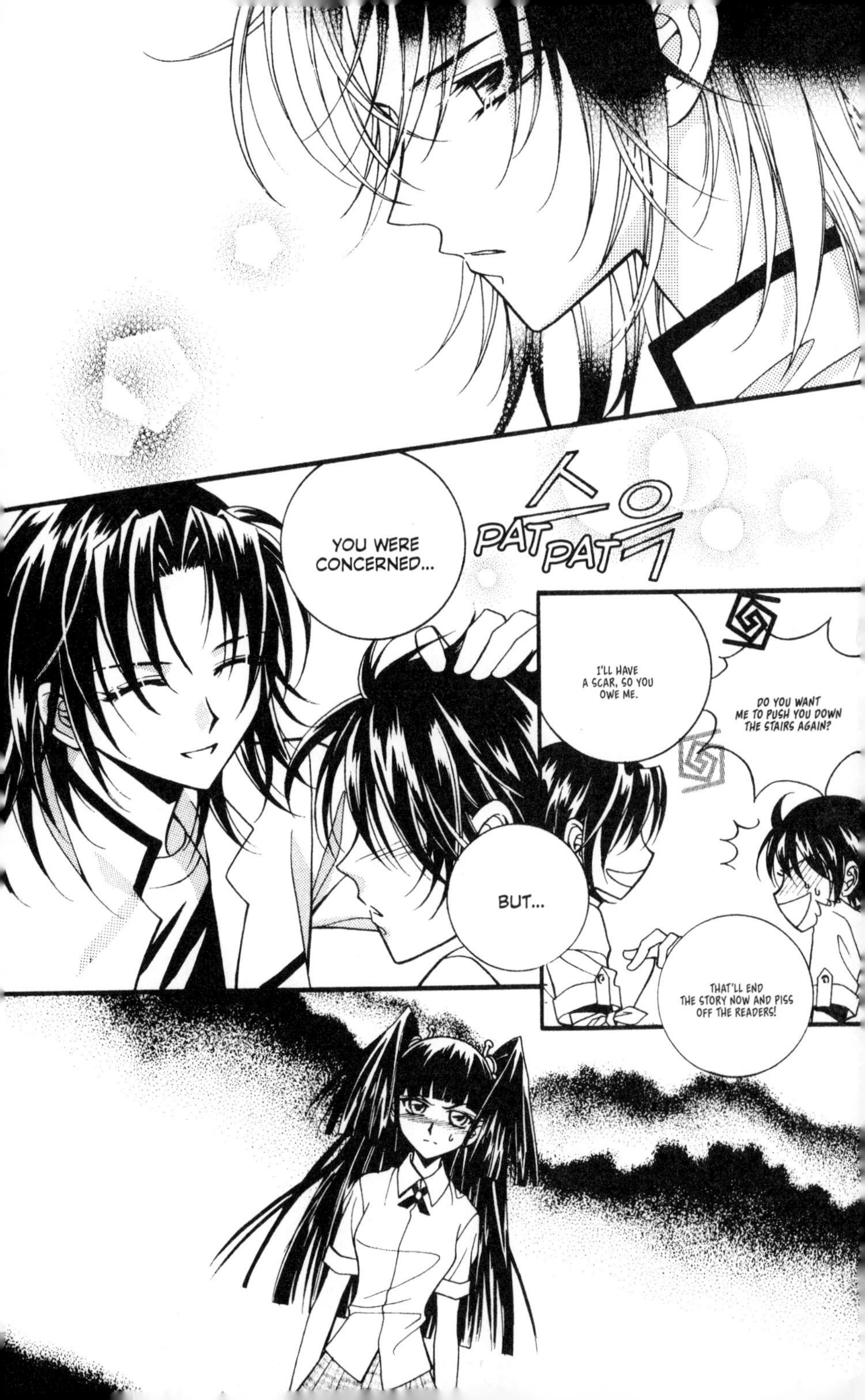
YOU WERE CONCERNED...
PAT PAT
BUT...
I'LL HAVE A SCAR, SO YOU OWE ME.
DO YOU WANT ME TO PUSH YOU DOWN THE STAIRS AGAIN?
THAT'LL END THE STORY NOW AND PISS OFF THE READERS!

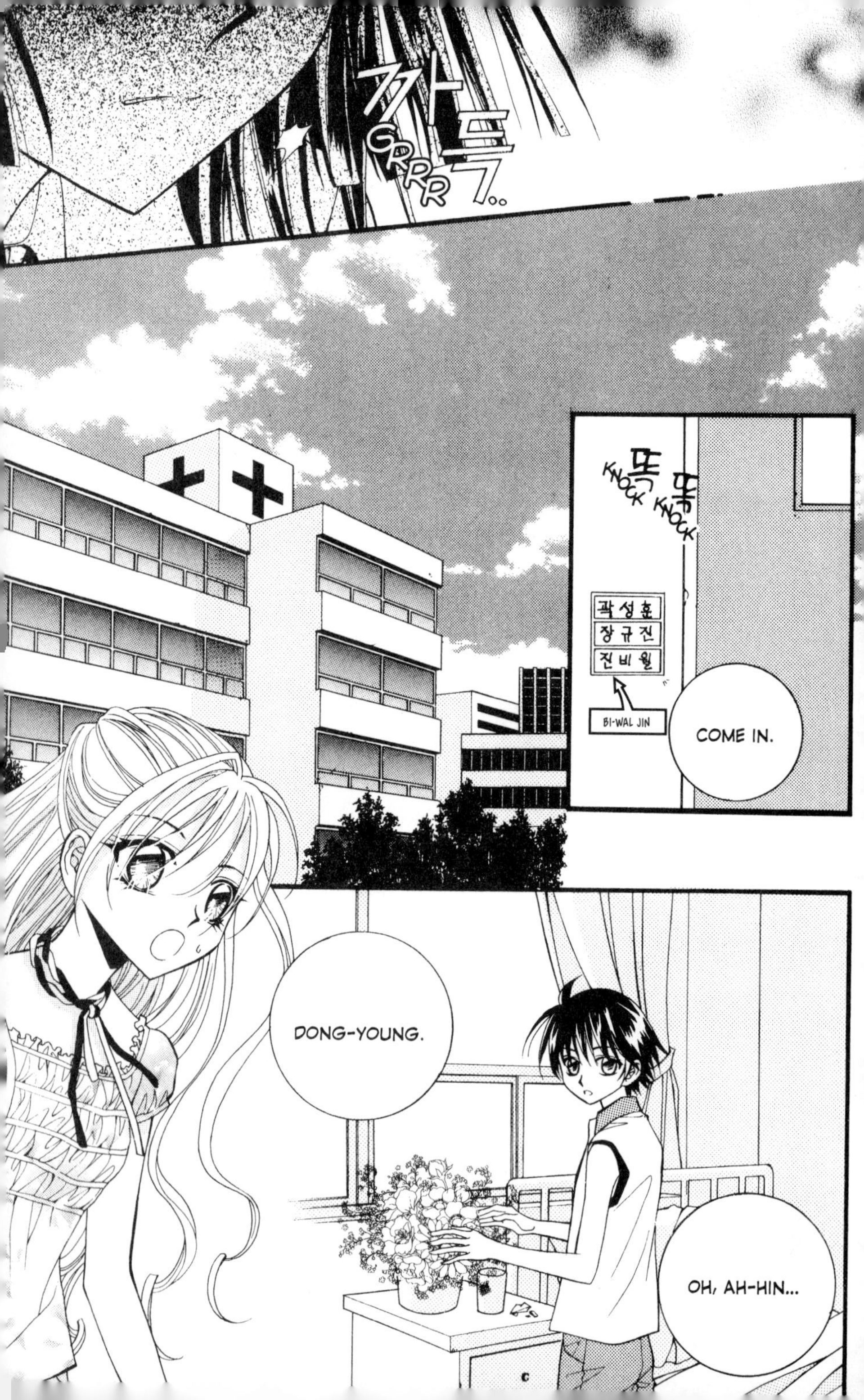

까드득
GRRRR..
똑 똑
KNOCK KNOCK
곽성훈
장규진
진비월
BI-WAL JIN
COME IN.
DONG-YOUNG.
OH, AH-HIN...

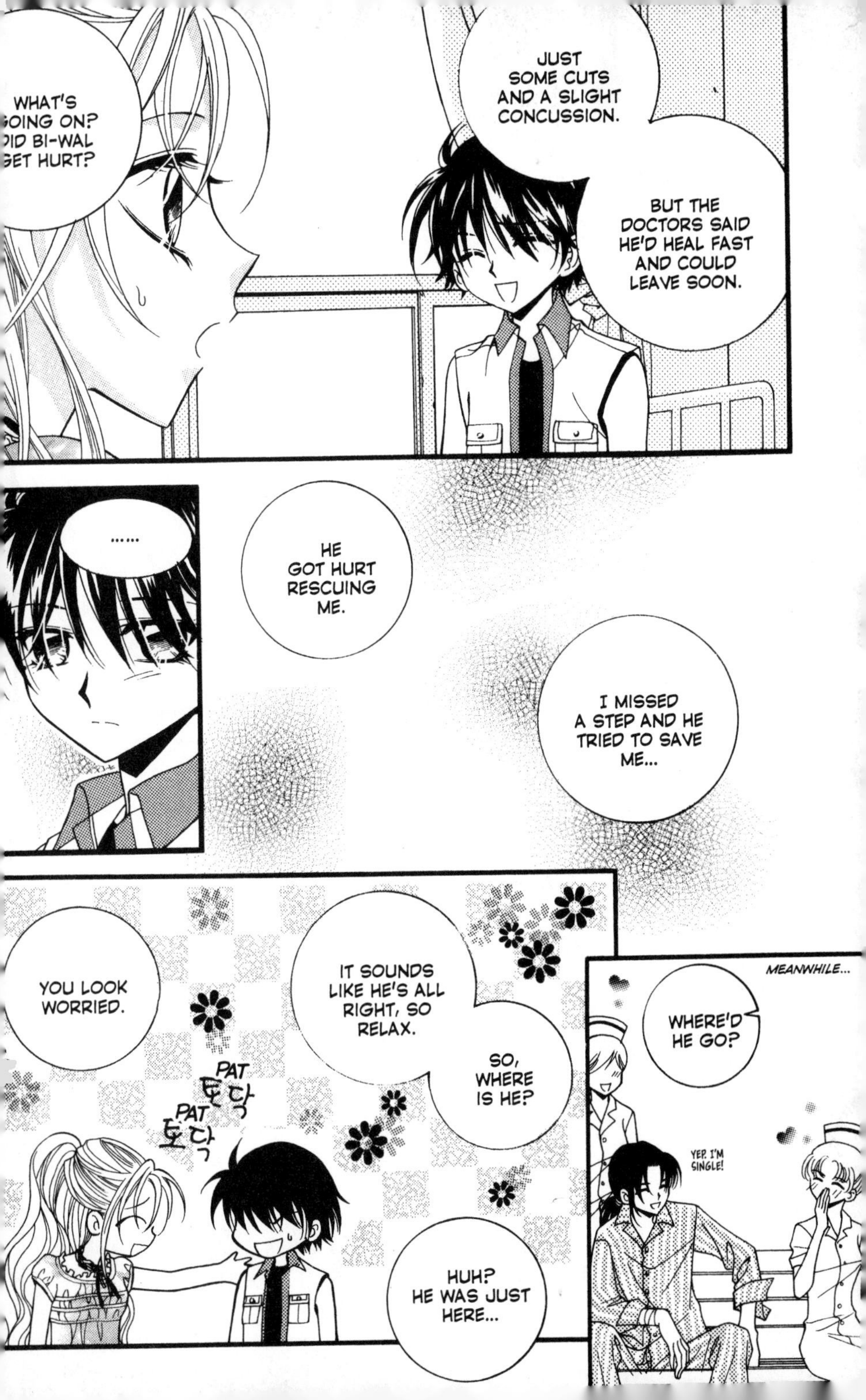
WHAT'S GOING ON? DID BI-WAL GET HURT?
JUST SOME CUTS AND A SLIGHT CONCUSSION.
BUT THE DOCTORS SAID HE'D HEAL FAST AND COULD LEAVE SOON.
......
HE GOT HURT RESCUING ME.
I MISSED A STEP AND HE TRIED TO SAVE ME...
YOU LOOK WORRIED.
IT SOUNDS LIKE HE'S ALL RIGHT, SO RELAX.
PAT 토닥
PAT 토닥
SO, WHERE IS HE?
HUH? HE WAS JUST HERE...
MEANWHILE...
WHERE'D HE GO?
YEP, I'M SINGLE!

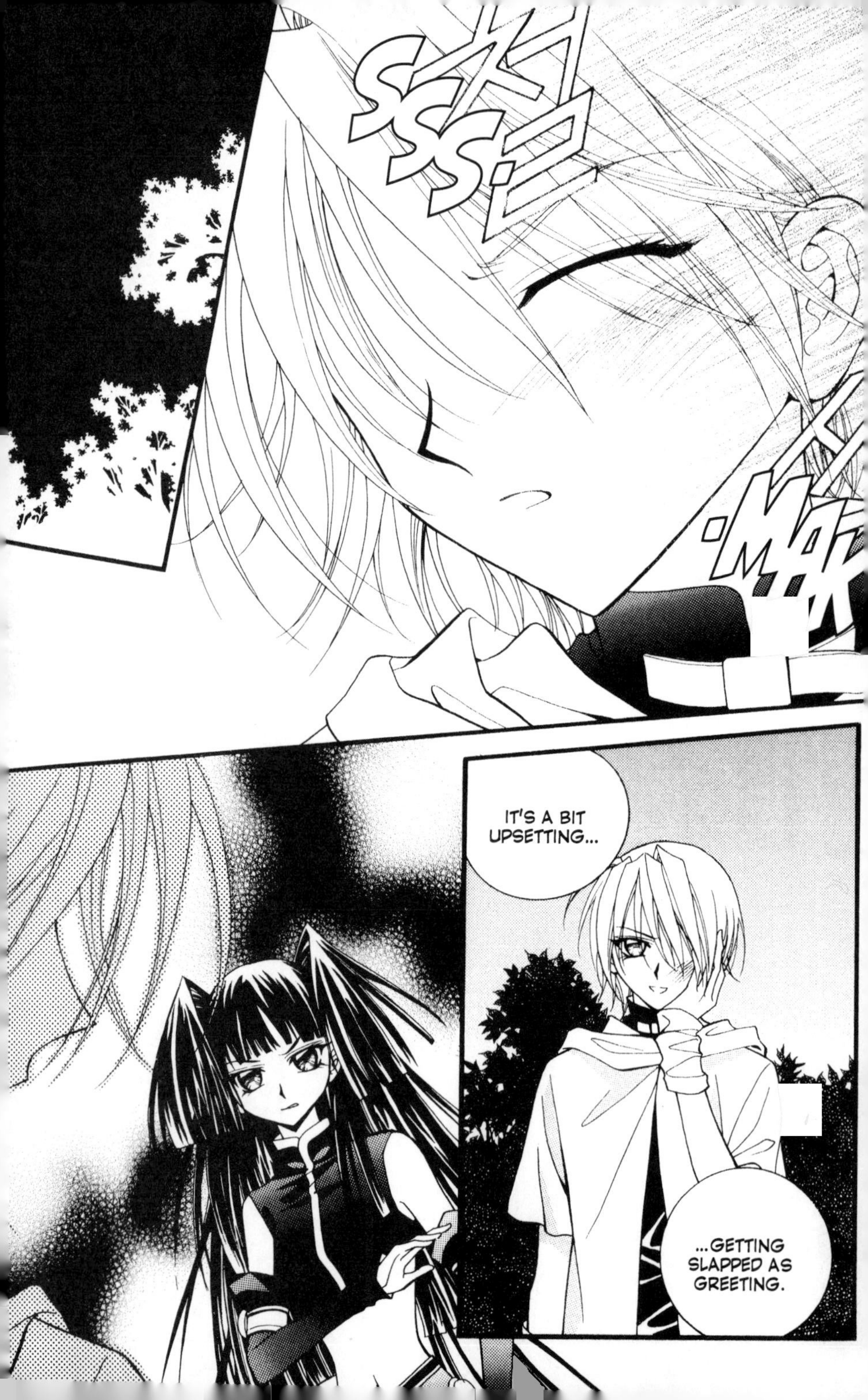
SSS
IT'S A BIT UPSETTING...
...GETTING SLAPPED AS GREETING.

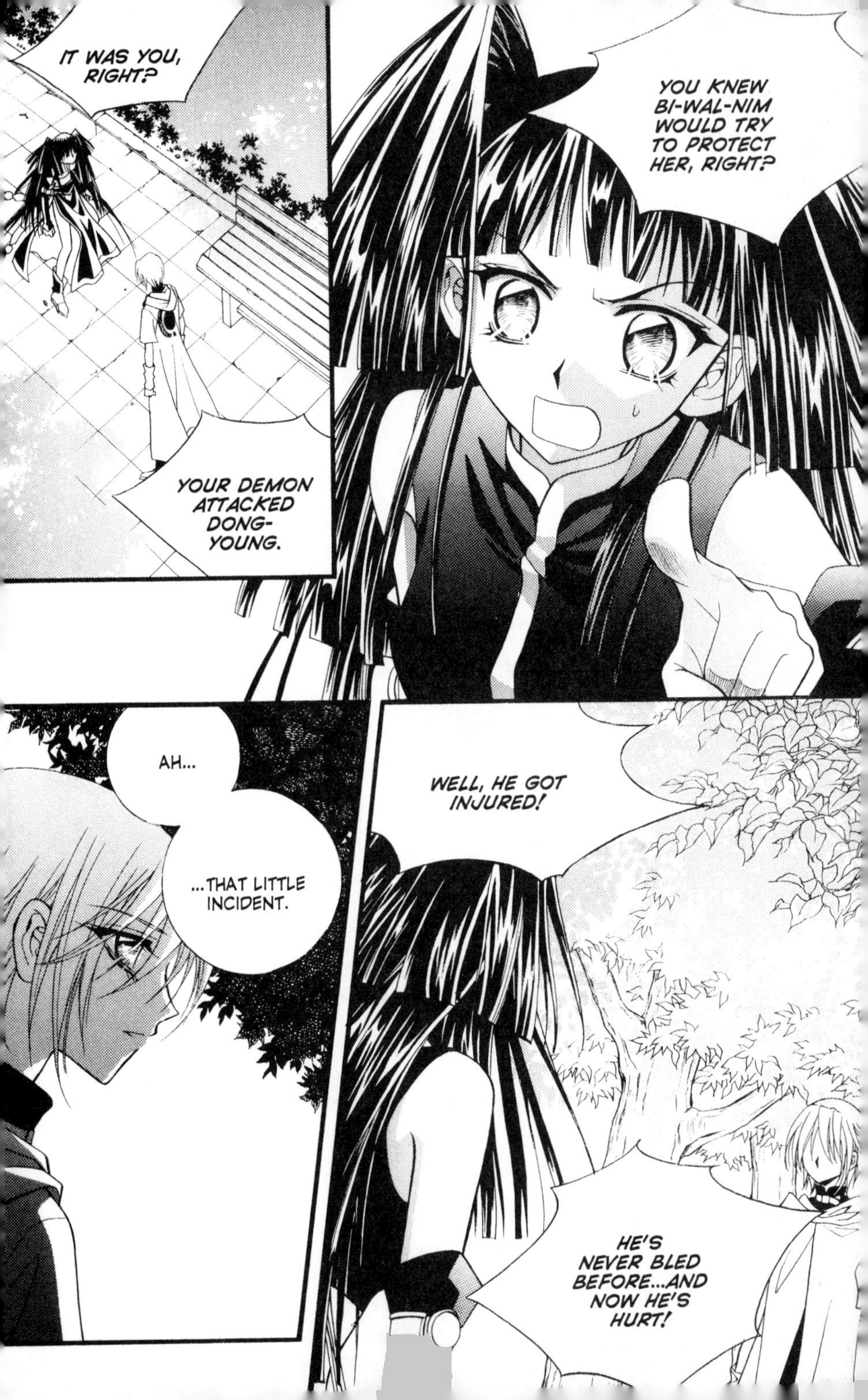
IT WAS YOU, RIGHT?
YOUR DEMON ATTACKED DONG-YOUNG.
YOU KNEW BI-WAL-NIM WOULD TRY TO PROTECT HER, RIGHT?
AH...
...THAT LITTLE INCIDENT.
WELL, HE GOT INJURED!
HE'S NEVER BLED BEFORE...AND NOW HE'S HURT!

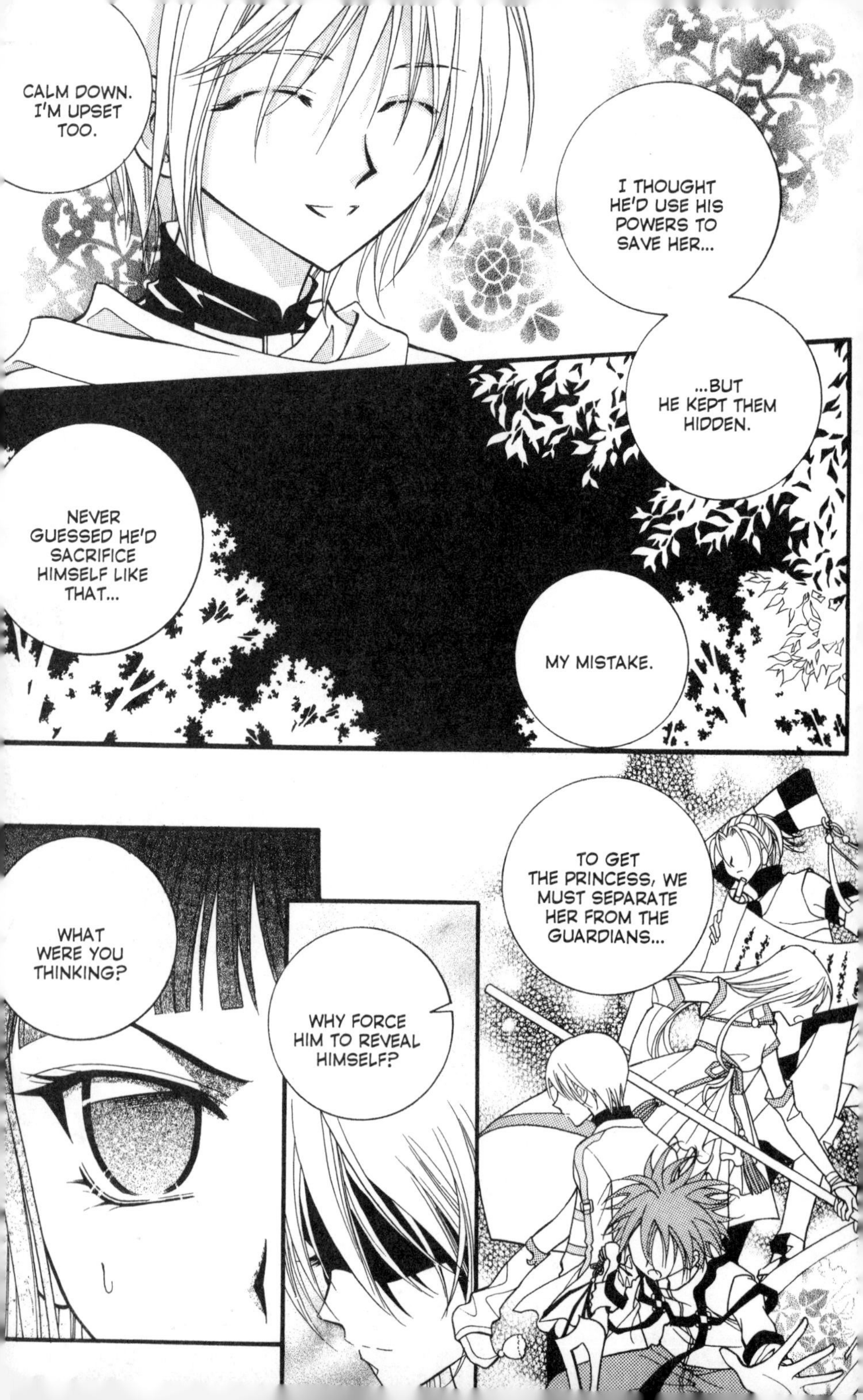
CALM DOWN. I'M UPSET TOO.
I THOUGHT HE'D USE HIS POWERS TO SAVE HER...
...BUT HE KEPT THEM HIDDEN.
NEVER GUESSED HE'D SACRIFICE HIMSELF LIKE THAT...
MY MISTAKE.
WHAT WERE YOU THINKING?
WHY FORCE HIM TO REVEAL HIMSELF?
TO GET THE PRINCESS, WE MUST SEPARATE HER FROM THE GUARDIANS...

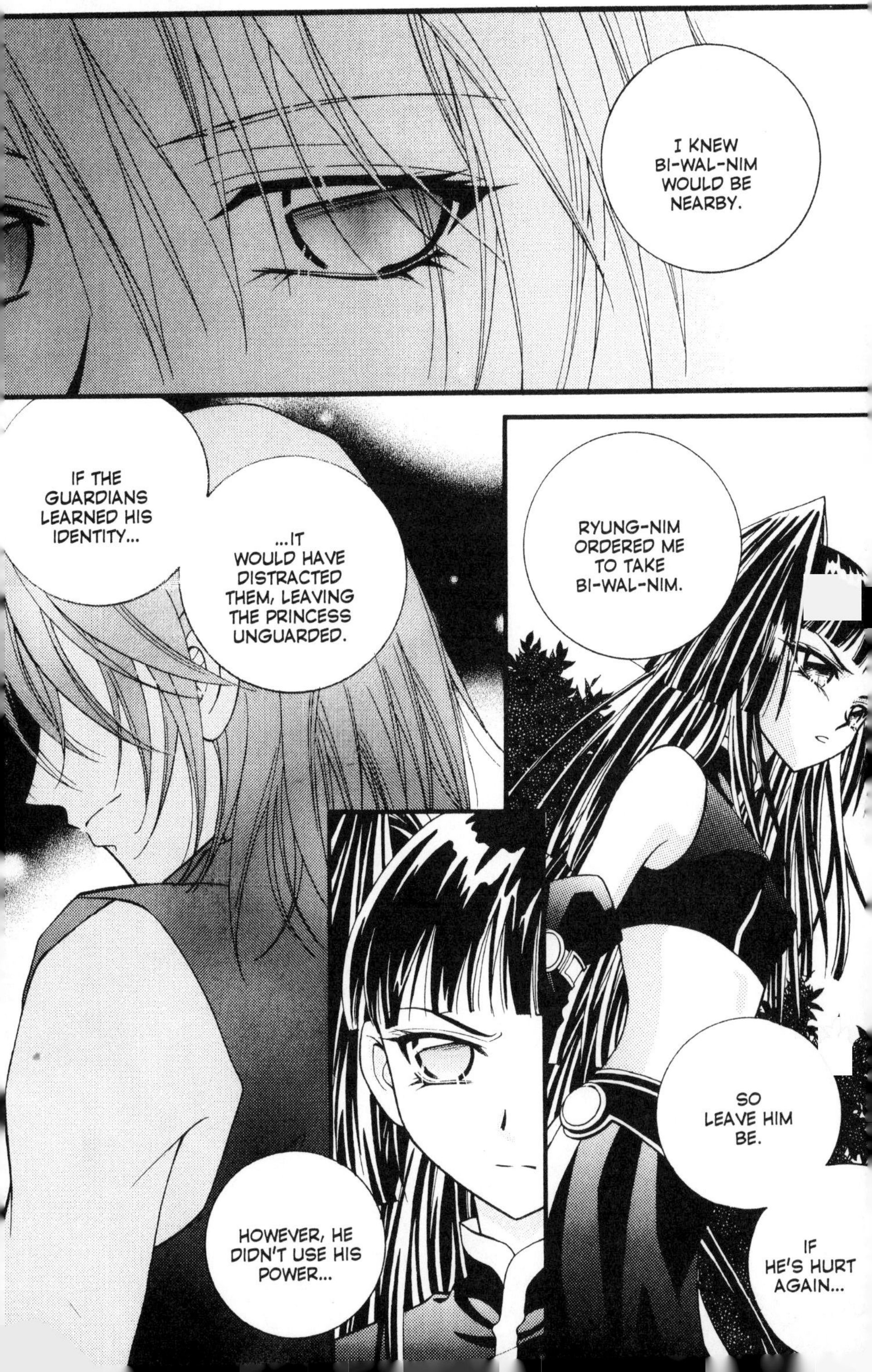
I KNEW BI-WAL-NIM WOULD BE NEARBY.
IF THE GUARDIANS LEARNED HIS IDENTITY...
...IT WOULD HAVE DISTRACTED THEM, LEAVING THE PRINCESS UNGUARDED.
RYUNG-NIM ORDERED ME TO TAKE BI-WAL-NIM.
HOWEVER, HE DIDN'T USE HIS POWER...
SO LEAVE HIM BE.
IF HE'S HURT AGAIN...

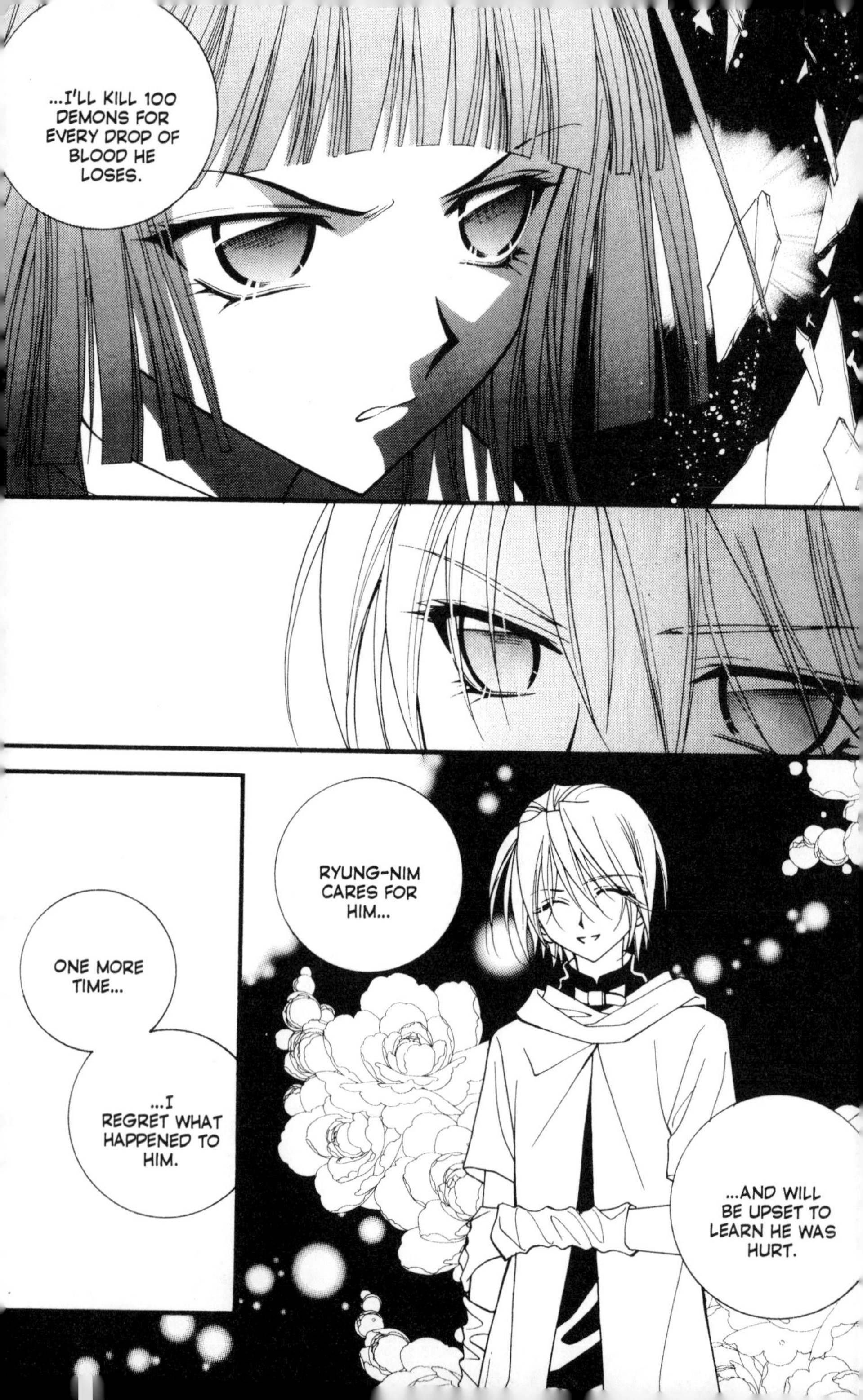
...I'LL KILL 100 DEMONS FOR EVERY DROP OF BLOOD HE LOSES.
ONE MORE TIME...
...I REGRET WHAT HAPPENED TO HIM.
RYUNG-NIM CARES FOR HIM...
...AND WILL BE UPSET TO LEARN HE WAS HURT.

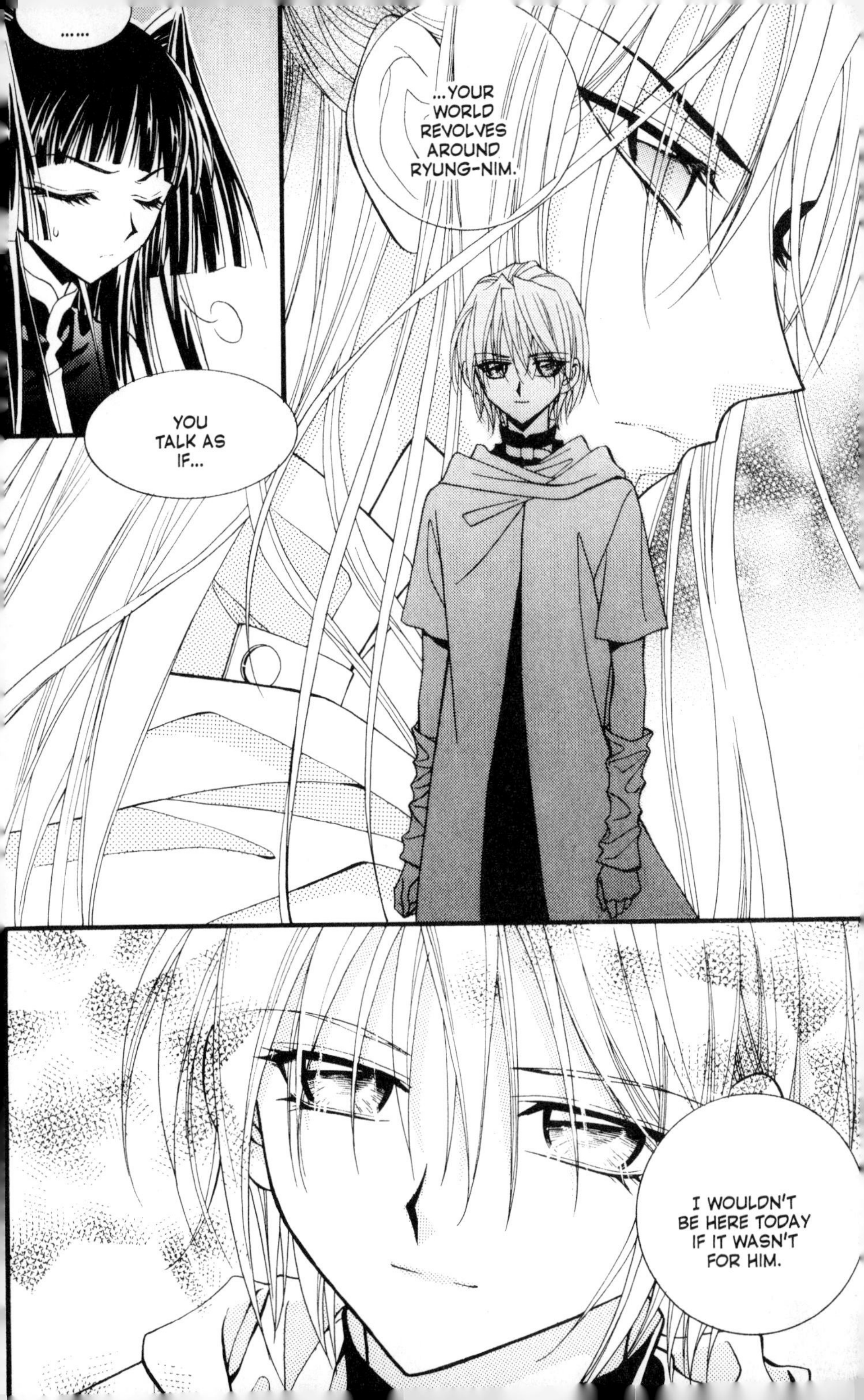
......
YOU TALK AS IF...
...YOUR WORLD REVOLVES AROUND RYUNG-NIM.
I WOULDN'T BE HERE TODAY IF IT WASN'T FOR HIM.

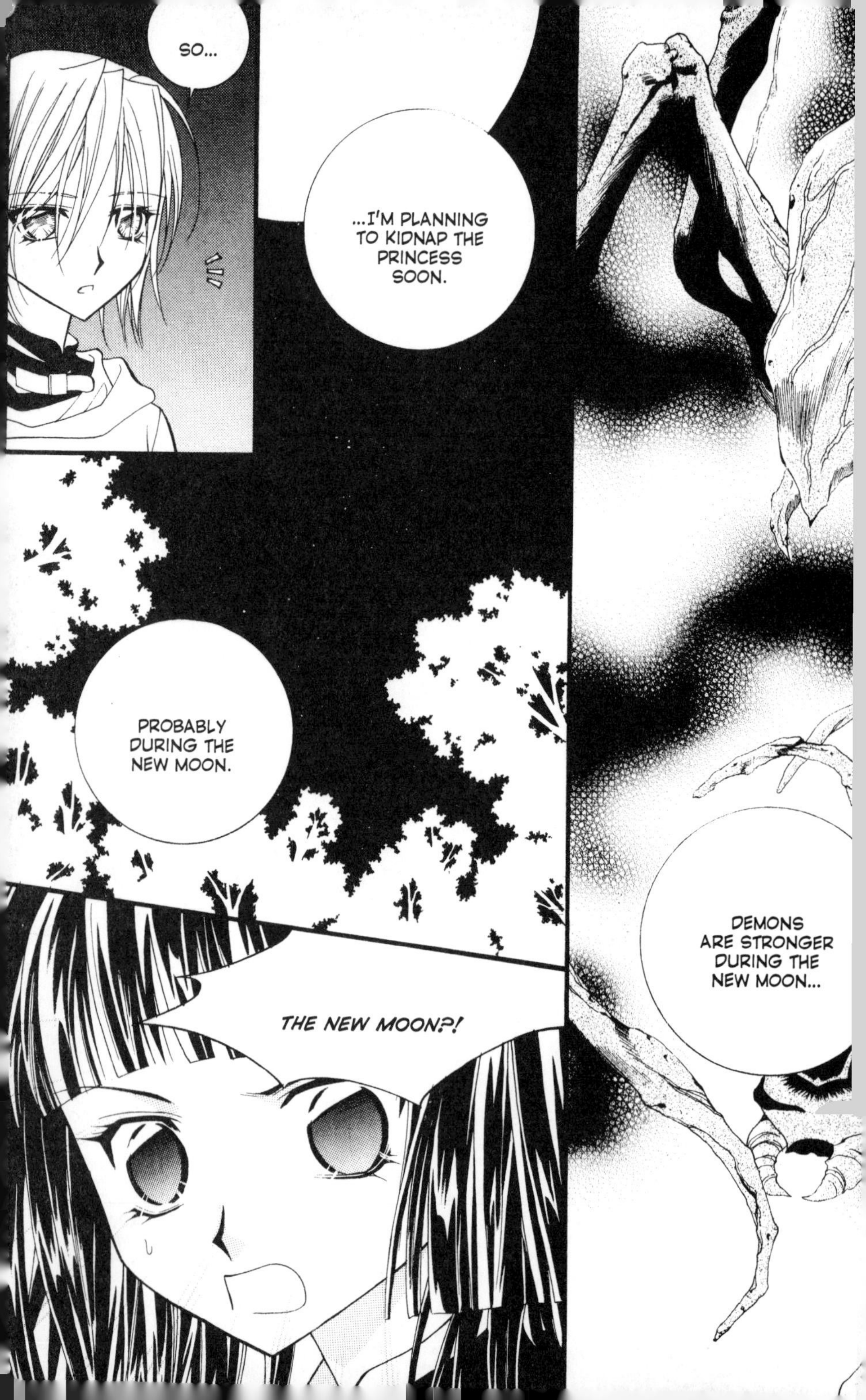
SO...
...I'M PLANNING TO KIDNAP THE PRINCESS SOON.
PROBABLY DURING THE NEW MOON.
THE NEW MOON?!
DEMONS ARE STRONGER DURING THE NEW MOON...

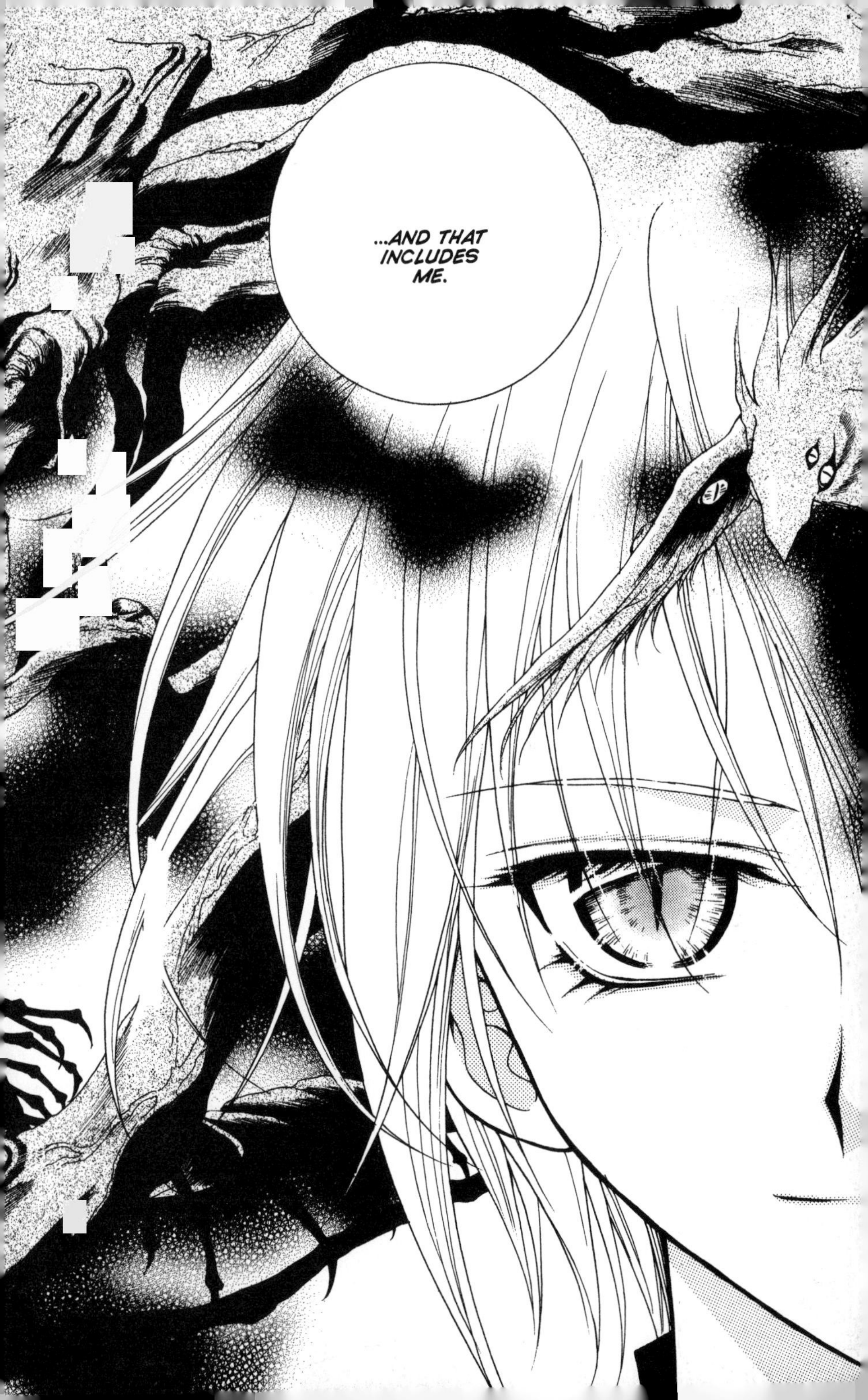
...AND THAT INCLUDES ME.

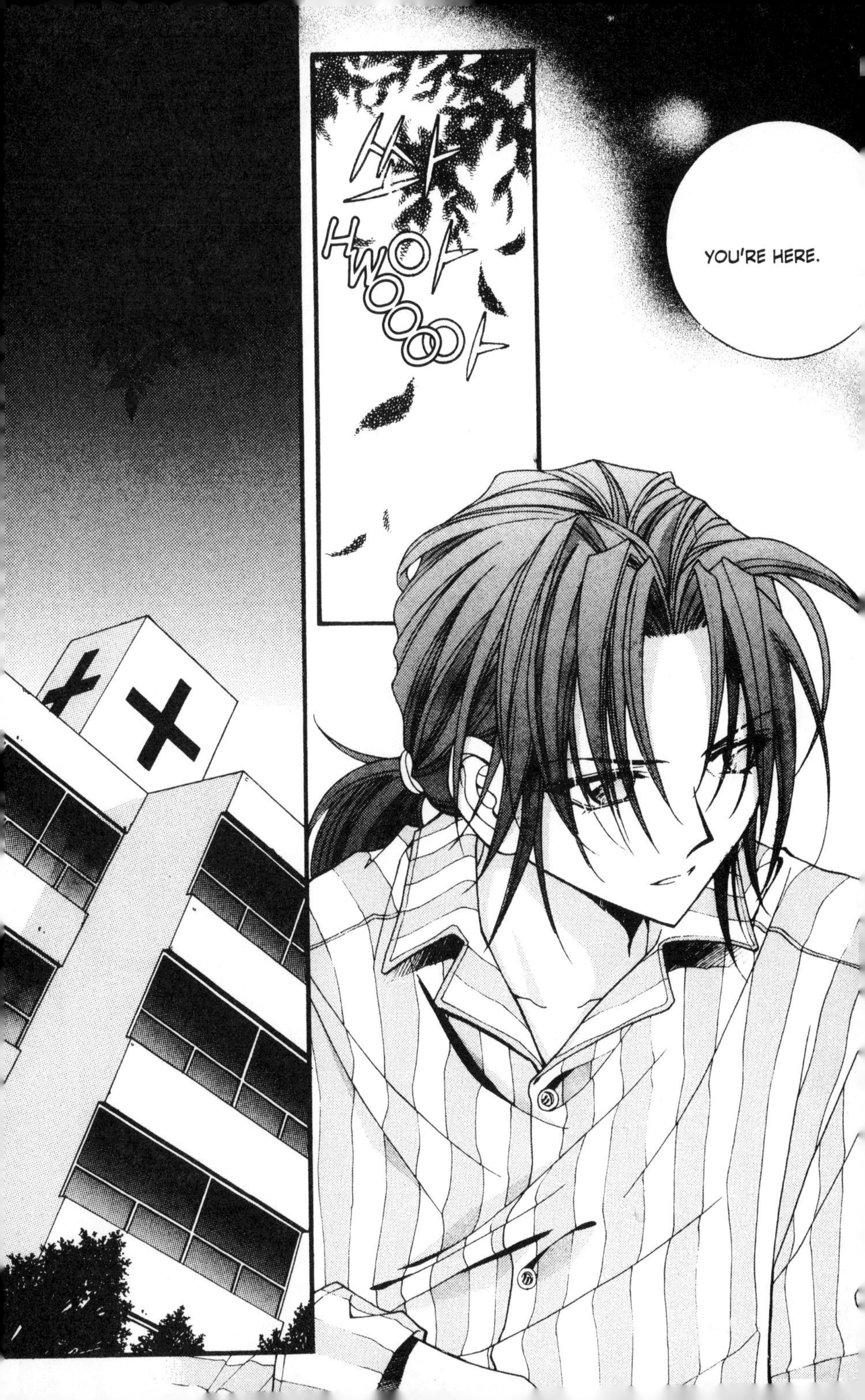
HWOOOO!
YOU'RE HERE.

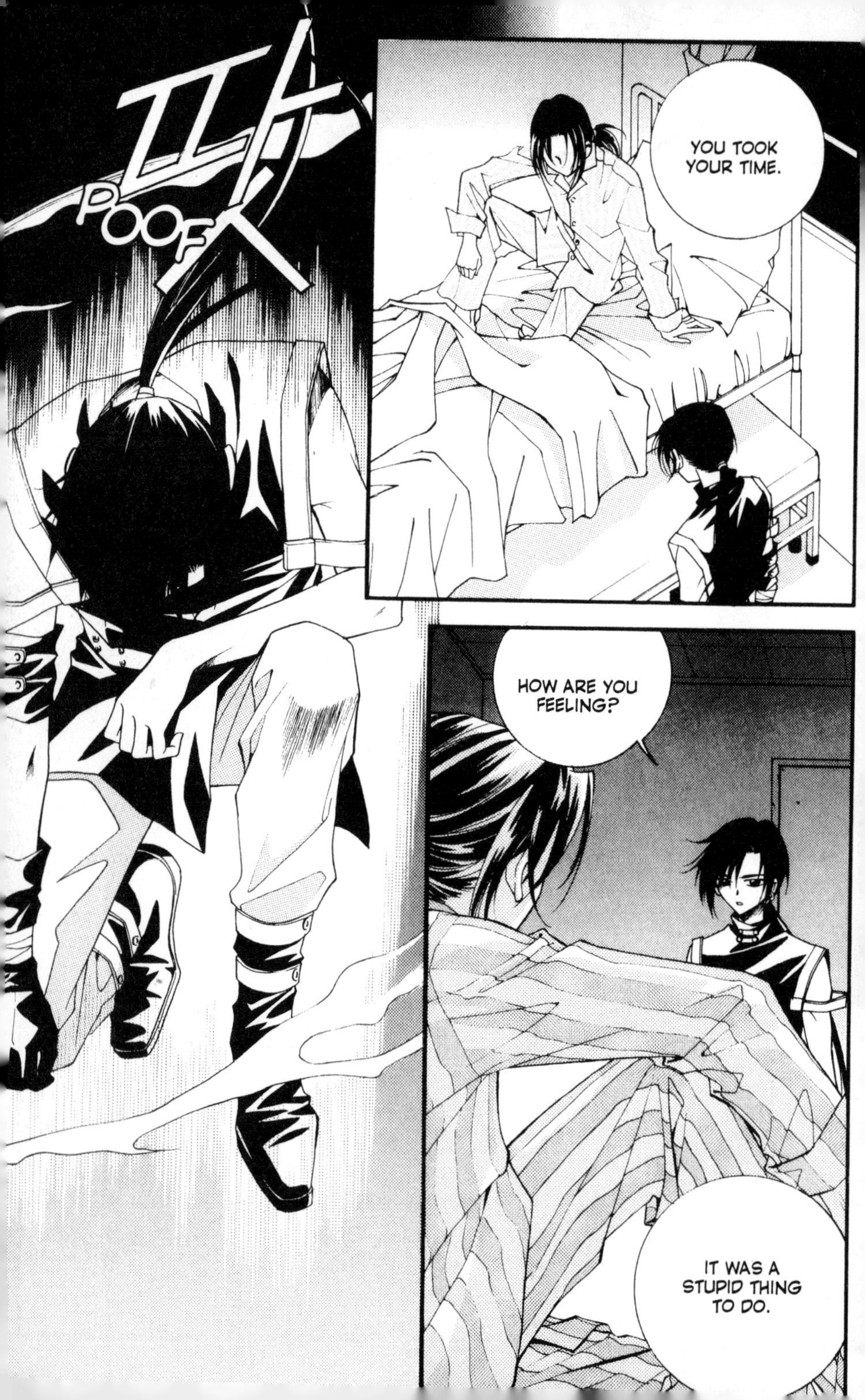
POOF
YOU TOOK YOUR TIME.
HOW ARE YOU FEELING?
IT WAS A STUPID THING TO DO.

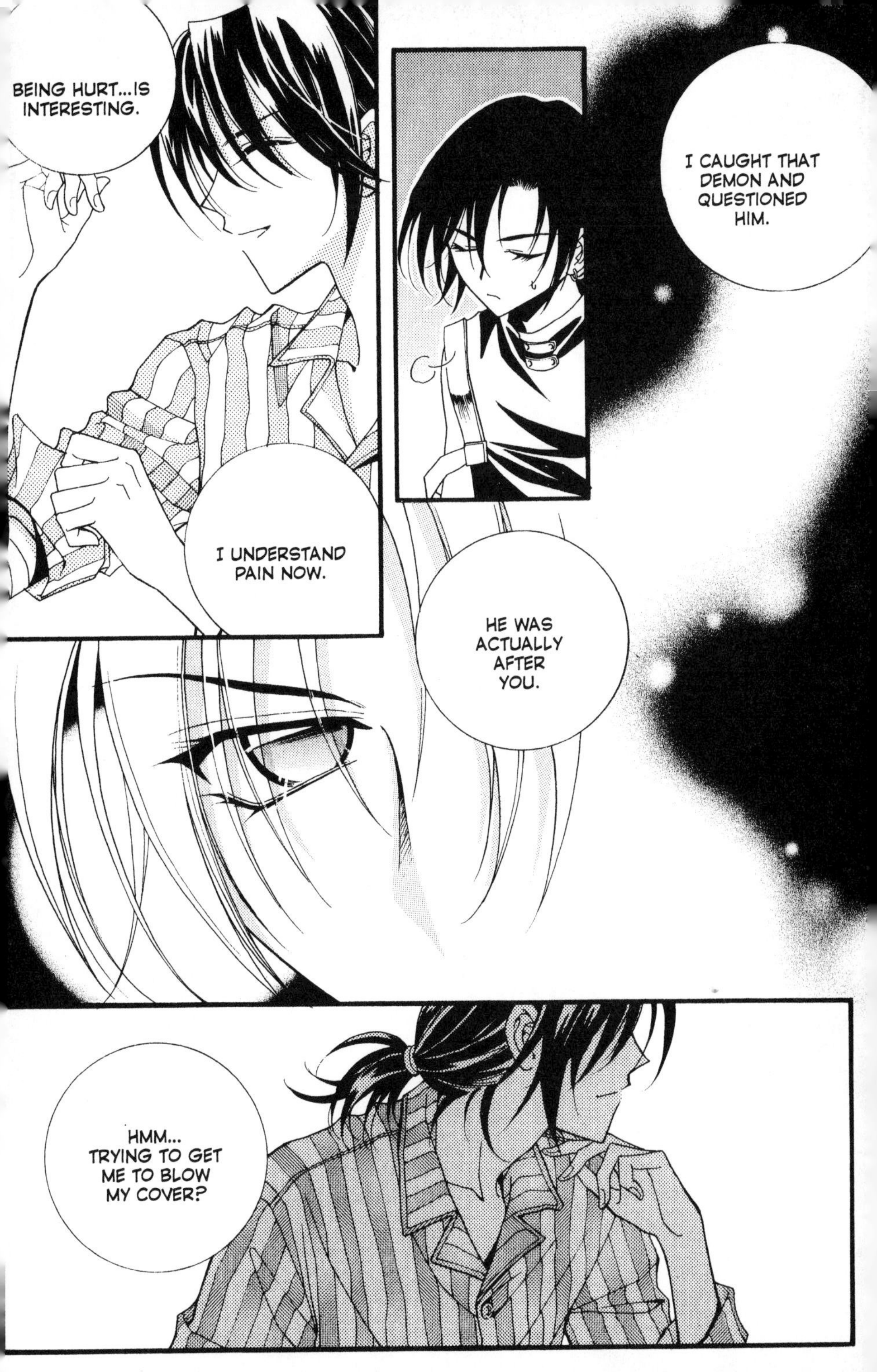
BEING HURT...IS INTERESTING.
I UNDERSTAND PAIN NOW.
I CAUGHT THAT DEMON AND QUESTIONED HIM.
HE WAS ACTUALLY AFTER YOU.
HMM... TRYING TO GET ME TO BLOW MY COVER?

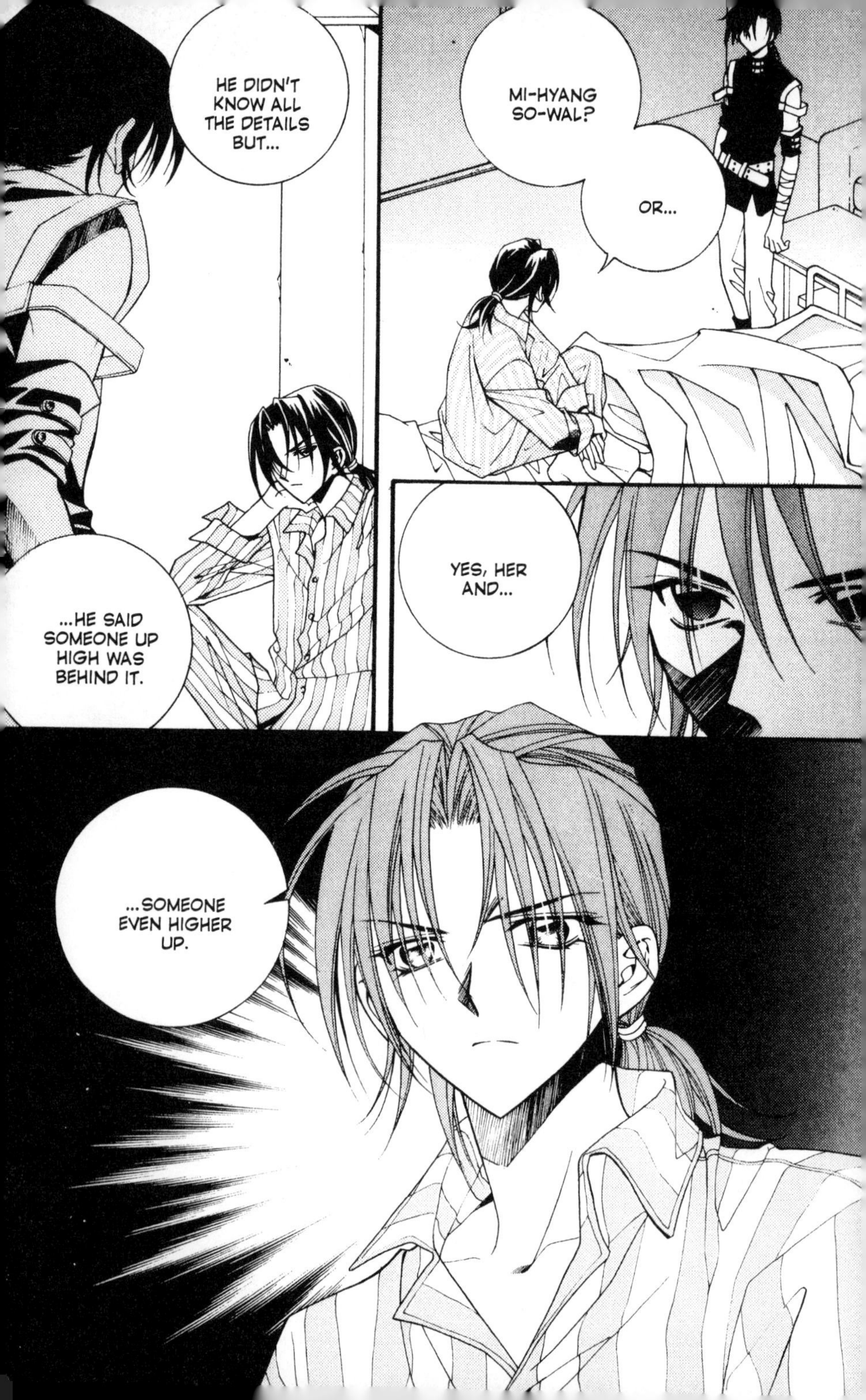
HE DIDN'T KNOW ALL THE DETAILS BUT...
...HE SAID SOMEONE UP HIGH WAS BEHIND IT.
MI-HYANG SO-WAL?
OR...
YES, HER AND...
...SOMEONE EVEN HIGHER UP.

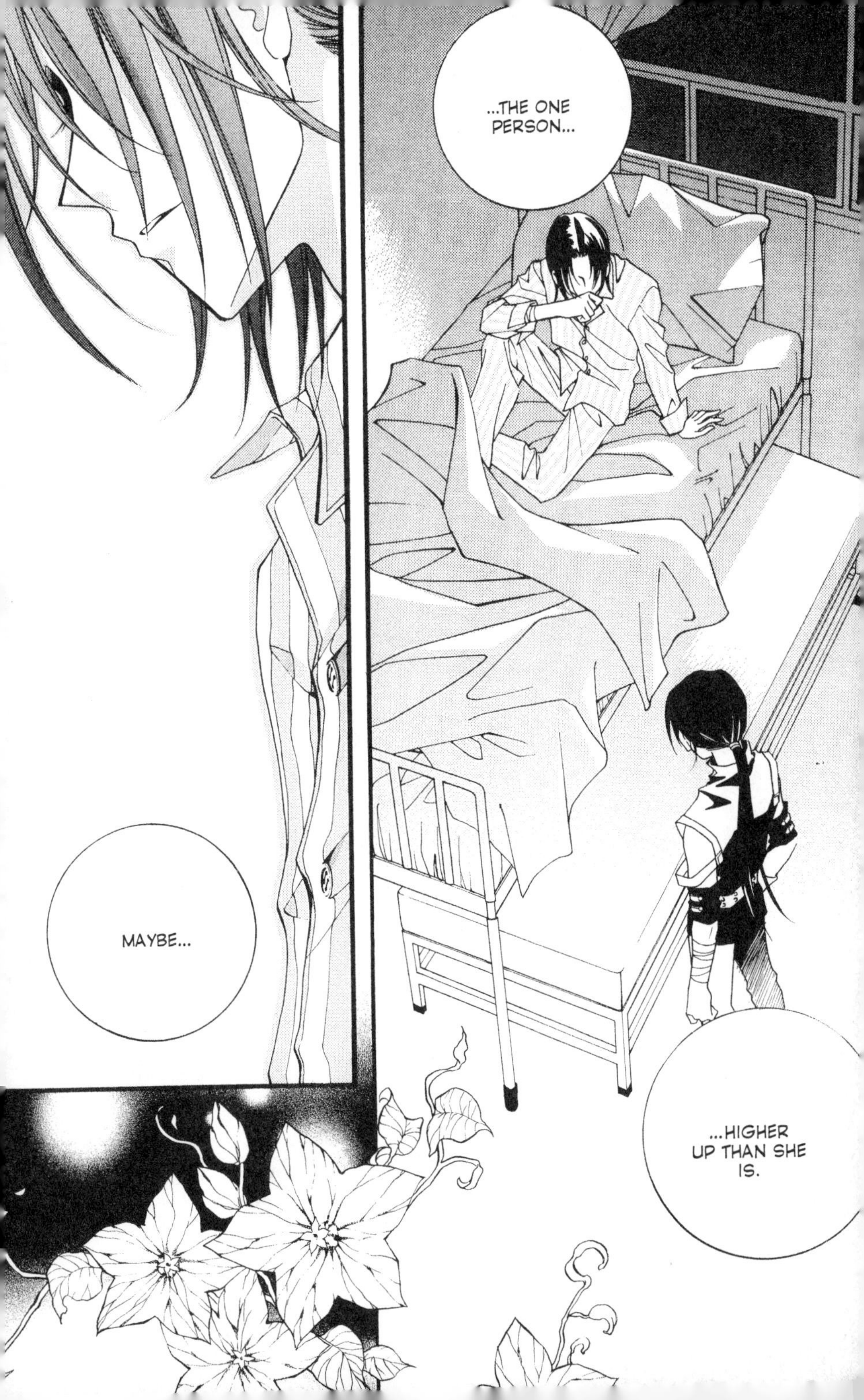
MAYBE...
...THE ONE PERSON...
...HIGHER UP THAN SHE IS.

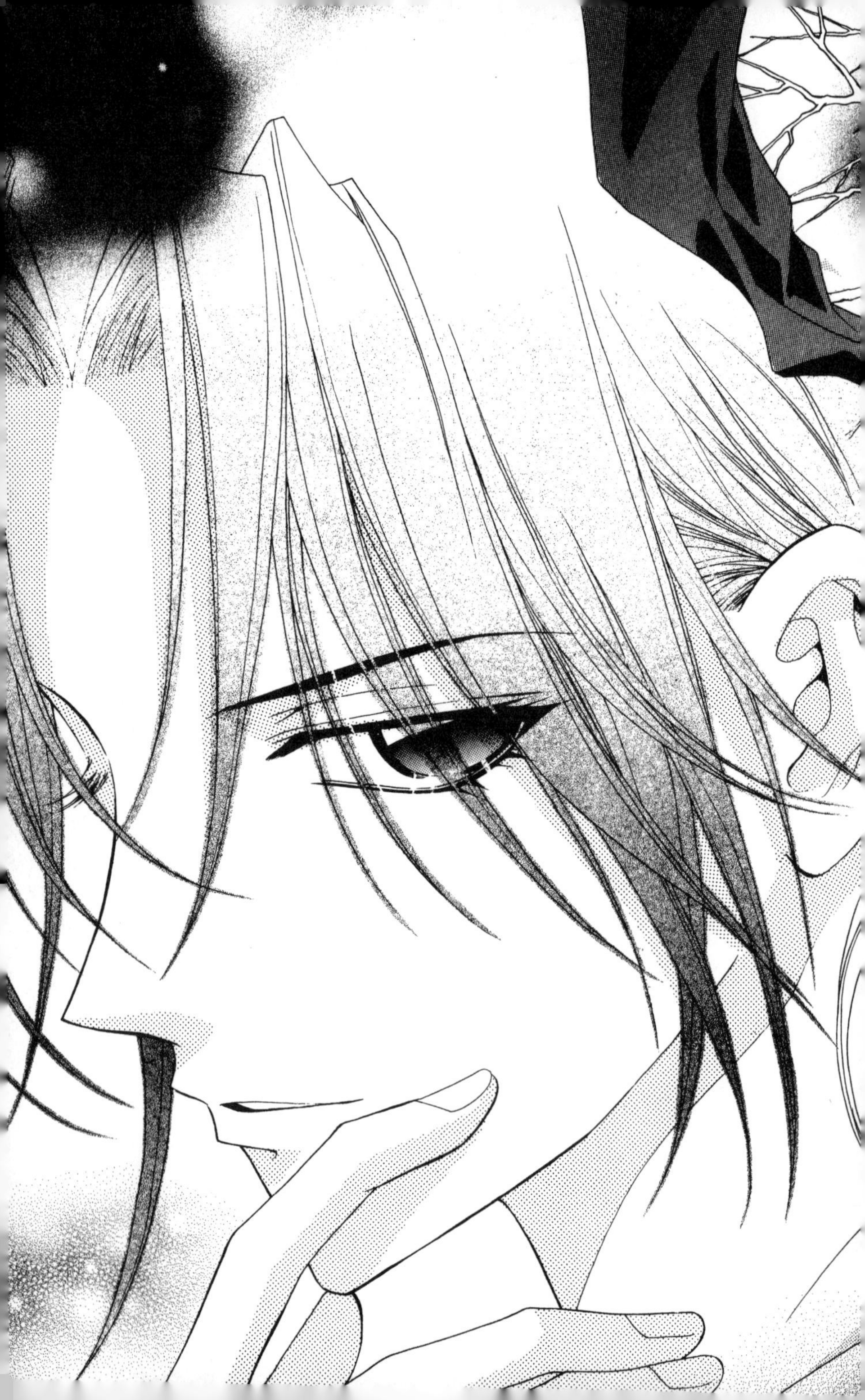

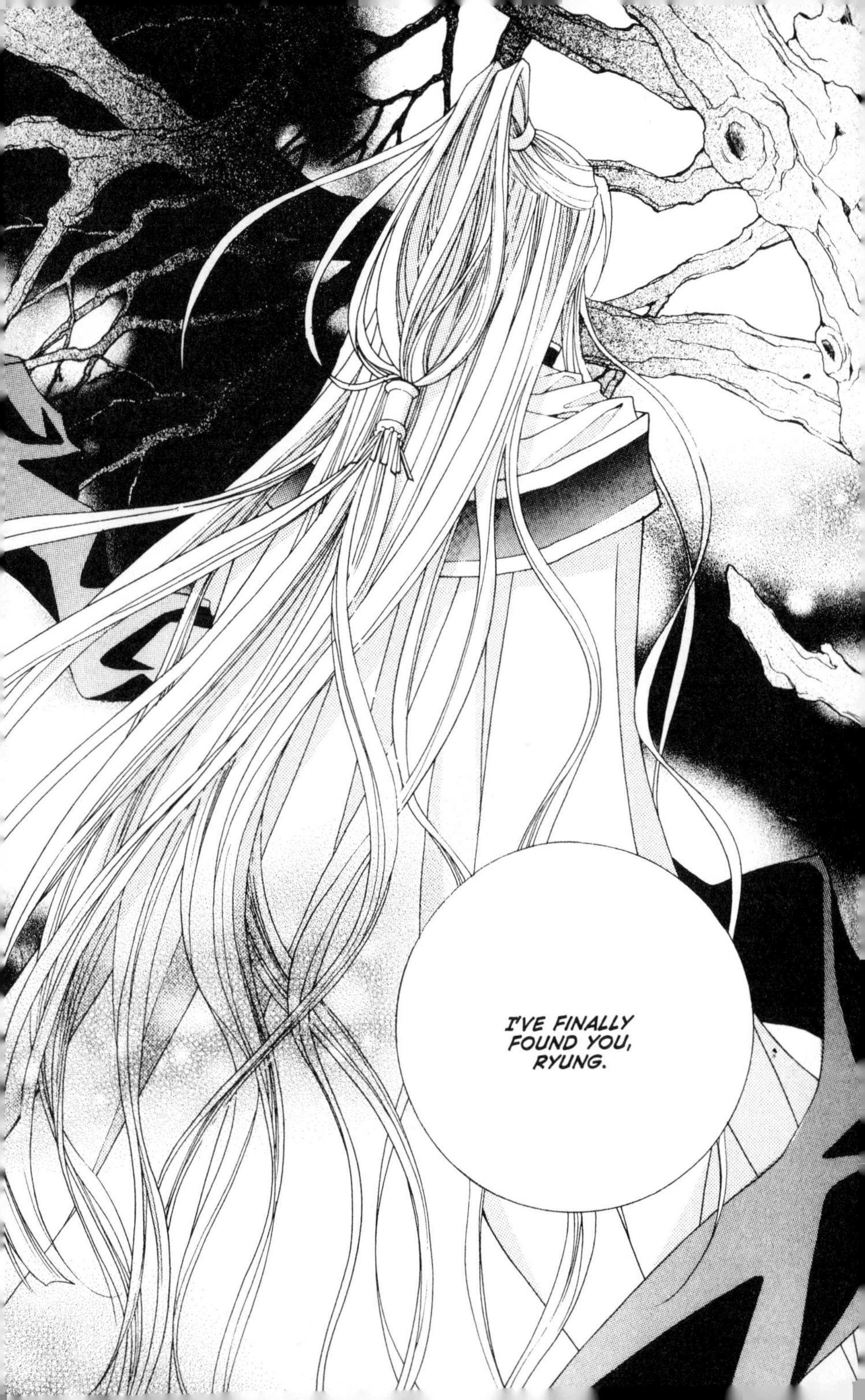
I'VE FINALLY FOUND YOU, RYUNG.

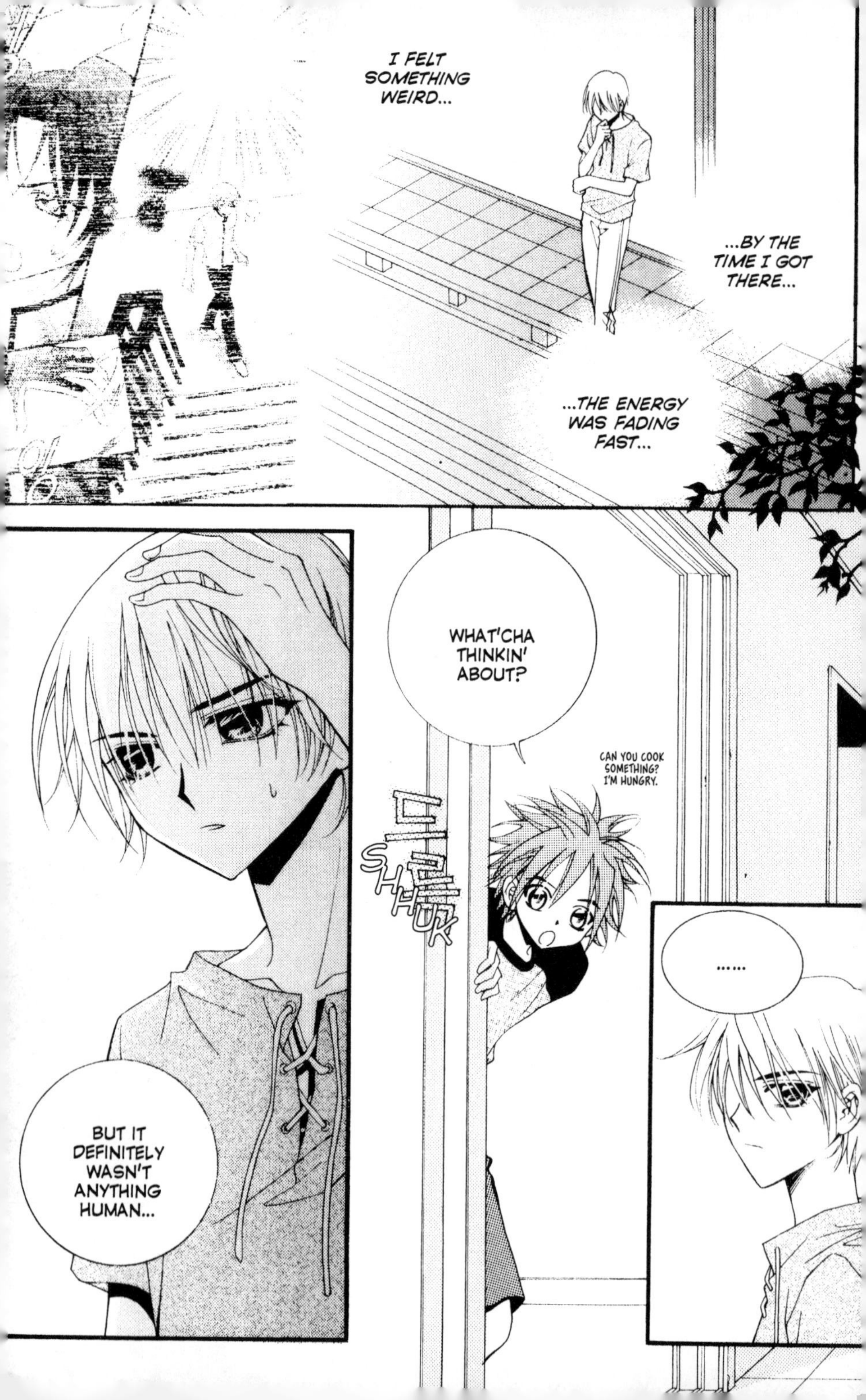
I FELT SOMETHING WEIRD...
...BY THE TIME I GOT THERE...
...THE ENERGY WAS FADING FAST...
BUT IT DEFINITELY WASN'T ANYTHING HUMAN...
WHAT'CHA THINKIN' ABOUT?
SHHUK
CAN YOU COOK SOMETHING? I'M HUNGRY.
......

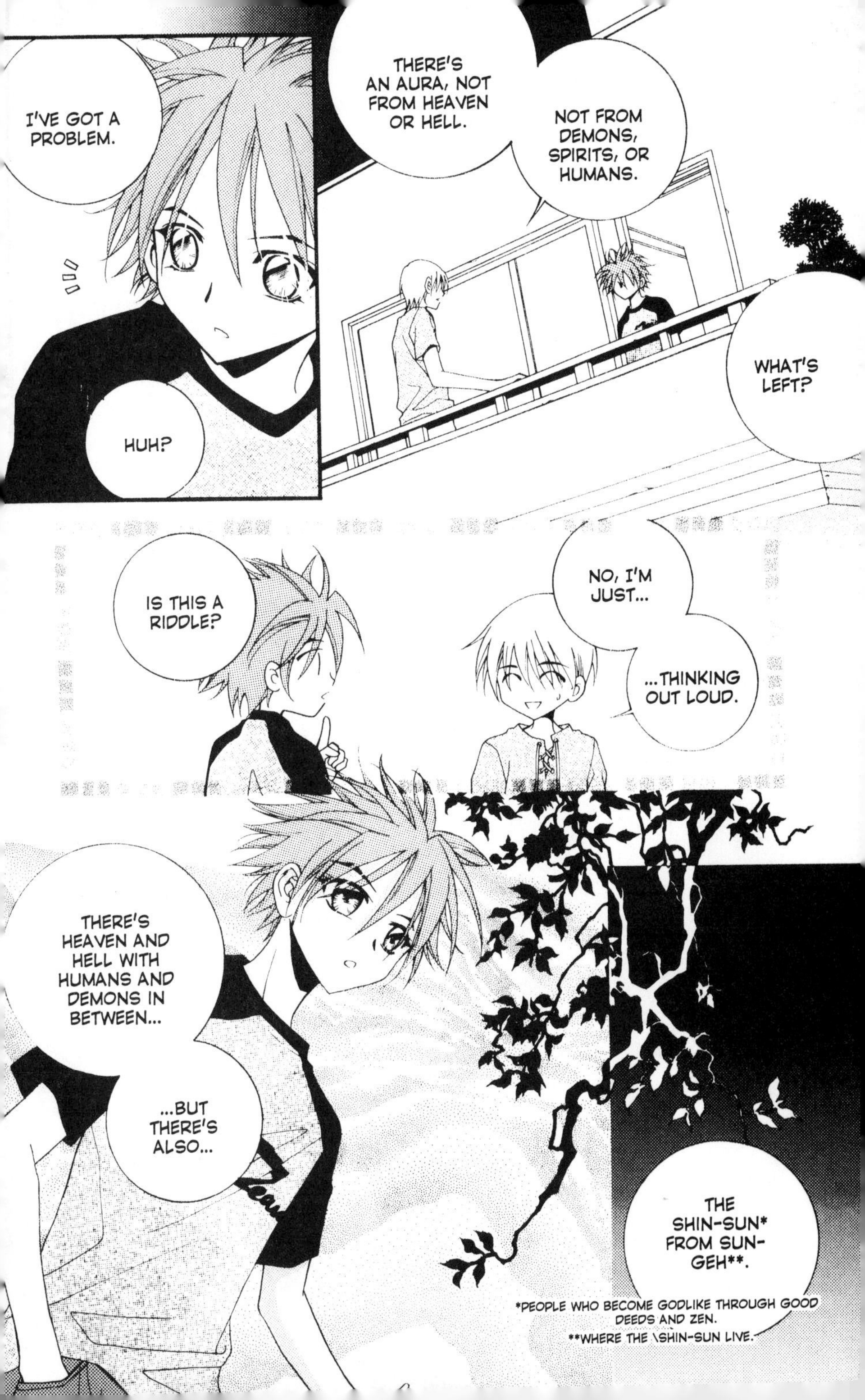
I'VE GOT A PROBLEM.
HUH?
THERE'S AN AURA, NOT FROM HEAVEN OR HELL.
NOT FROM DEMONS, SPIRITS, OR HUMANS.
WHAT'S LEFT?
IS THIS A RIDDLE?
NO, I'M JUST...
...THINKING OUT LOUD.
THERE'S HEAVEN AND HELL WITH HUMANS AND DEMONS IN BETWEEN...
...BUT THERE'S ALSO...
THE SHIN-SUN* FROM SUN-GEH**.

*PEOPLE WHO BECOME GODLIKE THROUGH GOOD DEEDS AND ZEN.

**WHERE THE SHIN-SUN LIVE.

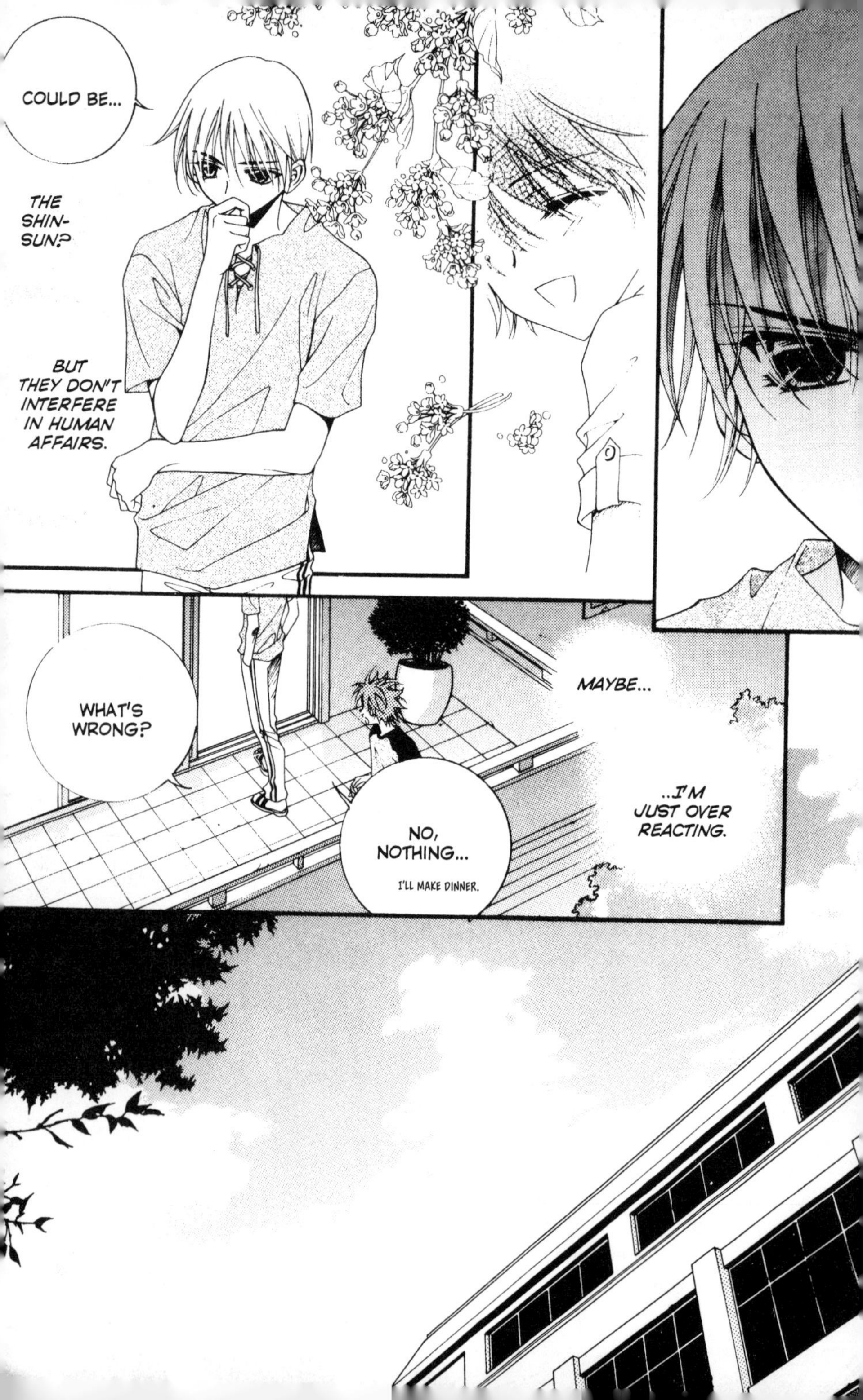
COULD BE...
THE SHIN-SUN?
BUT THEY DON'T INTERFERE IN HUMAN AFFAIRS.
WHAT'S WRONG?
NO, NOTHING...
I'LL MAKE DINNER.
MAYBE...
..I'M JUST OVER REACTING.

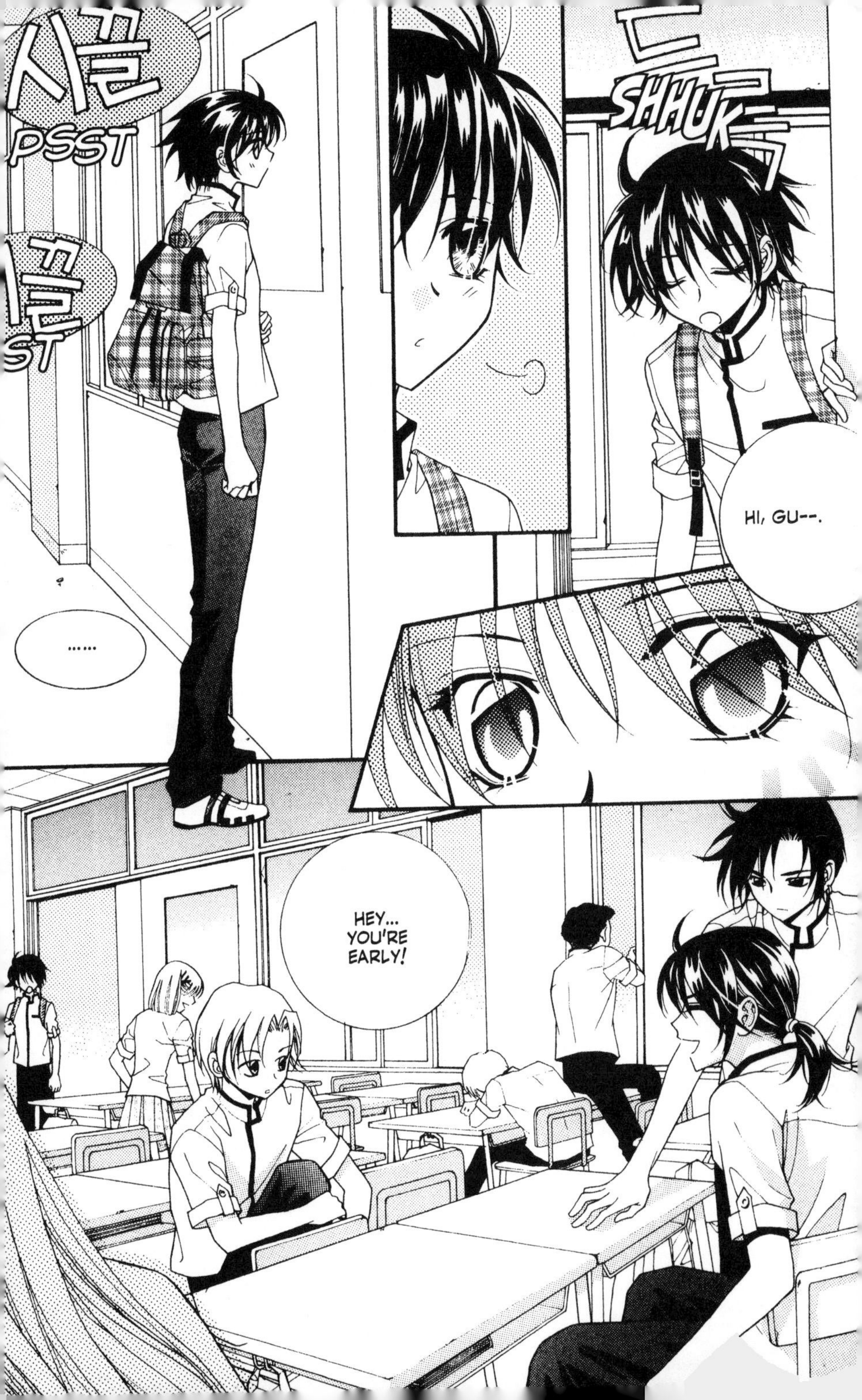
PSST
ST
......
SHHUK
HI, GU--.
HEY... YOU'RE EARLY!

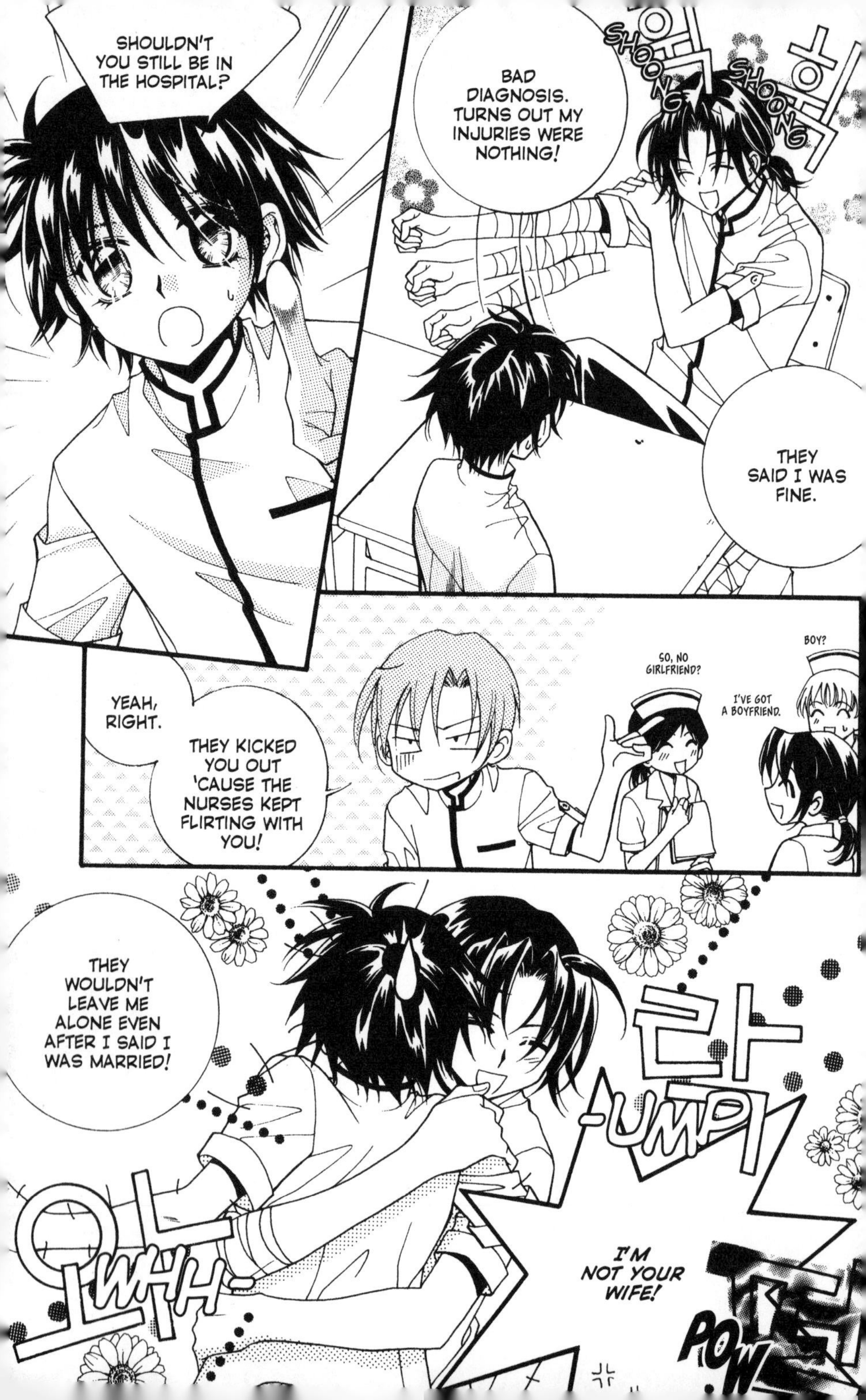

SHOULDN'T YOU STILL BE IN THE HOSPITAL?
SHOONG
SHOONG
BAD DIAGNOSIS. TURNS OUT MY INJURIES WERE NOTHING!
THEY SAID I WAS FINE.
YEAH, RIGHT.
THEY KICKED YOU OUT 'CAUSE THE NURSES KEPT FLIRTING WITH YOU!
SO, NO GIRLFRIEND?
I'VE GOT A BOYFRIEND.
BOY?
THEY WOULDN'T LEAVE ME ALONE EVEN AFTER I SAID I WAS MARRIED!
WHH-
-UMP!
I'M NOT YOUR WIFE!
POW

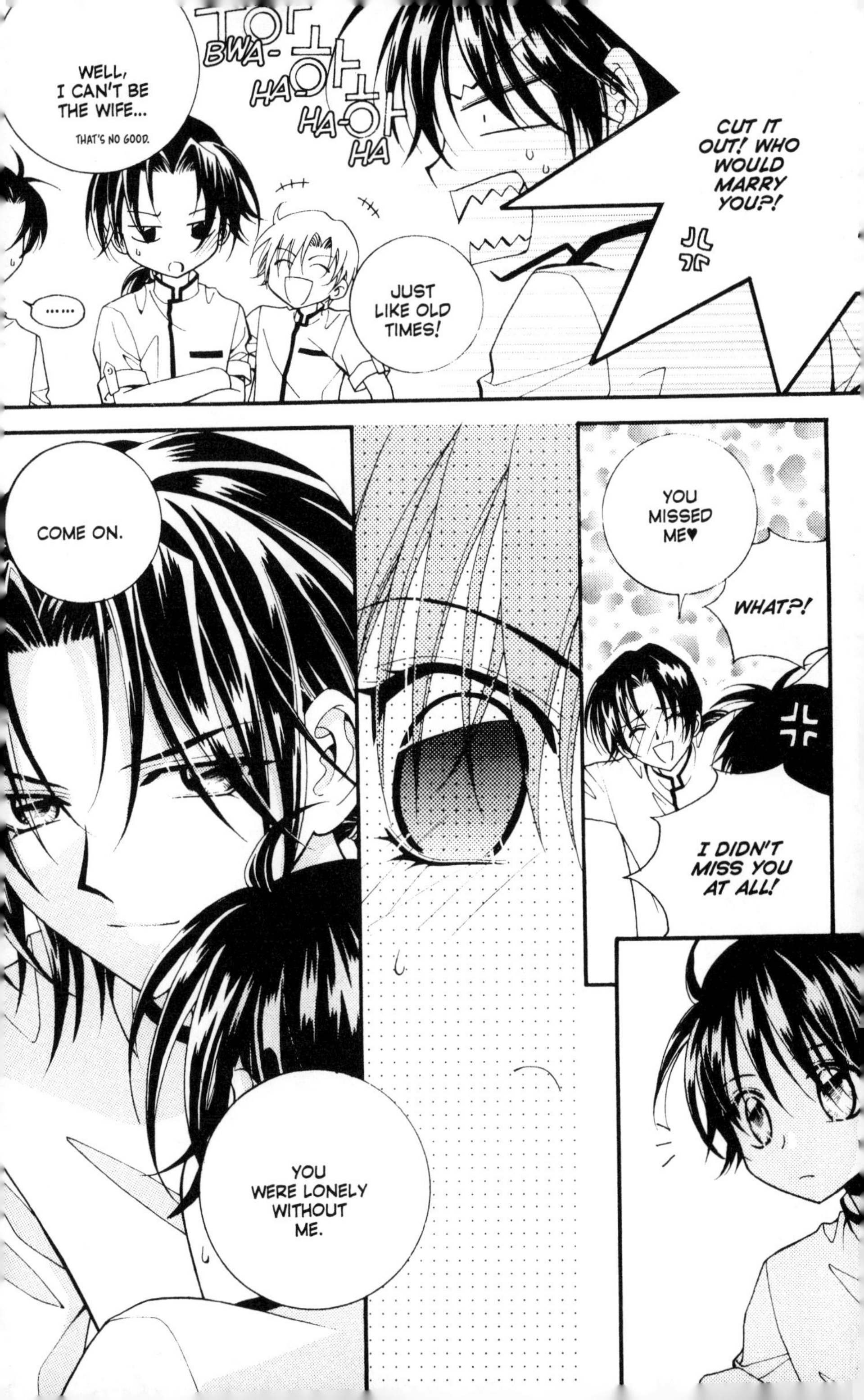
WELL, I CAN'T BE THE WIFE...
THAT'S NO GOOD.
BWA-HA-HA-HA
......
JUST LIKE OLD TIMES!
CUT IT OUT! WHO WOULD MARRY YOU?!
COME ON.
YOU WERE LONELY WITHOUT ME.
YOU MISSED ME♥
WHAT?!
I DIDN'T MISS YOU AT ALL!

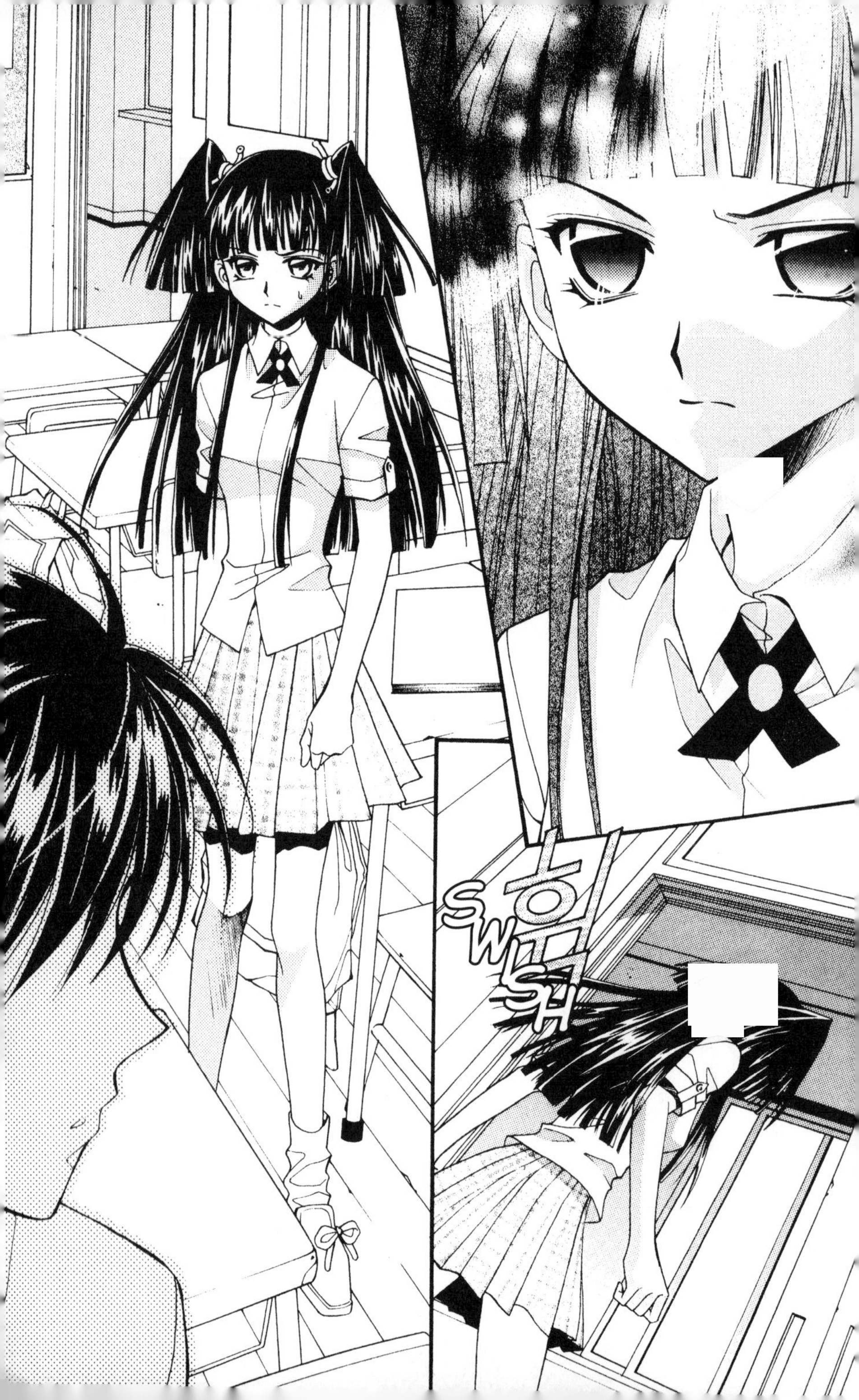
휙
SWISH

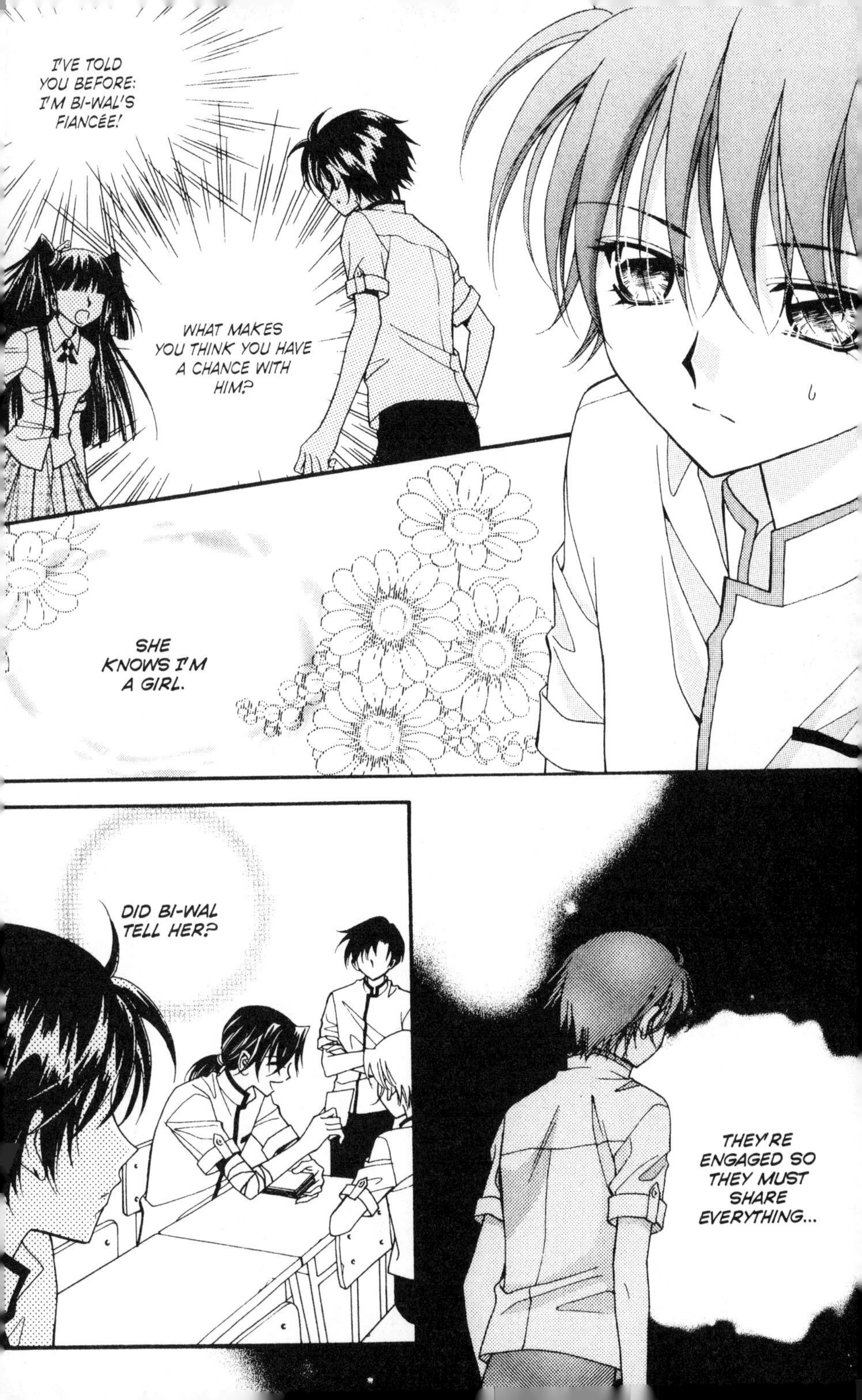
I'VE TOLD YOU BEFORE: I'M BI-WAL'S FIANCÉE!
WHAT MAKES YOU THINK YOU HAVE A CHANCE WITH HIM?
SHE KNOWS I'M A GIRL.
DID BI-WAL TELL HER?
THEY'RE ENGAGED SO THEY MUST SHARE EVERYTHING...

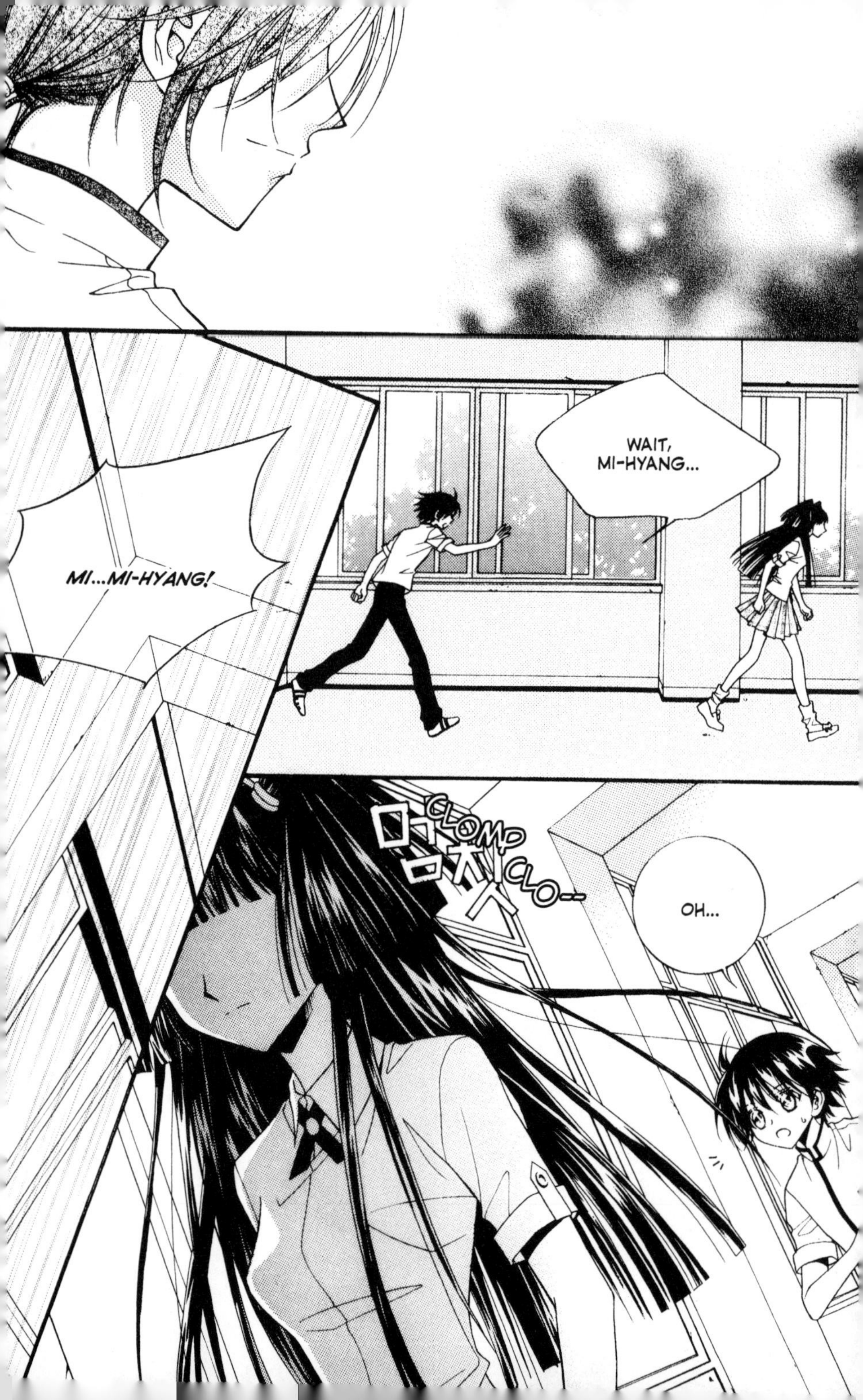
MI...MI-HYANG!
WAIT, MI-HYANG...
CLOMP CLO--
OH...

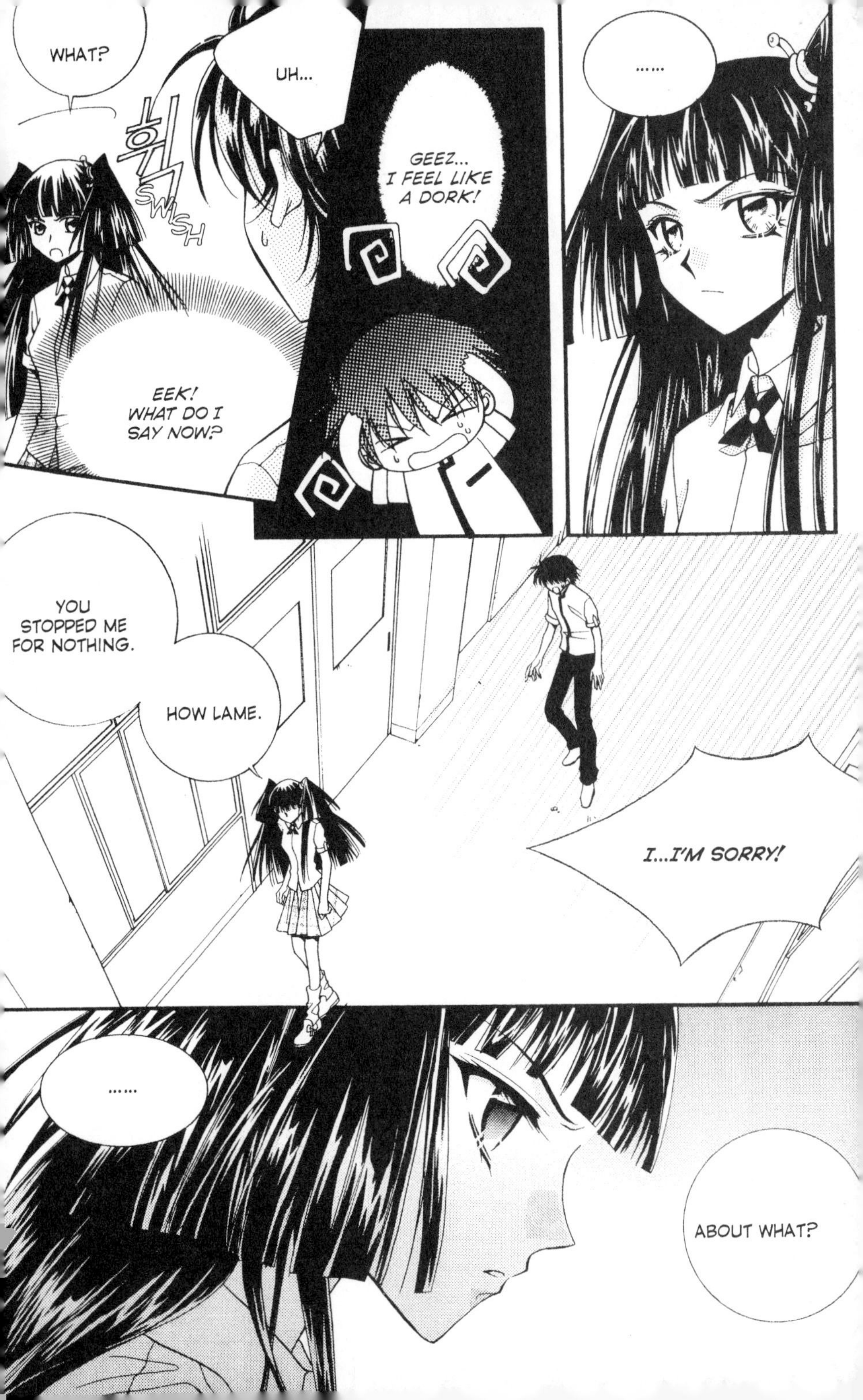
WHAT?
휙
SWISH
UH...
EEK! WHAT DO I SAY NOW?
GEEZ... I FEEL LIKE A DORK!
......
YOU STOPPED ME FOR NOTHING.
HOW LAME.
I...I'M SORRY!
......
ABOUT WHAT?

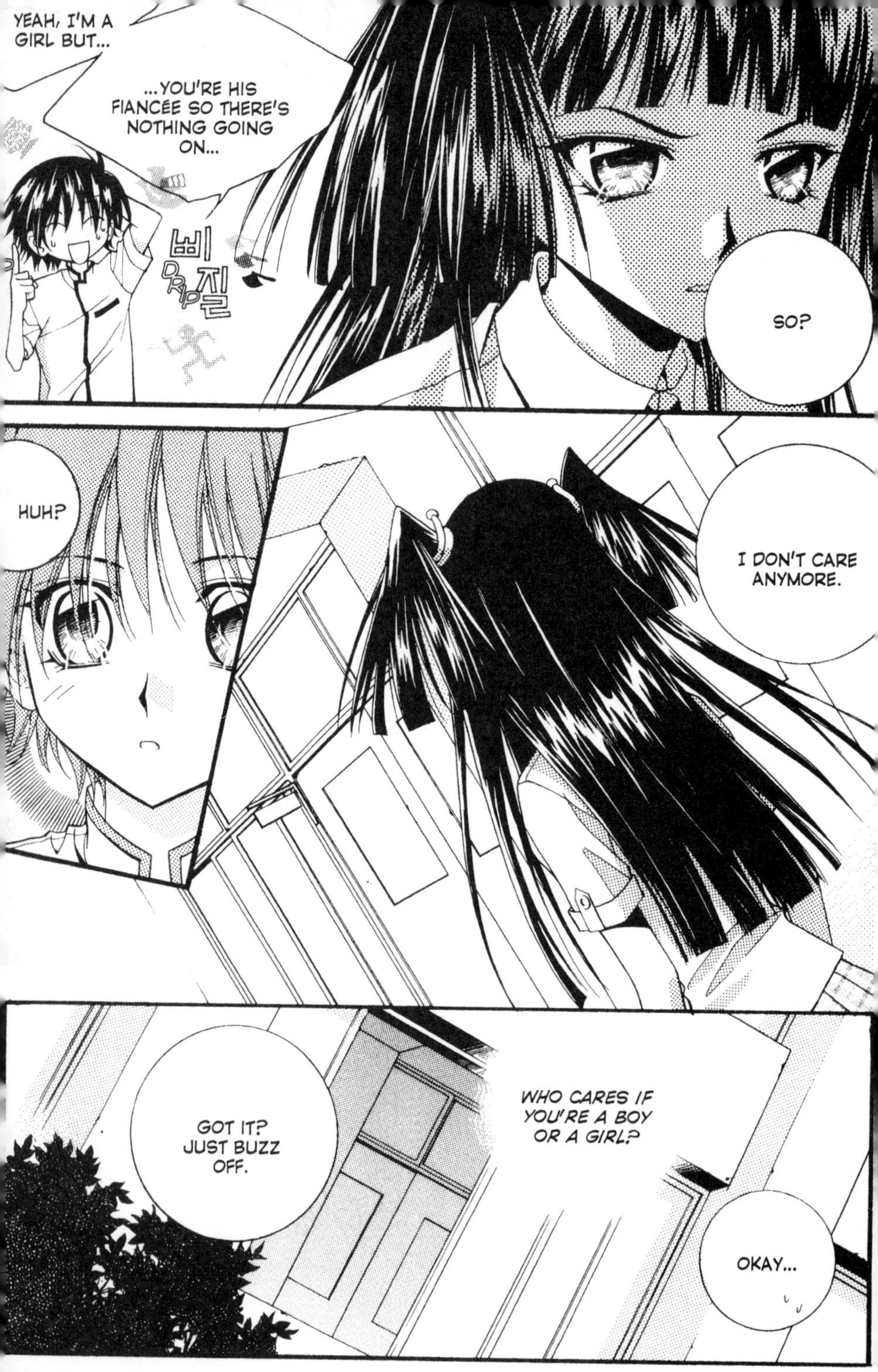
YEAH, I'M A GIRL BUT...
...YOU'RE HIS FIANCÉE SO THERE'S NOTHING GOING ON...
삐질
DRIP
SO?
HUH?
I DON'T CARE ANYMORE.
GOT IT? JUST BUZZ OFF.
WHO CARES IF YOU'RE A BOY OR A GIRL?
OKAY...

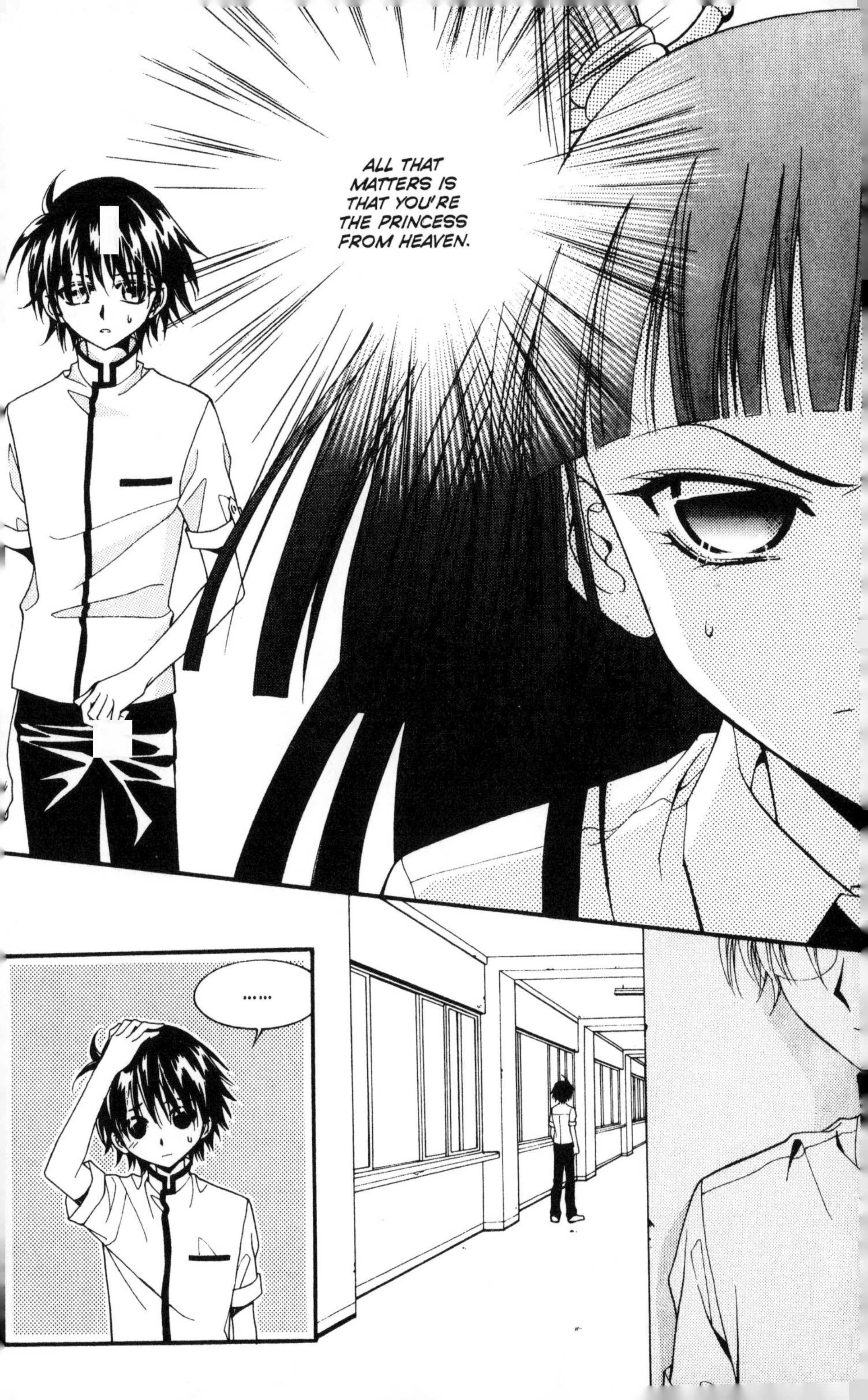
ALL THAT MATTERS IS THAT YOU'RE THE PRINCESS FROM HEAVEN.
......

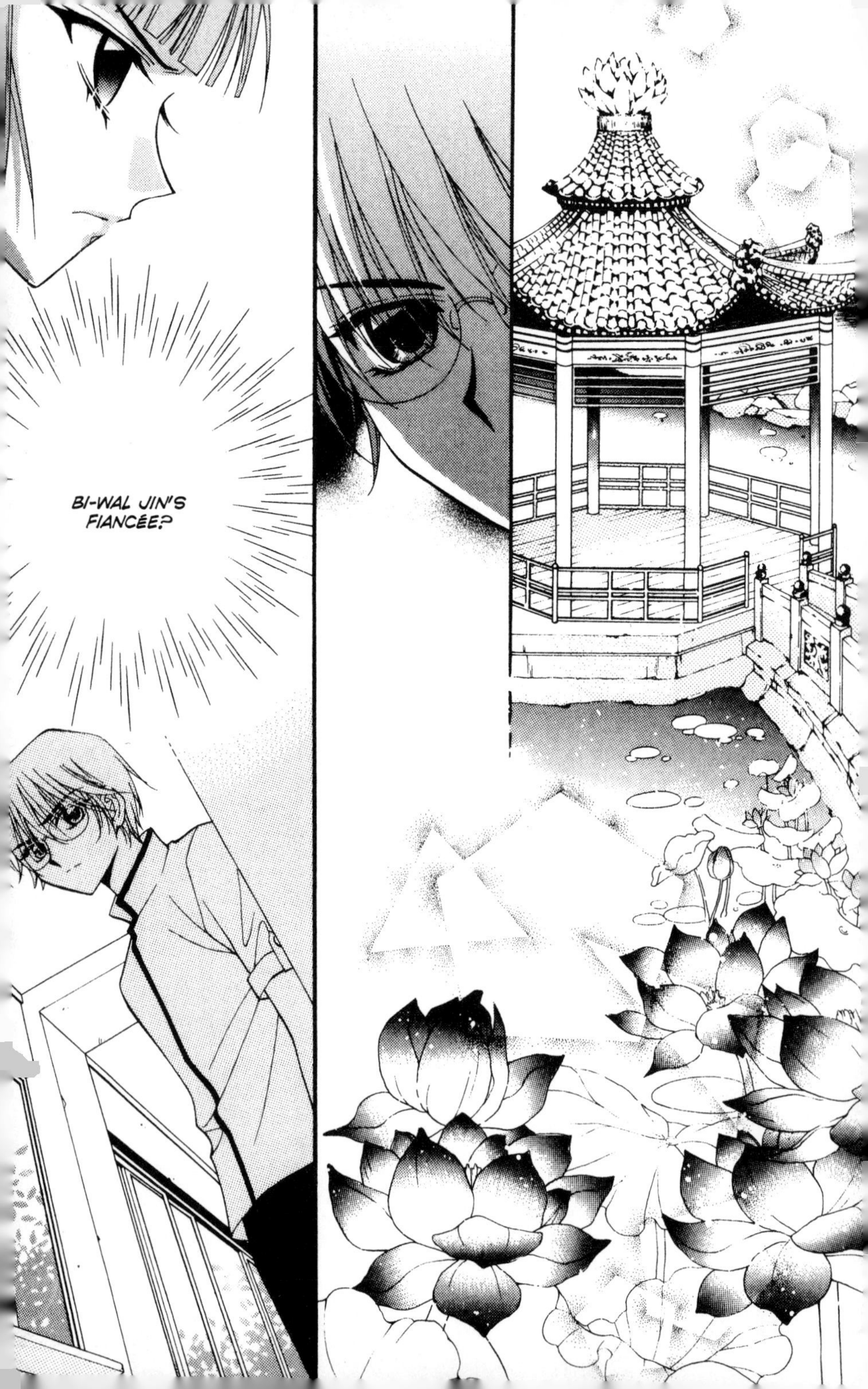
BI-WAL JIN'S FIANCÉE?

SO NOW ALL FOUR GUARDIANS ARE PROTECTING DONG-YOUNG-NIM.

THE BLACK TURTLE WAS SUPPOSED TO BE LOYAL TO HIS ORDERS.

HE HAD NO CHOICE. HIS PRIDE WOULD'VE BEEN HURT...

...IF THE DEMONS TOOK DONG-YOUNG-NIM RIGHT IN FRONT OF HIM.

BUT HE WENT AGAINST HIS ORDERS.

AND THESE DAYS, THE DEMONS ARE TRYING EVEN HARDER...

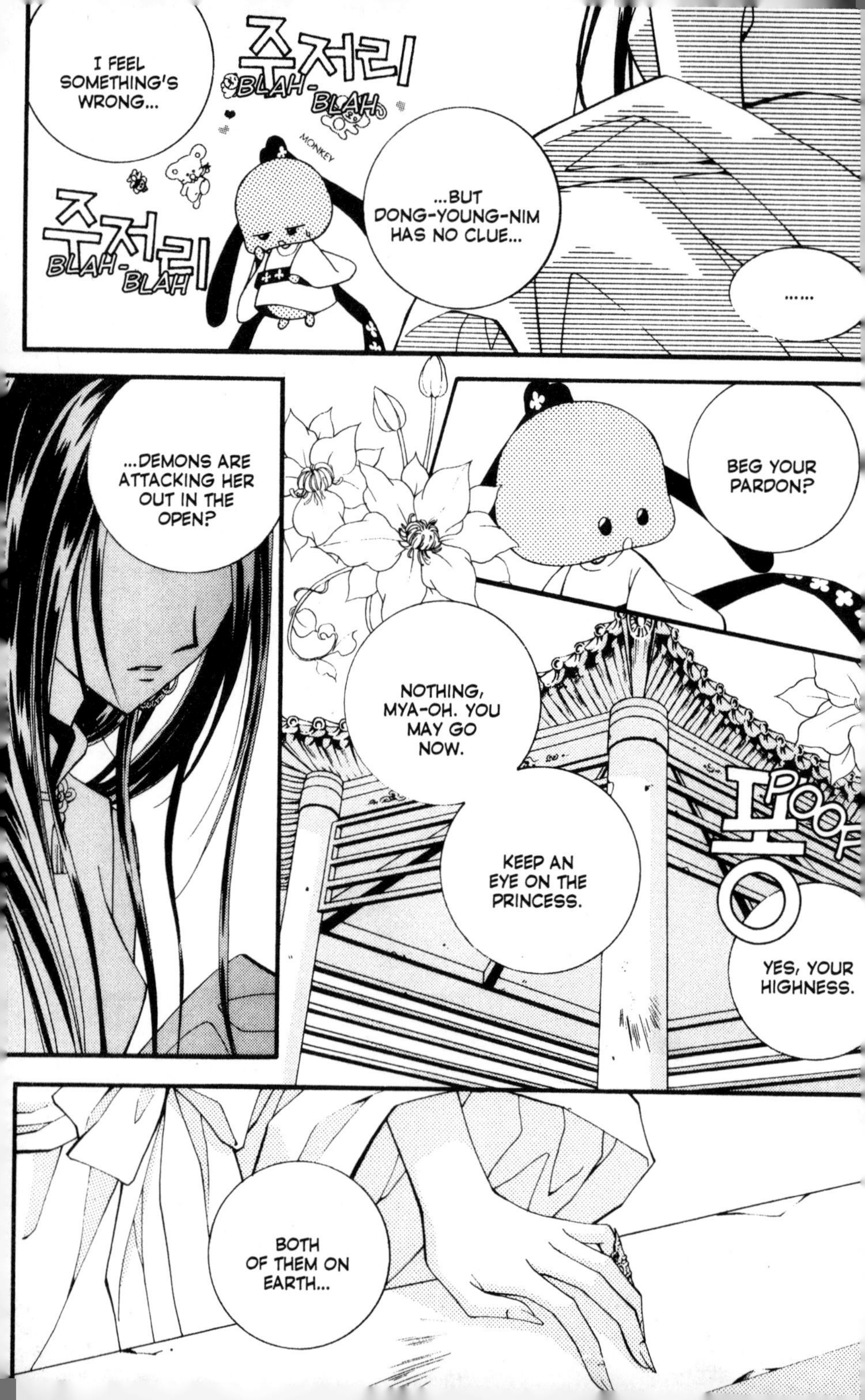

I FEEL SOMETHING'S WRONG...
주저리
BLAH-BLAH
MONKEY
주저리
BLAH-BLAH
...BUT DONG-YOUNG-NIM HAS NO CLUE...
......
...DEMONS ARE ATTACKING HER OUT IN THE OPEN?
BEG YOUR PARDON?
NOTHING, MYA-OH. YOU MAY GO NOW.
KEEP AN EYE ON THE PRINCESS.
포
POOK
YES, YOUR HIGHNESS.
BOTH OF THEM ON EARTH...

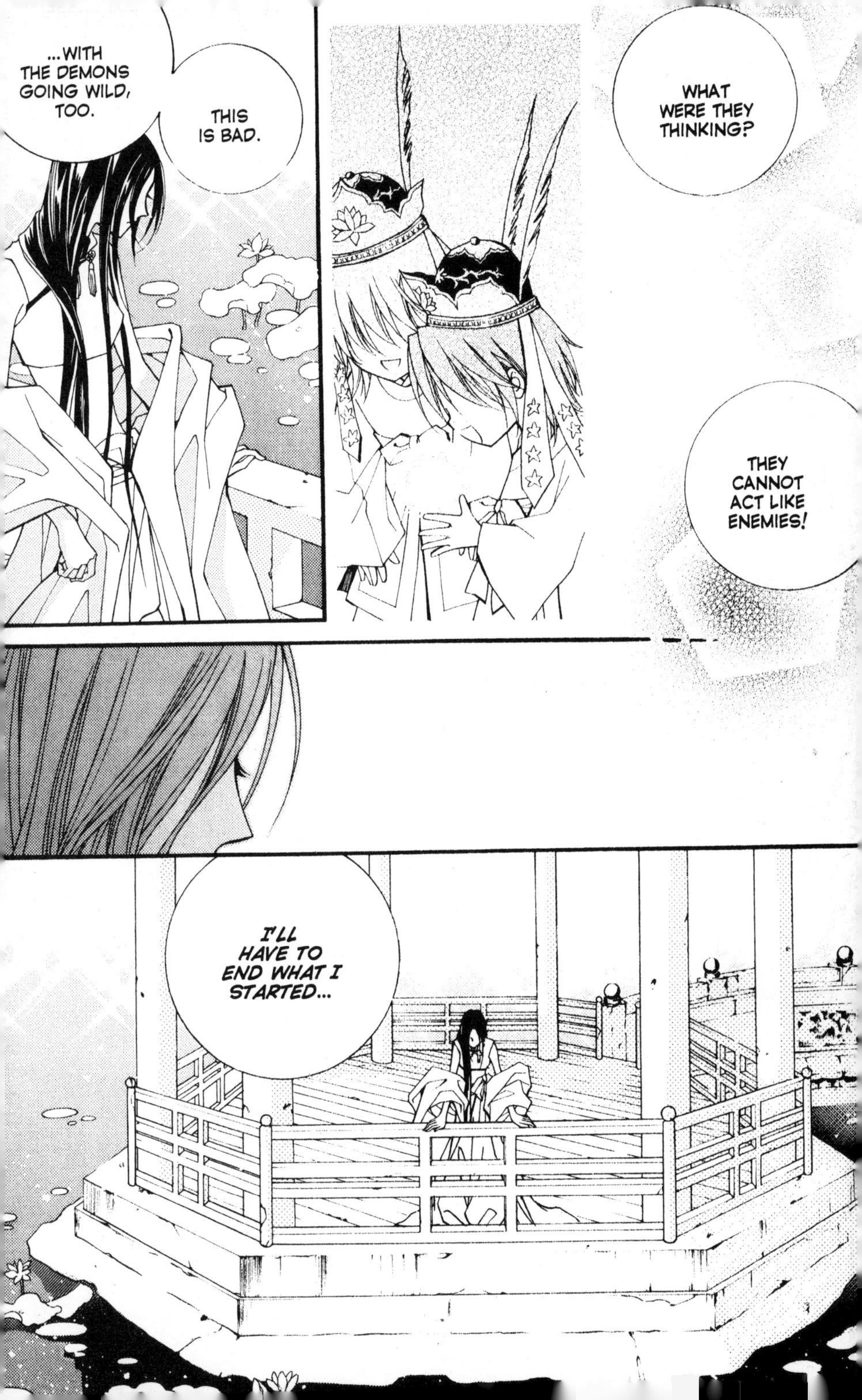
WHAT WERE THEY THINKING?
THEY CANNOT ACT LIKE ENEMIES!
THIS IS BAD.
...WITH THE DEMONS GOING WILD, TOO.
I'LL HAVE TO END WHAT I STARTED...

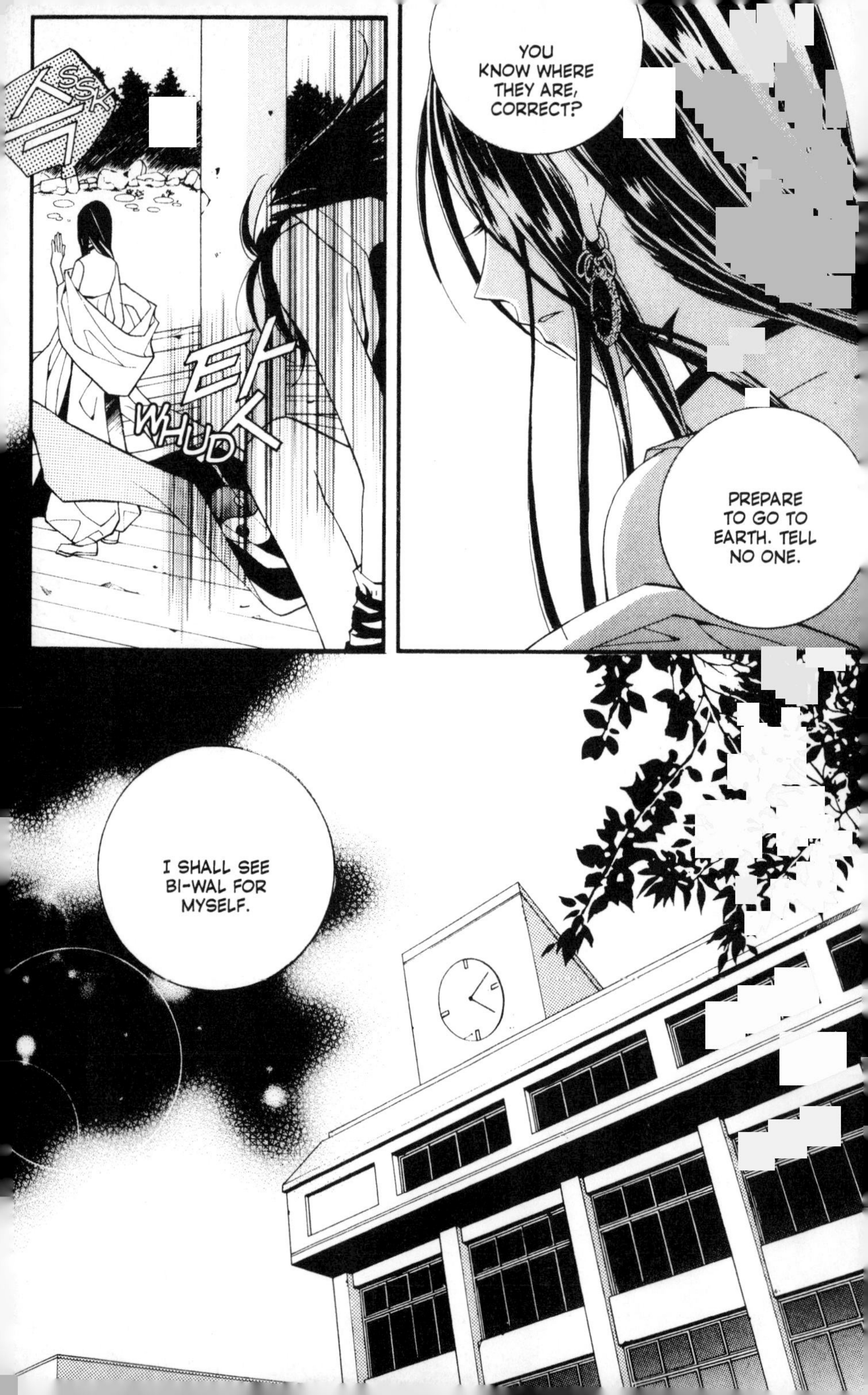
SSK
WHUD
YOU KNOW WHERE THEY ARE, CORRECT?
PREPARE TO GO TO EARTH. TELL NO ONE.
I SHALL SEE BI-WAL FOR MYSELF.

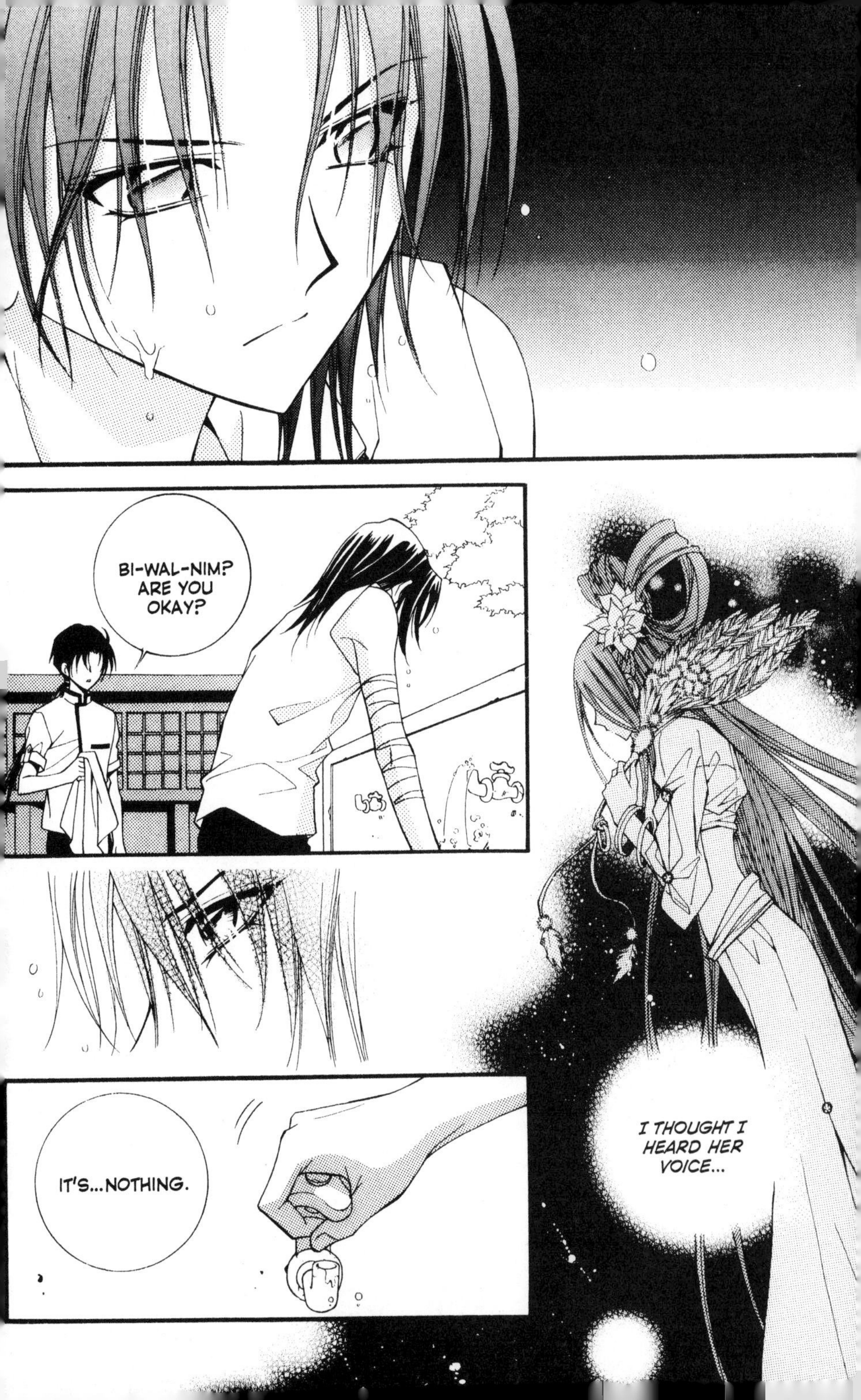
BI-WAL-NIM? ARE YOU OKAY?
IT'S...NOTHING.
I THOUGHT I HEARD HER VOICE...

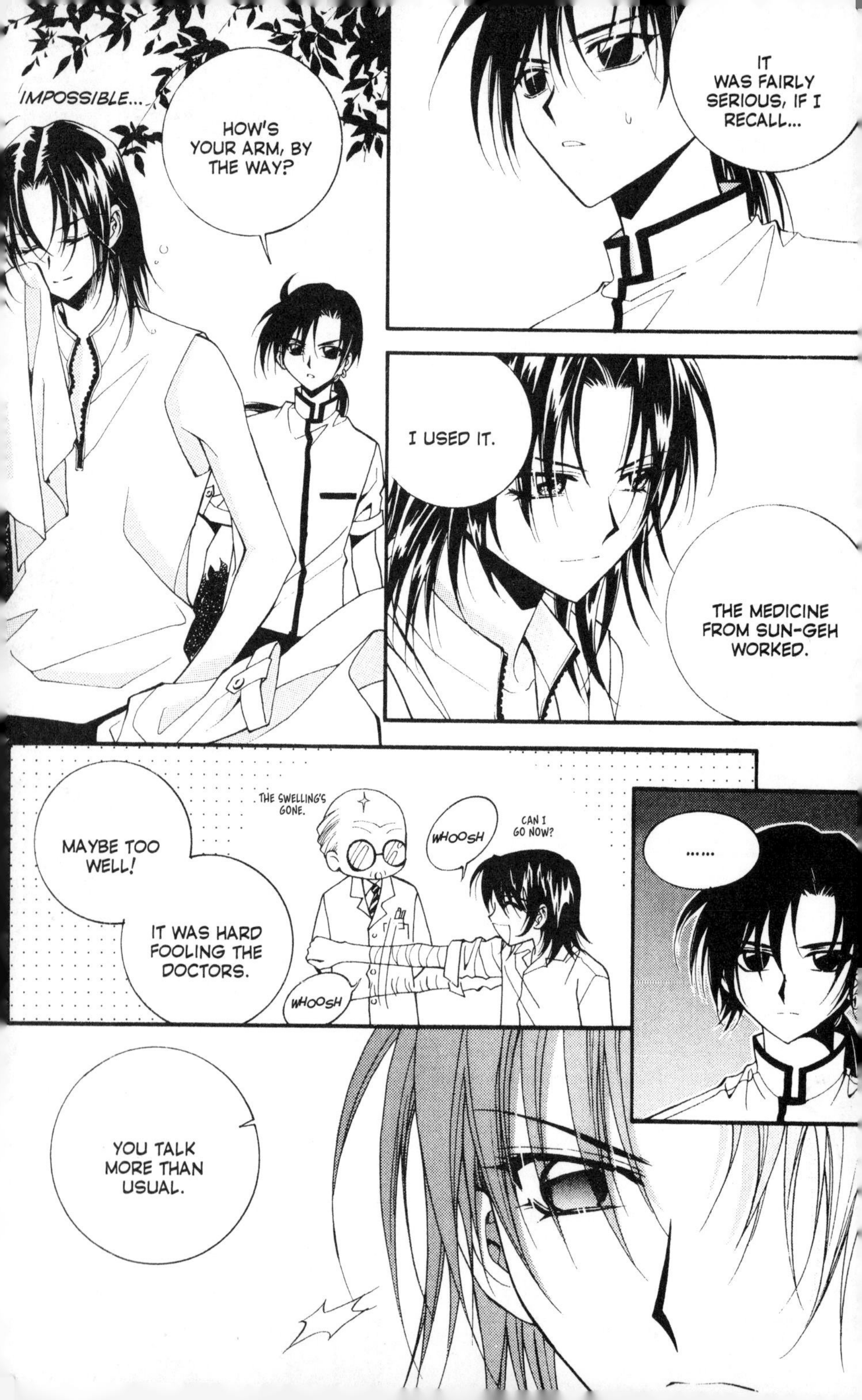
IMPOSSIBLE...
HOW'S YOUR ARM, BY THE WAY?
IT WAS FAIRLY SERIOUS, IF I RECALL...
I USED IT.
THE MEDICINE FROM SUN-GEH WORKED.
MAYBE TOO WELL!
IT WAS HARD FOOLING THE DOCTORS.
THE SWELLING'S GONE.
WHOOSH
CAN I GO NOW?
WHOOSH
......
YOU TALK MORE THAN USUAL.

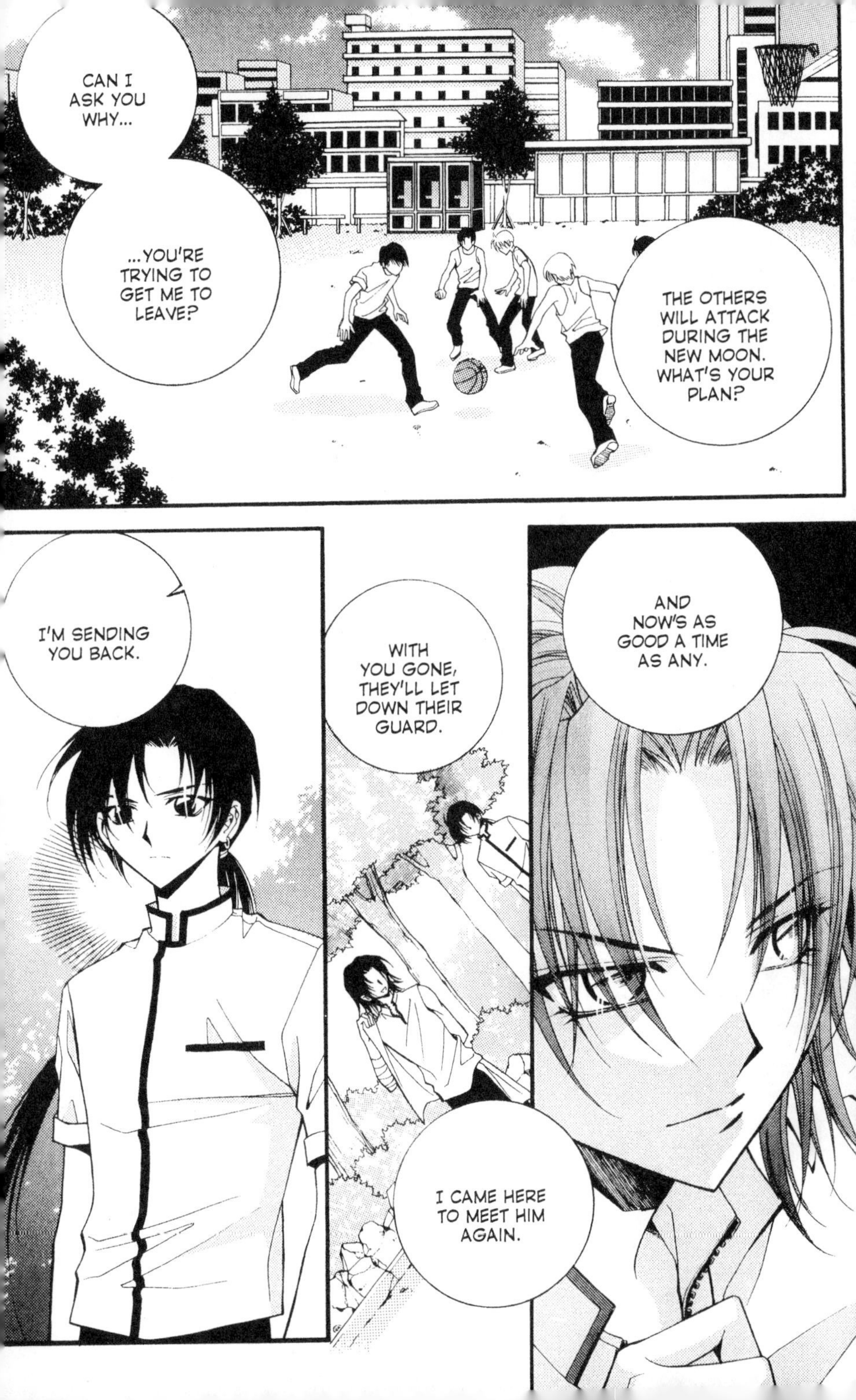
CAN I ASK YOU WHY...
...YOU'RE TRYING TO GET ME TO LEAVE?
THE OTHERS WILL ATTACK DURING THE NEW MOON. WHAT'S YOUR PLAN?
I'M SENDING YOU BACK.
WITH YOU GONE, THEY'LL LET DOWN THEIR GUARD.
AND NOW'S AS GOOD A TIME AS ANY.
I CAME HERE TO MEET HIM AGAIN.

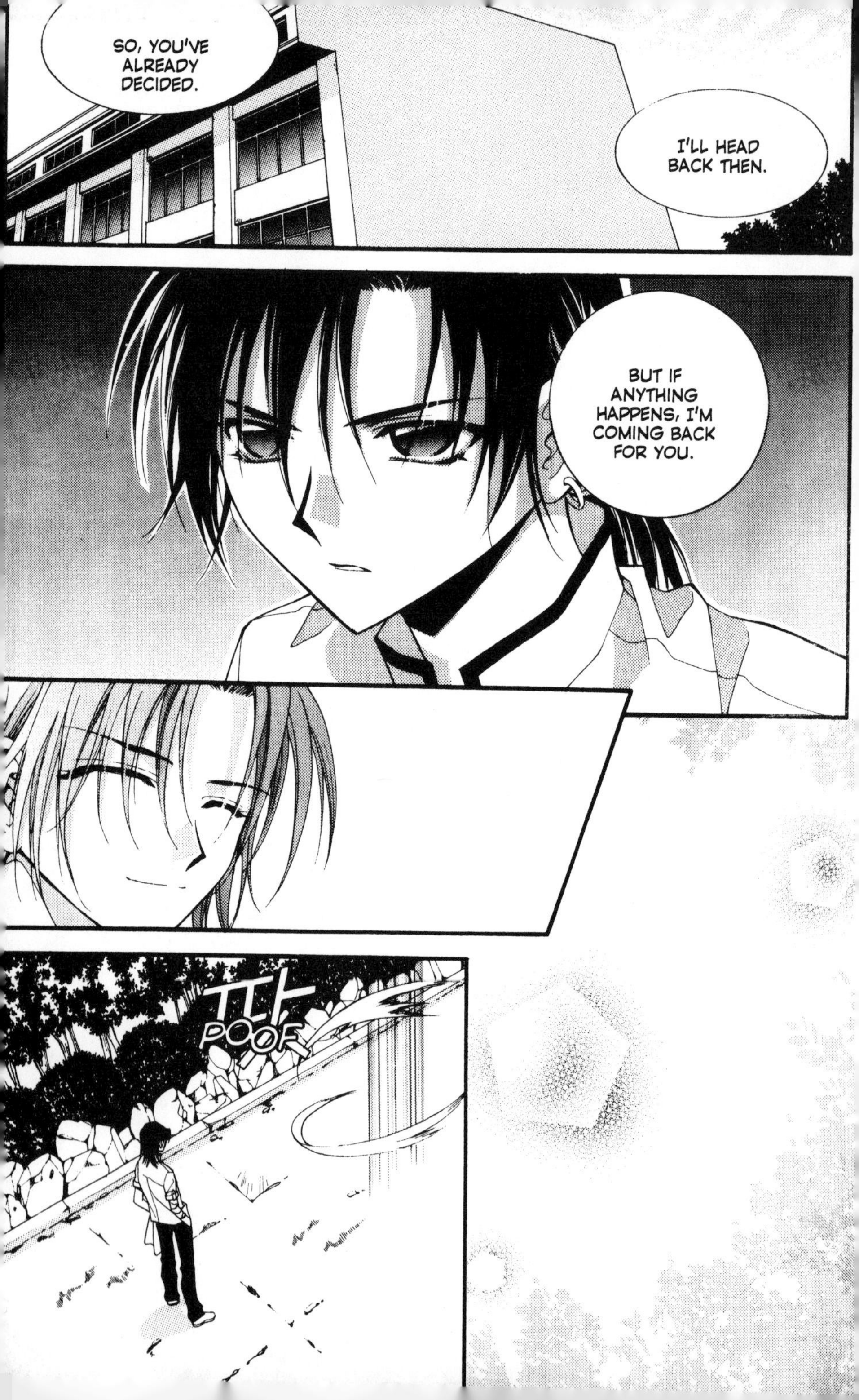
SO, YOU'VE ALREADY DECIDED.
I'LL HEAD BACK THEN.
BUT IF ANYTHING HAPPENS, I'M COMING BACK FOR YOU.
POOF

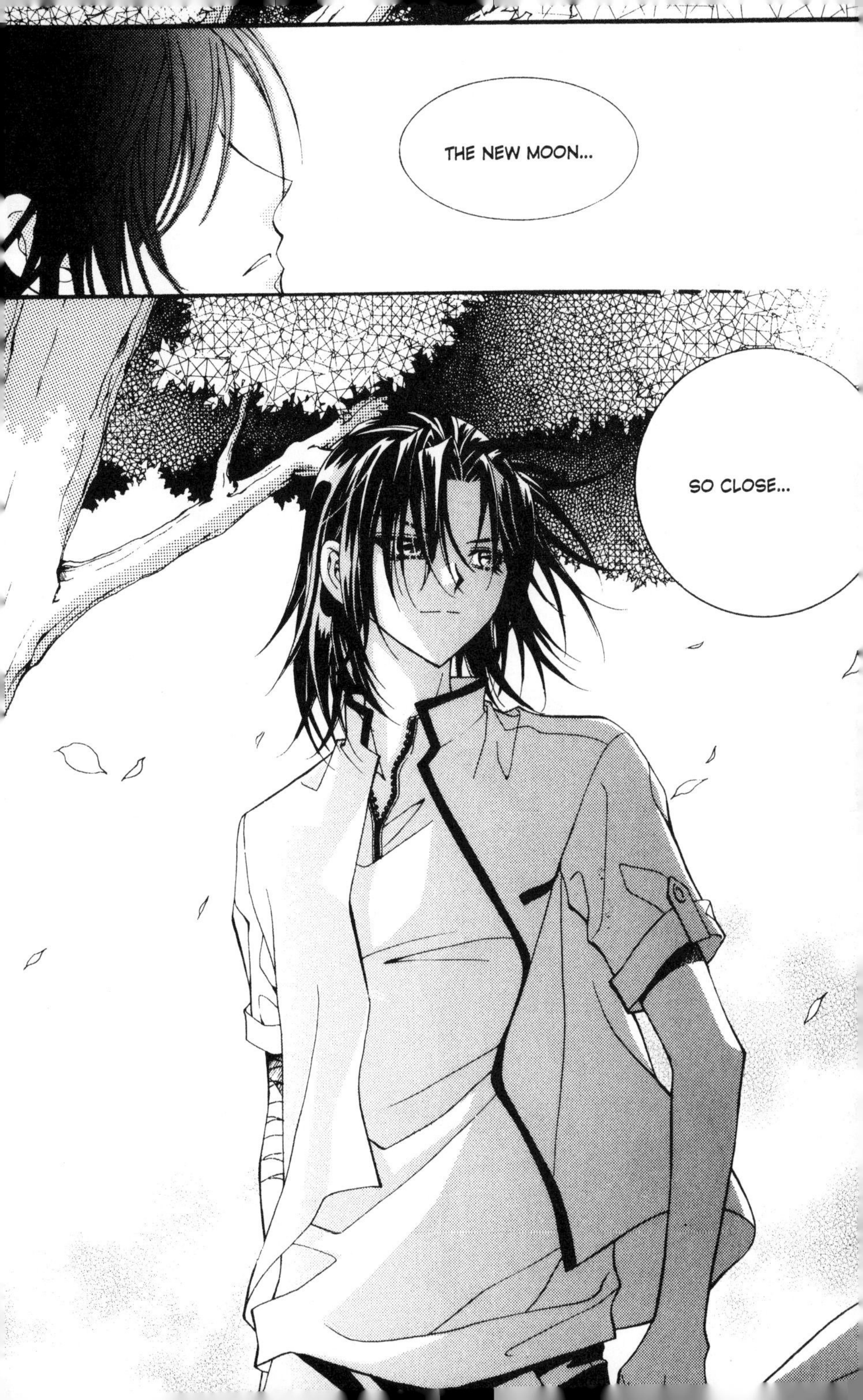
THE NEW MOON...
SO CLOSE...

VI THE PRINCESS IS KIDNAPPED!

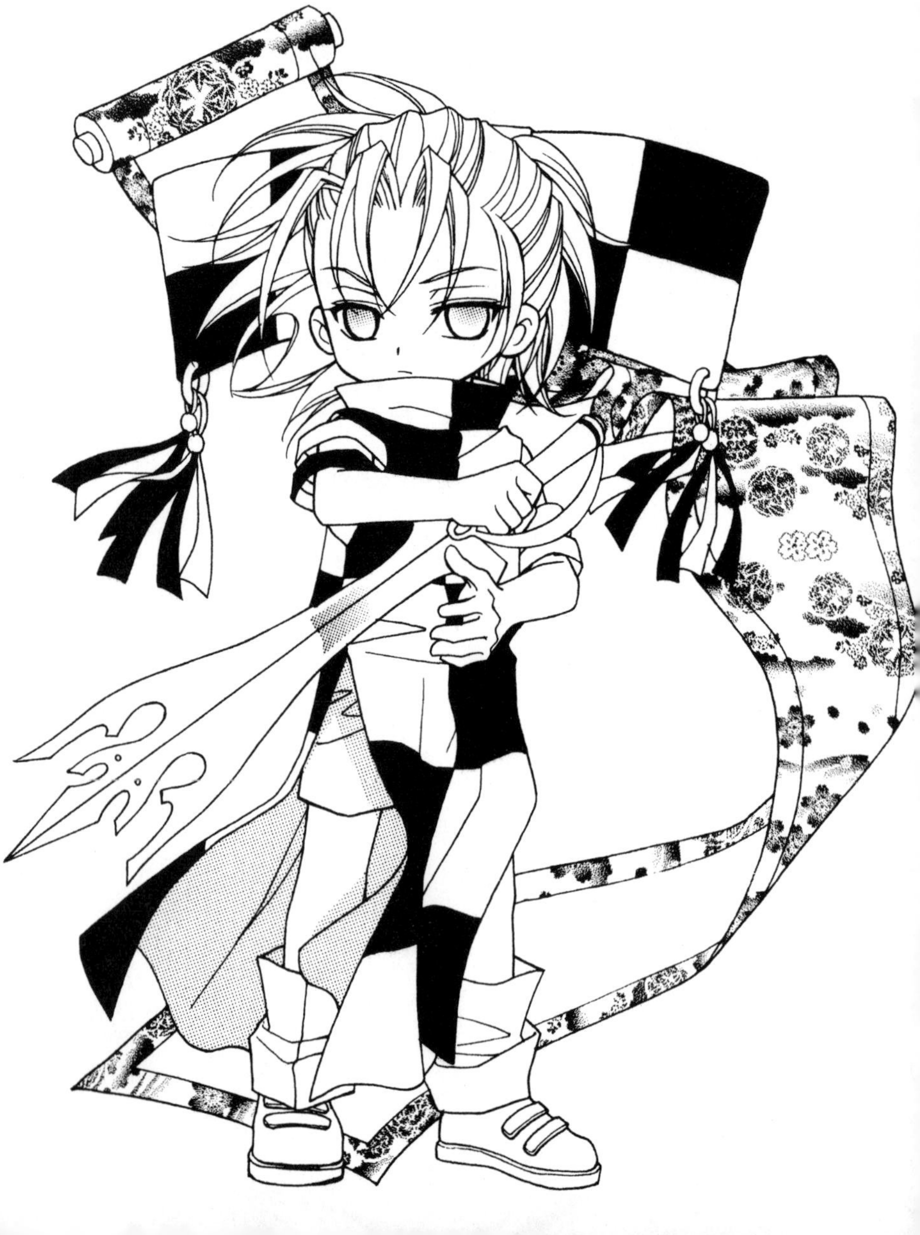

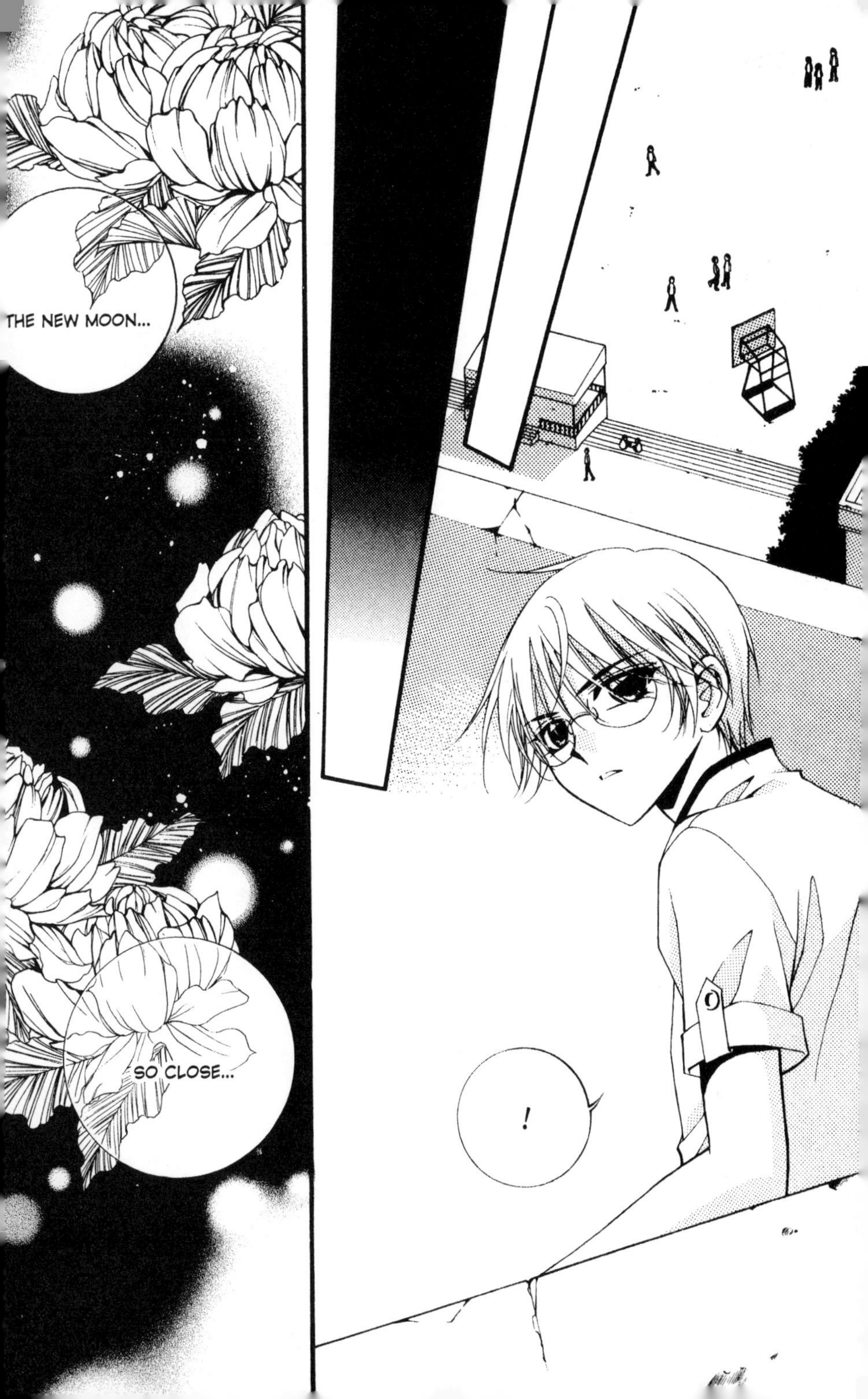
THE NEW MOON...
SO CLOSE...
!

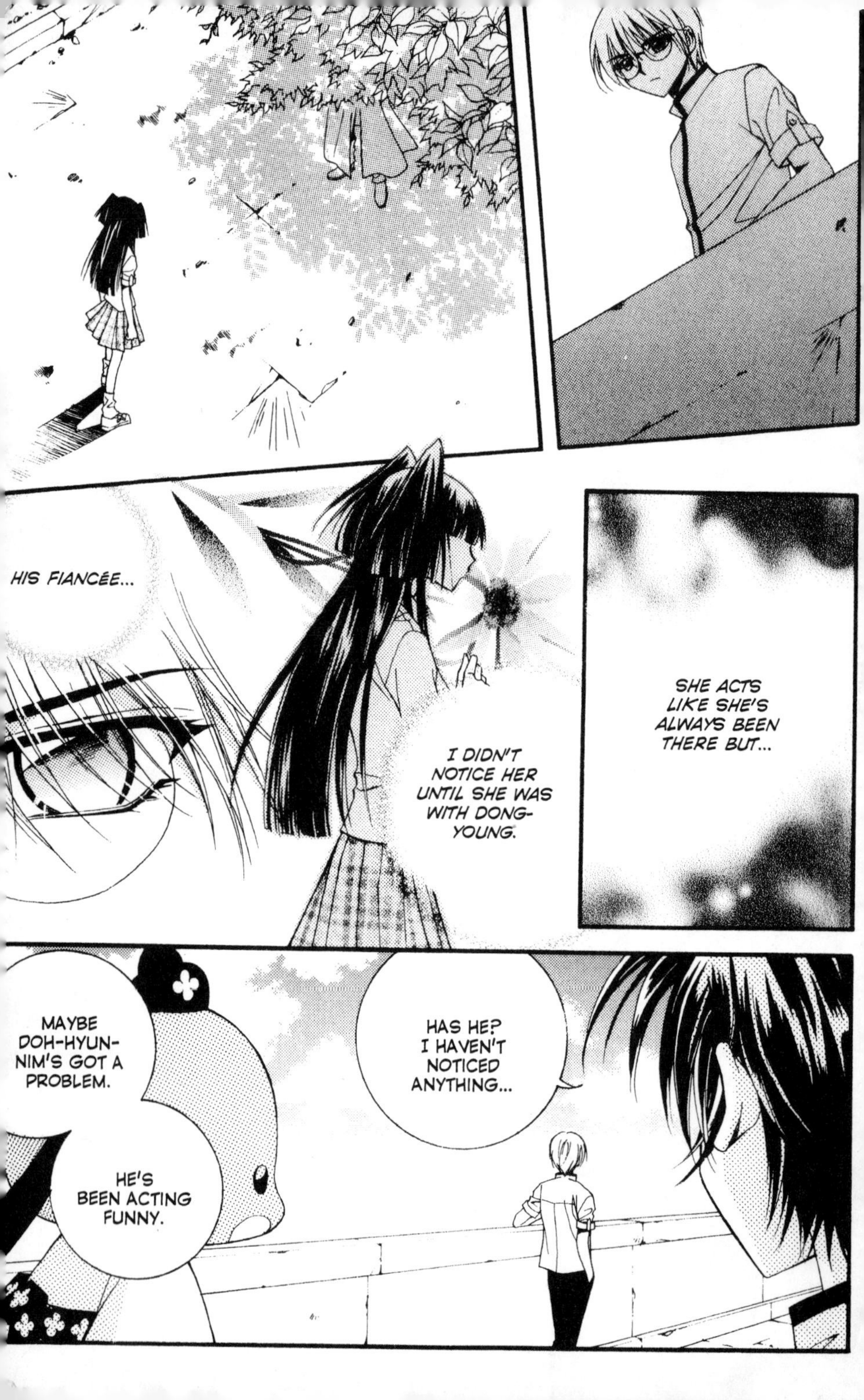
HIS FIANCÉE...
I DIDN'T NOTICE HER UNTIL SHE WAS WITH DONG-YOUNG.
SHE ACTS LIKE SHE'S ALWAYS BEEN THERE BUT...
MAYBE DOH-HYUN-NIM'S GOT A PROBLEM.
HE'S BEEN ACTING FUNNY.
HAS HE? I HAVEN'T NOTICED ANYTHING...

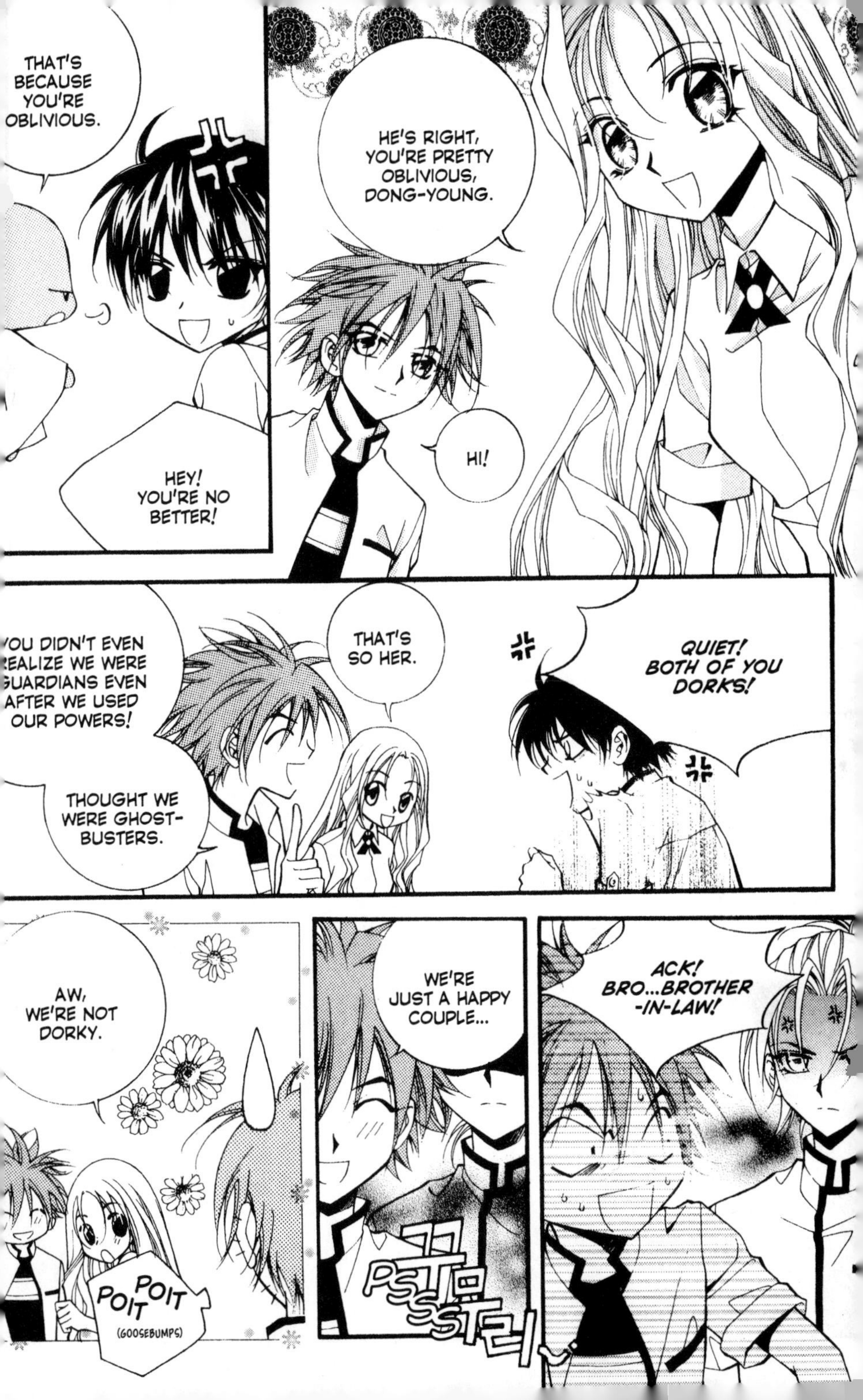
THAT'S BECAUSE YOU'RE OBLIVIOUS.
HEY! YOU'RE NO BETTER!
HE'S RIGHT, YOU'RE PRETTY OBLIVIOUS, DONG-YOUNG.
HI!
YOU DIDN'T EVEN REALIZE WE WERE GUARDIANS EVEN AFTER WE USED OUR POWERS!
THOUGHT WE WERE GHOST-BUSTERS.
THAT'S SO HER.
QUIET! BOTH OF YOU DORKS!
AW, WE'RE NOT DORKY.
POIT POIT
(GOOSEBUMPS)
WE'RE JUST A HAPPY COUPLE...
PSSSST
ACK! BRO...BROTHER-IN-LAW!

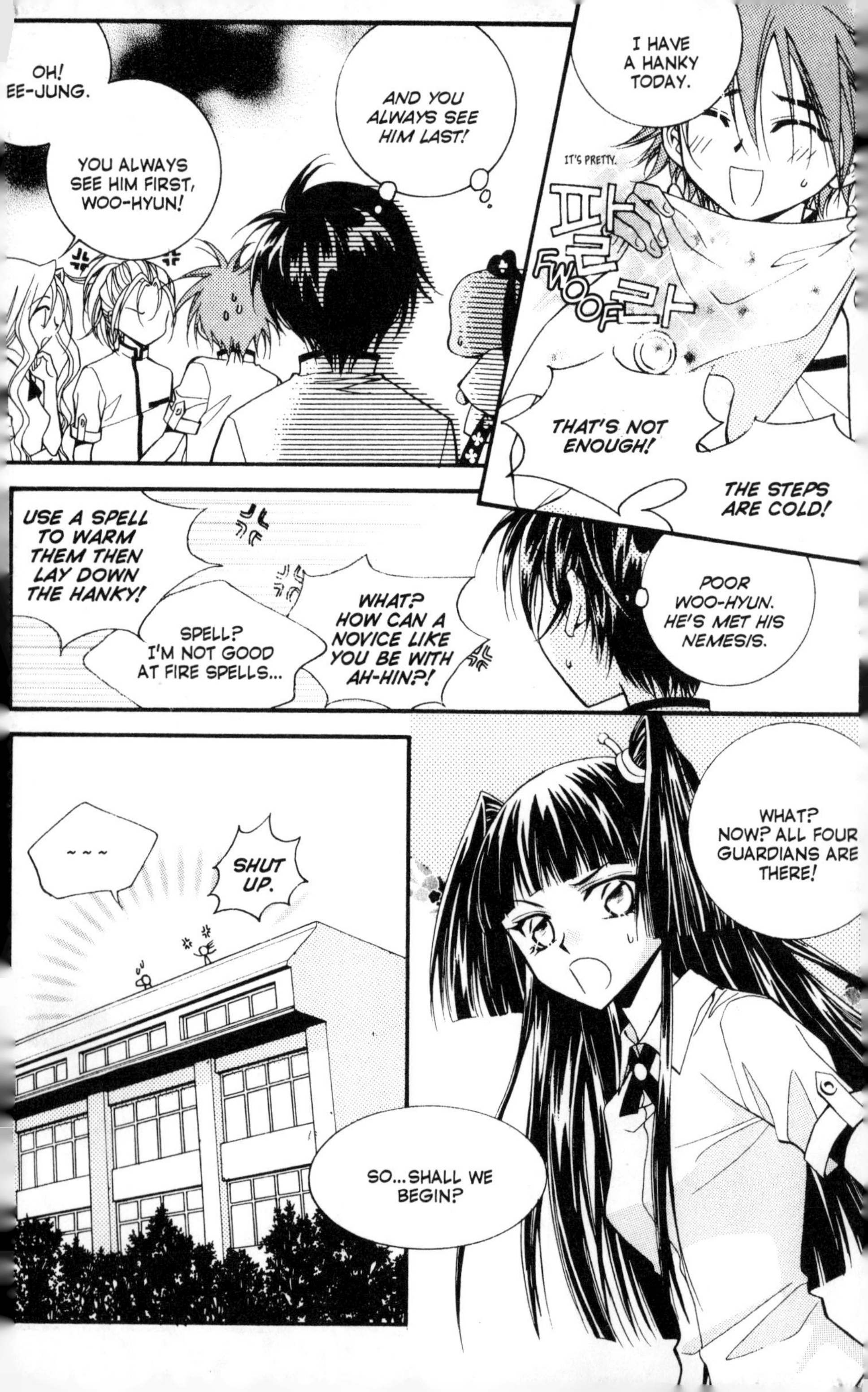
OH! EE-JUNG.
YOU ALWAYS SEE HIM FIRST, WOO-HYUN!
AND YOU ALWAYS SEE HIM LAST!
I HAVE A HANKY TODAY.
IT'S PRETTY.
FWOOF
THAT'S NOT ENOUGH!
THE STEPS ARE COLD!
USE A SPELL TO WARM THEM THEN LAY DOWN THE HANKY!
SPELL? I'M NOT GOOD AT FIRE SPELLS...
WHAT? HOW CAN A NOVICE LIKE YOU BE WITH AH-HIN?!
POOR WOO-HYUN. HE'S MET HIS NEMESIS.
~ ~ ~
SHUT UP.
WHAT? NOW? ALL FOUR GUARDIANS ARE THERE!
SO...SHALL WE BEGIN?

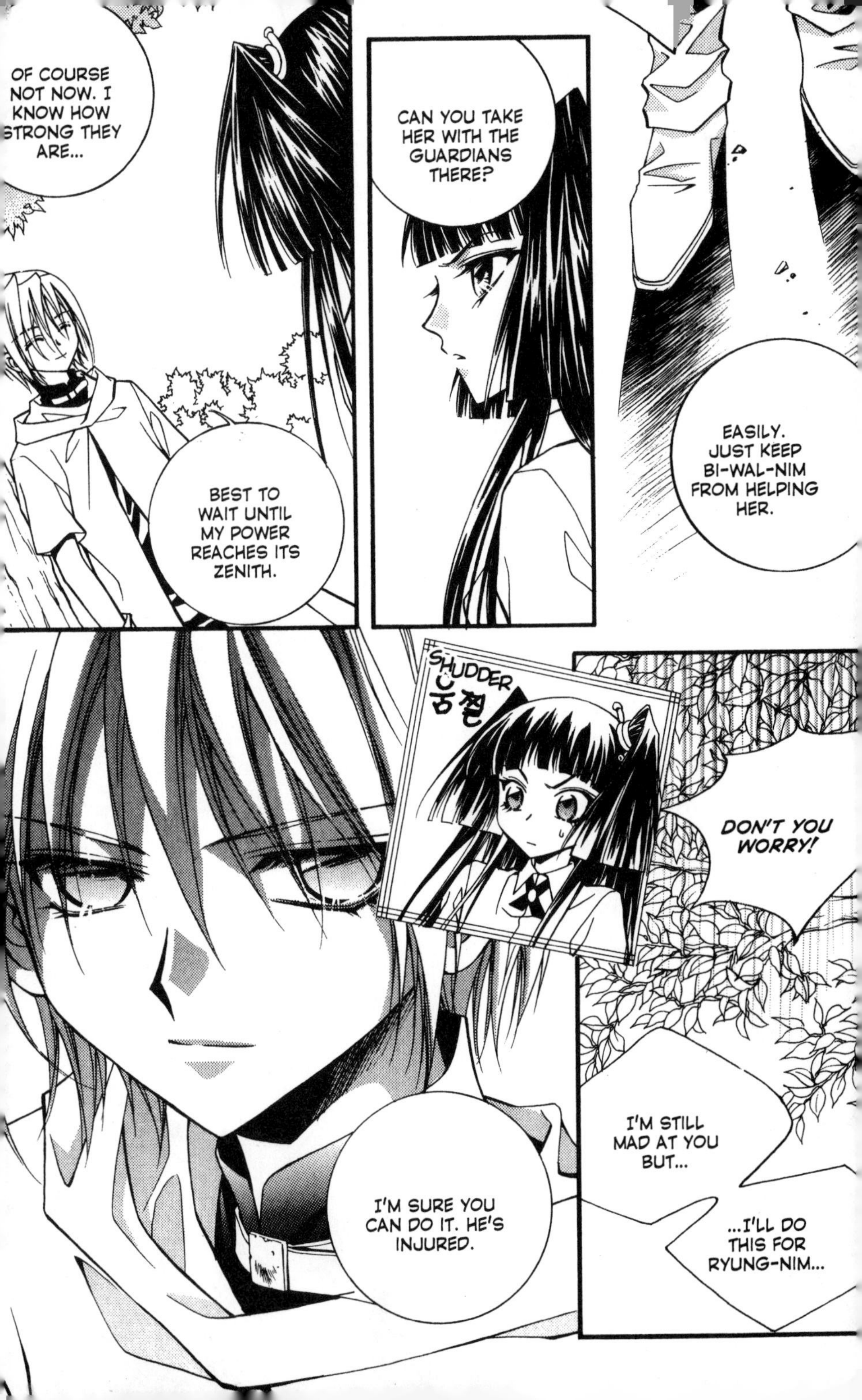
OF COURSE NOT NOW. I KNOW HOW STRONG THEY ARE...
BEST TO WAIT UNTIL MY POWER REACHES ITS ZENITH.
CAN YOU TAKE HER WITH THE GUARDIANS THERE?
EASILY. JUST KEEP BI-WAL-NIM FROM HELPING HER.
I'M SURE YOU CAN DO IT. HE'S INJURED.
SHUDDER
움찔
DON'T YOU WORRY!
I'M STILL MAD AT YOU BUT...
...I'LL DO THIS FOR RYUNG-NIM...

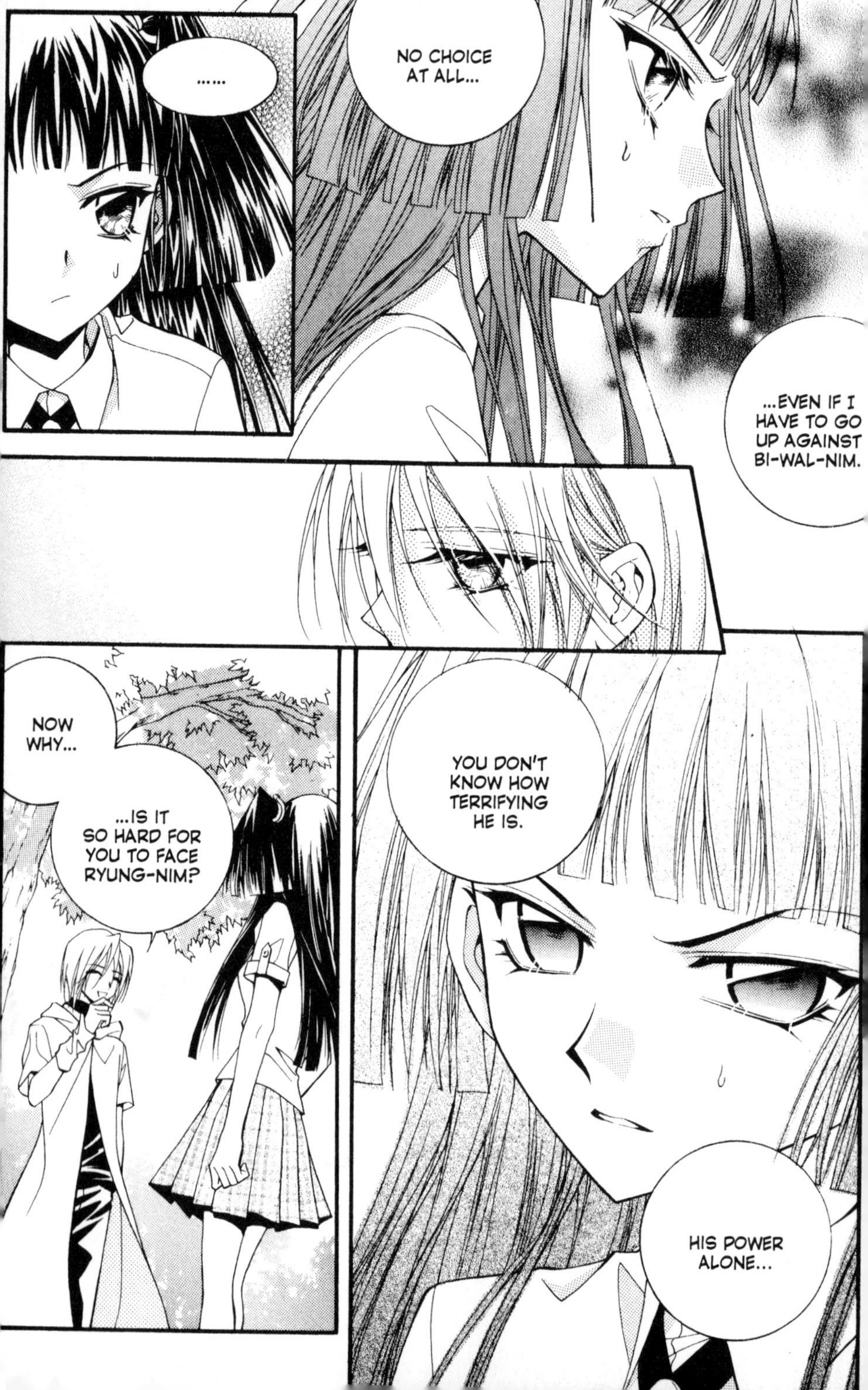
……
NO CHOICE AT ALL...
...EVEN IF I HAVE TO GO UP AGAINST BI-WAL-NIM.
NOW WHY...
...IS IT SO HARD FOR YOU TO FACE RYUNG-NIM?
YOU DON'T KNOW HOW TERRIFYING HE IS.
HIS POWER ALONE...

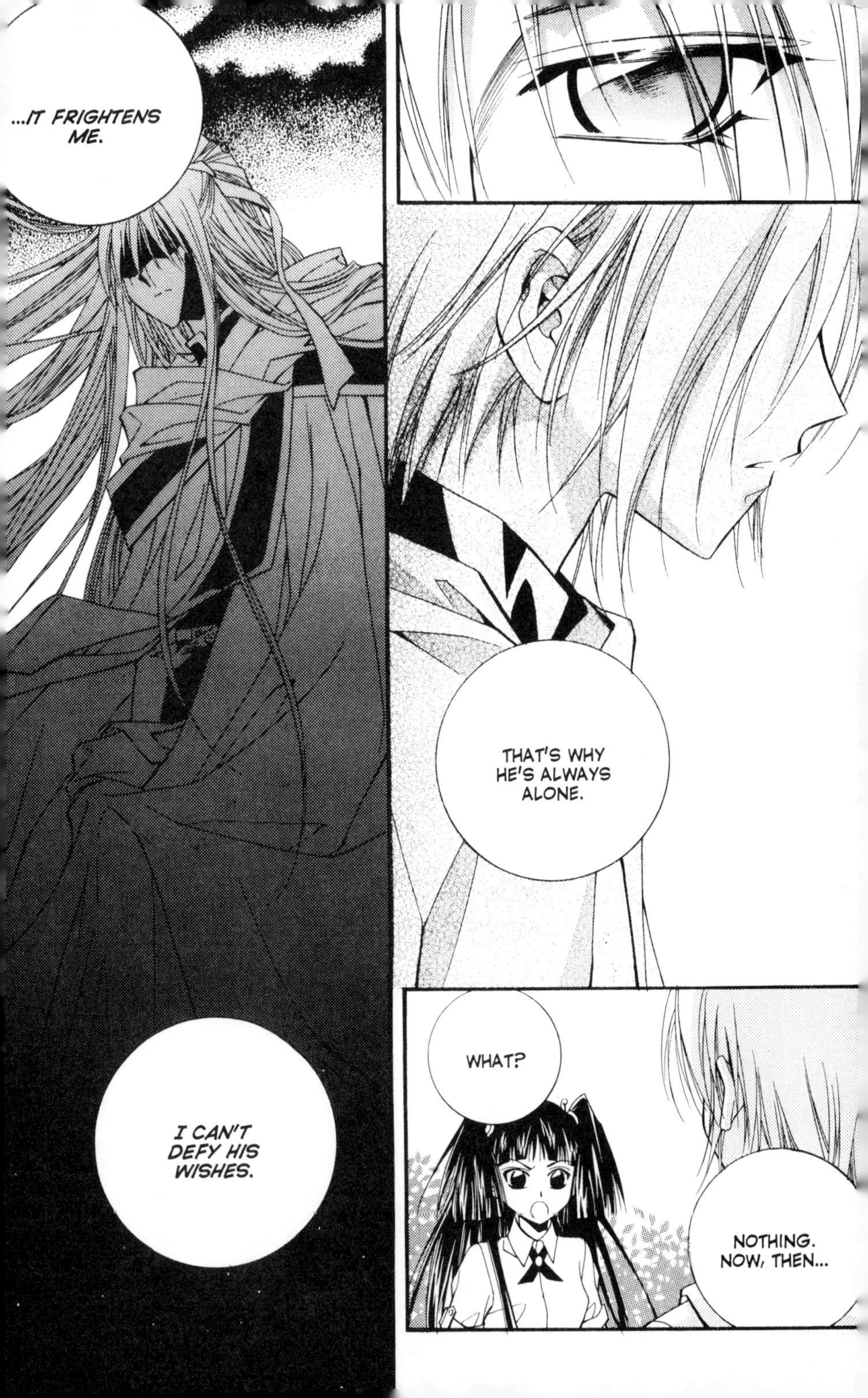
...IT FRIGHTENS ME.
I CAN'T DEFY HIS WISHES.
THAT'S WHY HE'S ALWAYS ALONE.
WHAT?
NOTHING. NOW, THEN...

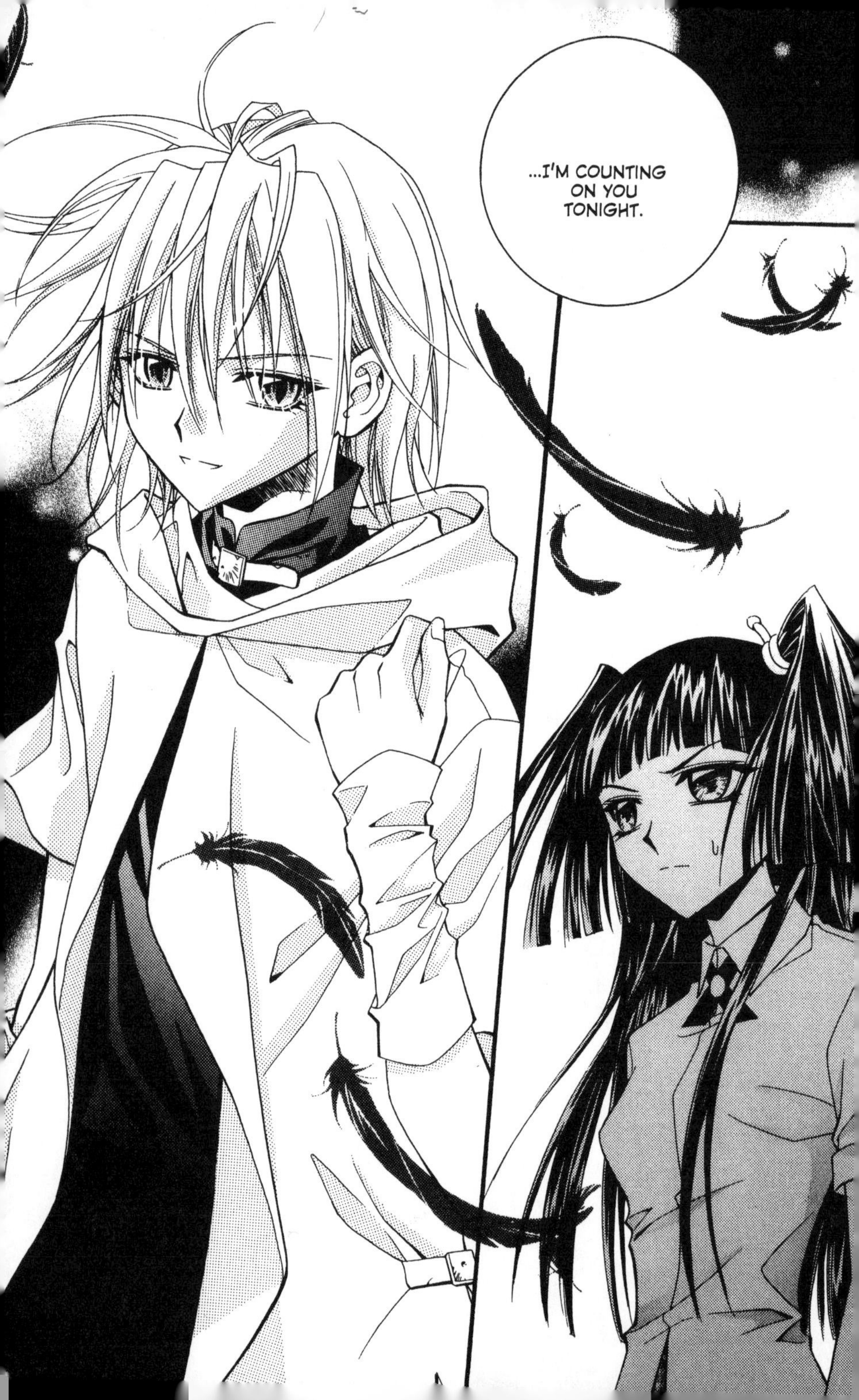
...I'M COUNTING ON YOU TONIGHT.

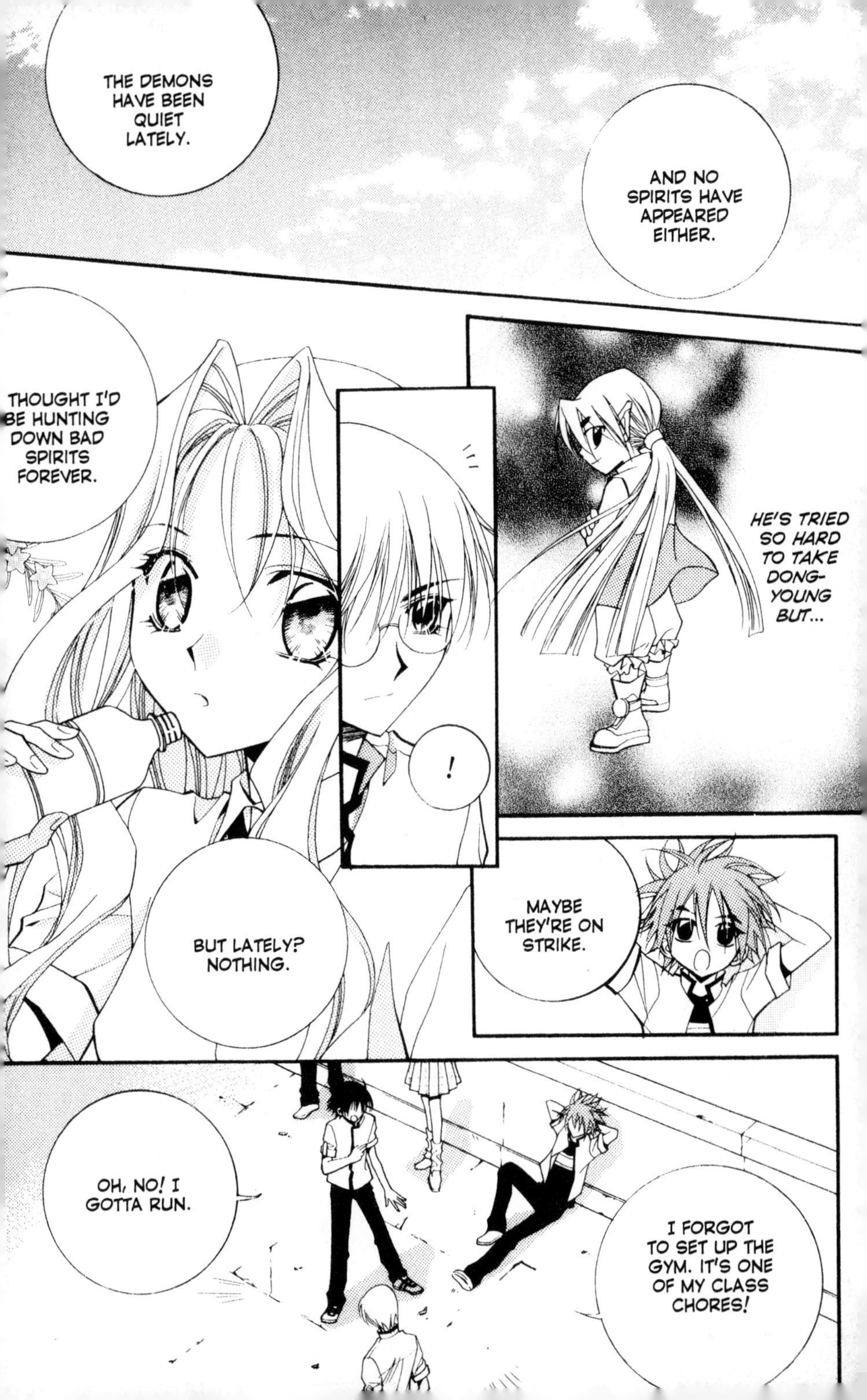
THE DEMONS HAVE BEEN QUIET LATELY.
AND NO SPIRITS HAVE APPEARED EITHER.
THOUGHT I'D BE HUNTING DOWN BAD SPIRITS FOREVER.
!
HE'S TRIED SO HARD TO TAKE DONG-YOUNG BUT...
BUT LATELY? NOTHING.
MAYBE THEY'RE ON STRIKE.
OH, NO! I GOTTA RUN.
I FORGOT TO SET UP THE GYM. IT'S ONE OF MY CLASS CHORES!

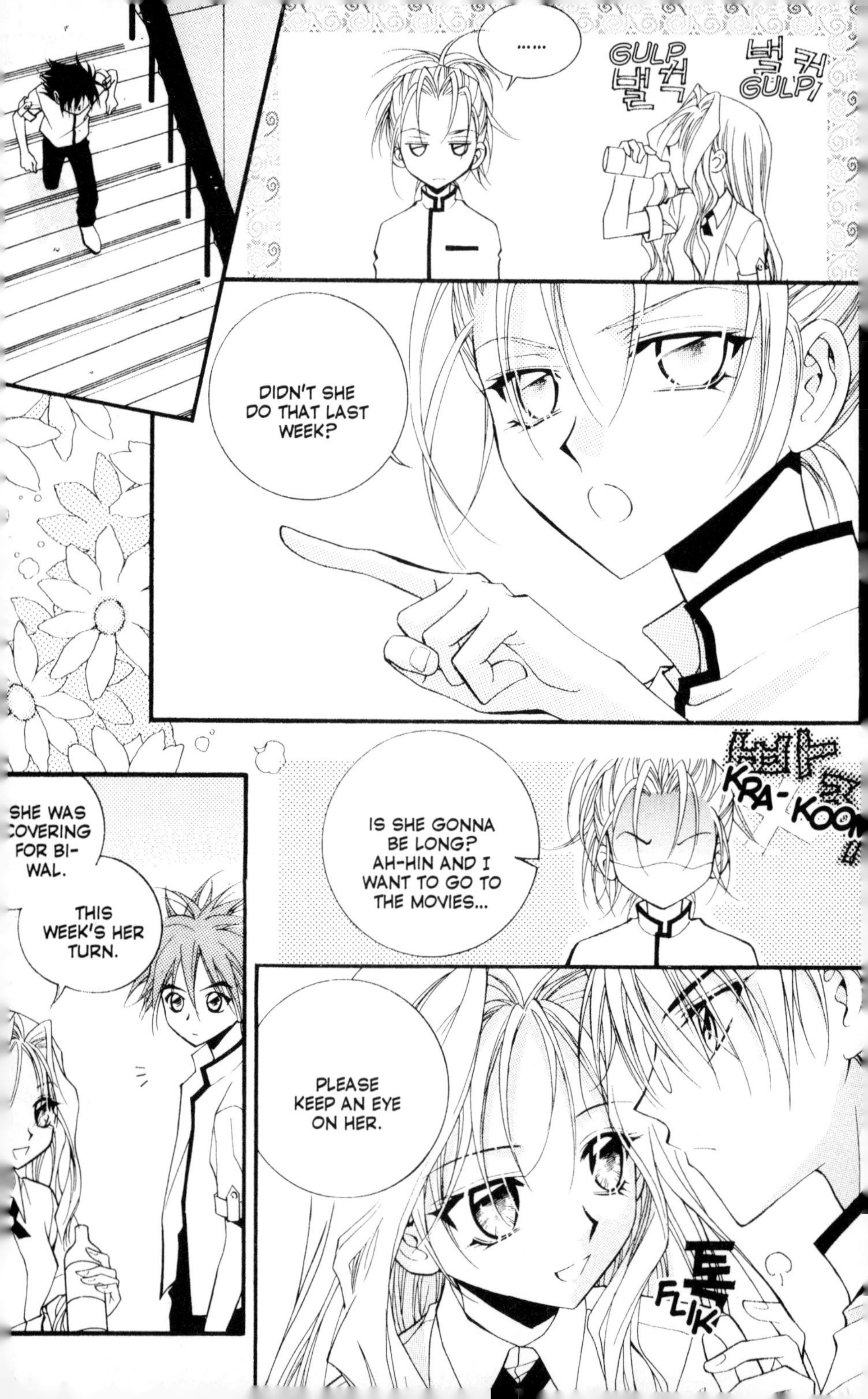
......
GULP
벌컥
벌컥
GULP!
DIDN'T SHE DO THAT LAST WEEK?
SHE WAS COVERING FOR BI-WAL.
THIS WEEK'S HER TURN.
IS SHE GONNA BE LONG? AH-HIN AND I WANT TO GO TO THE MOVIES...
KRA-KOON!!
PLEASE KEEP AN EYE ON HER.
FLIK!

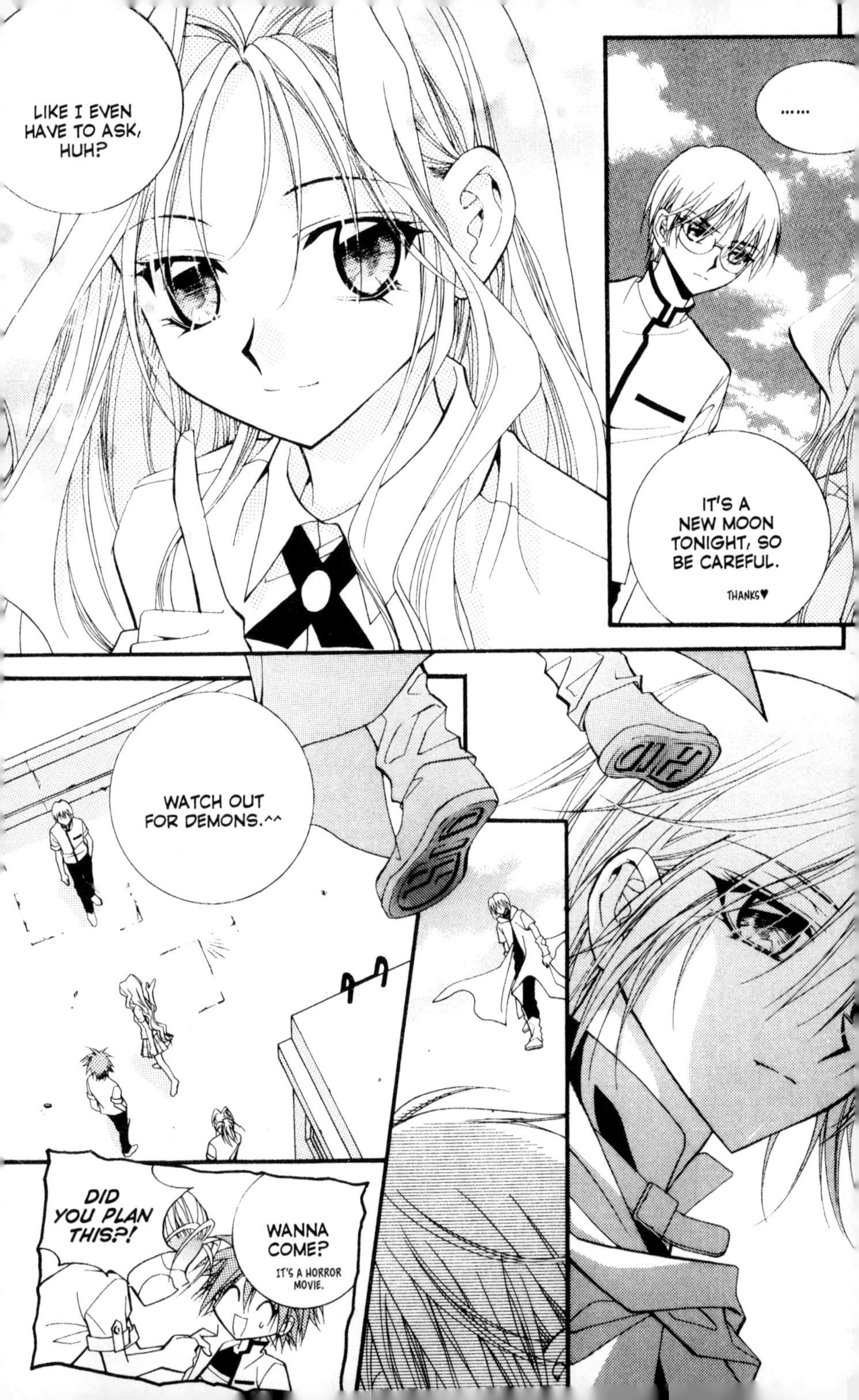
LIKE I EVEN HAVE TO ASK, HUH?
......
IT'S A NEW MOON TONIGHT, SO BE CAREFUL.
THANKS♥
WATCH OUT FOR DEMONS.^^
DID YOU PLAN THIS?!
WANNA COME?
IT'S A HORROR MOVIE.

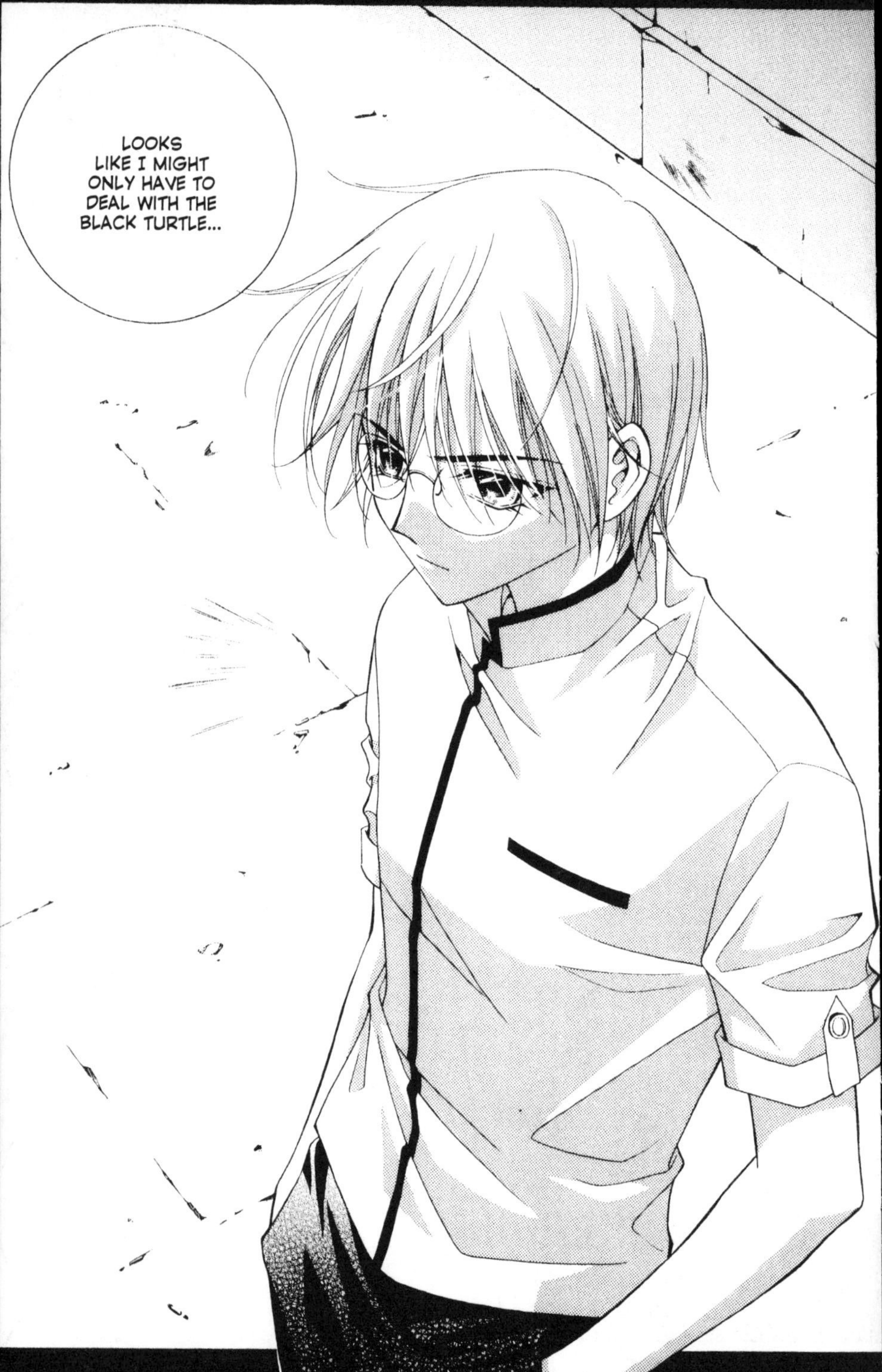
LOOKS LIKE I MIGHT ONLY HAVE TO DEAL WITH THE BLACK TURTLE...

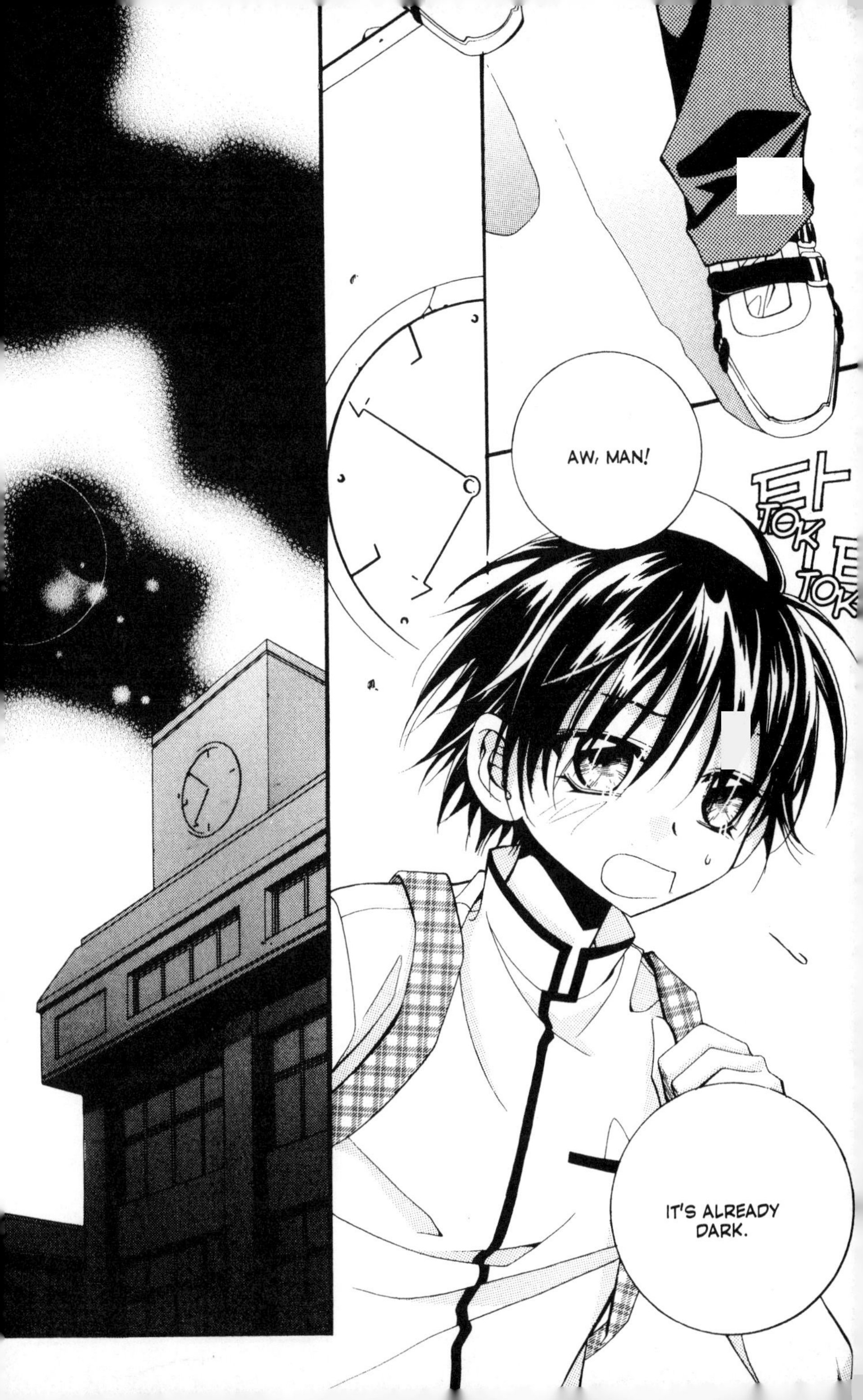
AW, MAN!
TOK
TOK
IT'S ALREADY DARK.

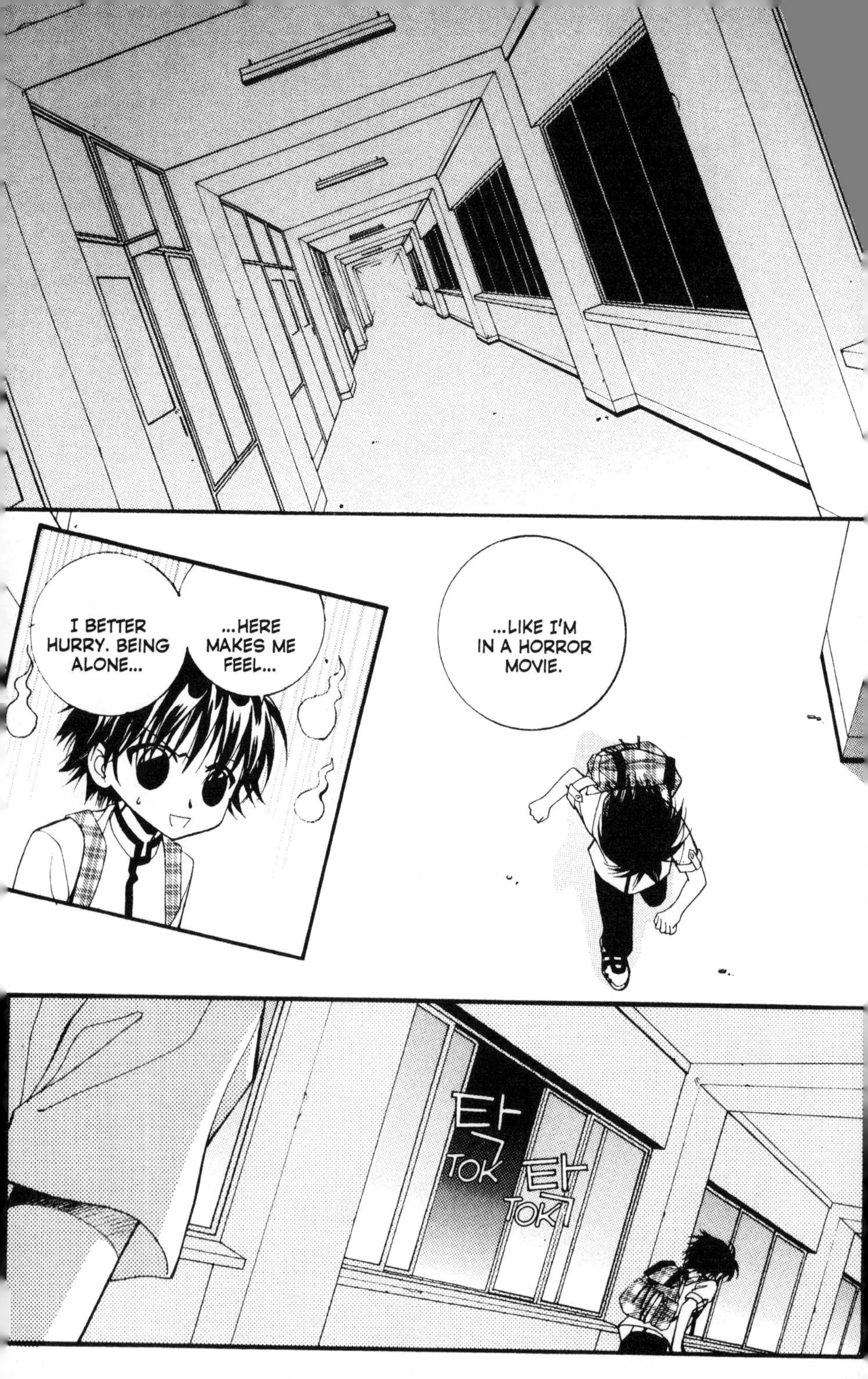
I BETTER HURRY. BEING ALONE...
...HERE MAKES ME FEEL...
...LIKE I'M IN A HORROR MOVIE.
탁 TOK
탁 TOK

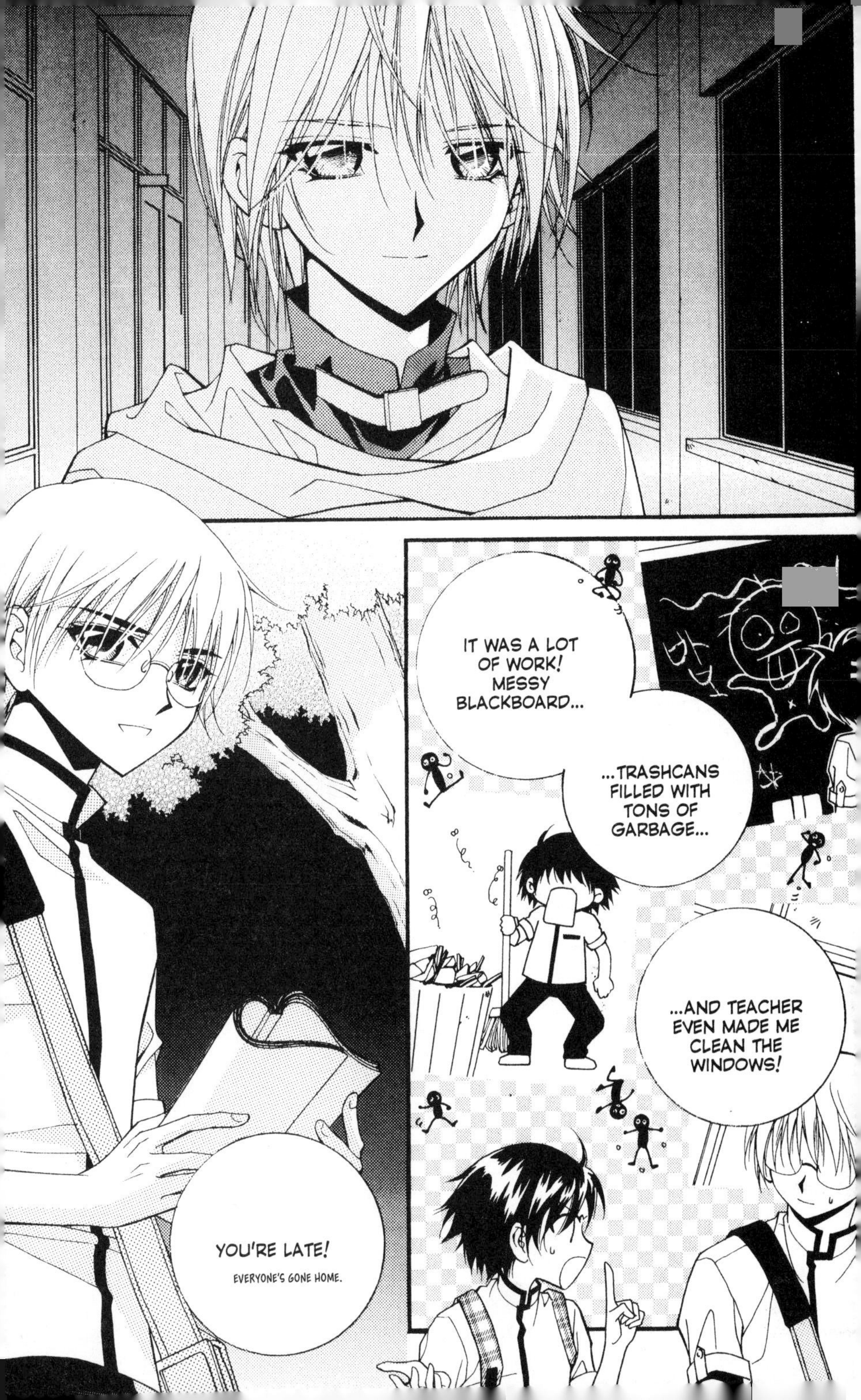
YOU'RE LATE!
EVERYONE'S GONE HOME.
IT WAS A LOT OF WORK! MESSY BLACKBOARD...
...TRASHCANS FILLED WITH TONS OF GARBAGE...
...AND TEACHER EVEN MADE ME CLEAN THE WINDOWS!

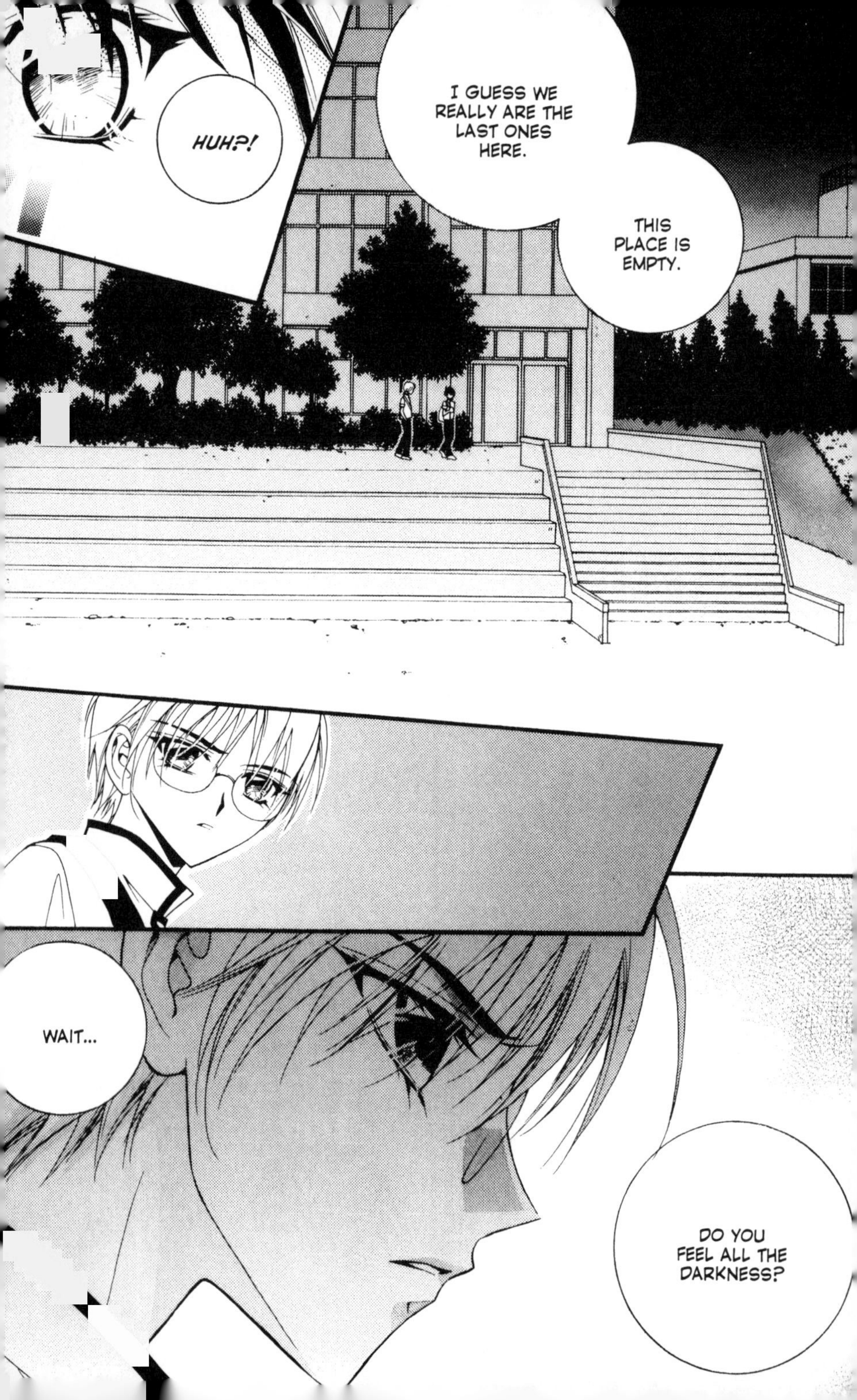
HUH?!
I GUESS WE REALLY ARE THE LAST ONES HERE.
THIS PLACE IS EMPTY.
WAIT...
DO YOU FEEL ALL THE DARKNESS?

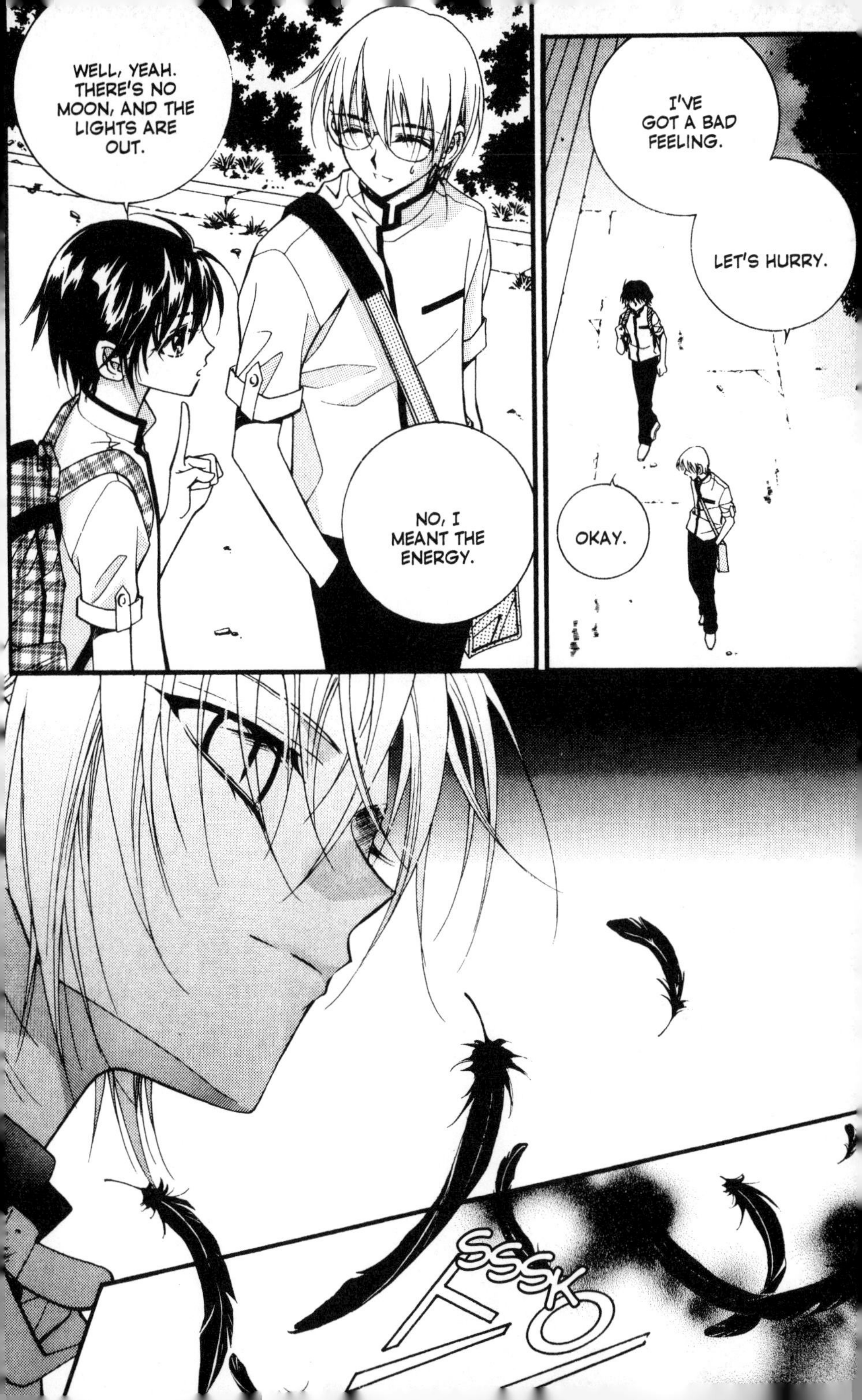
WELL, YEAH. THERE'S NO MOON, AND THE LIGHTS ARE OUT.
NO, I MEANT THE ENERGY.
I'VE GOT A BAD FEELING.
LET'S HURRY.
OKAY.
SSSKO

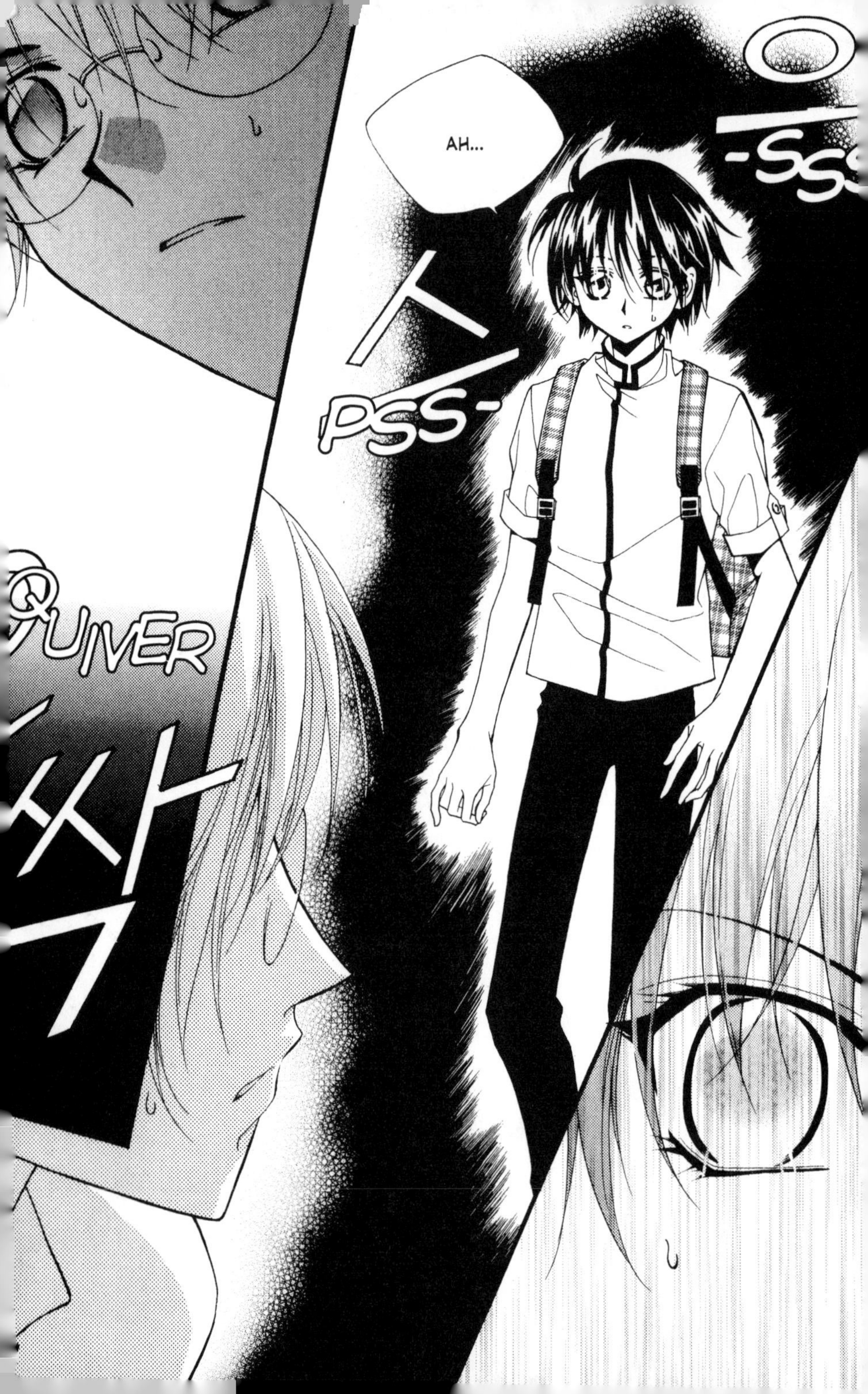
QUIVER
AH...
PSS-
-SSS

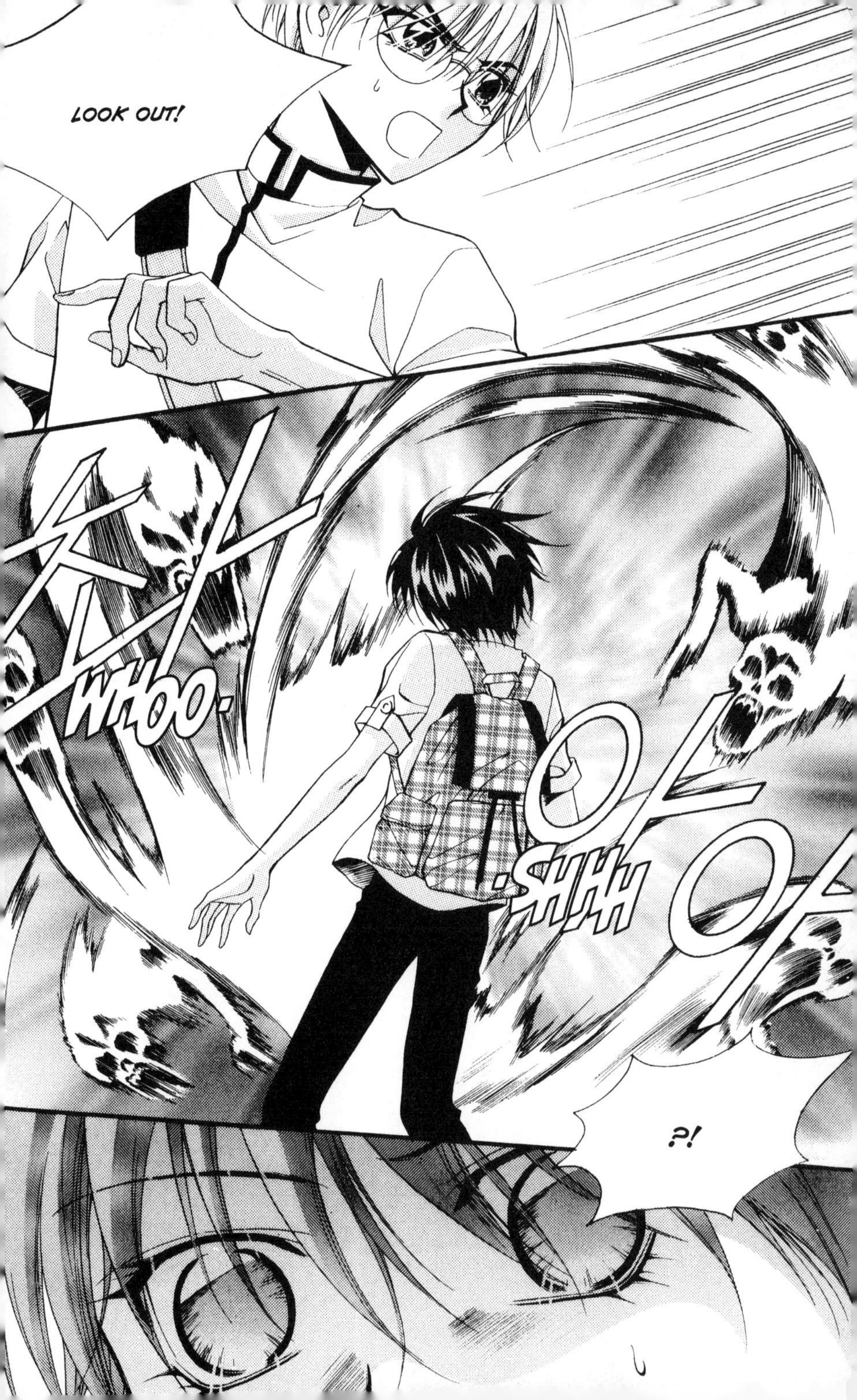
LOOK OUT!
WHOO-
.SHHH
?!

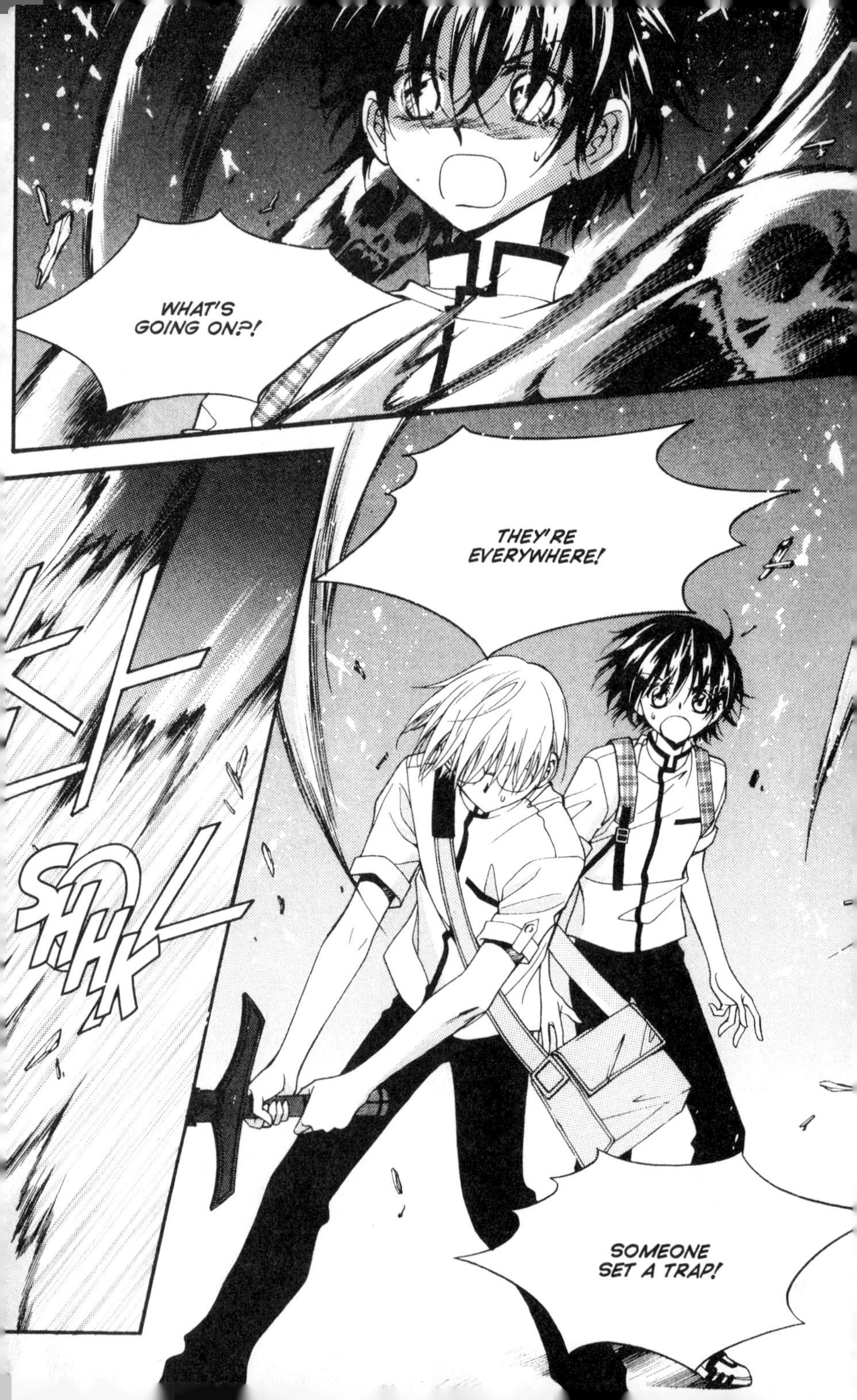
WHAT'S GOING ON?!
SHHK
THEY'RE EVERYWHERE!
SOMEONE SET A TRAP!

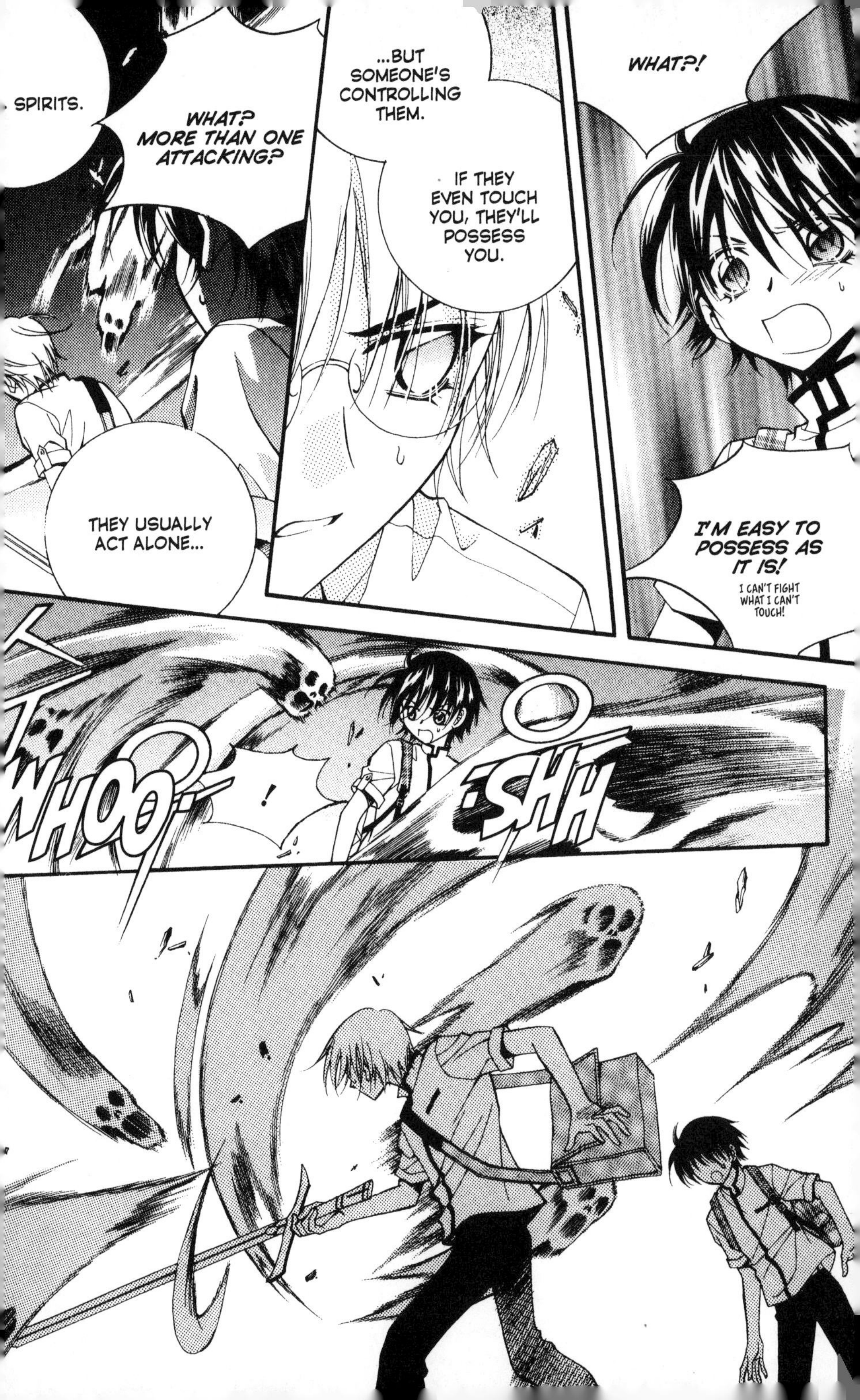

SPIRITS.
WHAT? MORE THAN ONE ATTACKING?
THEY USUALLY ACT ALONE...
...BUT SOMEONE'S CONTROLLING THEM.
IF THEY EVEN TOUCH YOU, THEY'LL POSSESS YOU.
WHAT?!
I'M EASY TO POSSESS AS IT IS!
I CAN'T FIGHT WHAT I CAN'T TOUCH!
WHOO
!
SHH

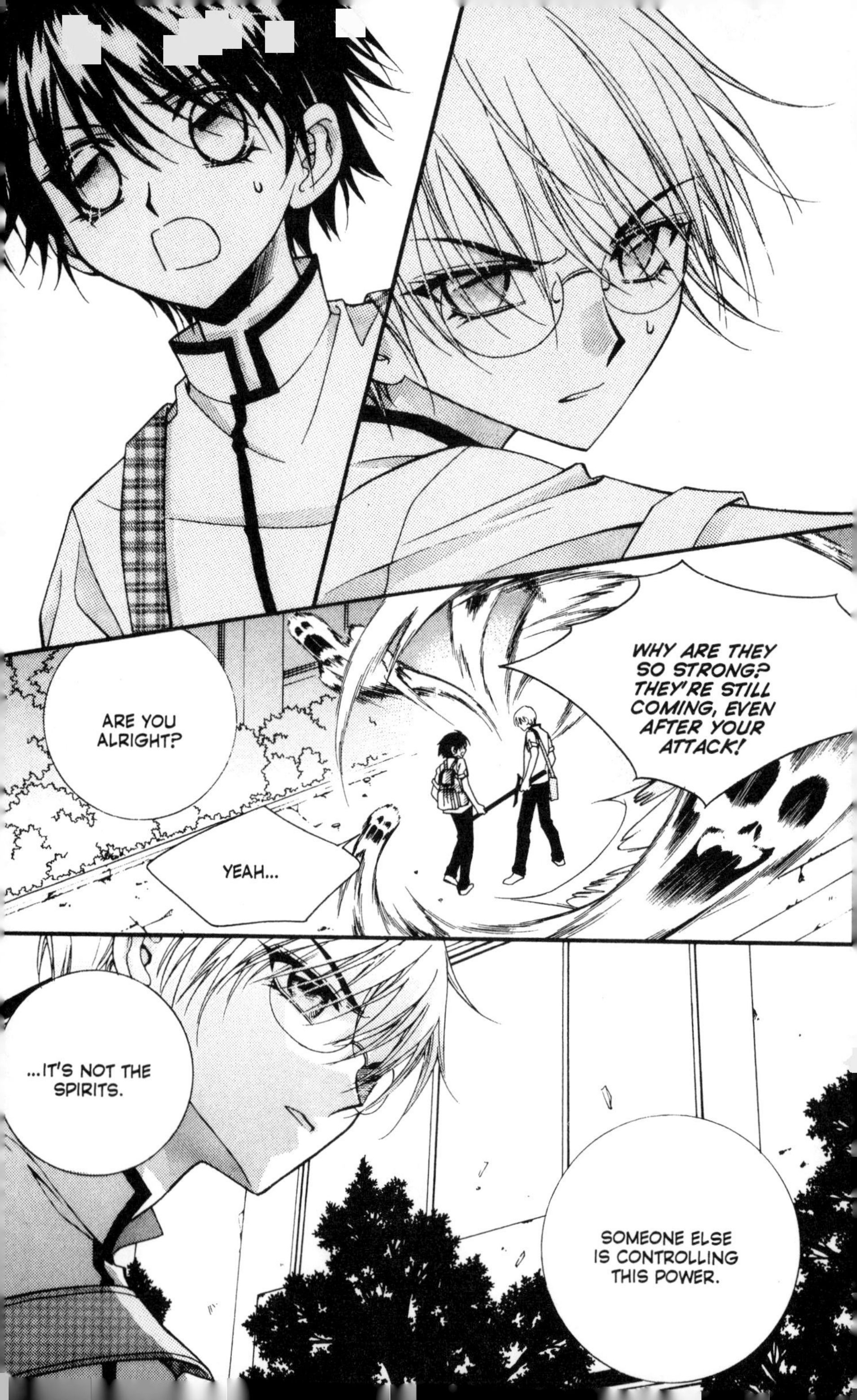
ARE YOU ALRIGHT?
YEAH...
WHY ARE THEY SO STRONG? THEY'RE STILL COMING, EVEN AFTER YOUR ATTACK!
...IT'S NOT THE SPIRITS.
SOMEONE ELSE IS CONTROLLING THIS POWER.

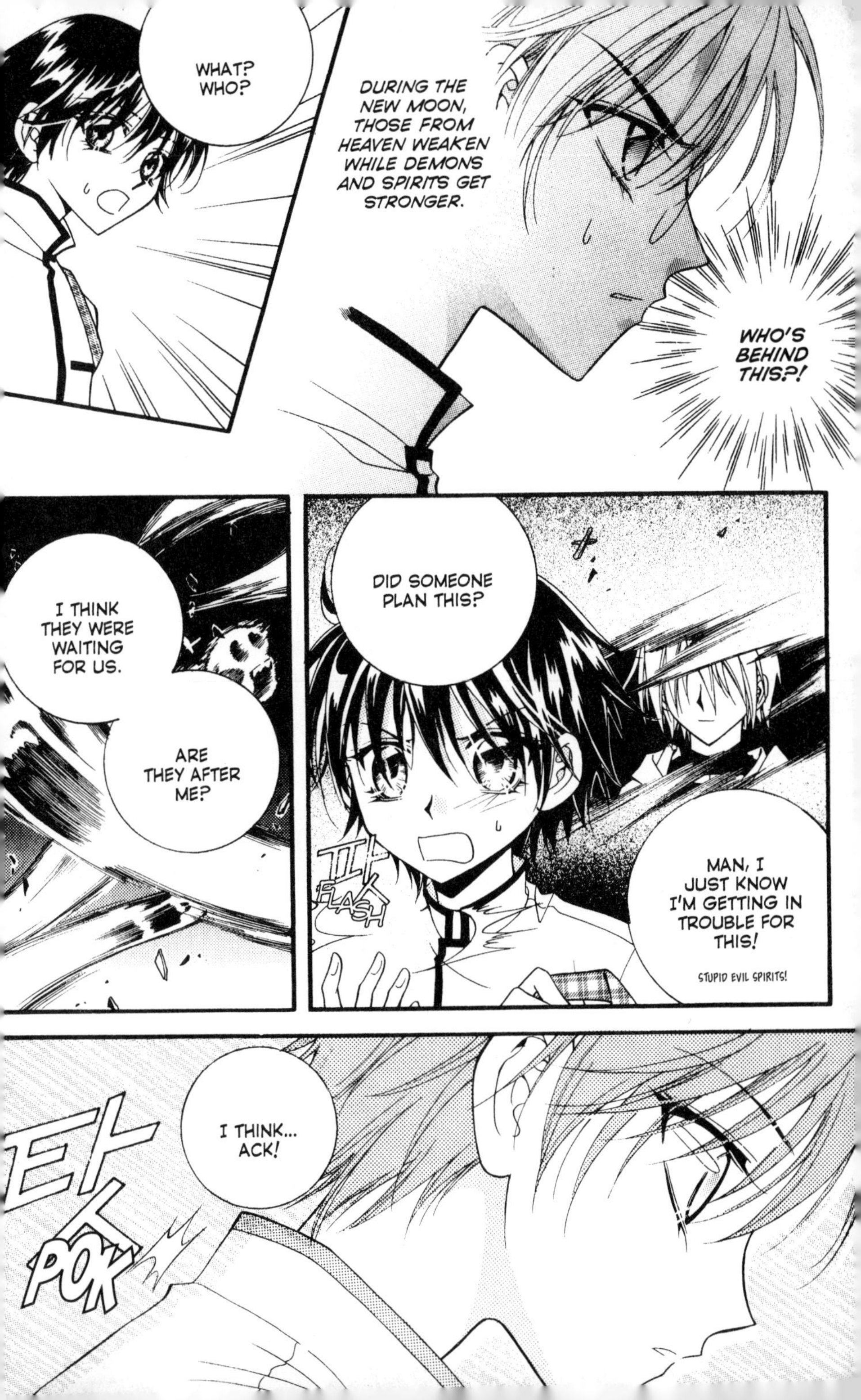
WHAT? WHO?
DURING THE NEW MOON, THOSE FROM HEAVEN WEAKEN WHILE DEMONS AND SPIRITS GET STRONGER.
WHO'S BEHIND THIS?!
I THINK THEY WERE WAITING FOR US.
ARE THEY AFTER ME?
DID SOMEONE PLAN THIS?
FLASH
MAN, I JUST KNOW I'M GETTING IN TROUBLE FOR THIS!
STUPID EVIL SPIRITS!
I THINK... ACK!
POK

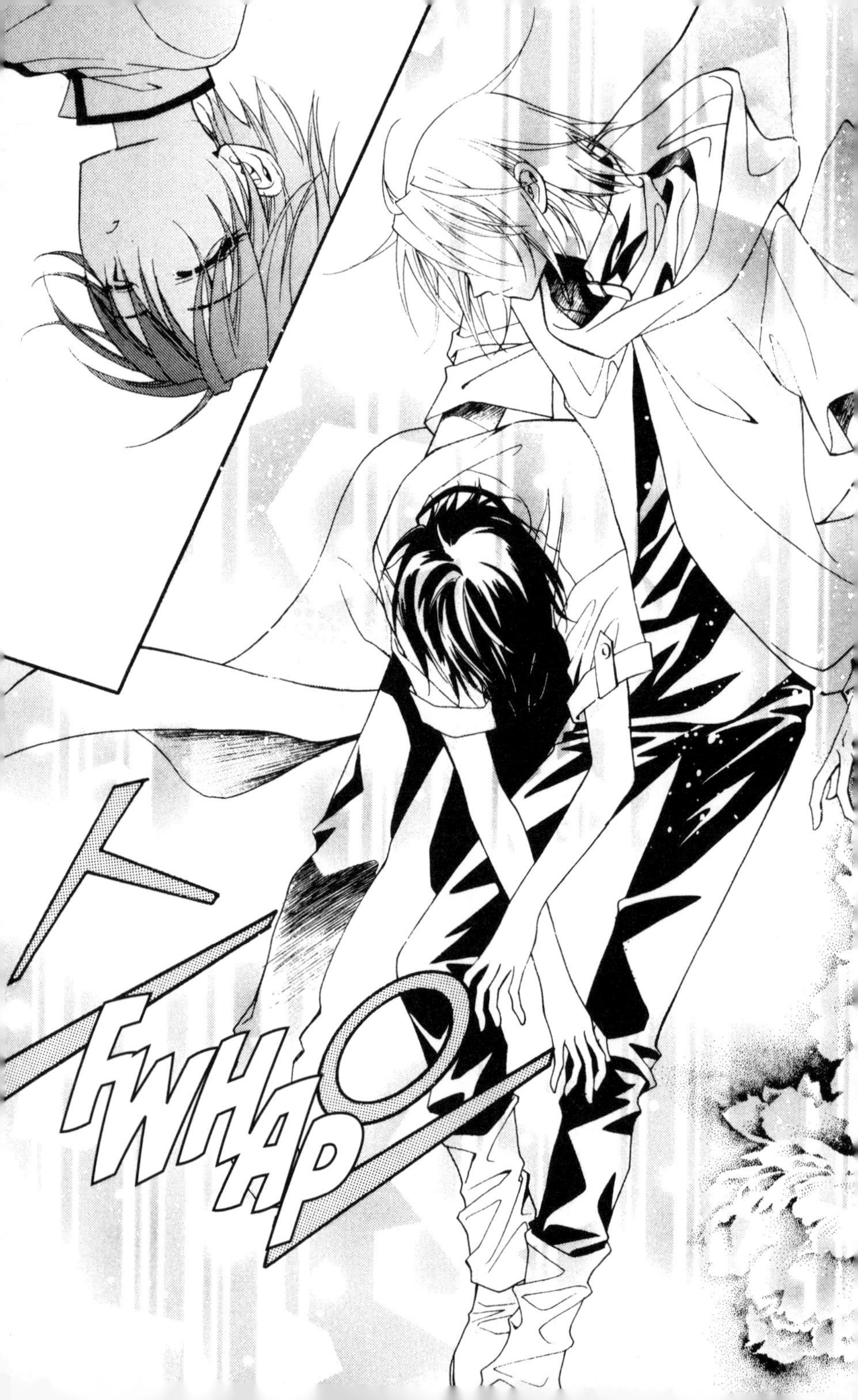
FWHAP

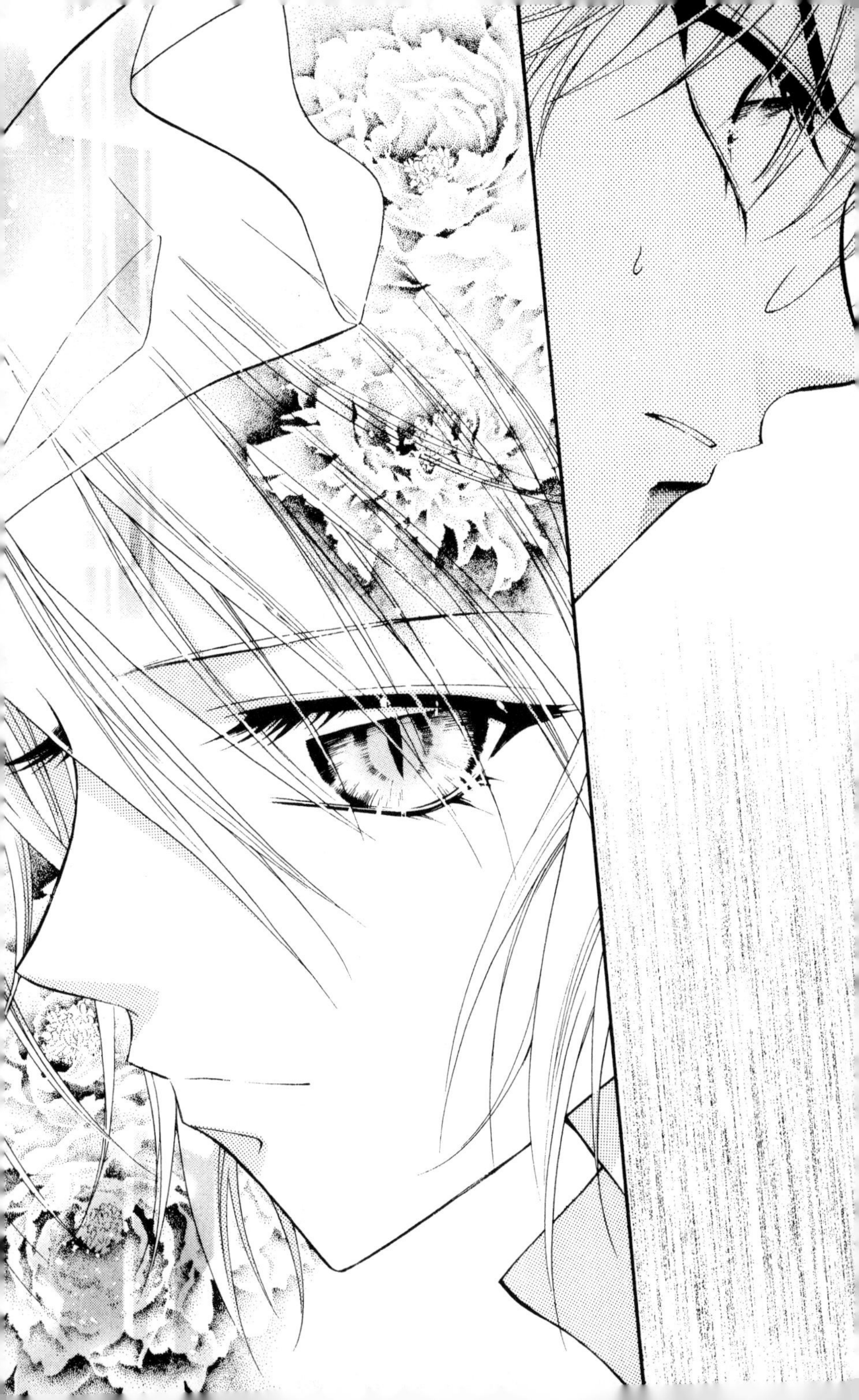

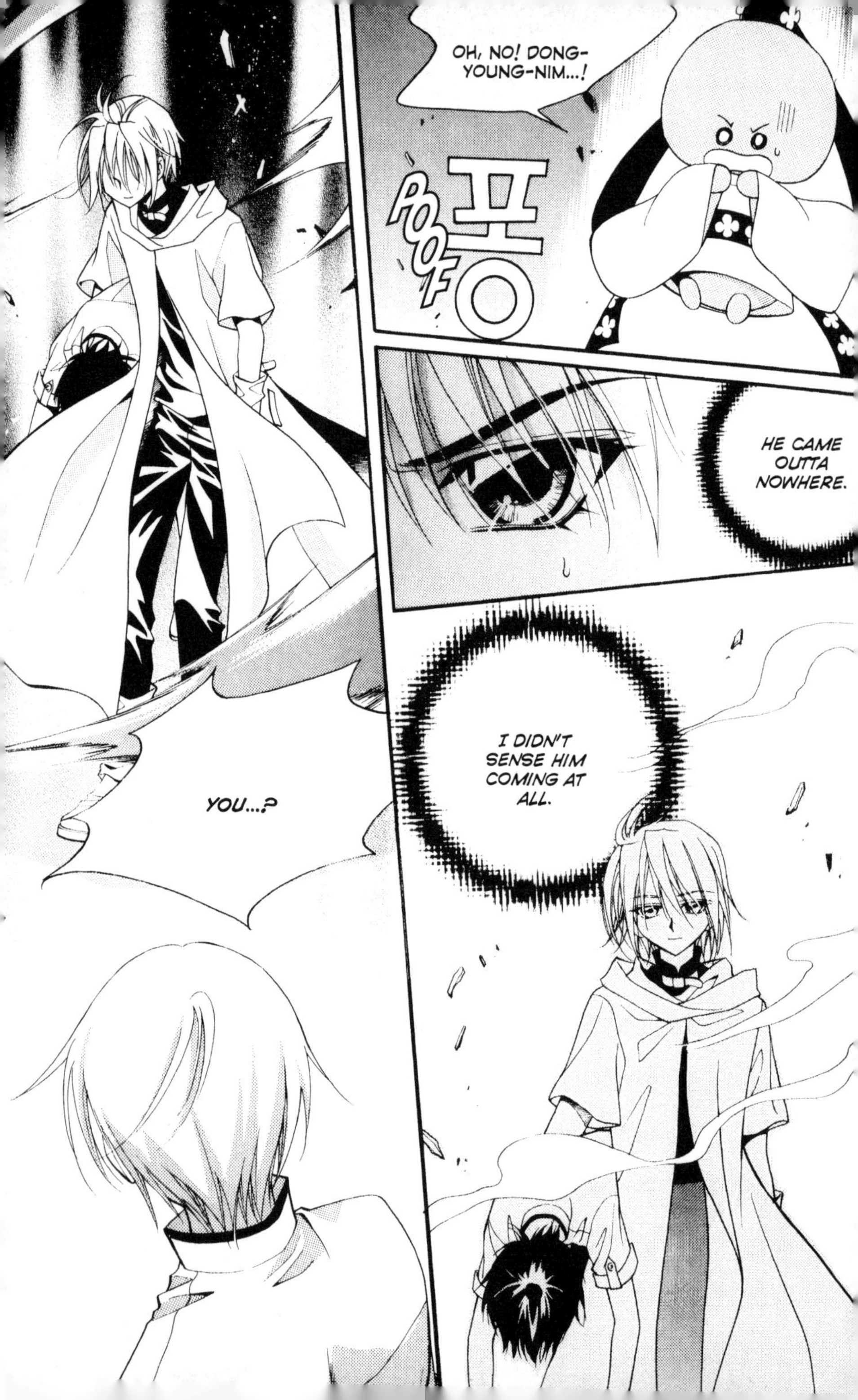
OH, NO! DONG-YOUNG-NIM...!
POOF
HE CAME OUTTA NOWHERE.
I DIDN'T SENSE HIM COMING AT ALL.
YOU...?

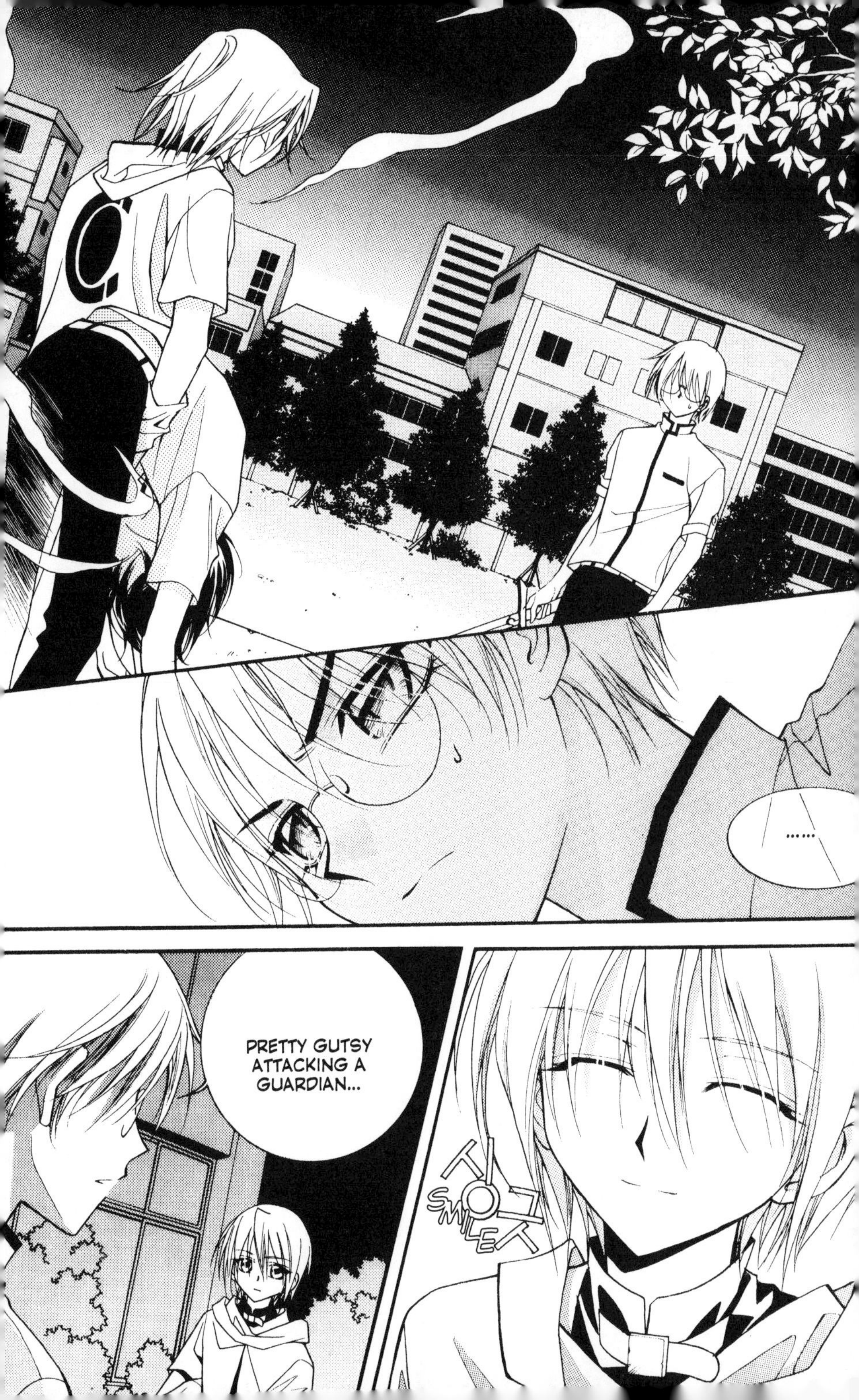

……
PRETTY GUTSY ATTACKING A GUARDIAN...
SMILE

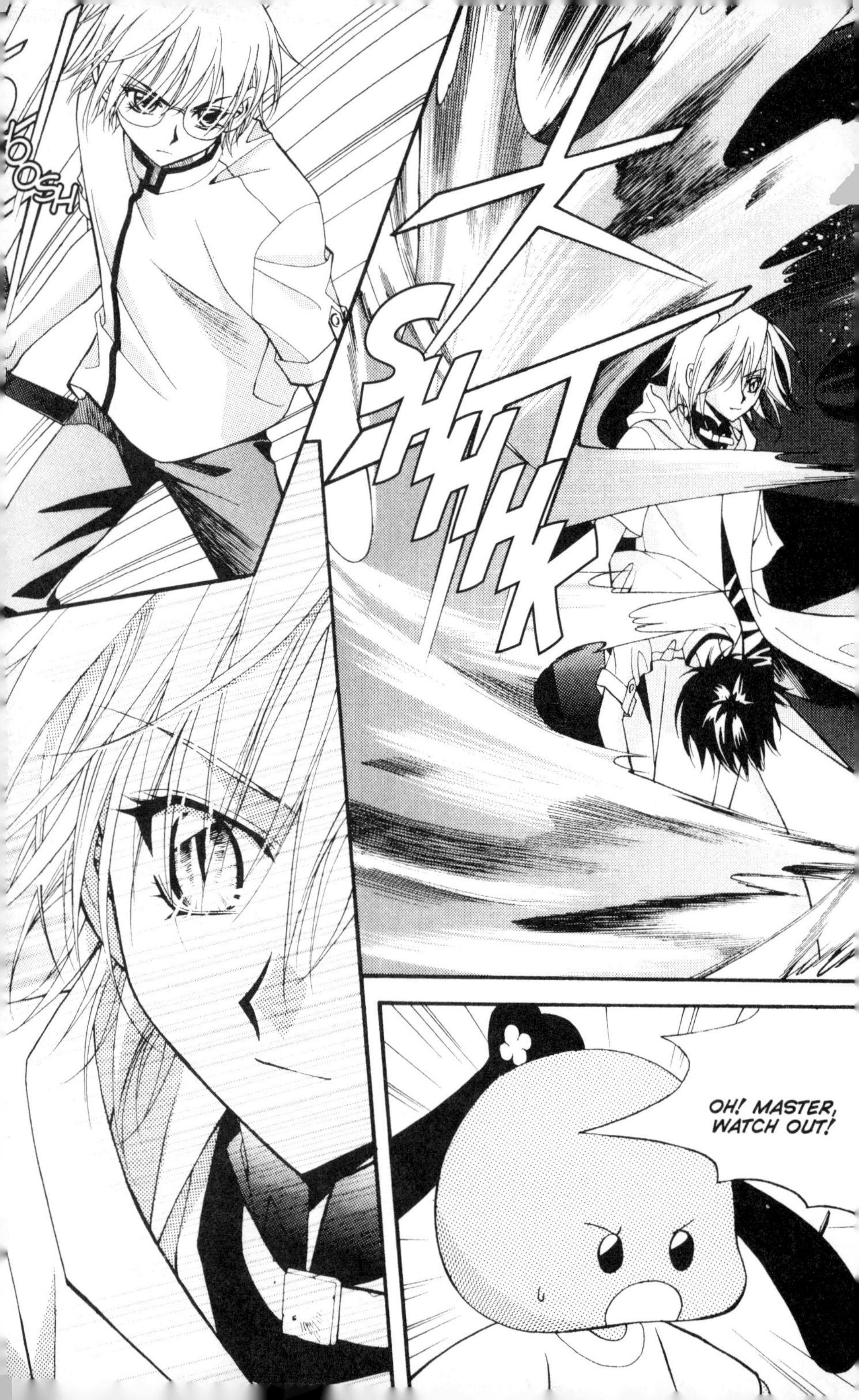
WOOSH
SHHHK
OH! MASTER, WATCH OUT!

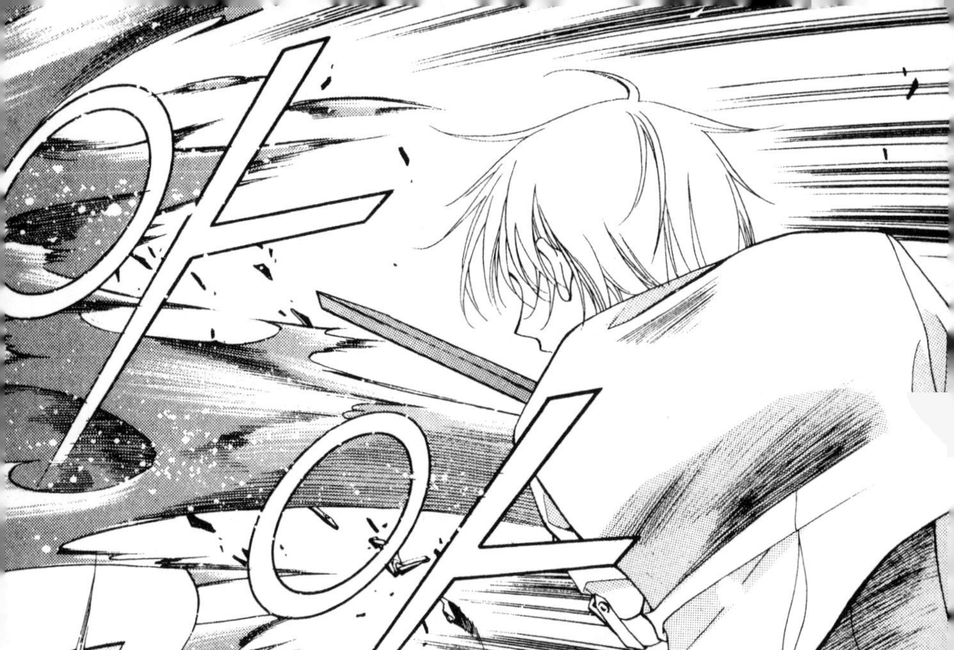
아
아
!!
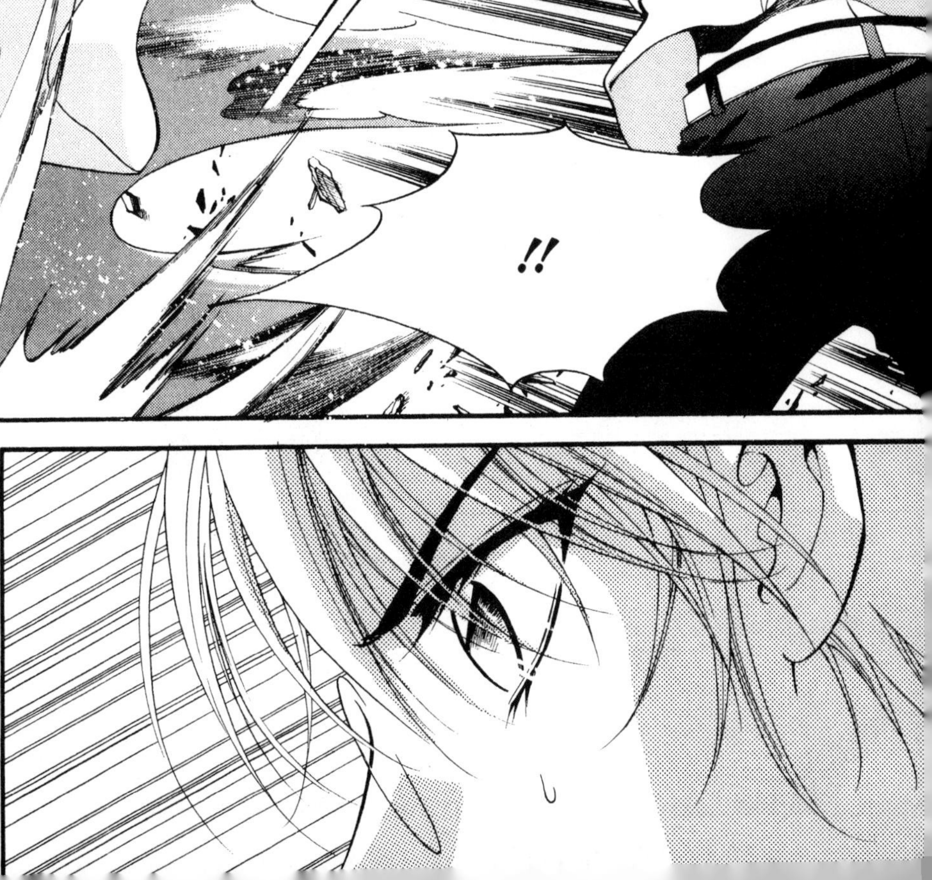

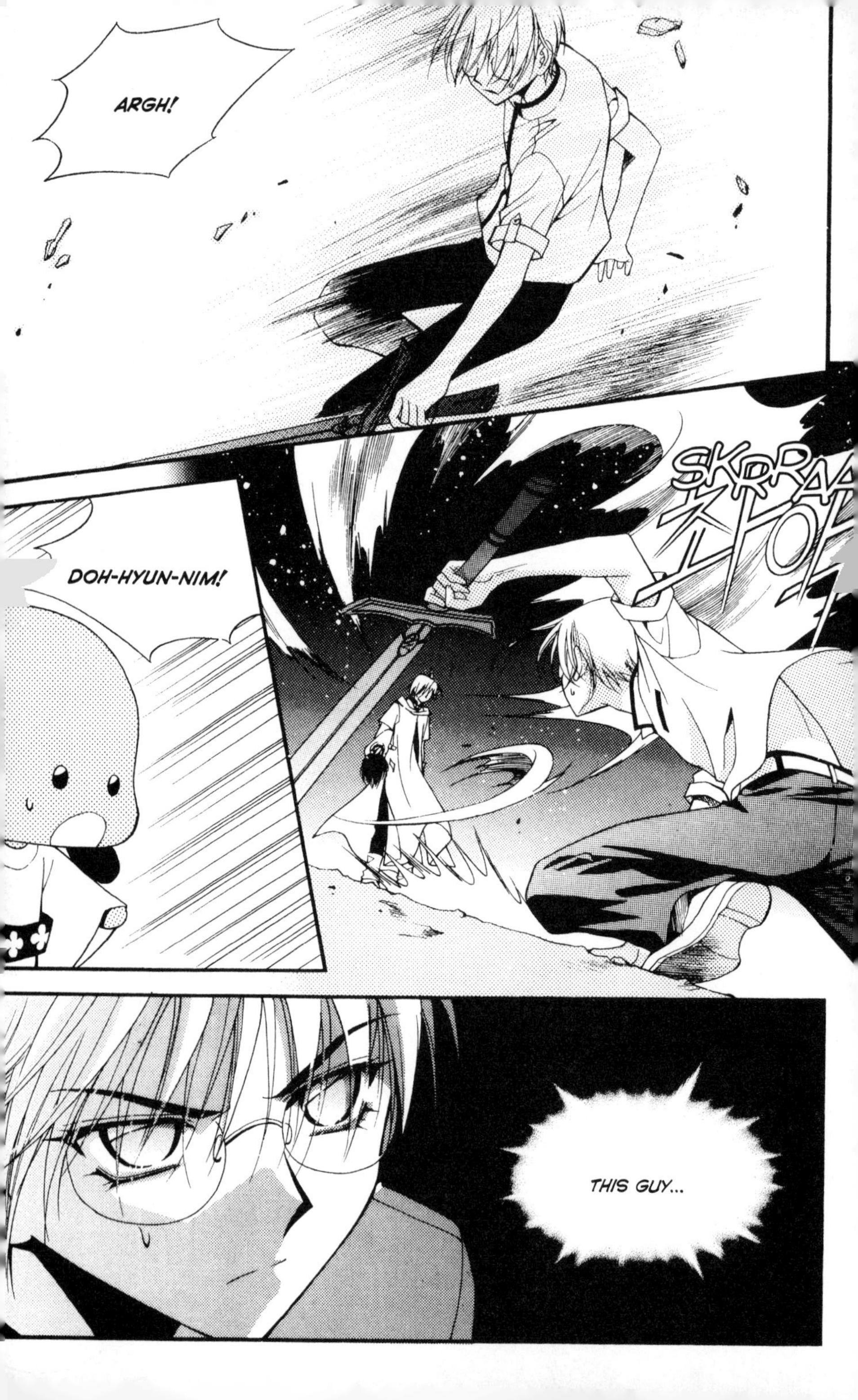
ARGH!
DOH-HYUN-NIM!
SKRRAA
THIS GUY...

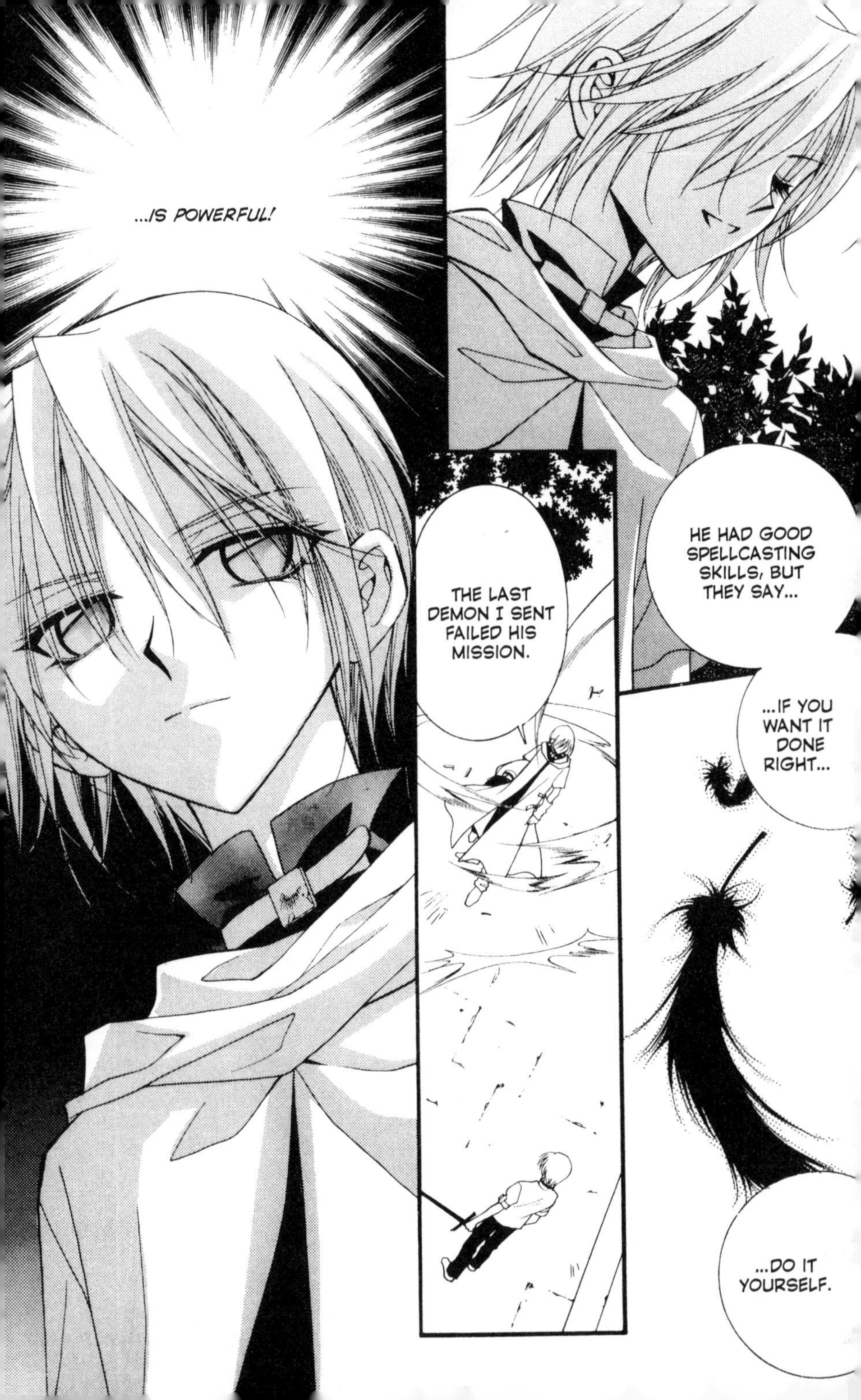
...IS POWERFUL!
THE LAST DEMON I SENT FAILED HIS MISSION.
HE HAD GOOD SPELLCASTING SKILLS, BUT THEY SAY...
...IF YOU WANT IT DONE RIGHT...
...DO IT YOURSELF.

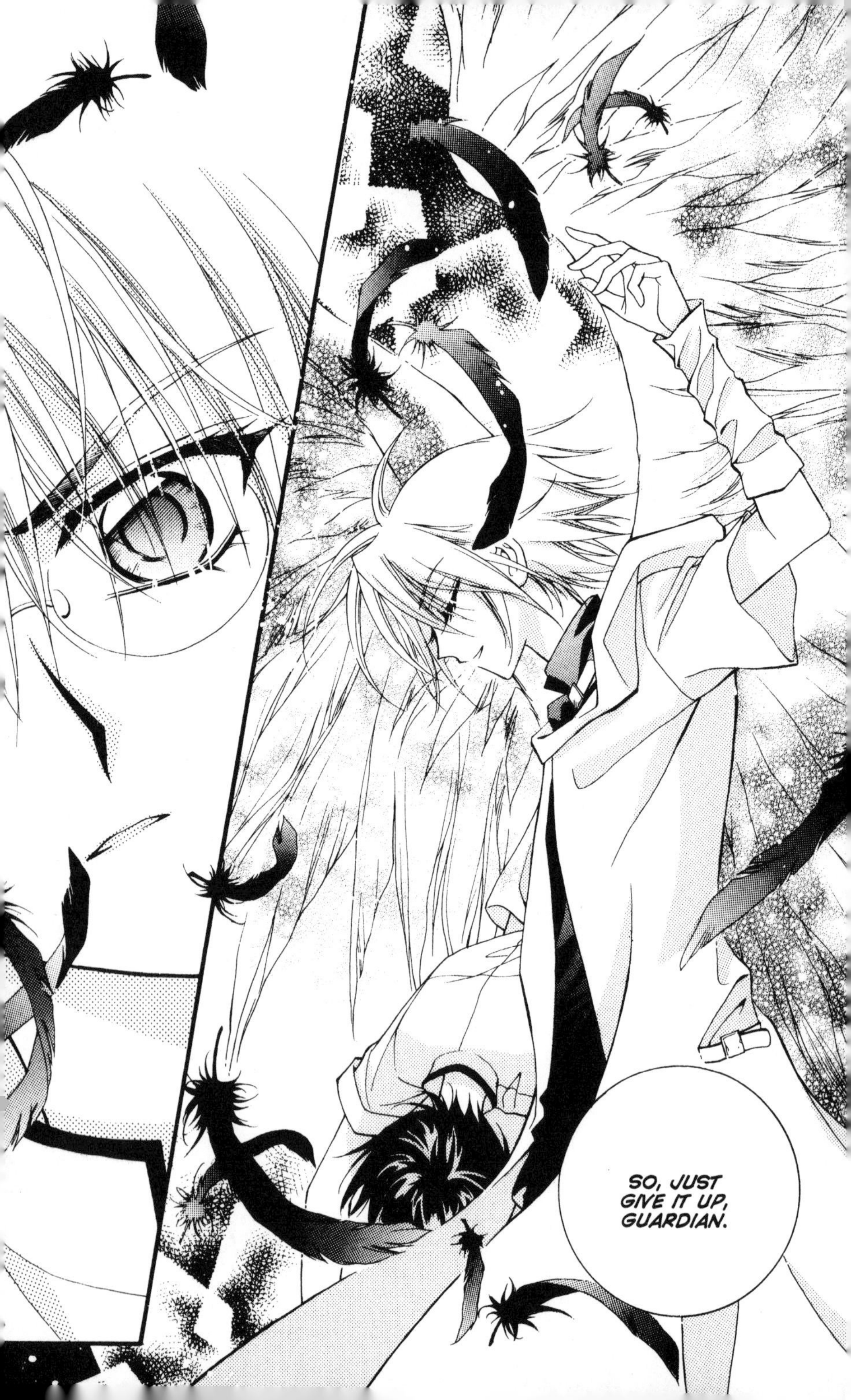
SO, JUST GIVE IT UP, GUARDIAN.

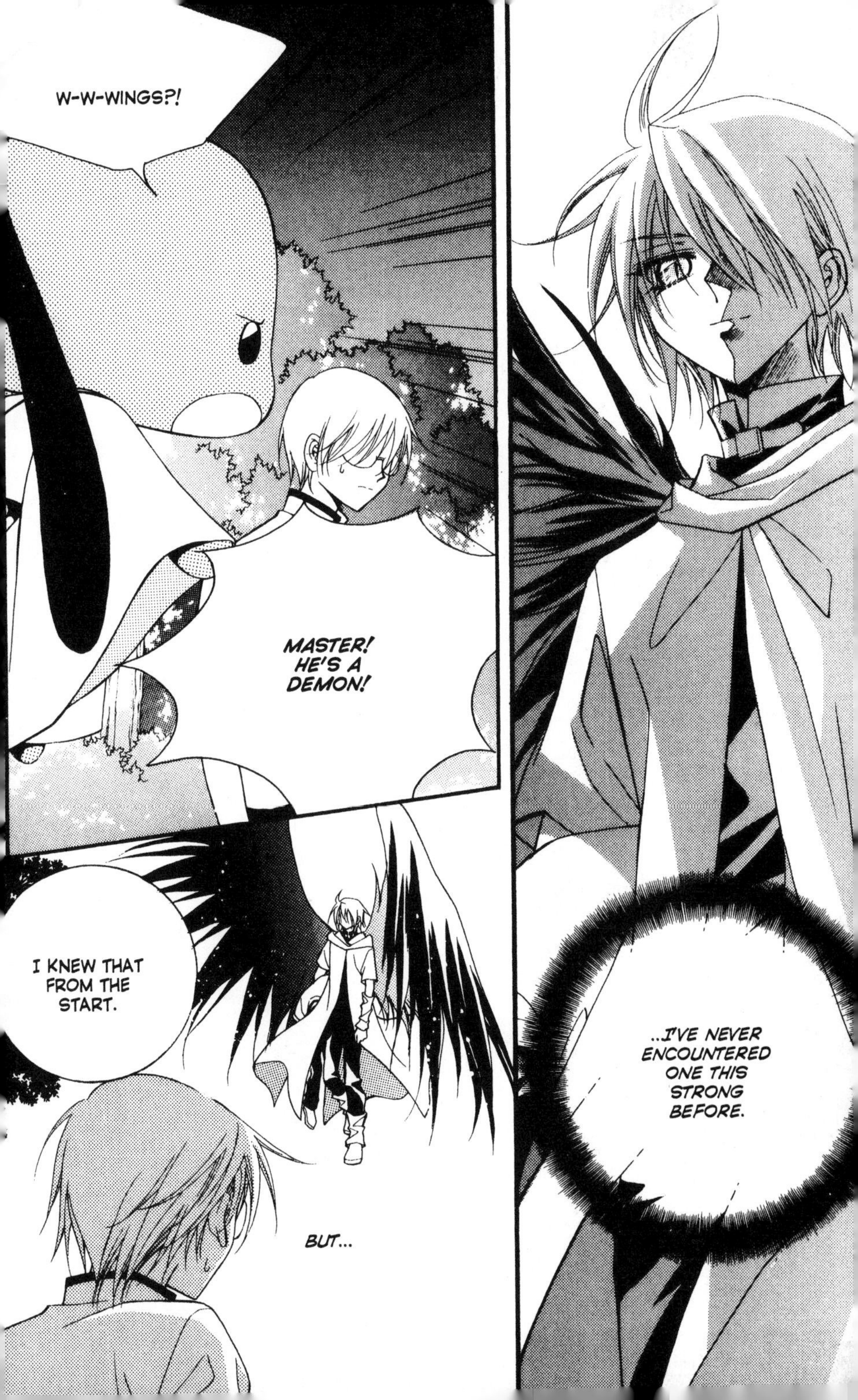
W-W-WINGS?!
MASTER! HE'S A DEMON!
I KNEW THAT FROM THE START.
BUT...
...I'VE NEVER ENCOUNTERED ONE THIS STRONG BEFORE.

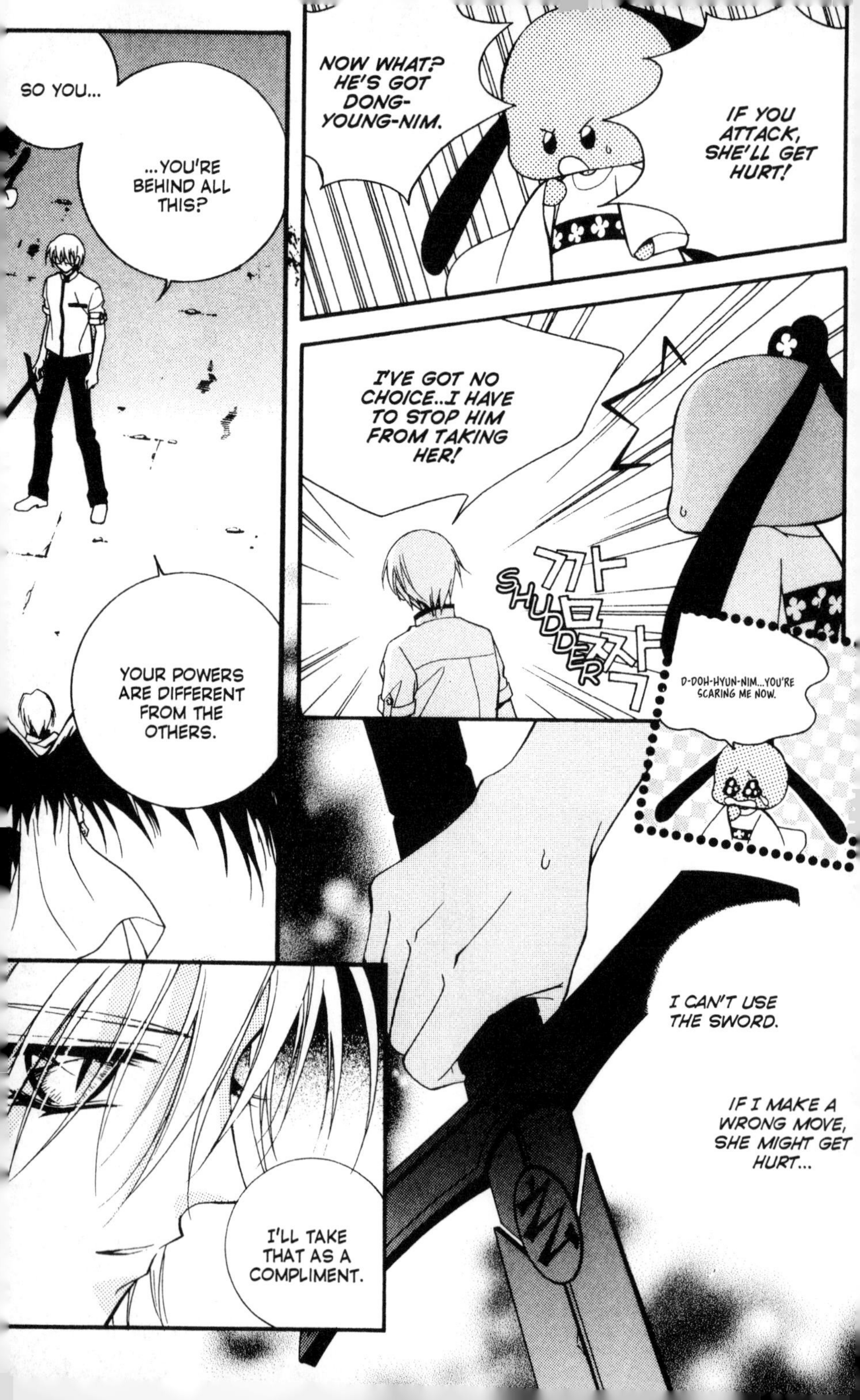

SO YOU...
...YOU'RE BEHIND ALL THIS?
YOUR POWERS ARE DIFFERENT FROM THE OTHERS.
I'LL TAKE THAT AS A COMPLIMENT.
NOW WHAT? HE'S GOT DONG-YOUNG-NIM.
IF YOU ATTACK, SHE'LL GET HURT!
I'VE GOT NO CHOICE...I HAVE TO STOP HIM FROM TAKING HER!
깜짝
SHUDDER
D-DOH-HYUN-NIM...YOU'RE SCARING ME NOW.
I CAN'T USE THE SWORD.
IF I MAKE A WRONG MOVE, SHE MIGHT GET HURT...

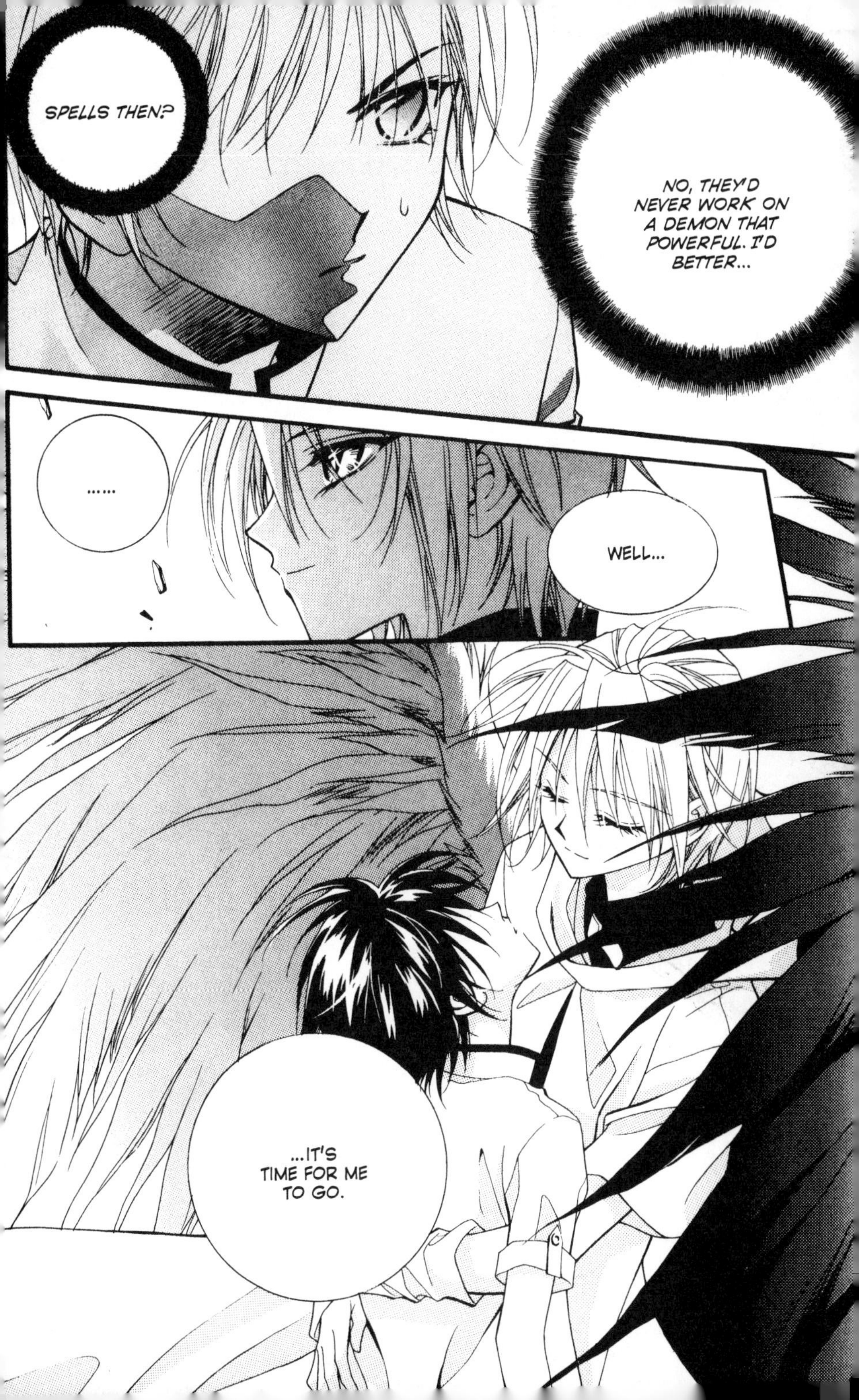
SPELLS THEN?
NO, THEY'D NEVER WORK ON A DEMON THAT POWERFUL. I'D BETTER...
......
WELL...
...IT'S TIME FOR ME TO GO.

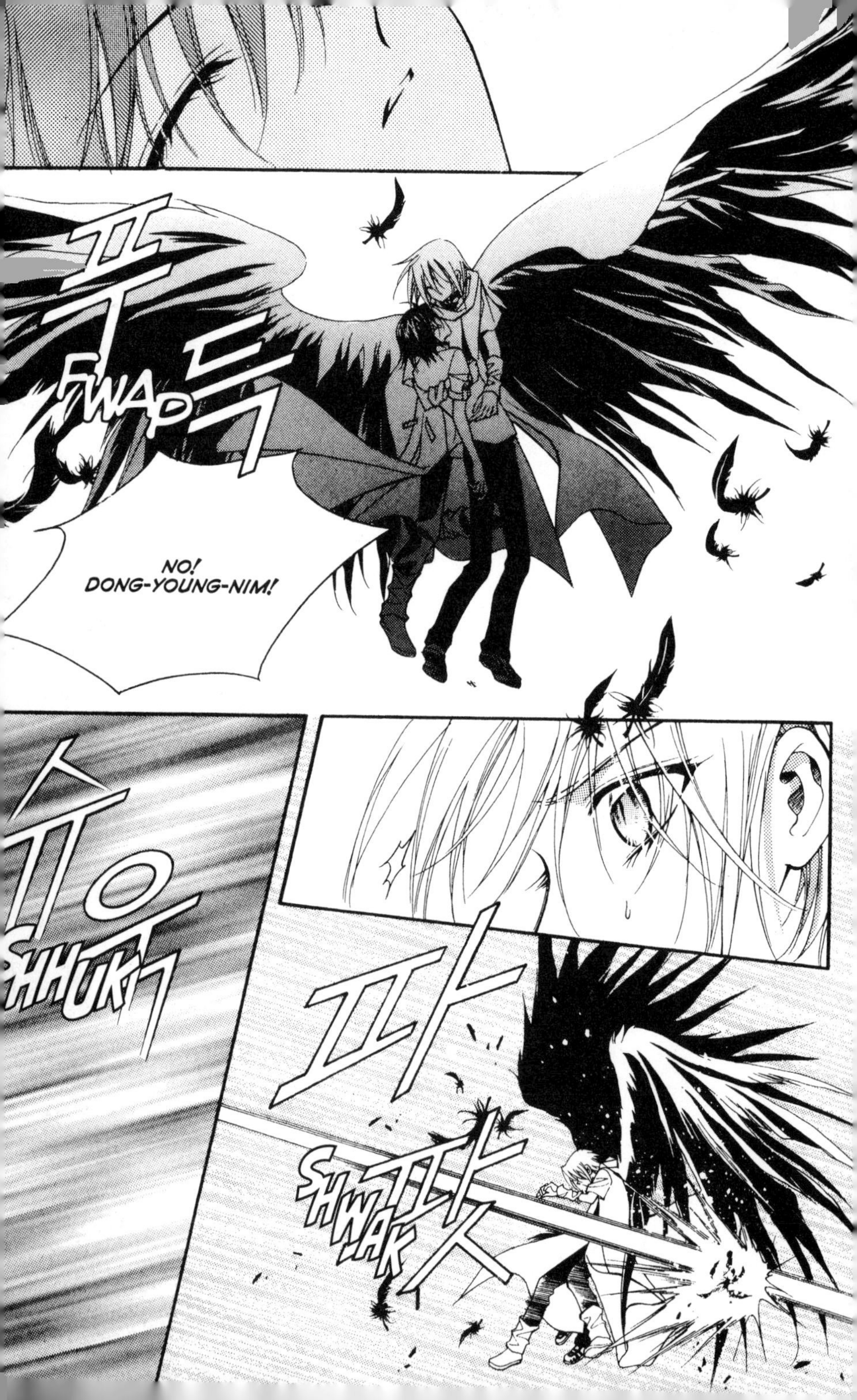
FWAP
NO! DONG-YOUNG-NIM!
SHHUK
SHWAK

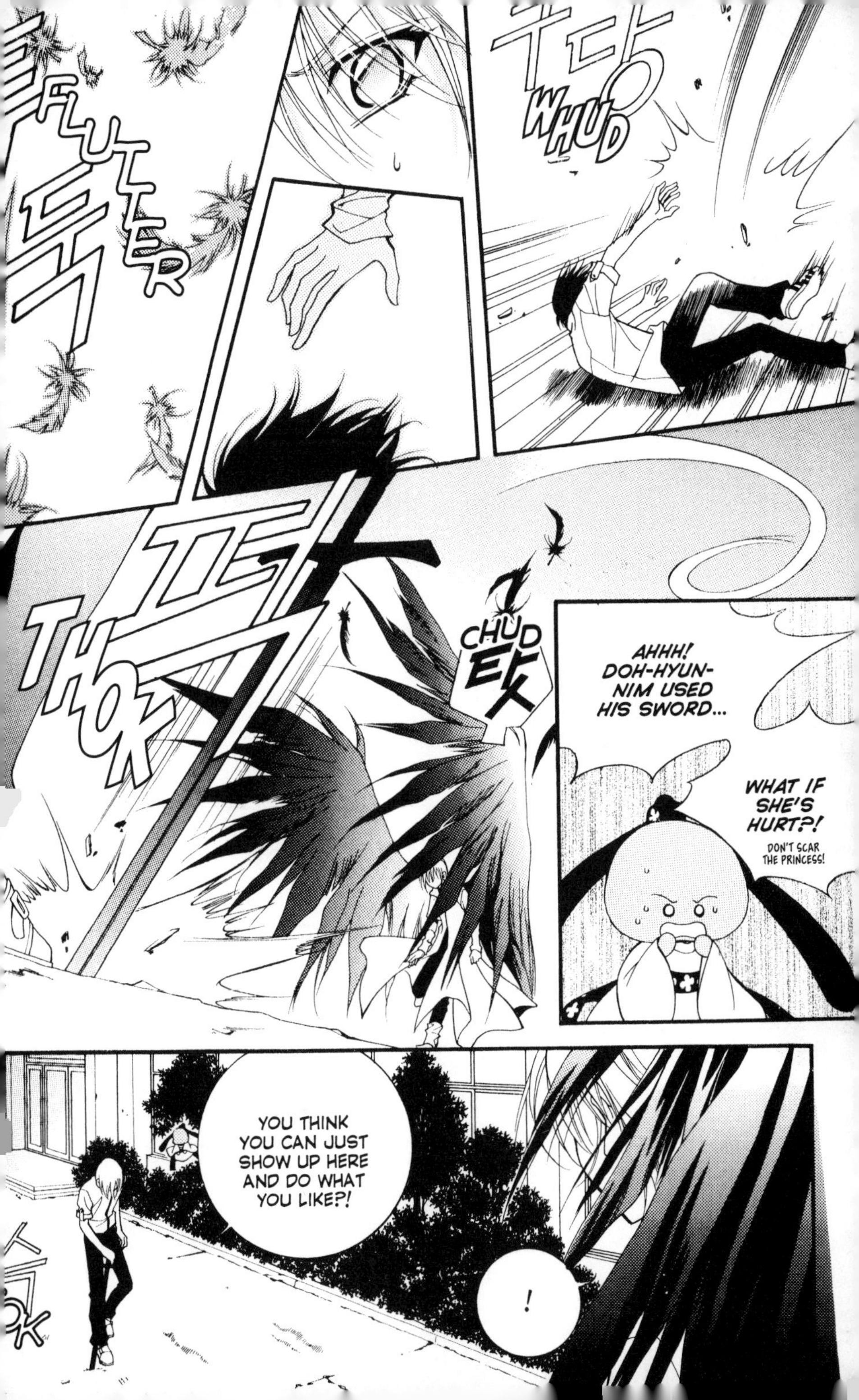

FLUTTER
WHUD
THOK
CHUD
AHHH! DOH-HYUN-NIM USED HIS SWORD...
WHAT IF SHE'S HURT?!
DON'T SCAR THE PRINCESS!
YOU THINK YOU CAN JUST SHOW UP HERE AND DO WHAT YOU LIKE?!
!
TOK

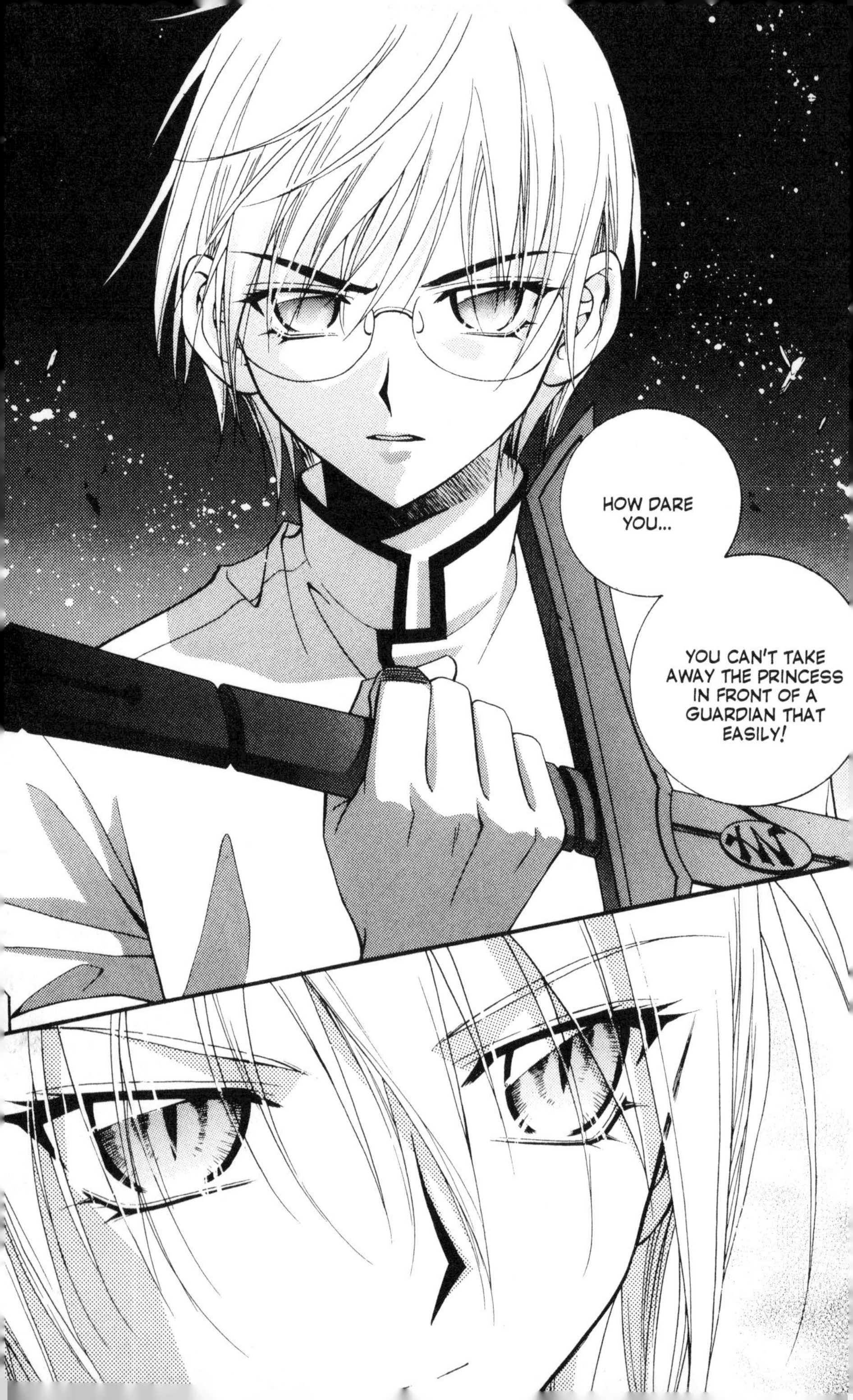
HOW DARE YOU...
YOU CAN'T TAKE AWAY THE PRINCESS IN FRONT OF A GUARDIAN THAT EASILY!

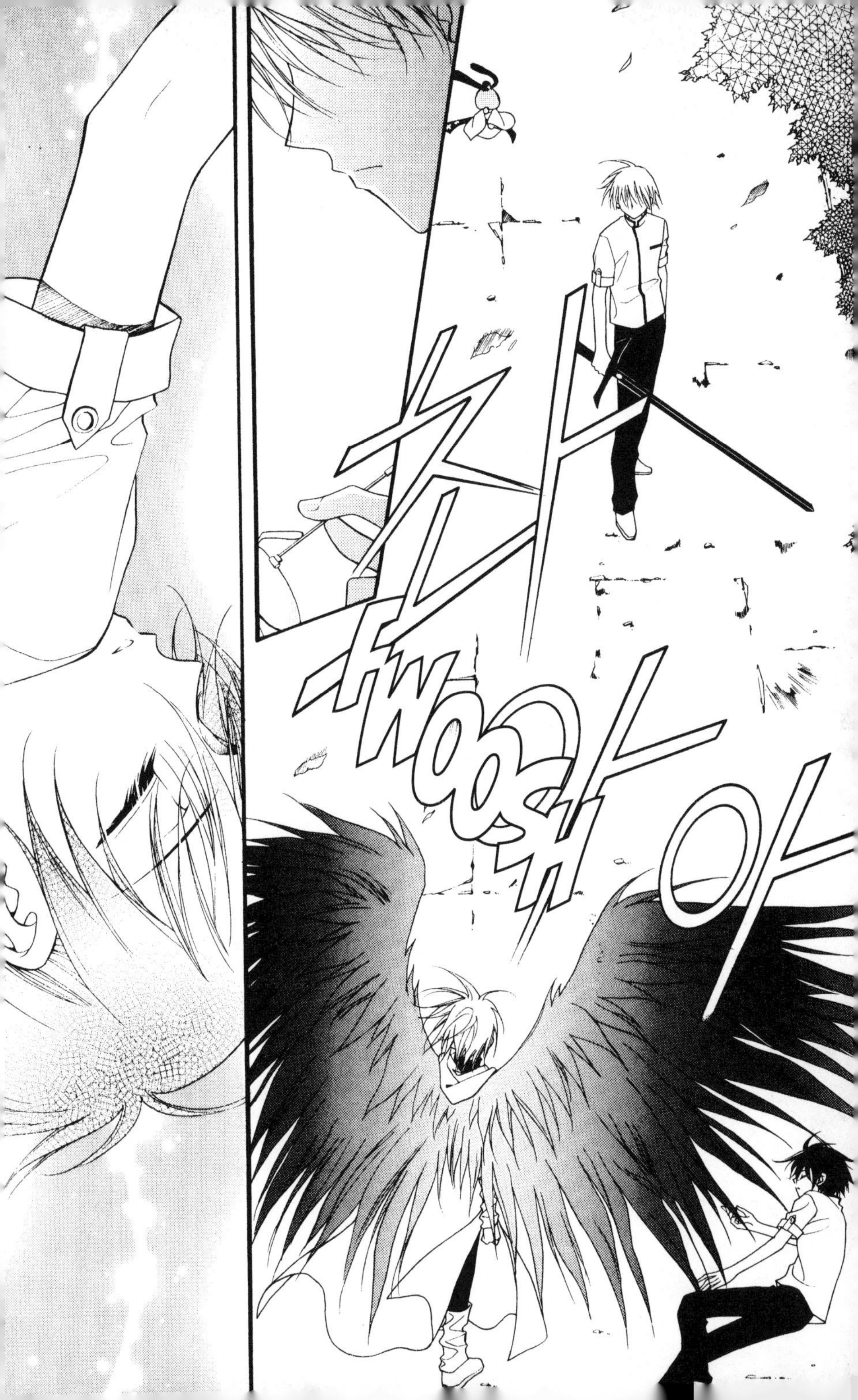
FWOOSH

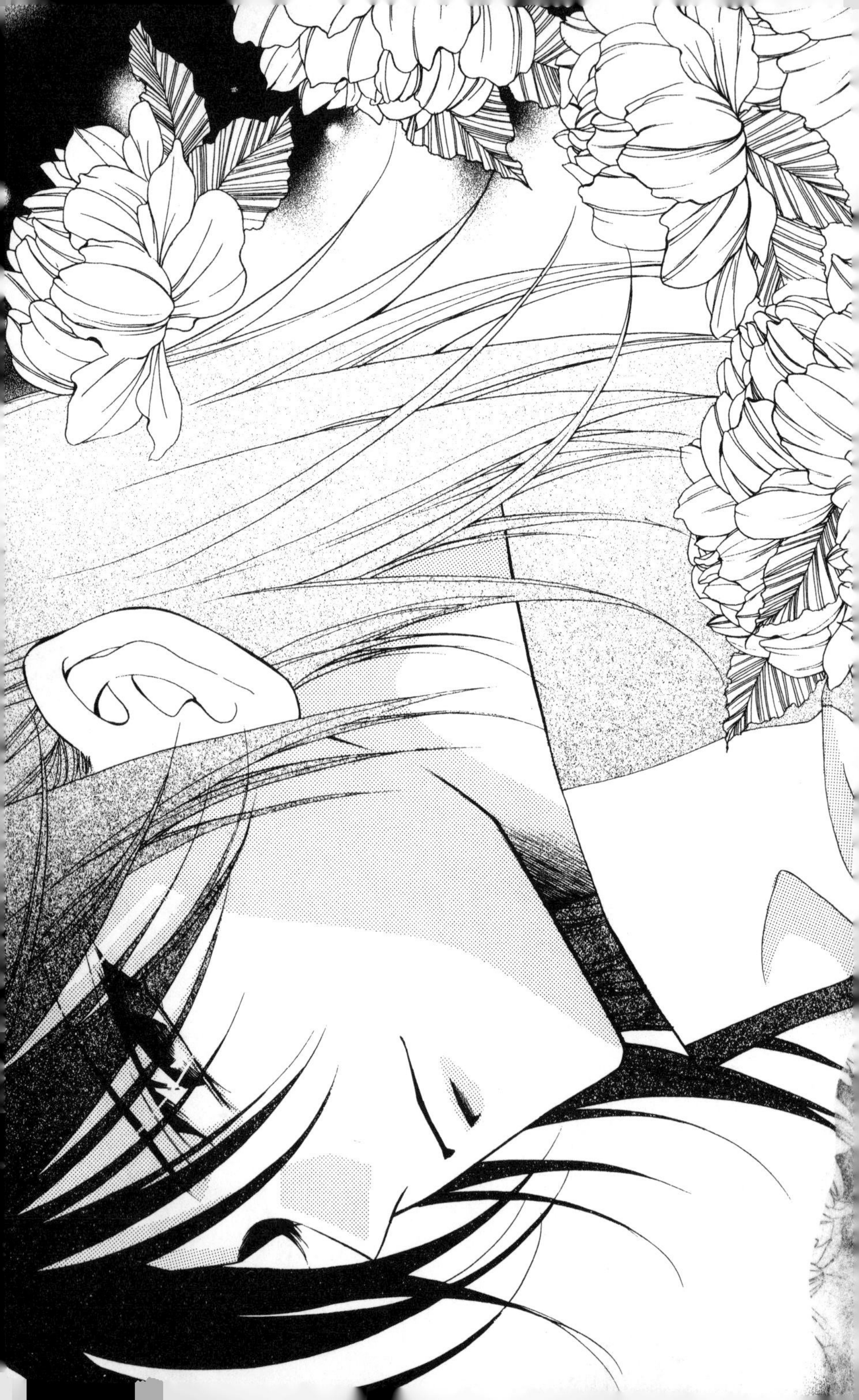

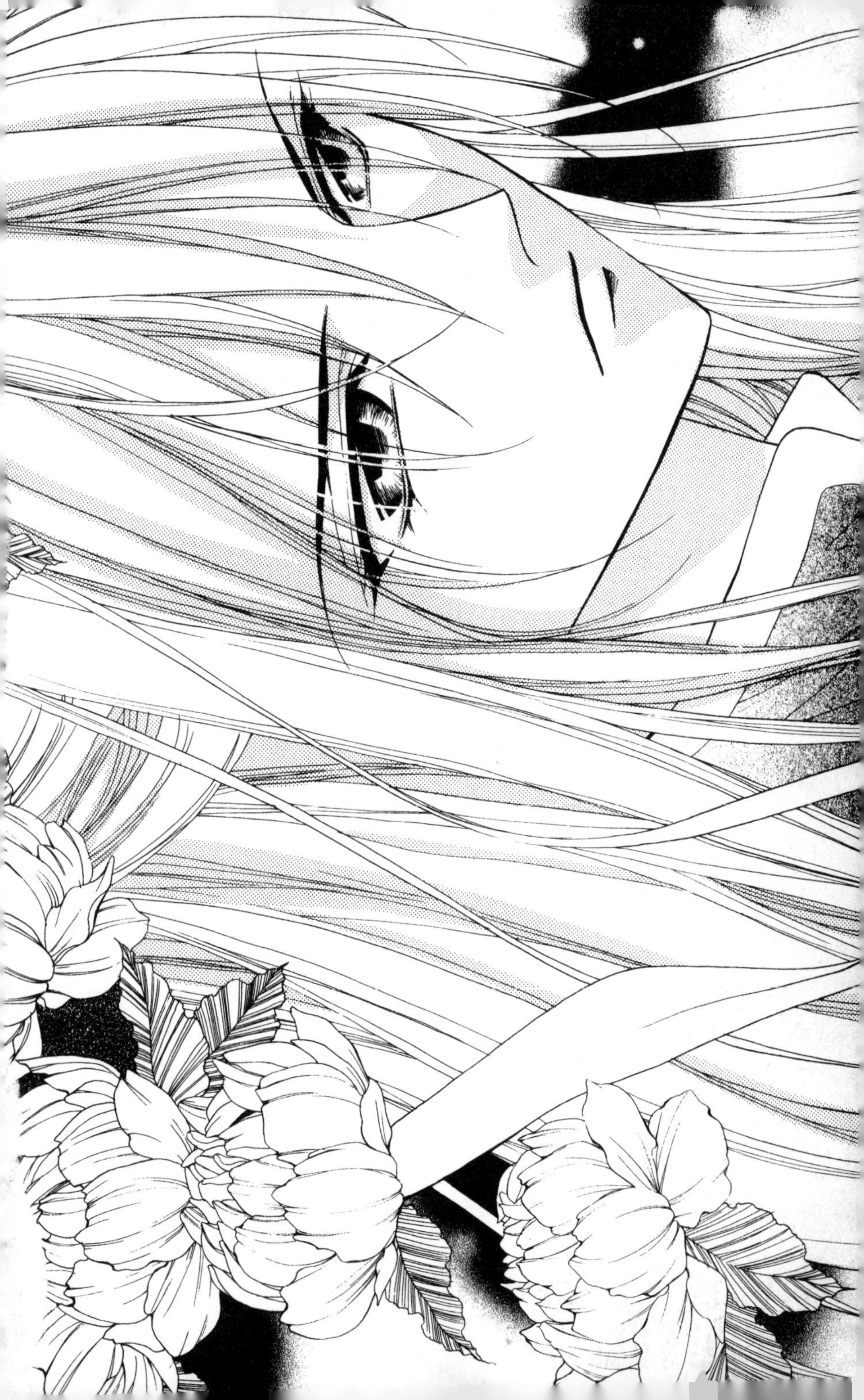

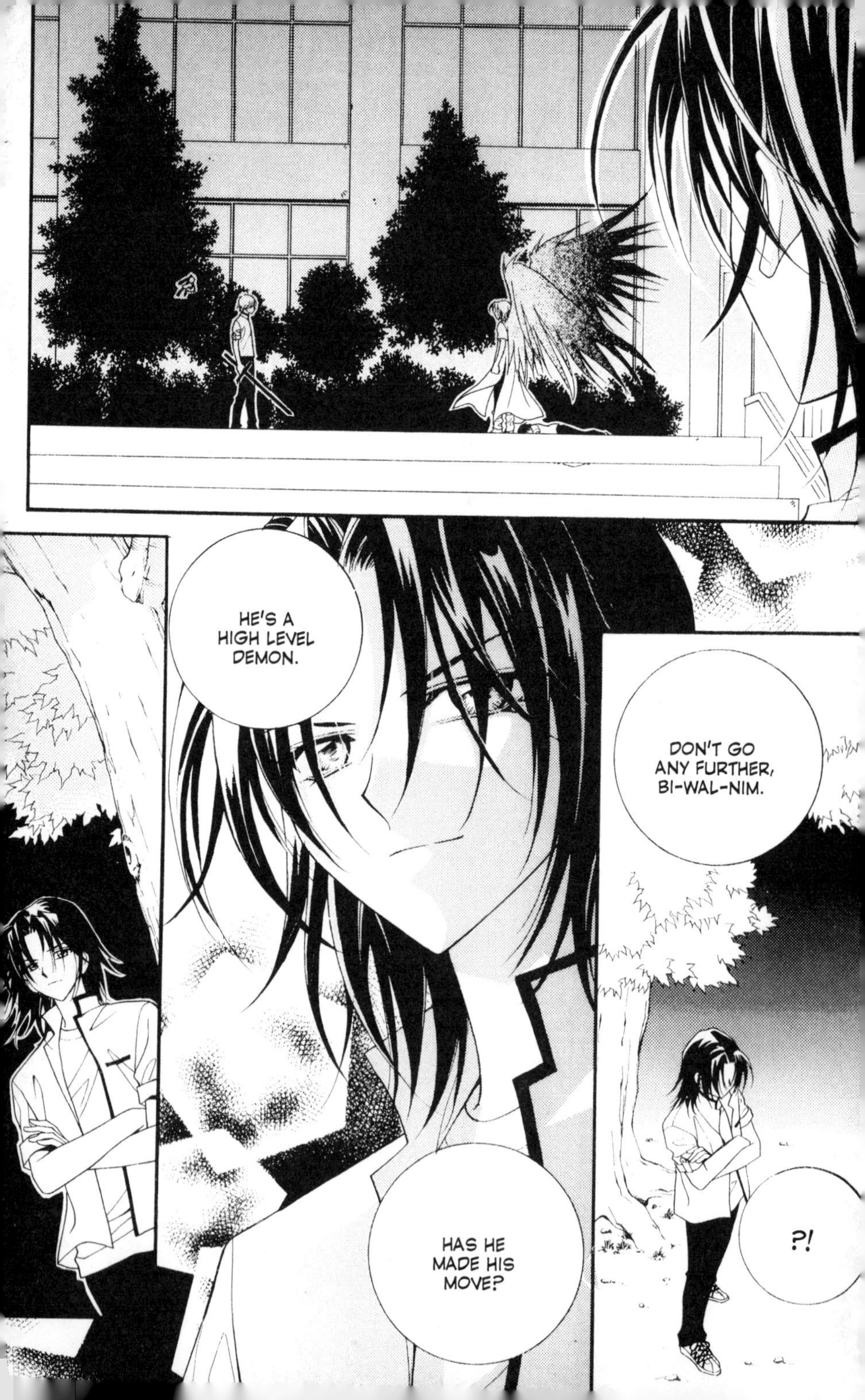
HE'S A HIGH LEVEL DEMON.
HAS HE MADE HIS MOVE?
DON'T GO ANY FURTHER, BI-WAL-NIM.
?!

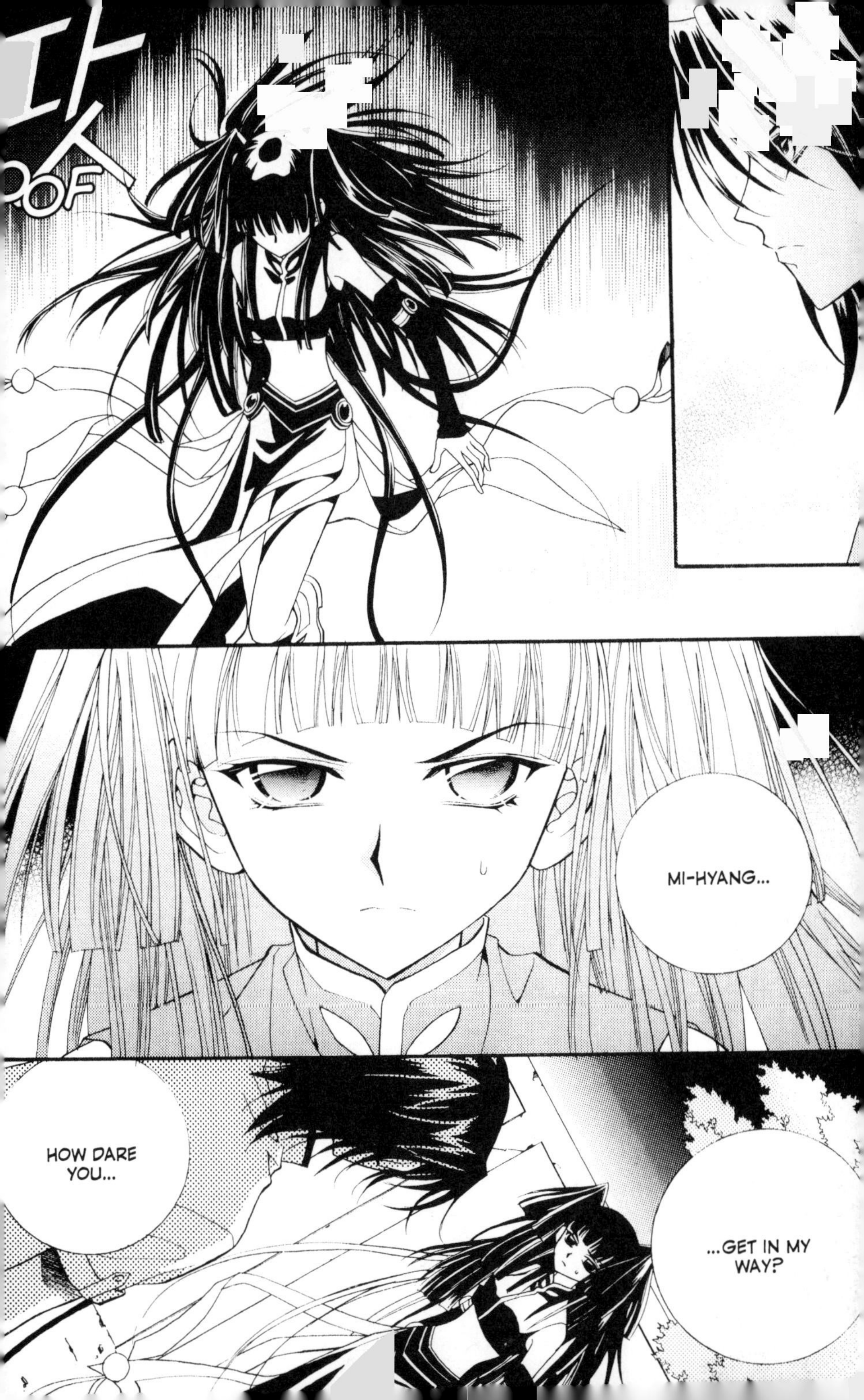
OOF
MI-HYANG...
HOW DARE YOU...
...GET IN MY WAY?

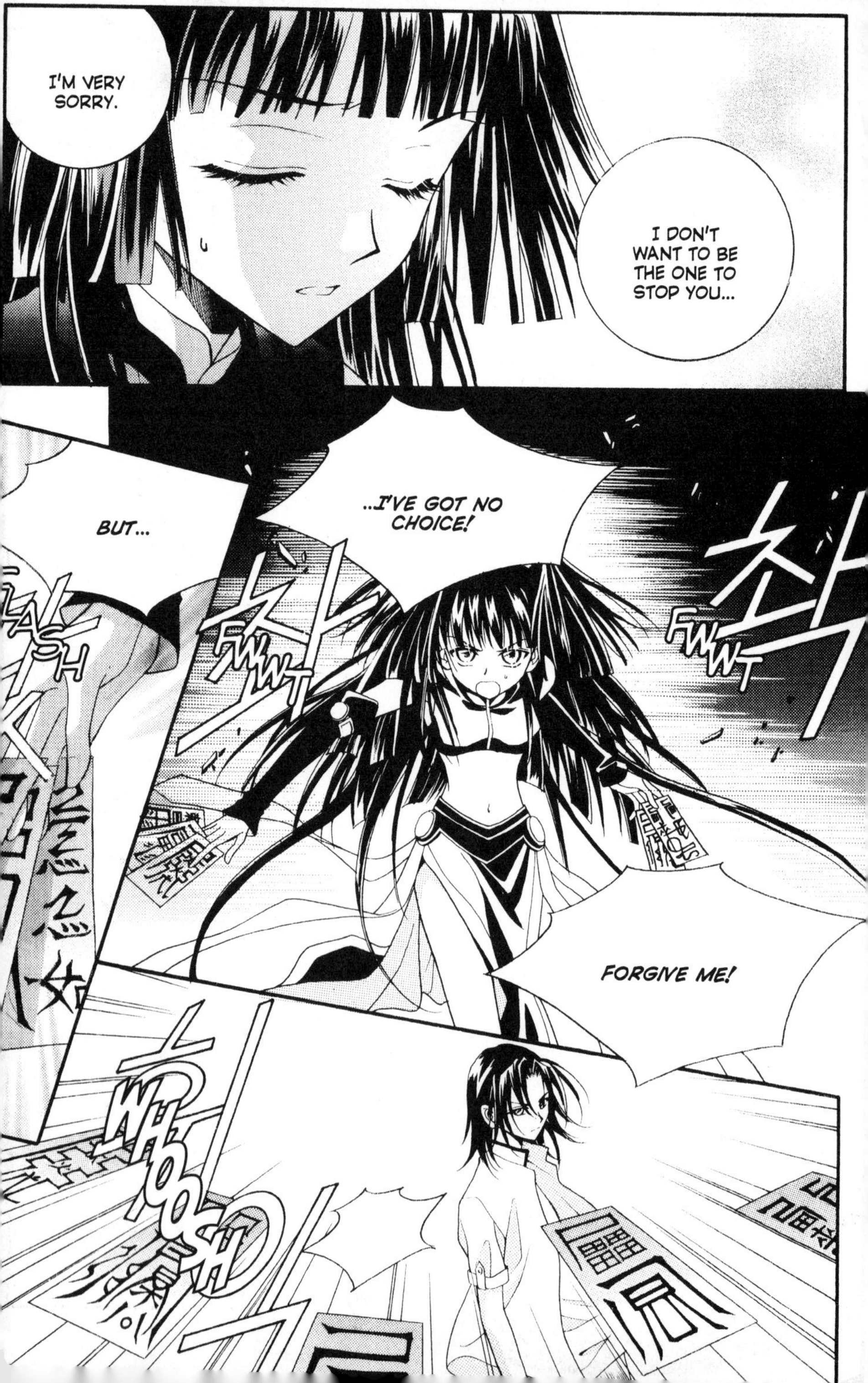
I'M VERY SORRY.
I DON'T WANT TO BE THE ONE TO STOP YOU...
BUT...
FLASH
...I'VE GOT NO CHOICE!
FWWT
FWWT
FORGIVE ME!
WHOOSH

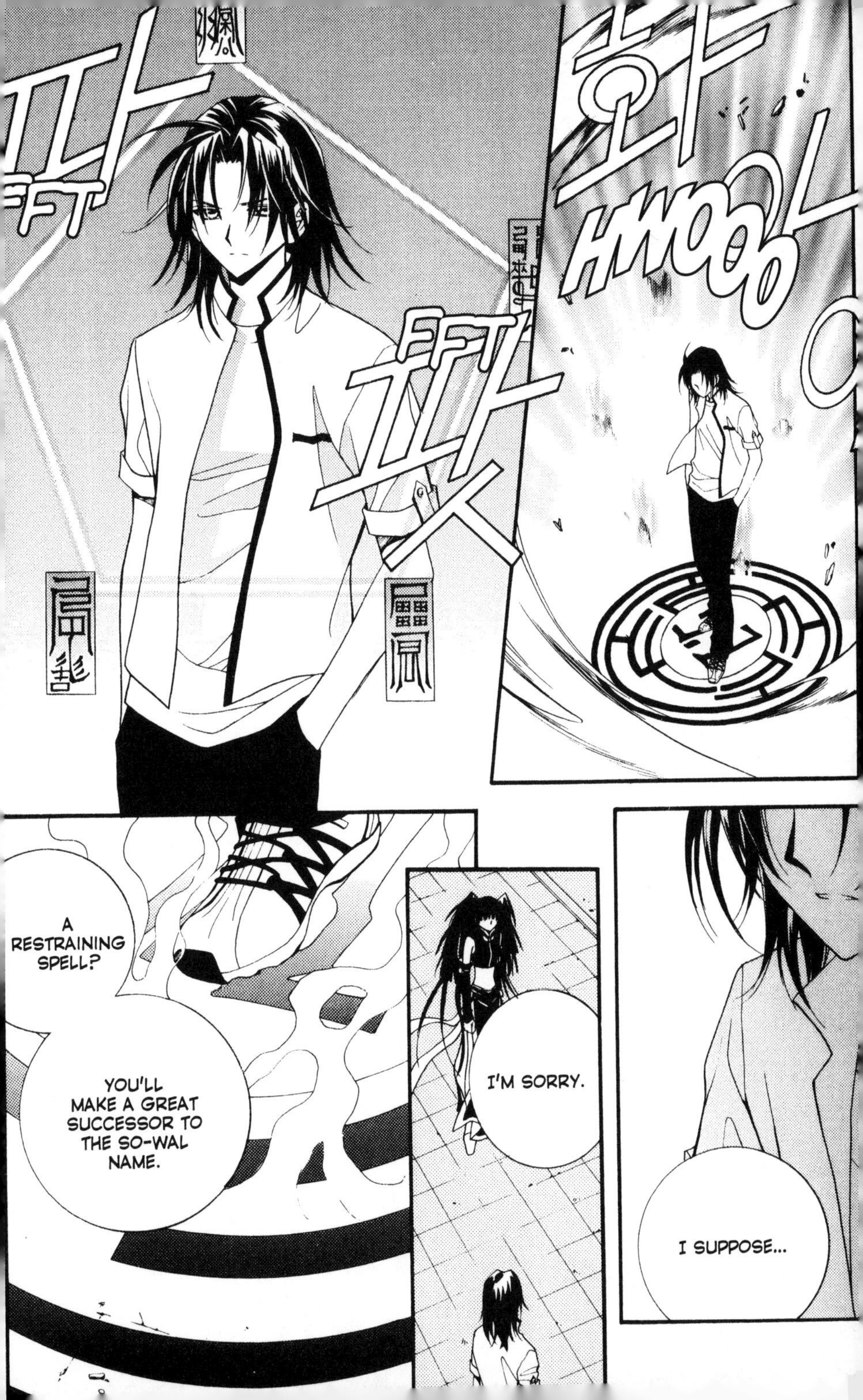
FFT
FFT
HWOOOO
A RESTRAINING SPELL?
YOU'LL MAKE A GREAT SUCCESSOR TO THE SO-WAL NAME.
I'M SORRY.
I SUPPOSE...

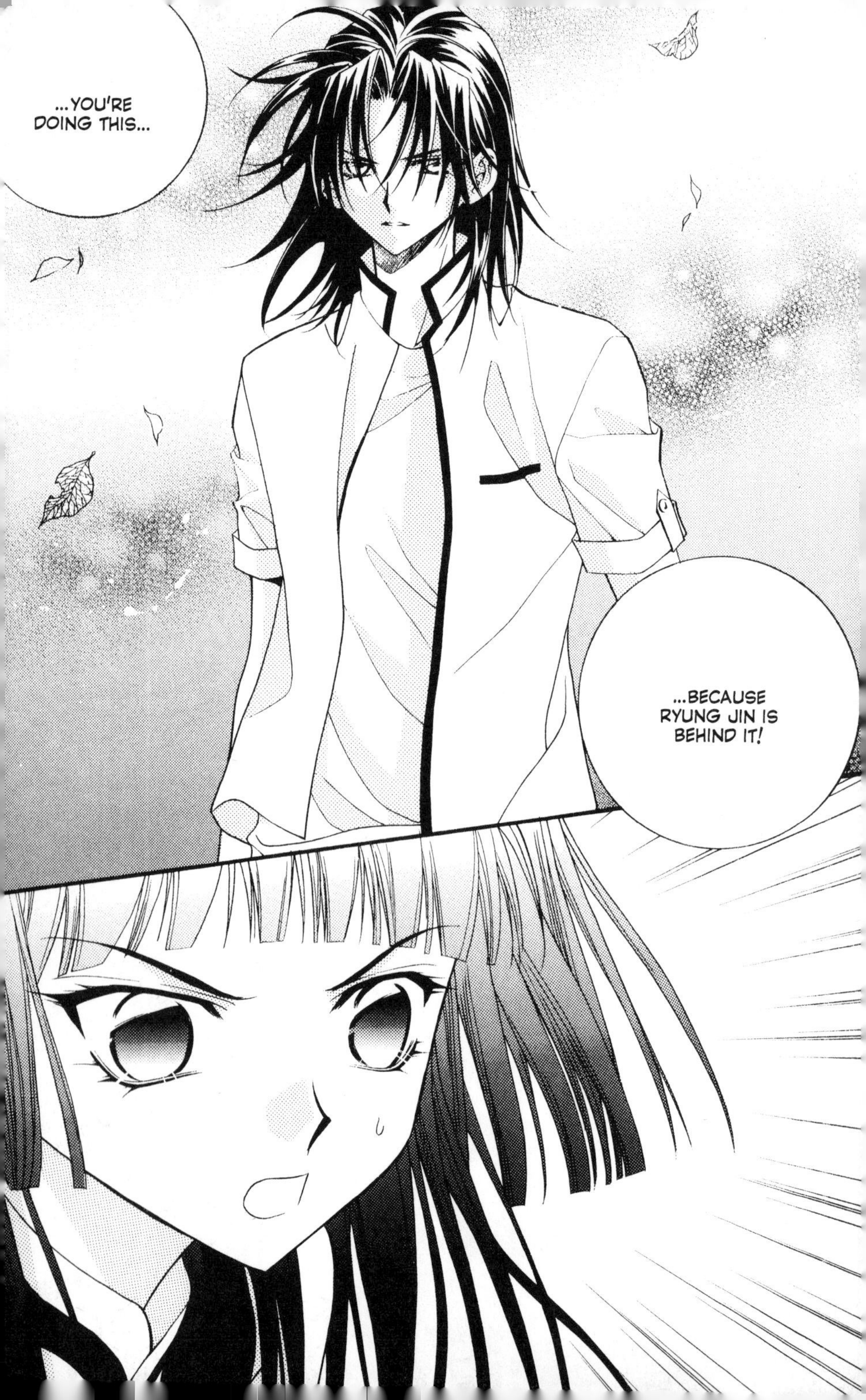
...YOU'RE DOING THIS...
...BECAUSE RYUNG JIN IS BEHIND IT!

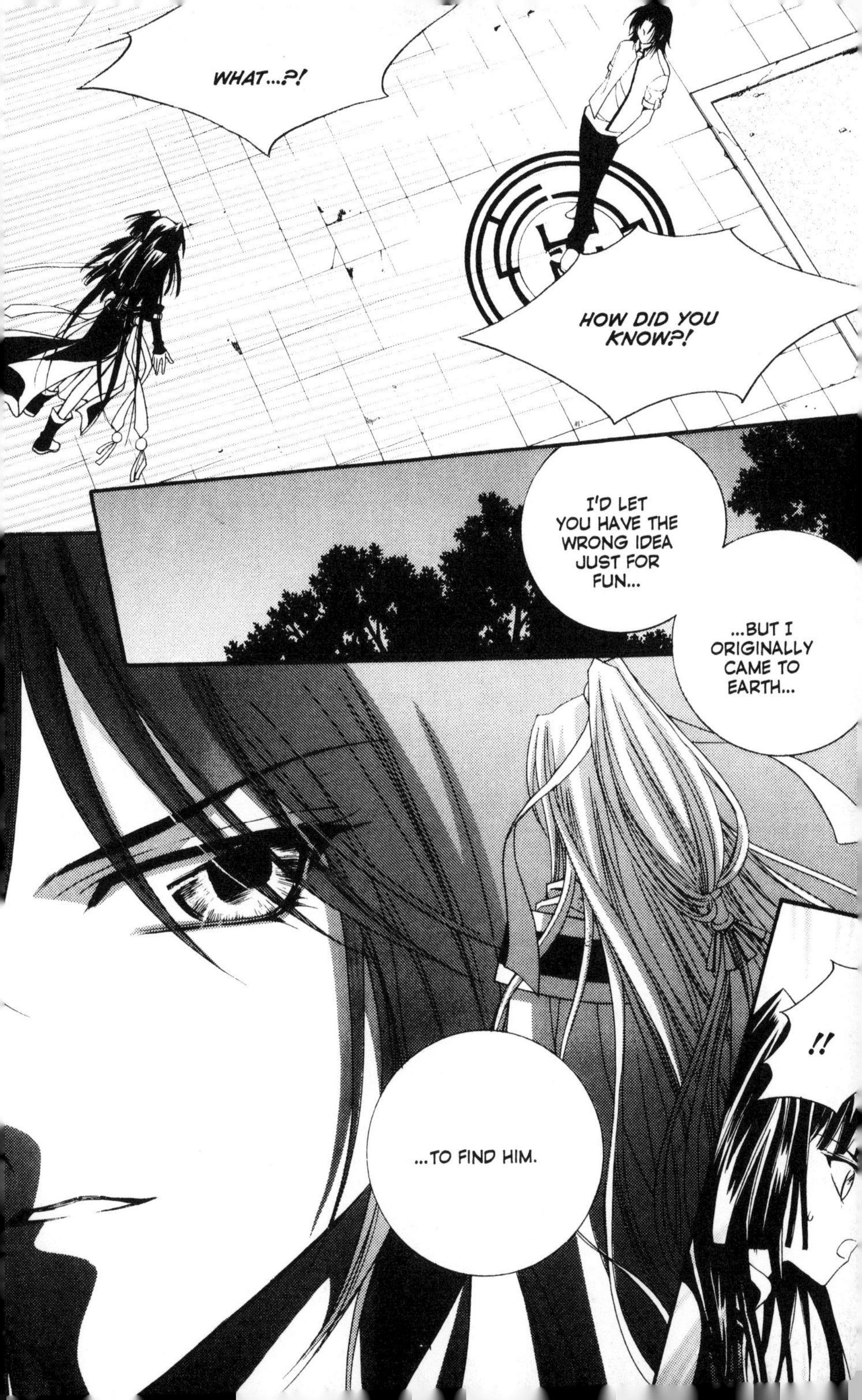
WHAT...?!
HOW DID YOU KNOW?!
I'D LET YOU HAVE THE WRONG IDEA JUST FOR FUN...
...BUT I ORIGINALLY CAME TO EARTH...
...TO FIND HIM.
!!

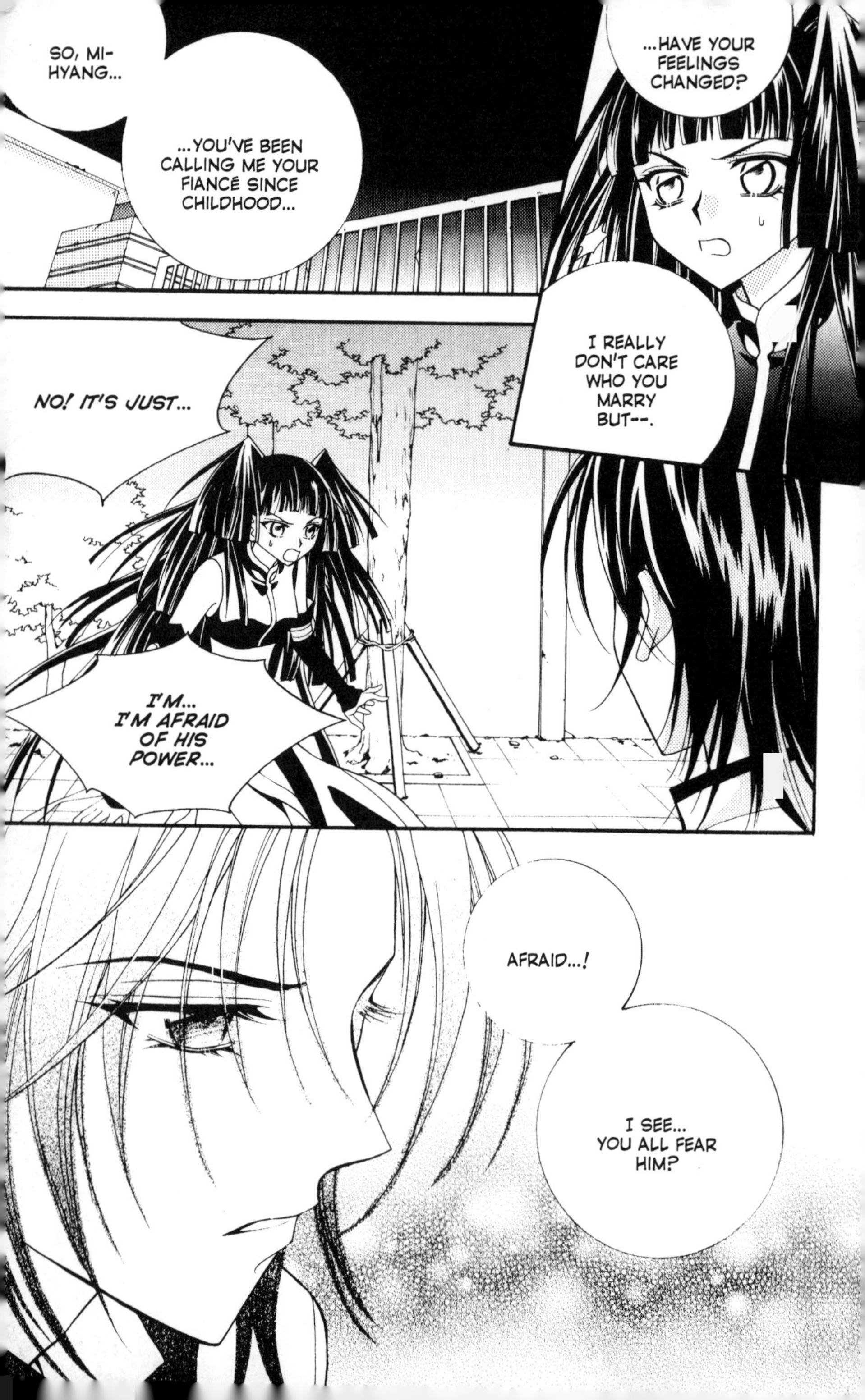
SO, MI-HYANG...
...YOU'VE BEEN CALLING ME YOUR FIANCÉ SINCE CHILDHOOD...
...HAVE YOUR FEELINGS CHANGED?
I REALLY DON'T CARE WHO YOU MARRY BUT--.
NO! IT'S JUST...
I'M... I'M AFRAID OF HIS POWER...
AFRAID...!
I SEE... YOU ALL FEAR HIM?

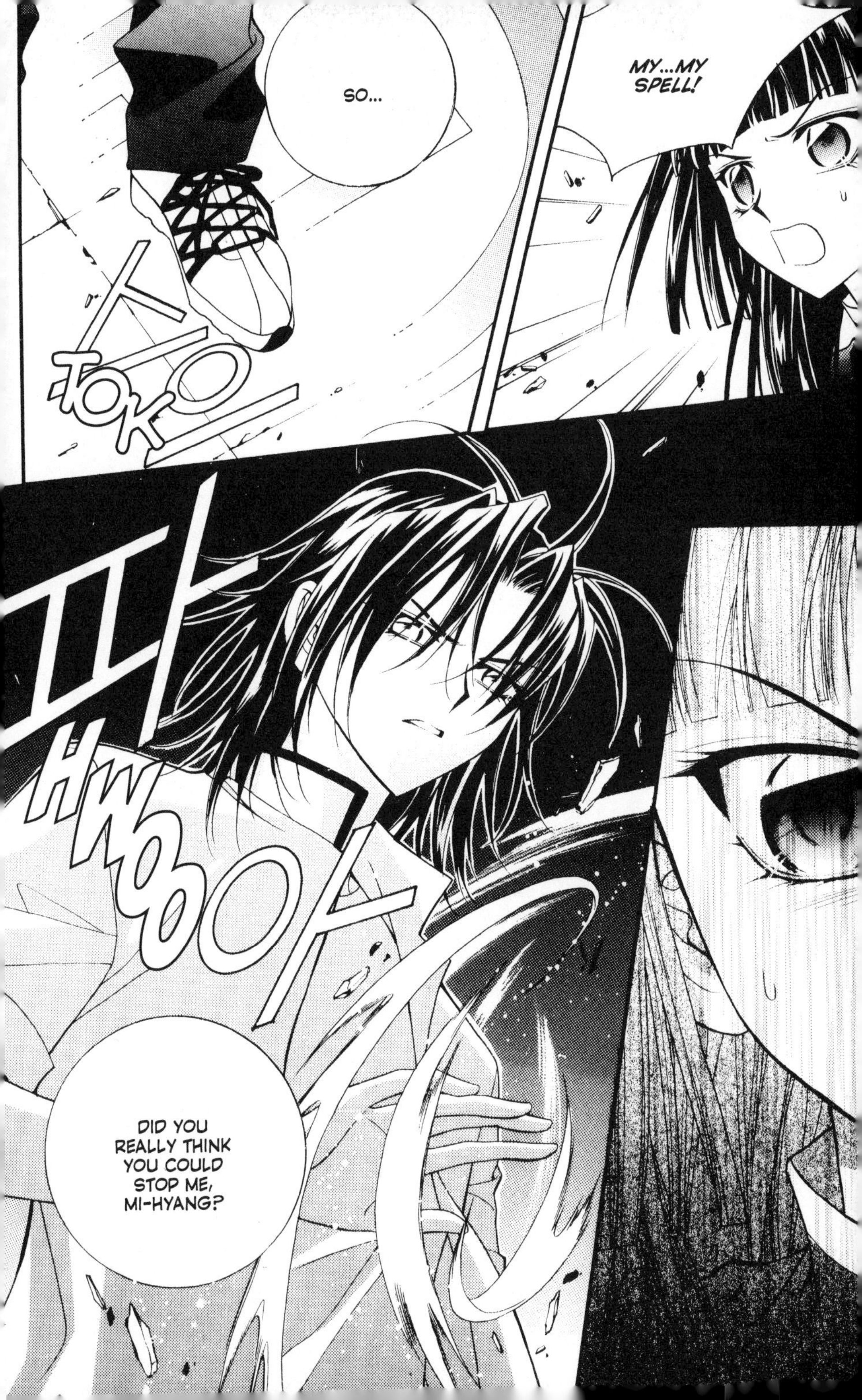
SO...
MY...MY SPELL!
DID YOU REALLY THINK YOU COULD STOP ME, MI-HYANG?

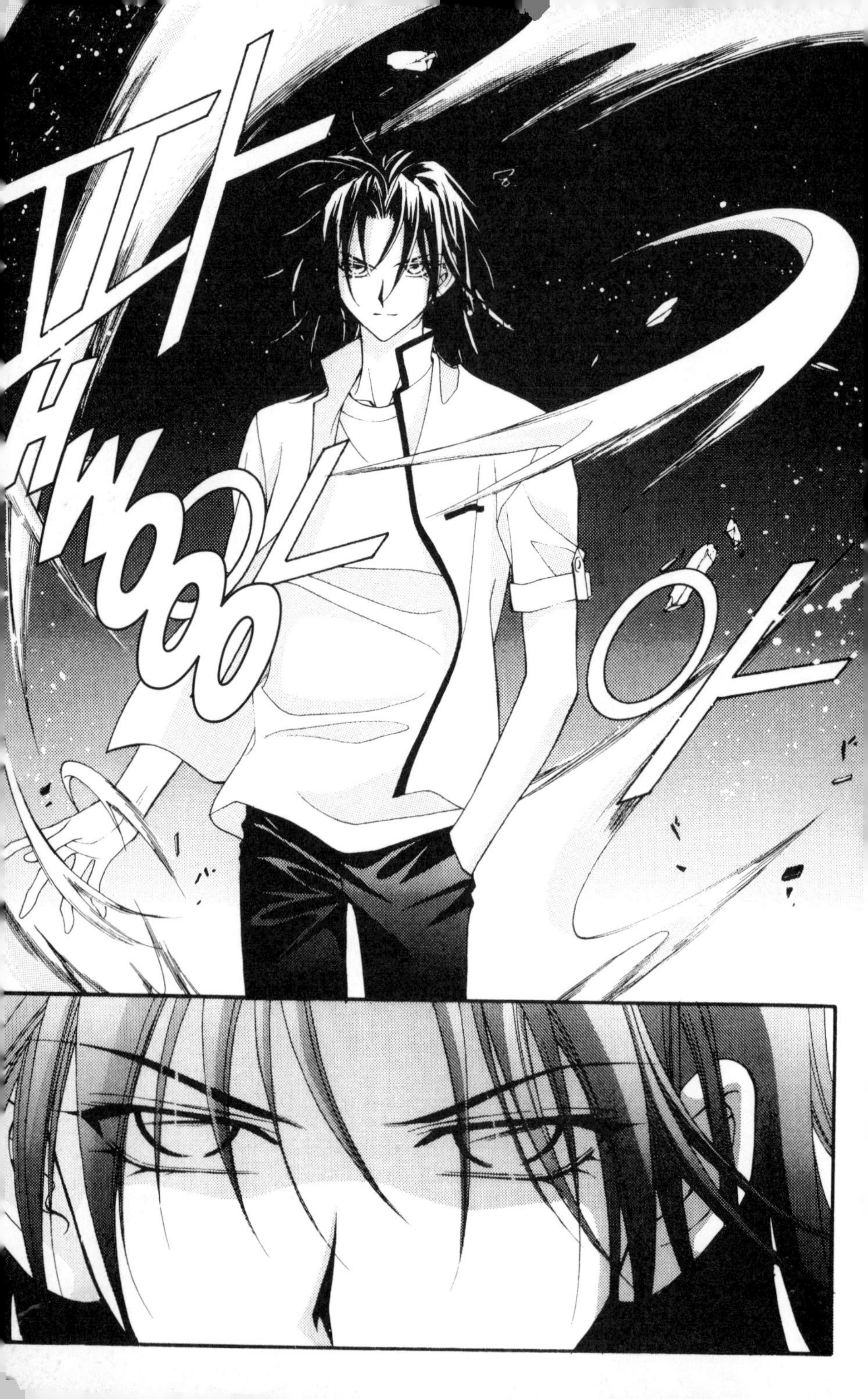

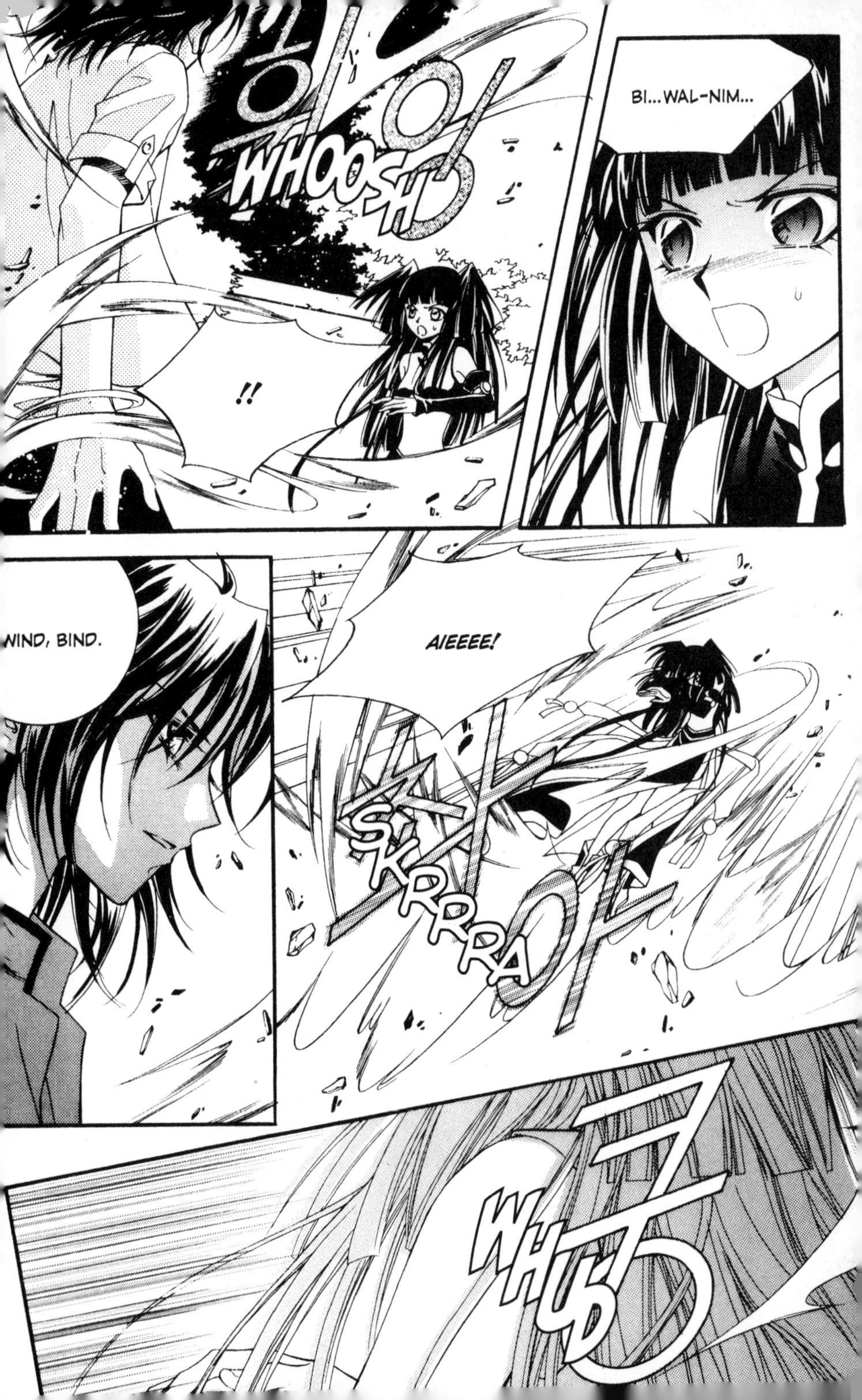

WHOOSH
!!
BI...WAL-NIM...
WIND, BIND.
AIEEEE!
SKRRRA
WHUD

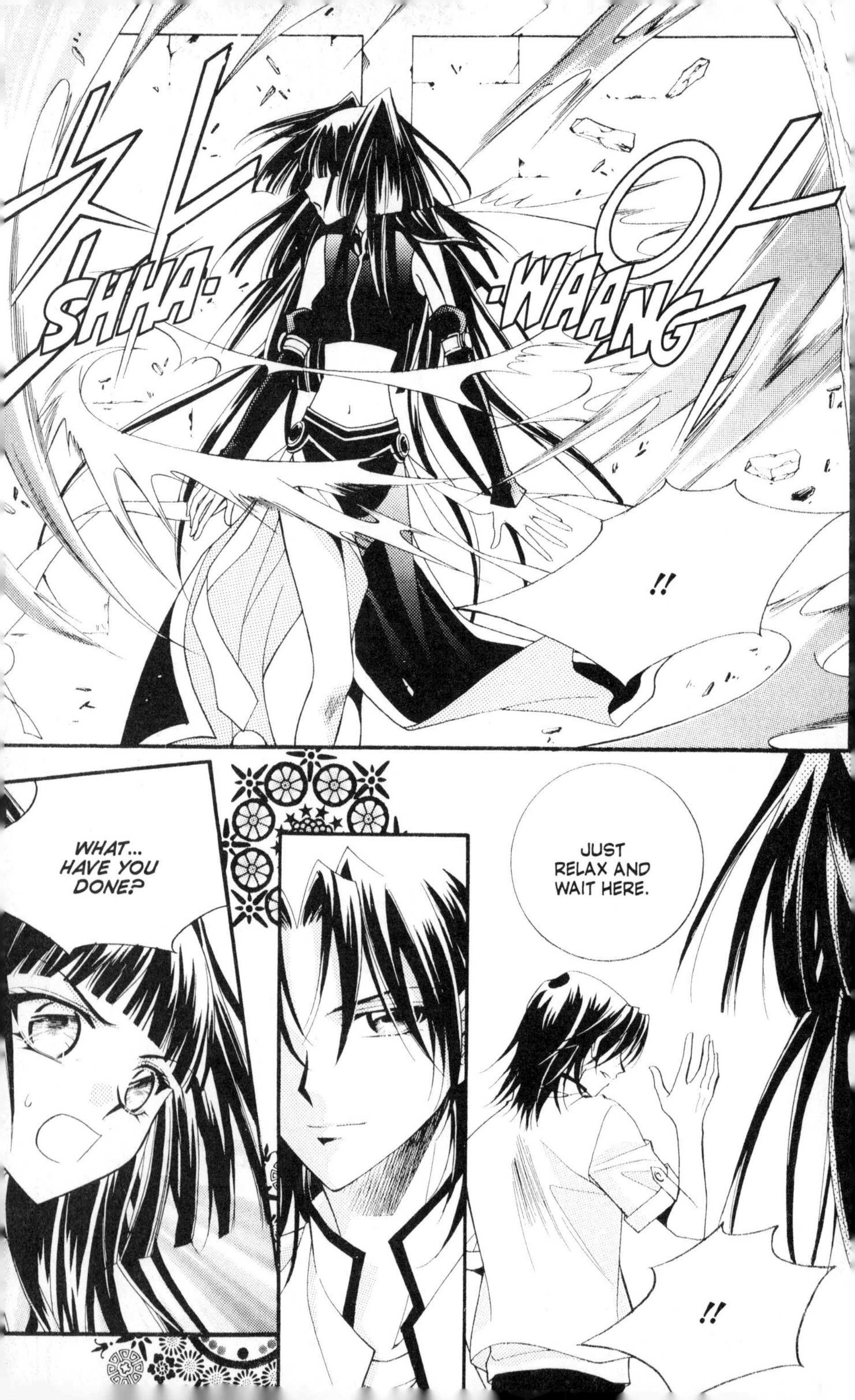
SHHA-
-WAAANG
!!
WHAT... HAVE YOU DONE?
JUST RELAX AND WAIT HERE.
!!

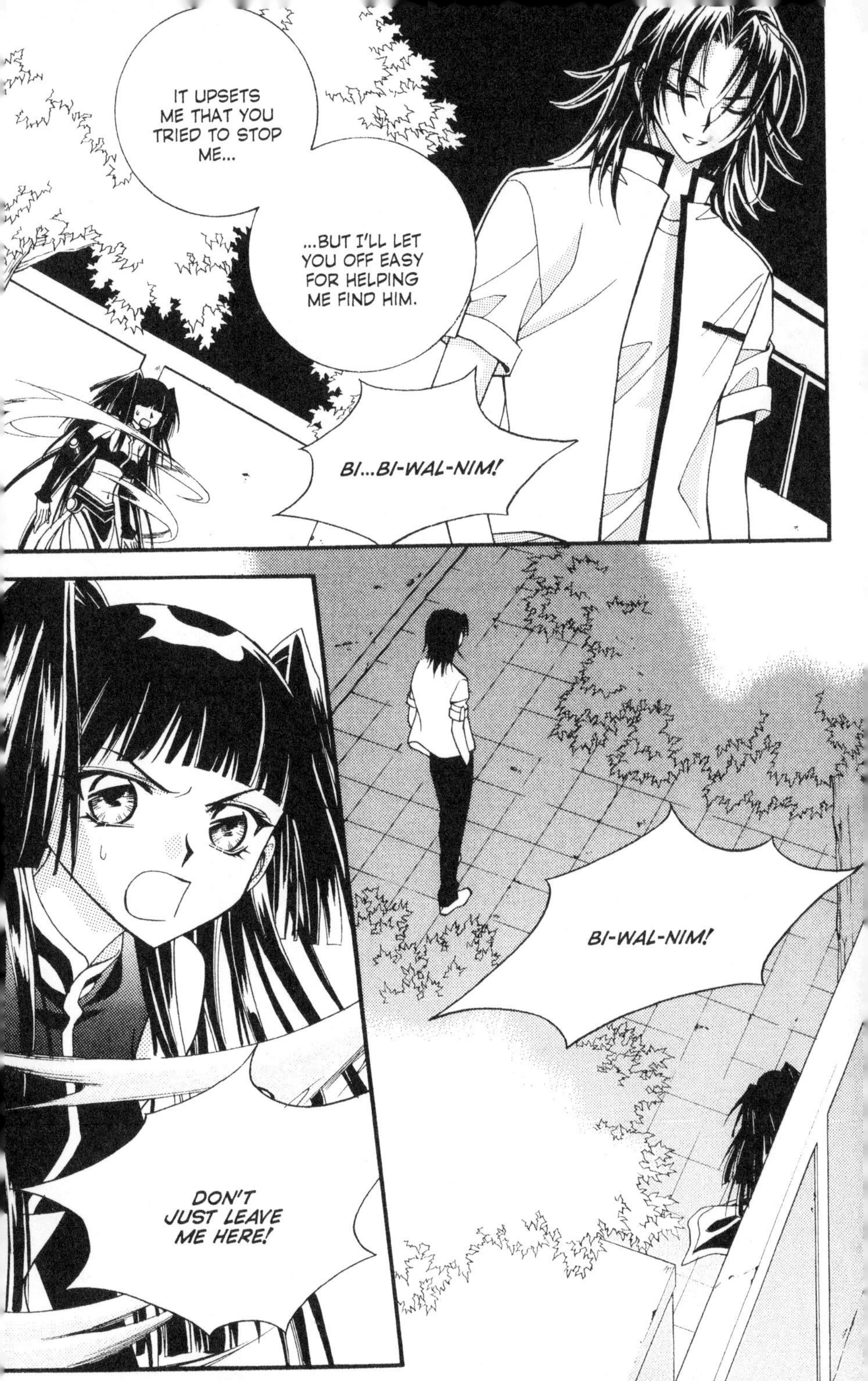
IT UPSETS ME THAT YOU TRIED TO STOP ME...
...BUT I'LL LET YOU OFF EASY FOR HELPING ME FIND HIM.
BI...BI-WAL-NIM!
DON'T JUST LEAVE ME HERE!
BI-WAL-NIM!

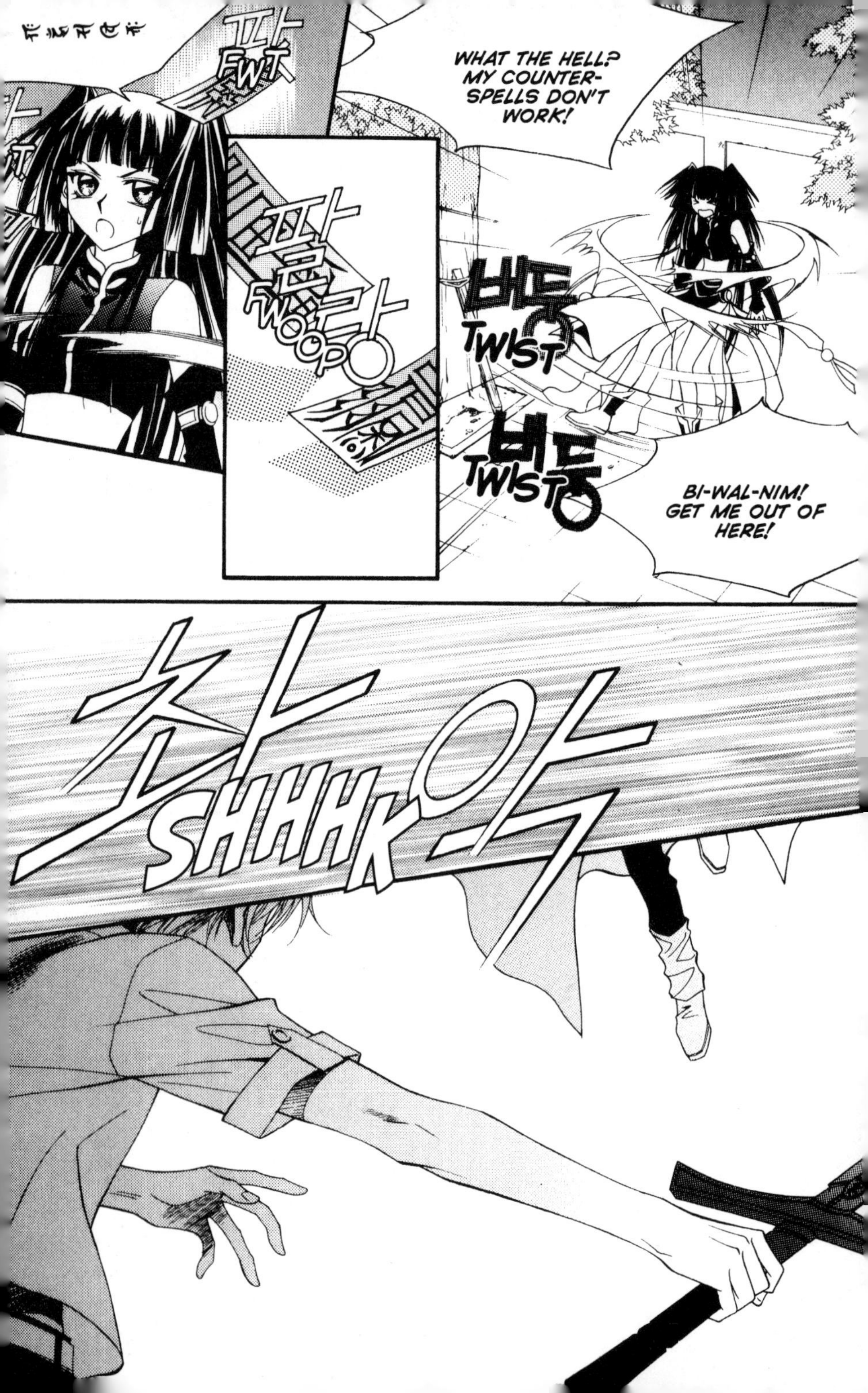
FWT
FWOOP
WHAT THE HELL? MY COUNTER-SPELLS DON'T WORK!
TWIST
TWIST
BI-WAL-NIM! GET ME OUT OF HERE!
SHHHK

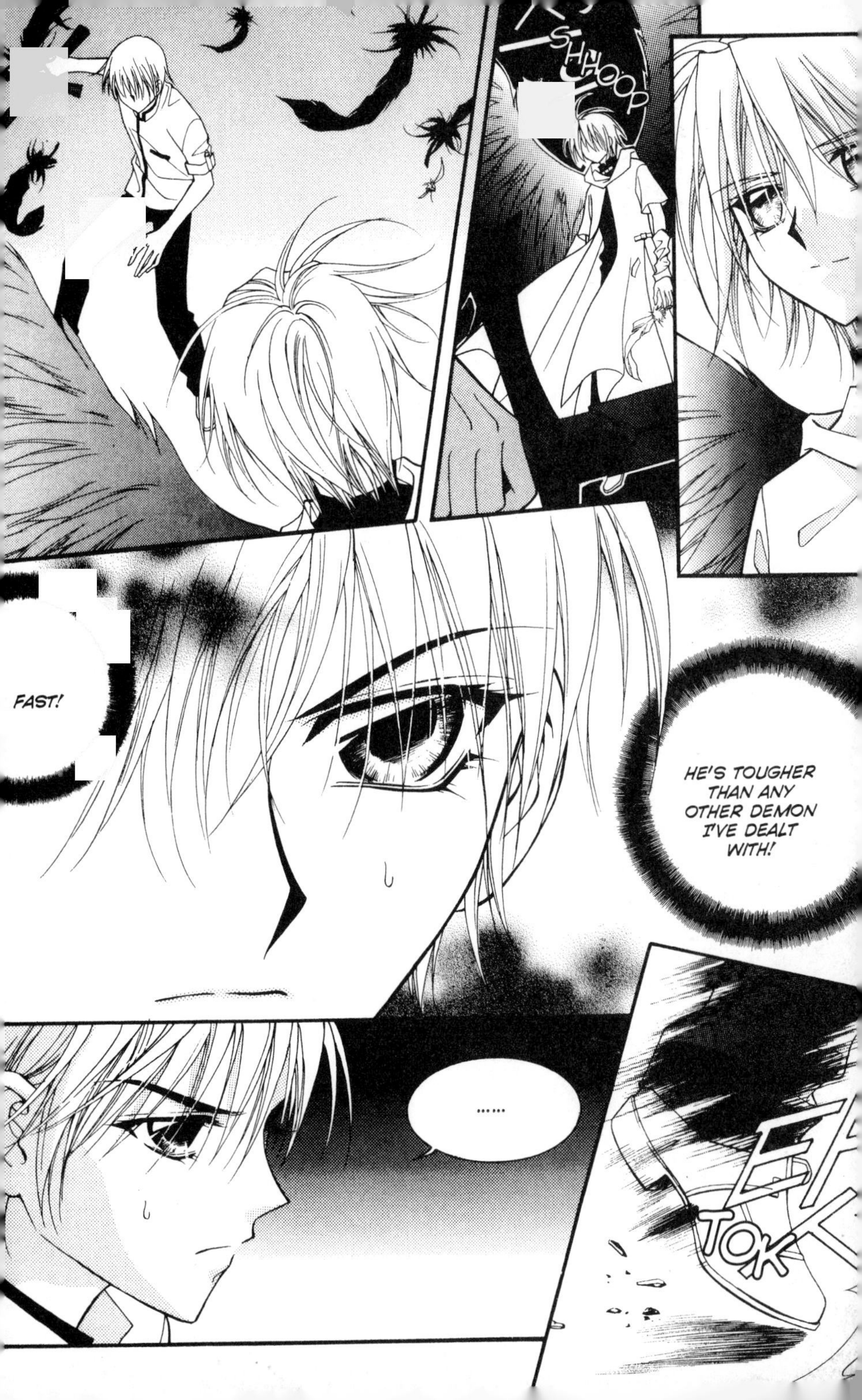

SHHOOP
FAST!
HE'S TOUGHER THAN ANY OTHER DEMON I'VE DEALT WITH!
......
TOK

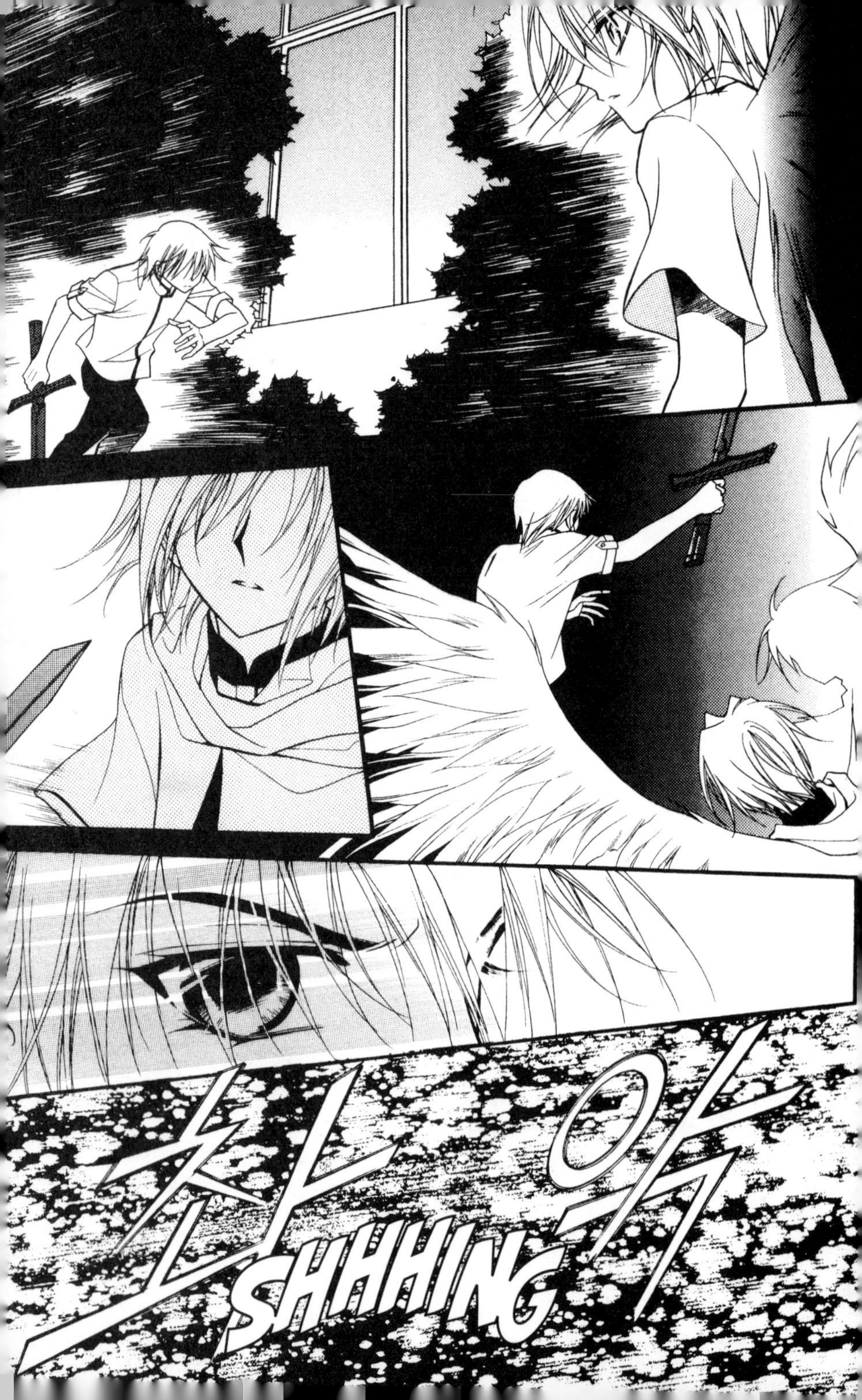
SHHHING

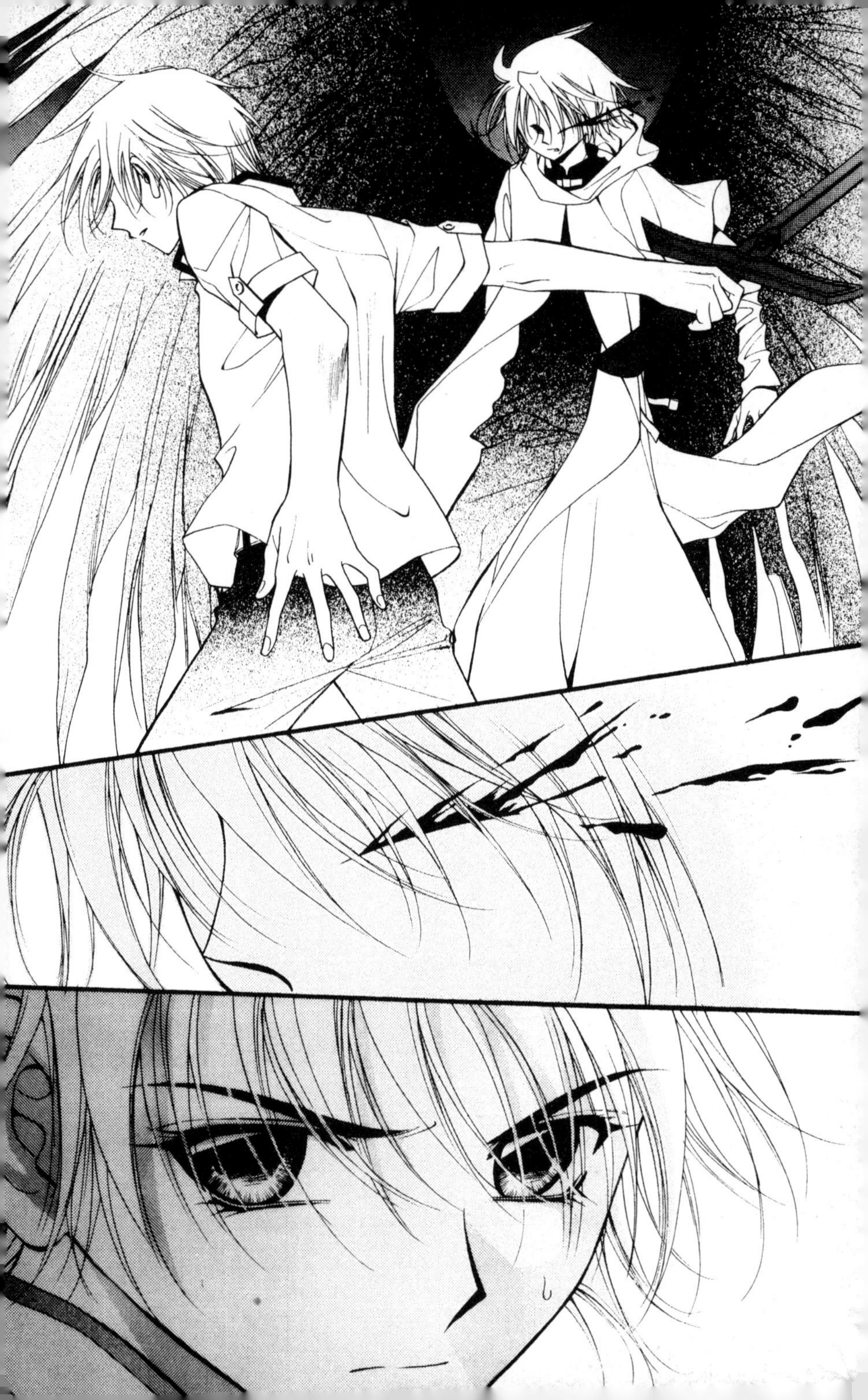

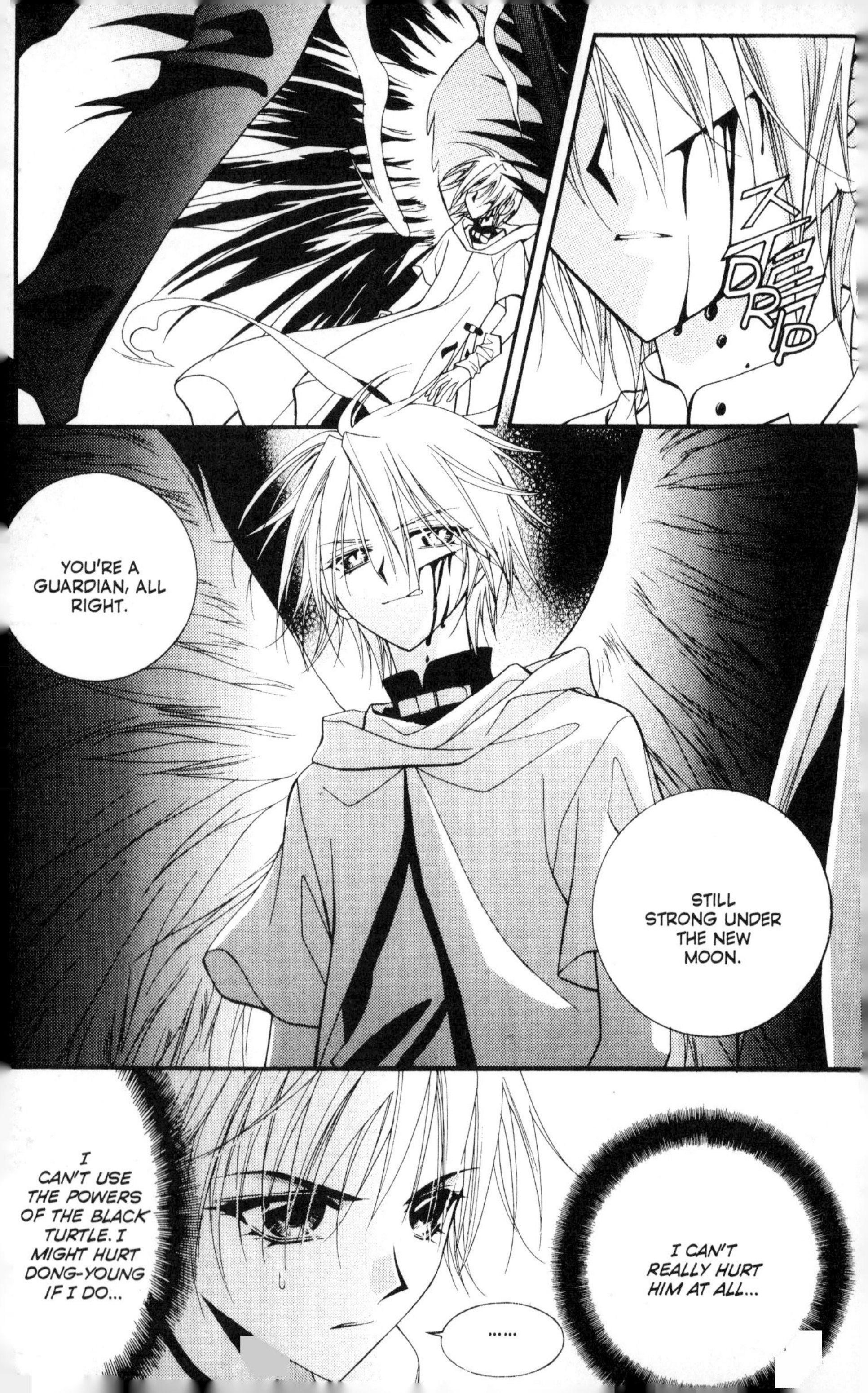
DRIP
YOU'RE A GUARDIAN, ALL RIGHT.
STILL STRONG UNDER THE NEW MOON.
I CAN'T USE THE POWERS OF THE BLACK TURTLE. I MIGHT HURT DONG-YOUNG IF I DO...
......
I CAN'T REALLY HURT HIM AT ALL...

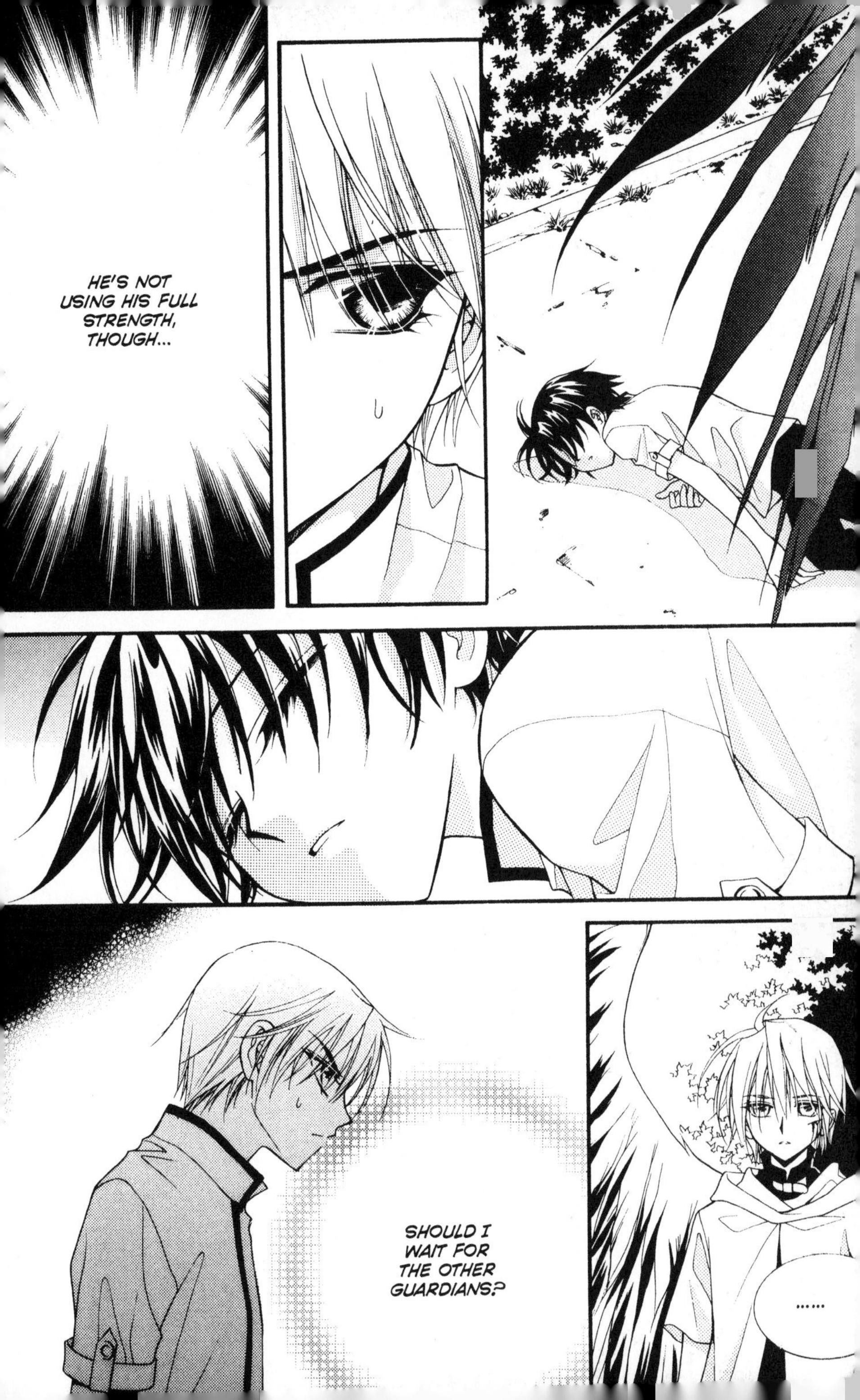
HE'S NOT USING HIS FULL STRENGTH, THOUGH...
SHOULD I WAIT FOR THE OTHER GUARDIANS?
......

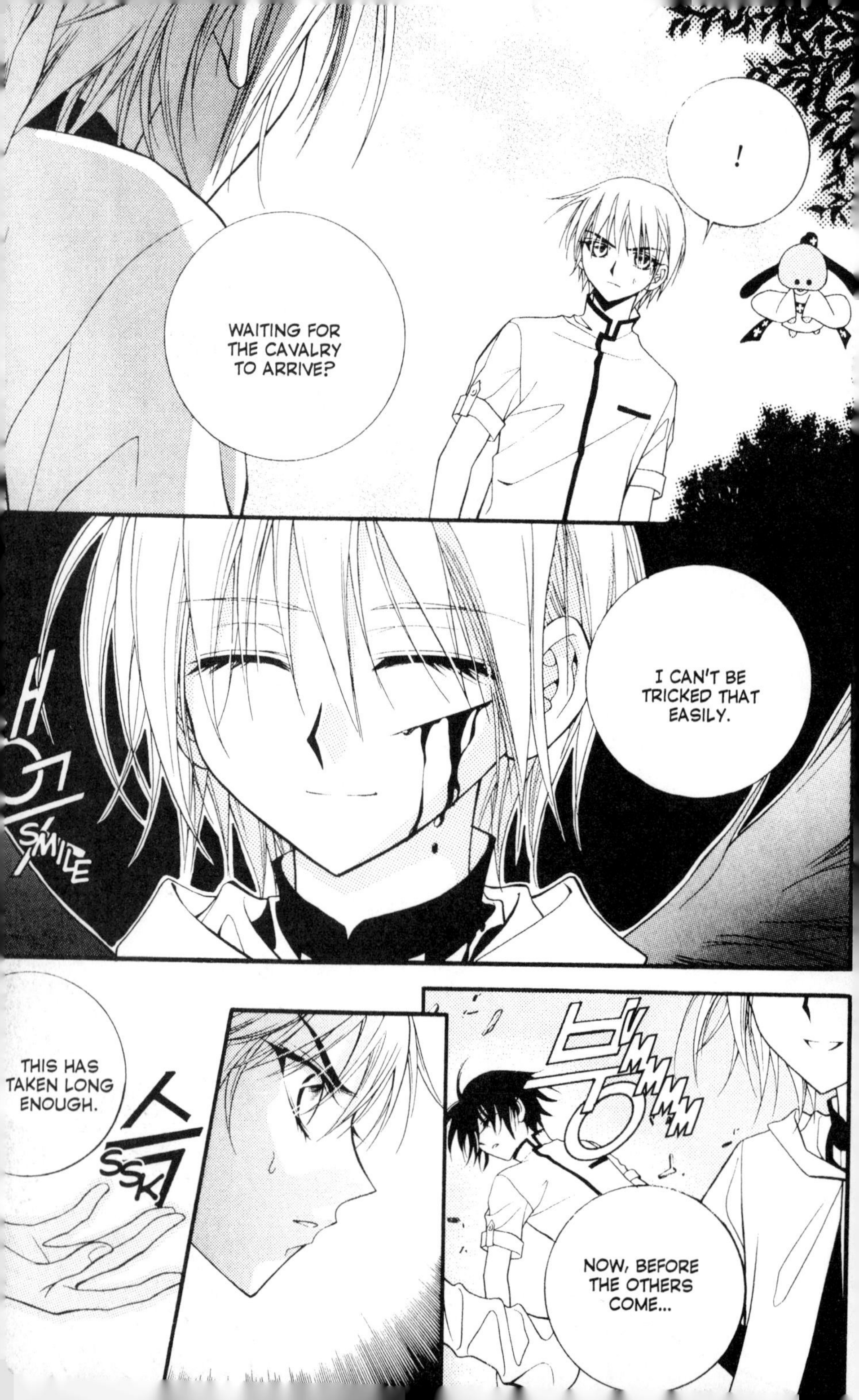
WAITING FOR THE CAVALRY TO ARRIVE?
!
SMILE
I CAN'T BE TRICKED THAT EASILY.
THIS HAS TAKEN LONG ENOUGH.
SSK
NOW, BEFORE THE OTHERS COME...

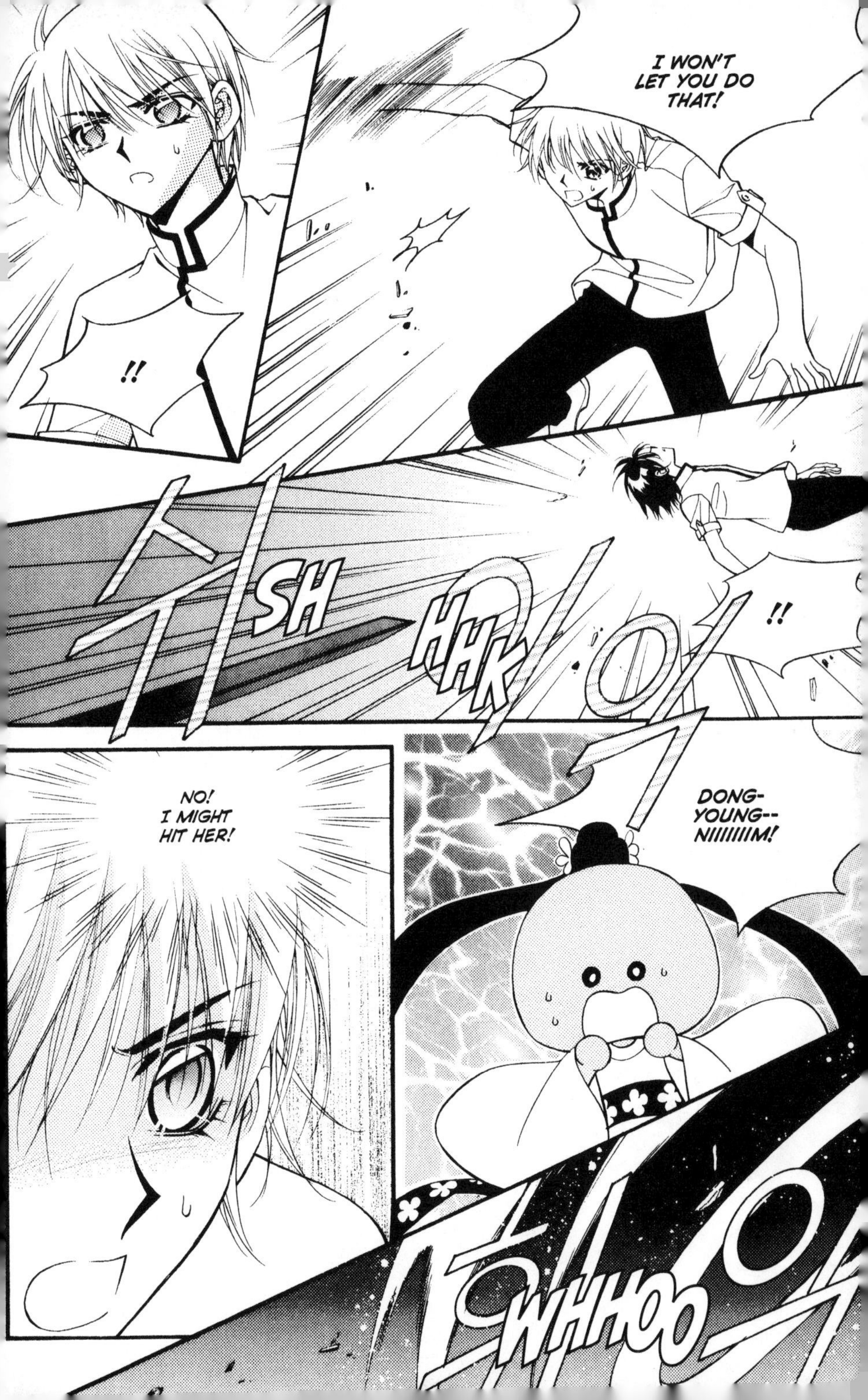
!!
I WON'T LET YOU DO THAT!
TSH
HHK
!!
NO! I MIGHT HIT HER!
DONG-YOUNG--NIIIIIIIM!
WHHOO

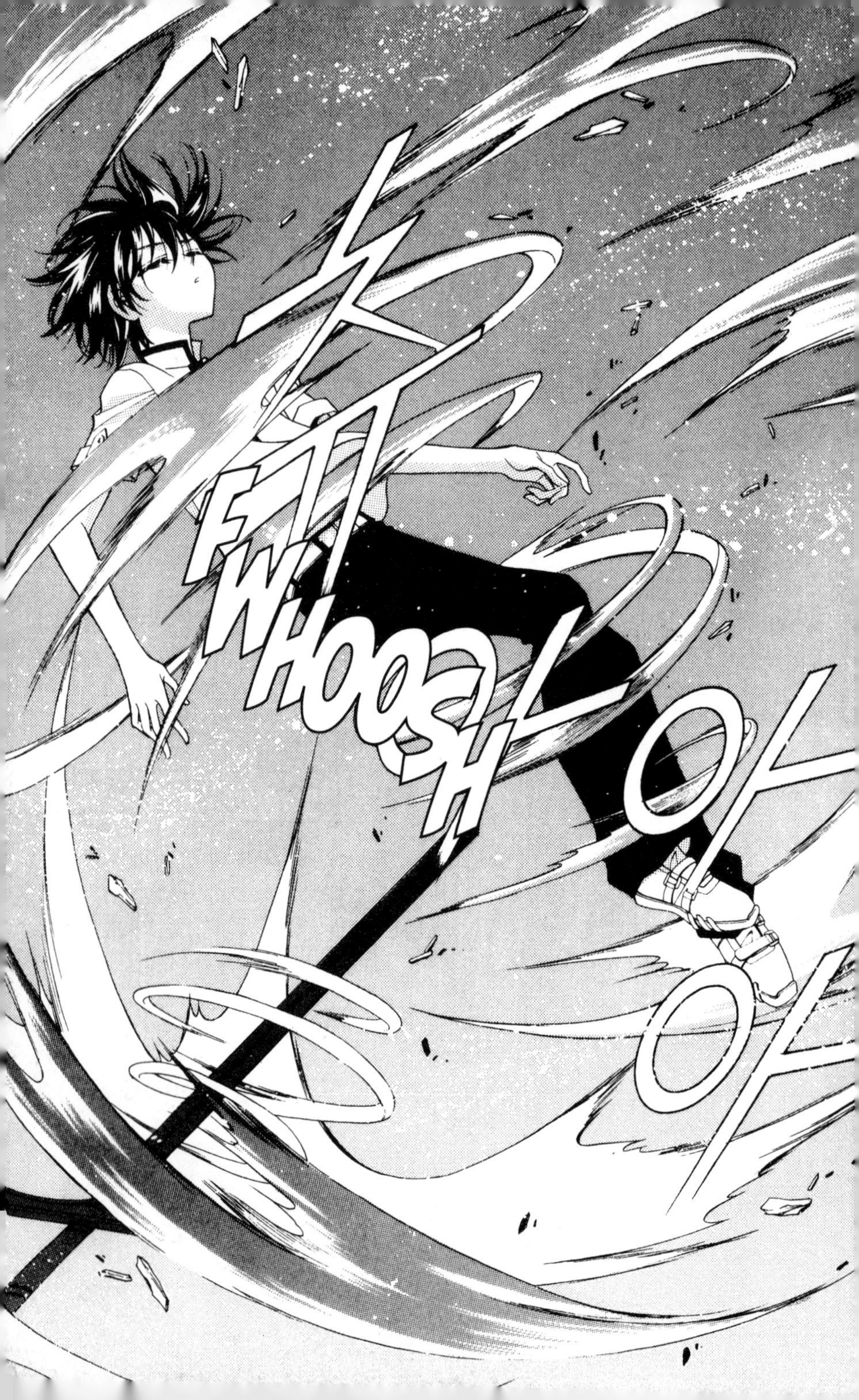
FWHOOSH

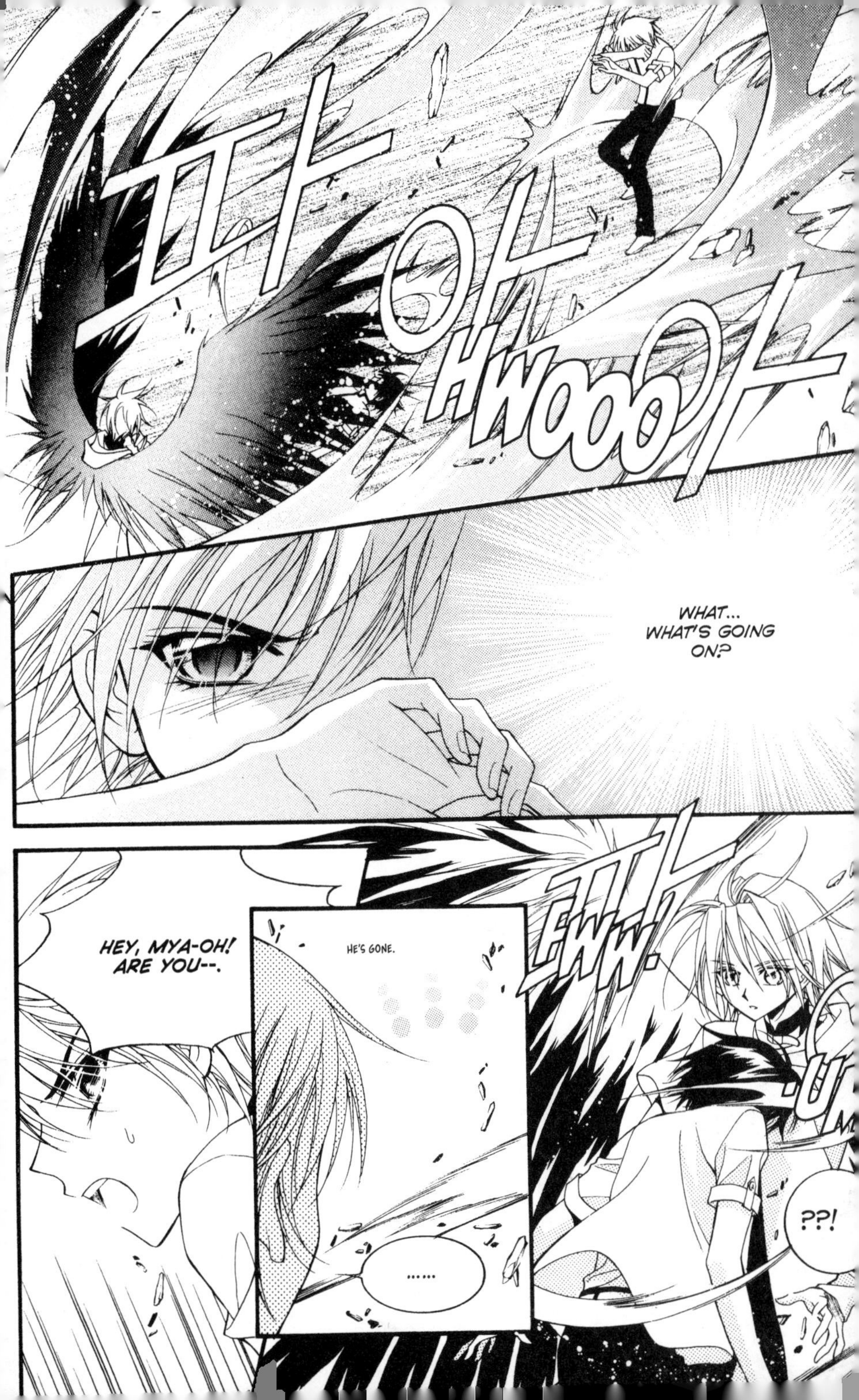
WHAT... WHAT'S GOING ON?
HEY, MYA-OH! ARE YOU--.
HE'S GONE.
......
??!

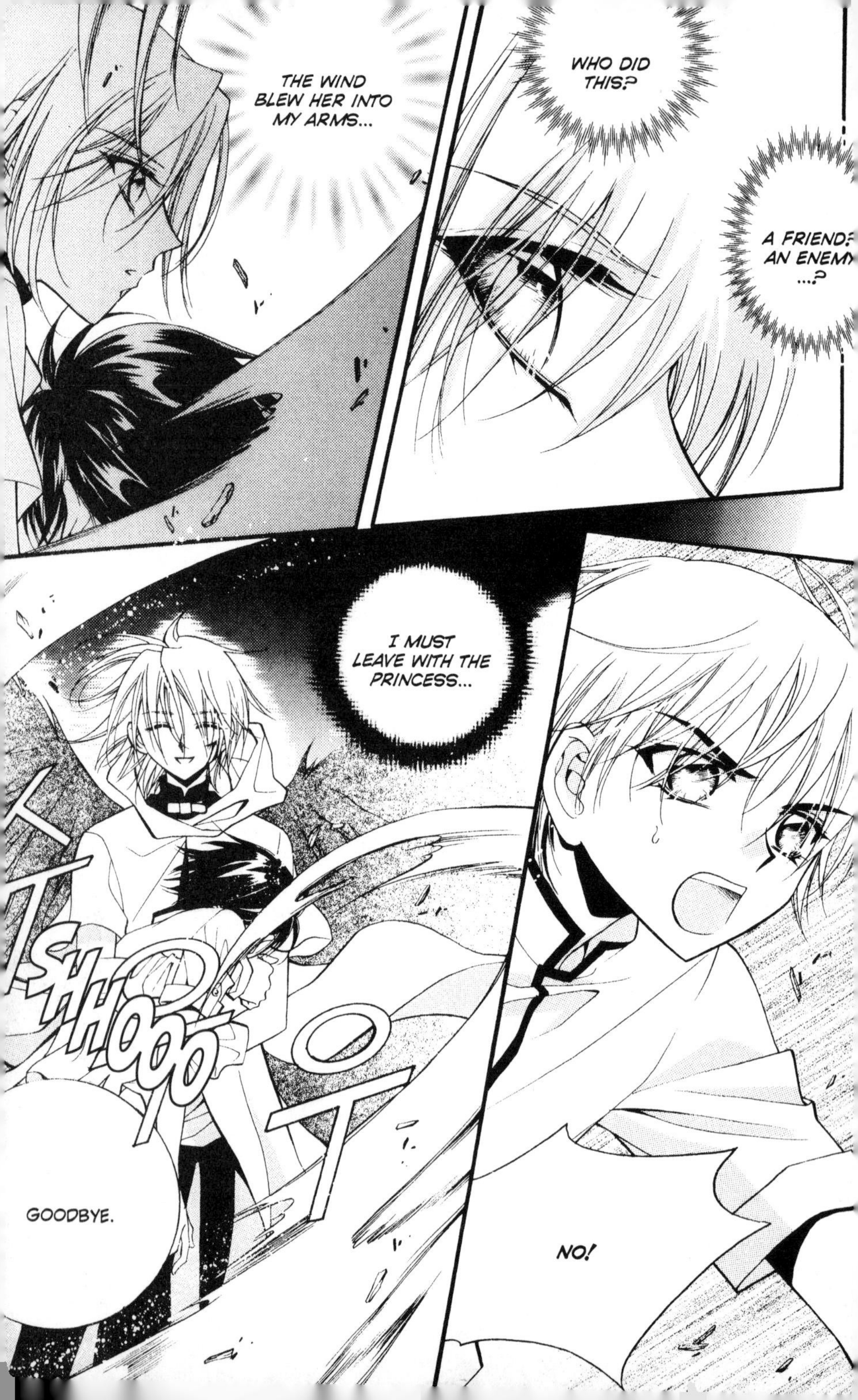
THE WIND BLEW HER INTO MY ARMS...
WHO DID THIS?
A FRIEND? AN ENEMY ...?
I MUST LEAVE WITH THE PRINCESS...
SHHOOOT
GOODBYE.
NO!

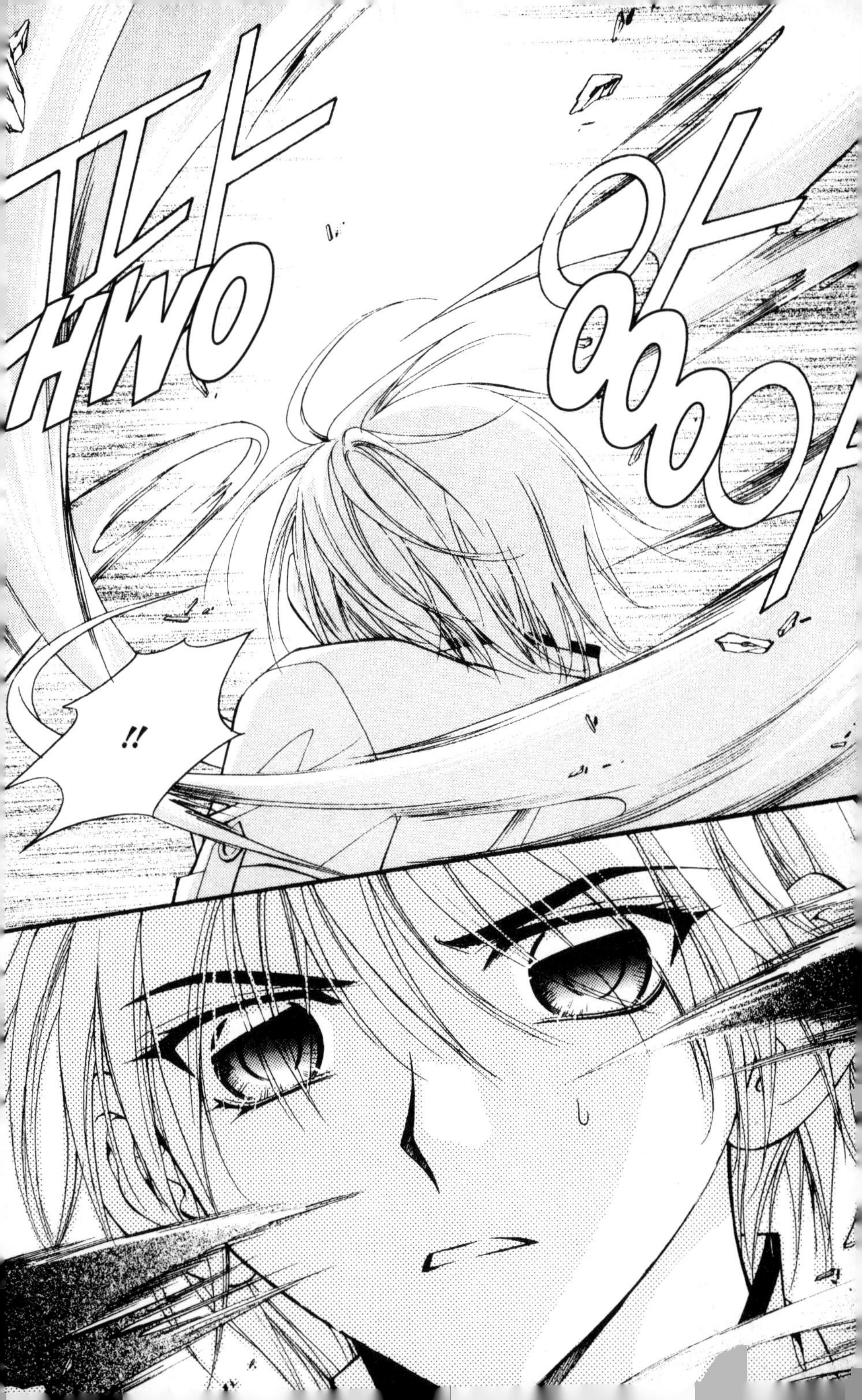
!!

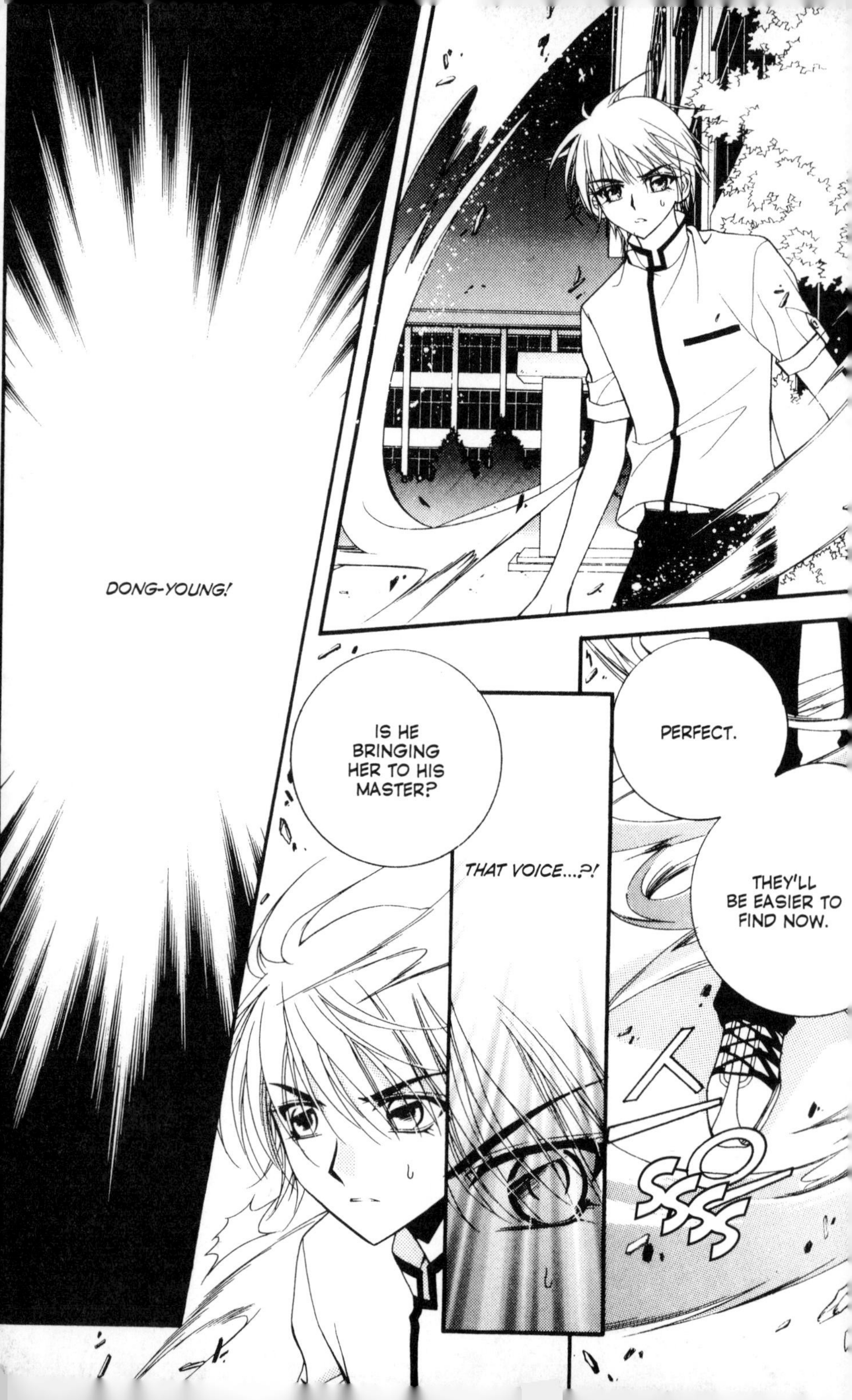
DONG-YOUNG!
IS HE BRINGING HER TO HIS MASTER?
THAT VOICE...?!
PERFECT.
THEY'LL BE EASIER TO FIND NOW.
SSS

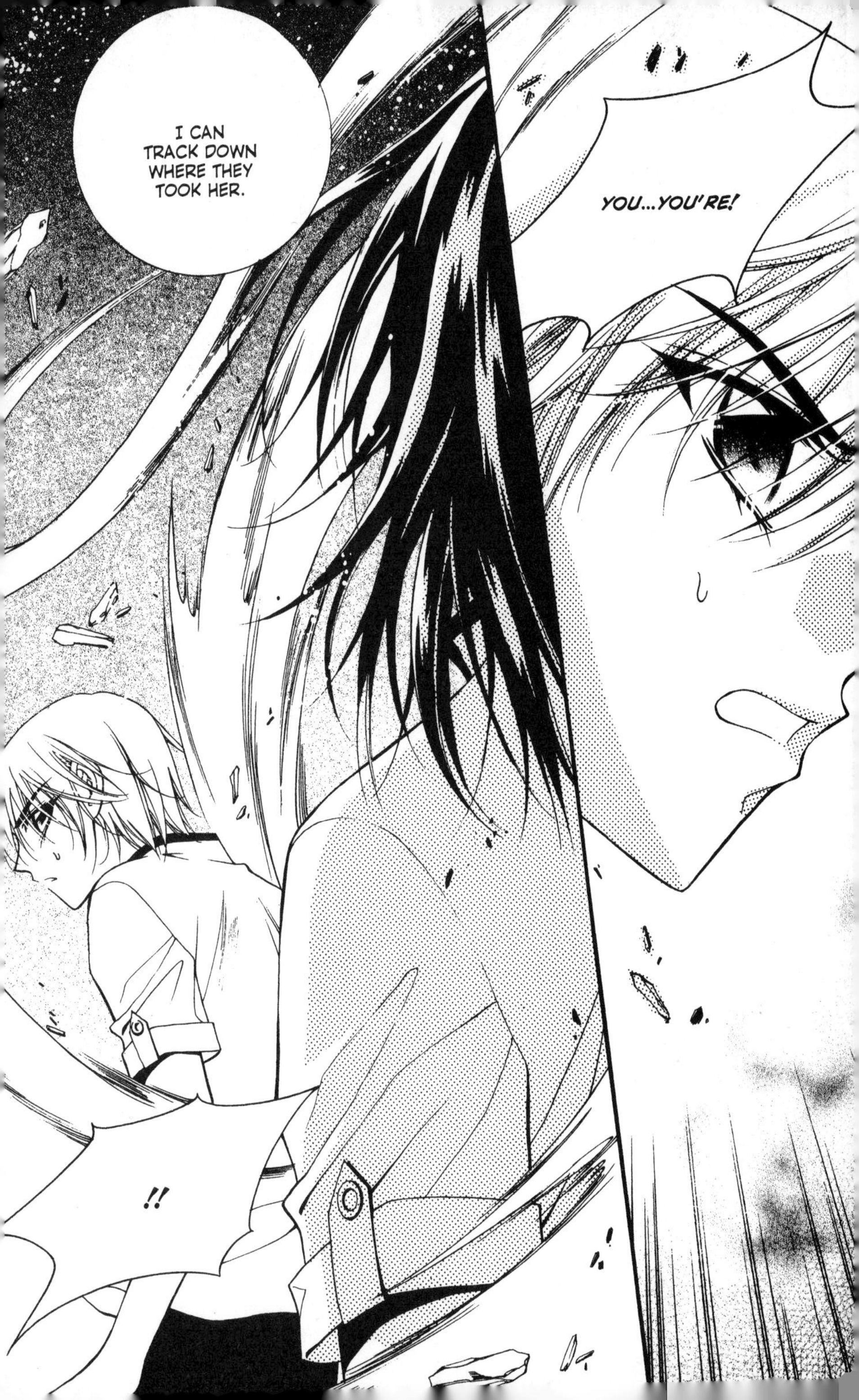
I CAN TRACK DOWN WHERE THEY TOOK HER.
YOU...YOU'RE!
!!

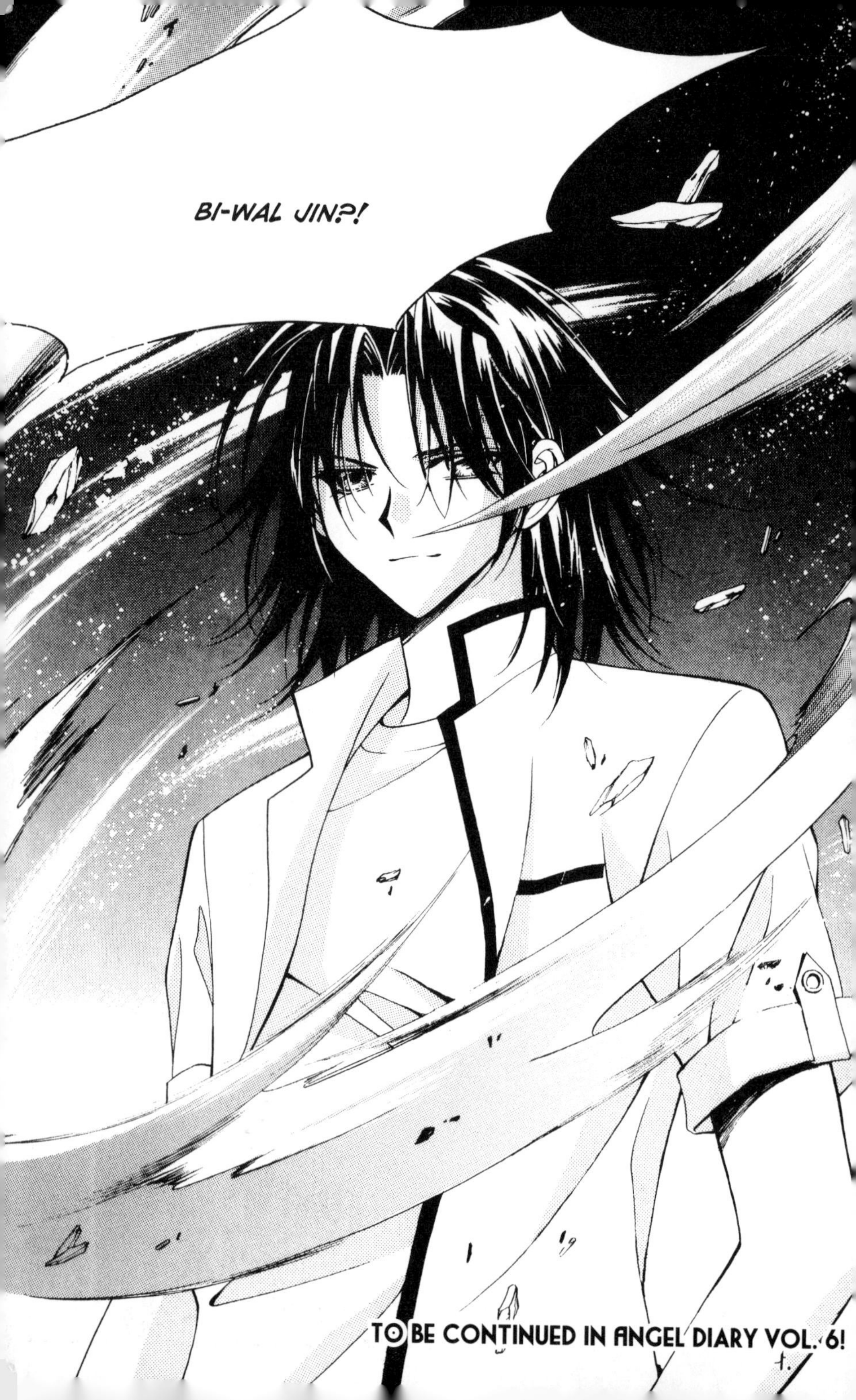
BI-WAL JIN?!
TO BE CONTINUED IN ANGEL DIARY VOL. 6!

THE FOUR GUARDIANS

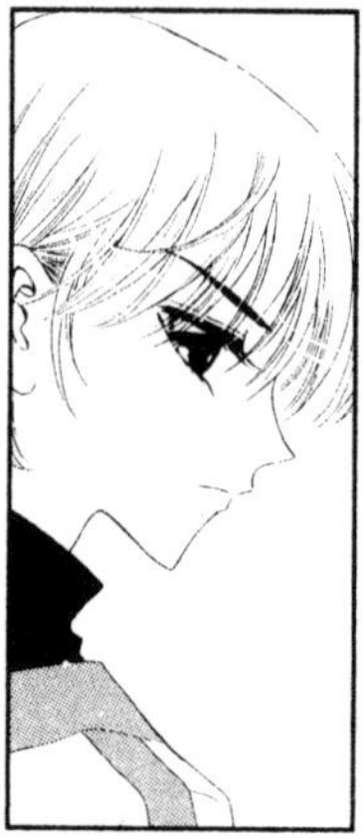

BLACK TURTLE

THE BLACK TURTLE GUARDS THE NORTHERN BORDERS OF HEAVEN. HE USES THE BLACK TURTLE SWORD, WHICH CAN TRANSFORM INTO SHA-OH, THE MINI TURTLE MASCOT.

HE LEADS THE FOUR GUARDIANS. HIS SWORDSMANSHIP SKILLS ARE LOWER THAN THE WHITE TIGER AND HIS SPELL CASTING IS LOWER THAN THE RED PHOENIX. HOWEVER, THE BLACK TURTLE IS QUITE PROFICIENT AND VERY BALANCED IN BOTH SKILLS, SO HE IS THE MOST POWERFUL AMONG THEM.

THE PREVIOUS BLACK TURTLE AND THE PREVIOUS BLUE DRAGON WERE FRIENDS. THE CURRENT BLACK TURTLE IS THE COUSIN OF THE CURRENT BLUE DRAGON.

HIS COLOR IS BLACK.

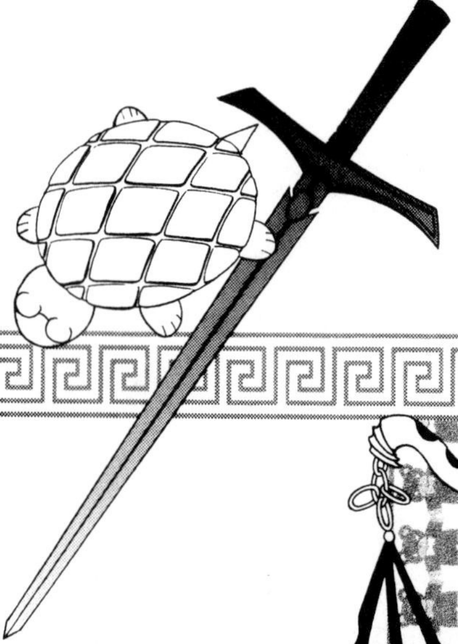

BLUE DRAGON

THE BLUE DRAGON GUARDS THE EASTERN BORDER OF HEAVEN. HE USES THE BLUE DRAGON SWORD, WHICH CAN TRANSFORM INTO PA-EE, THE MINI LIZARD-LIKE DRAGON MASCOT.

HE USUALLY USES HIS SWORD, BUT SOMETIMES HE USES SPELLS. HOWEVER, THE BLUE DRAGON ONLY HAS A BASIC KNOWLEDGE IN CASTING SPELLS. HE GREW UP WITH HIS COUSIN THE BLACK TURTLE.

HIS COLOR IS BLUE.

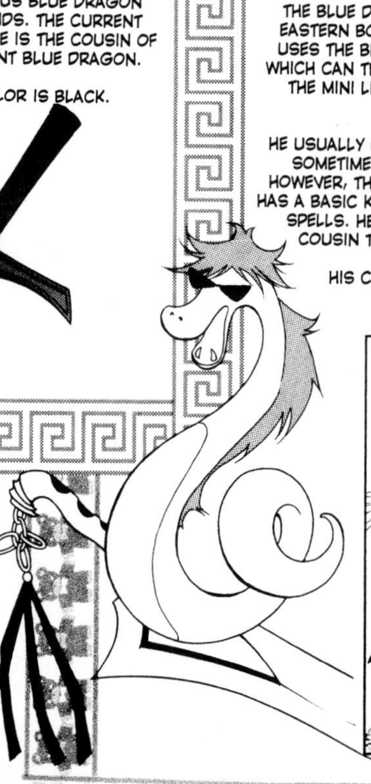

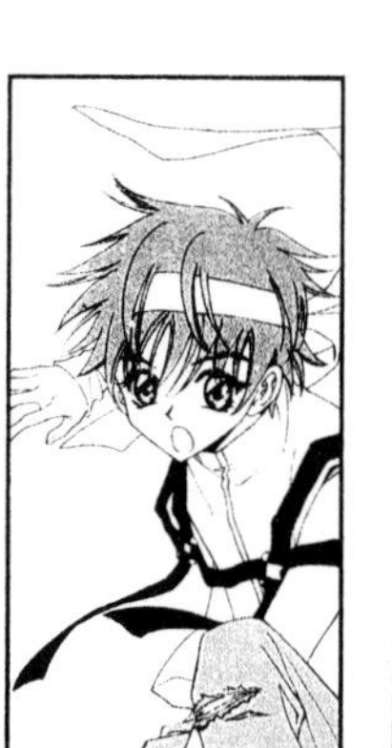

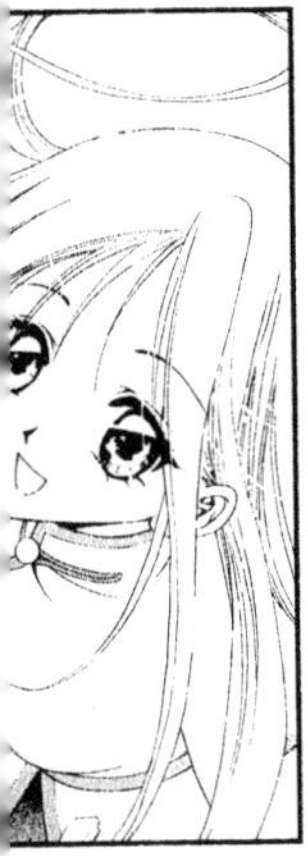

WHITE TIGER

THE WHITE TIGER GUARDS THE WESTERN BORDER OF HEAVEN. SHE USES THE WHITE DRAGON SWORD, WHICH CAN TRANSFORM INTO MI-NYANG, THE MINI CAT-LIKE TIGER MASCOT.

SHE COMES FROM A FAMILY WITH A LONG LINE OF WARRIORS, SO HER SWORDSMANSHIP IS EXCELLENT. HOWEVER, SHE'S TERRIBLE AT CASTING SPELLS.

SHE IS AN ILLEGITIMATE CHILD, SO SHE WAS NEVER MEANT TO BE A SUCCESSOR OF THE WHITE TIGER. BUT BECAUSE HER HALF BROTHER BECAME THE RED PHOENIX, AND BECAUSE OF HER FORMIDABLE SWORD TECHNIQUE, SHE BECAME THE WHITE TIGER.

SHE IS DATING THE BLUE DRAGON.

HER COLOR IS WHITE.

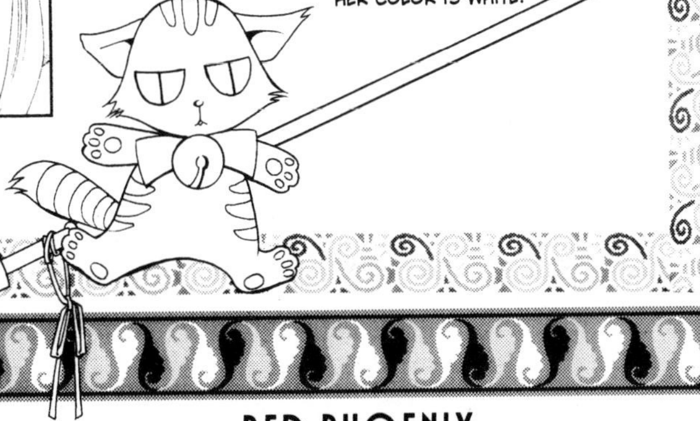

RED PHOENIX

THE RED PHOENIX GUARDS THE SOUTHERN BORDER OF HEAVEN. HE WIELDS THE RED PHOENIX SWORD WHICH CAN TRANSFORM INTO SU-EE, THE SPARROW-LIKE RED PHOENIX MASCOT. HOWEVER, HE DOESN'T USE THE SWORD MUCH. INSTEAD, HE USES THE SCROLL, ANOTHER TRANSFORMER OF SU-EE, TO CAST SPELLS.

THE RED PHOENIX IS THE BEST SPELLCASTER OUT OF THE FOUR GUARDIANS. HE'S ALSO THE SON OF THE PREVIOUS WHITE TIGER AND PREVIOUS RED PHOENIX. WHEN IT WAS REVEALED THAT HIS FATHER HAD HAD AN AFFAIR, HIS MOTHER TOOK HIM TO THE LAND OF THE RED PHOENIX WHERE HE BECAME A SUCCESSOR TO THE RED PHOENIX.

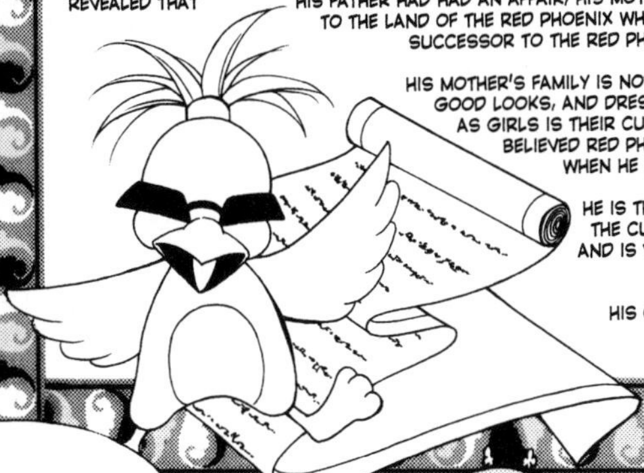

HIS MOTHER'S FAMILY IS NOTORIOUS FOR THEIR GOOD LOOKS, AND DRESSING YOUNG BOYS AS GIRLS IS THEIR CUSTOM. MANY PEOPLE BELIEVED RED PHOENIX WAS A GIRL WHEN HE WAS YOUNGER.

HE IS THE HALF BROTHER OF THE CURRENT WHITE TIGER, AND IS VERY PROTECTIVE OF HER.

HIS COLOR IS RED.

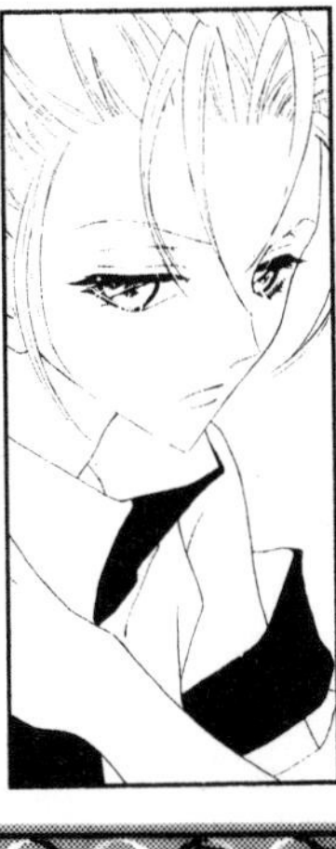

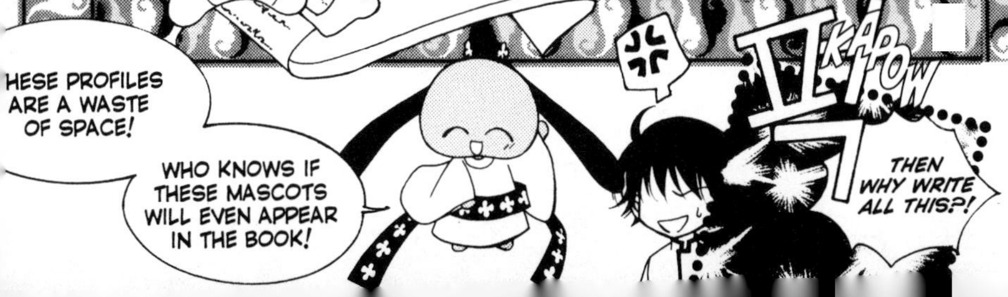
HESE PROFILES ARE A WASTE OF SPACE!
WHO KNOWS IF THESE MASCOTS WILL EVEN APPEAR IN THE BOOK!
KAPOW
THEN WHY WRITE ALL THIS?!

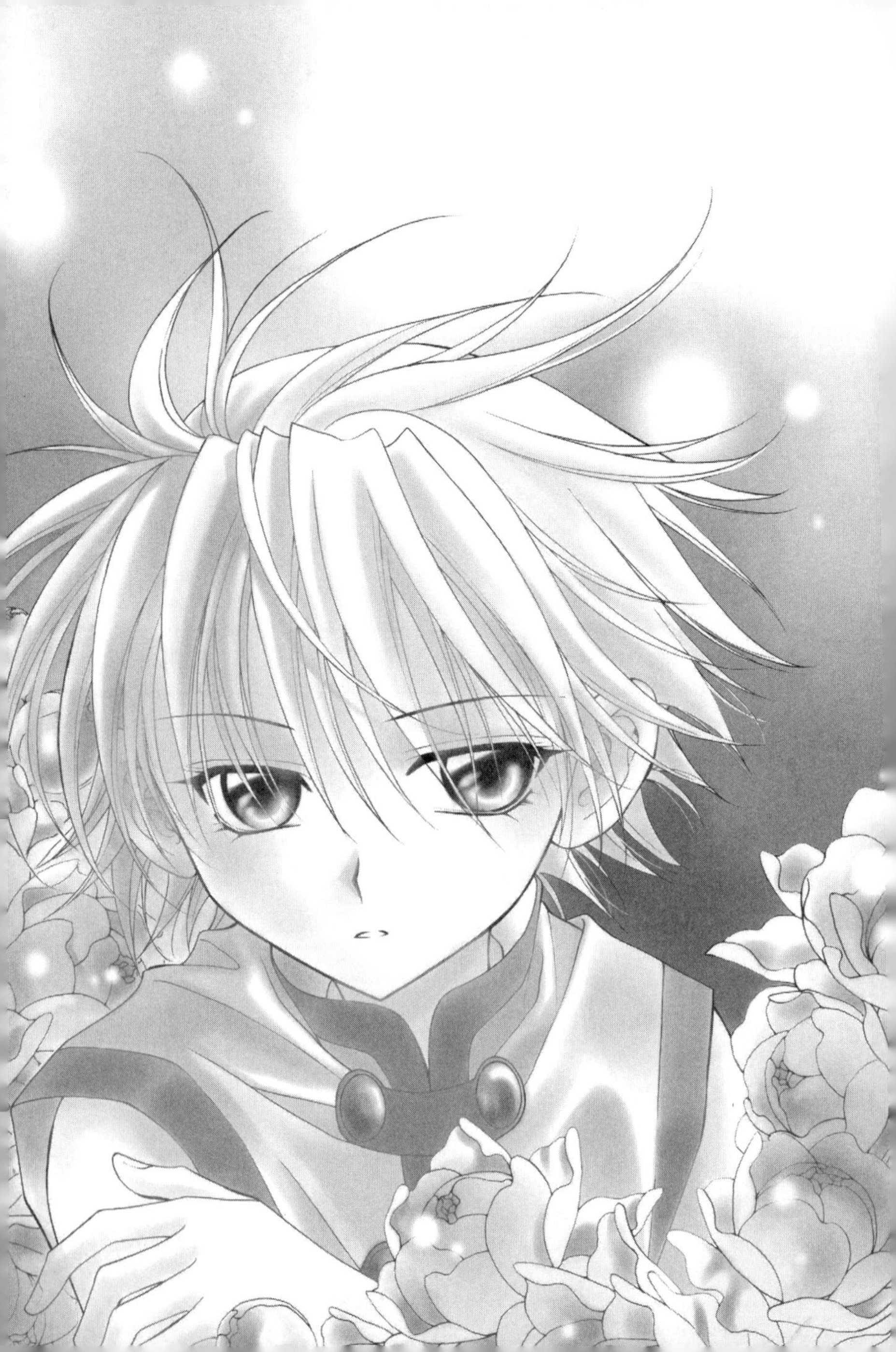

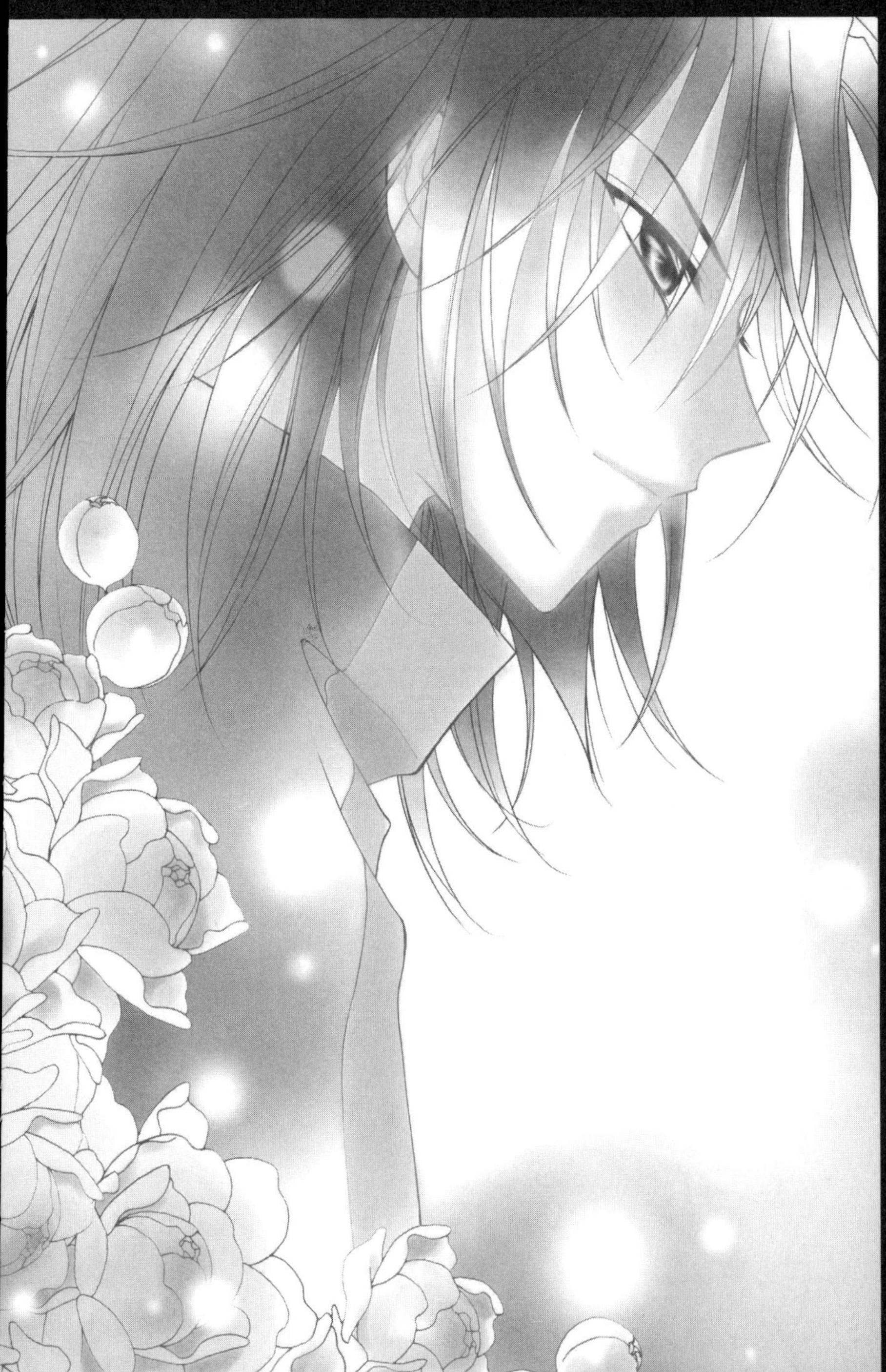

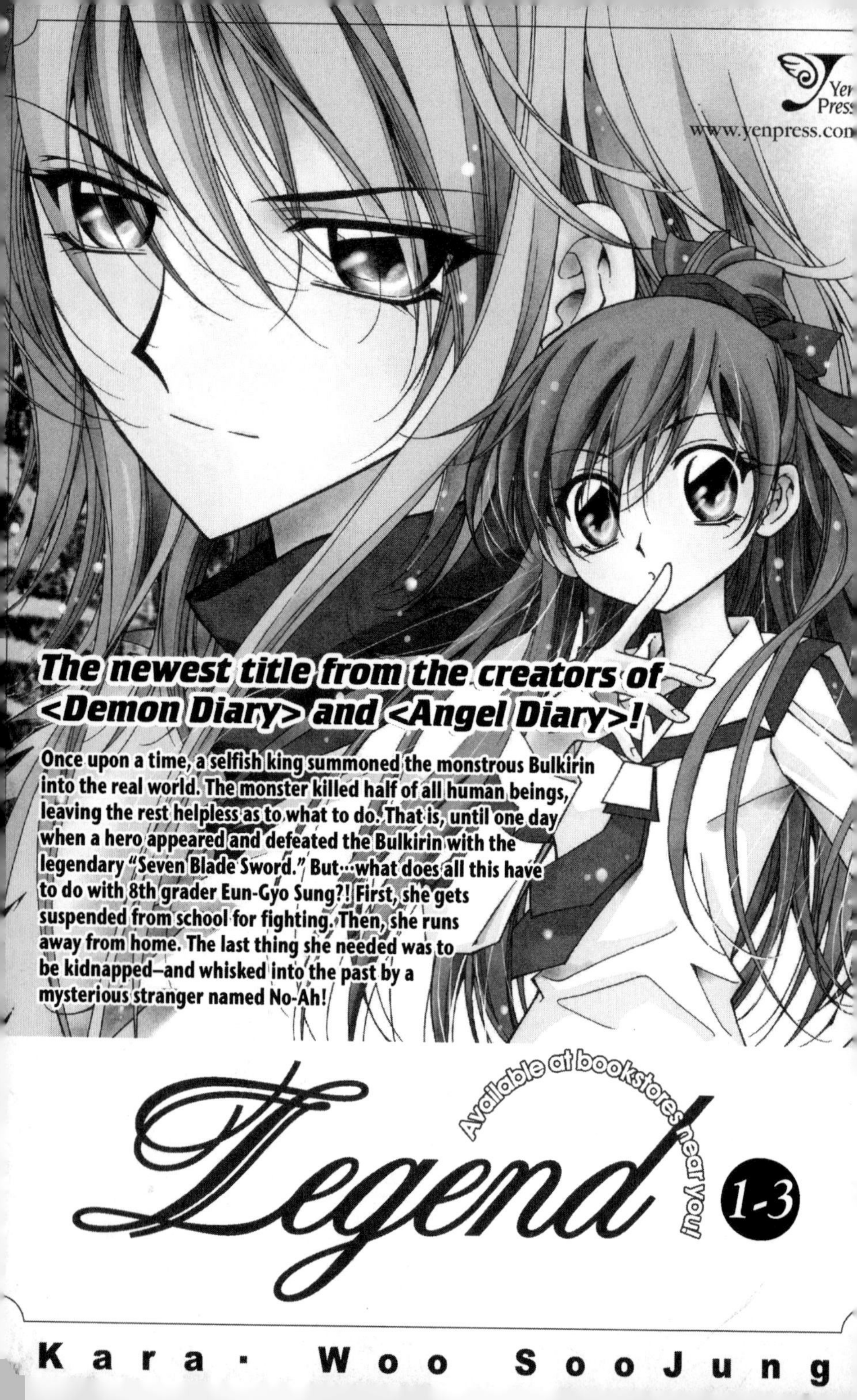
Yen Press
www.yenpress.com
The newest title from the creators of <Demon Diary> and <Angel Diary>!
Once upon a time, a selfish king summoned the monstrous Bulkirin into the real world. The monster killed half of all human beings, leaving the rest helpless as to what to do. That is, until one day when a hero appeared and defeated the Bulkirin with the legendary "Seven Blade Sword." But…what does all this have to do with 8th grader Eun-Gyo Sung?! First, she gets suspended from school for fighting. Then, she runs away from home. The last thing she needed was to be kidnapped–and whisked into the past by a mysterious stranger named No-Ah!
Legend
Available at bookstores near you!
1-3
Kara · Woo SooJung

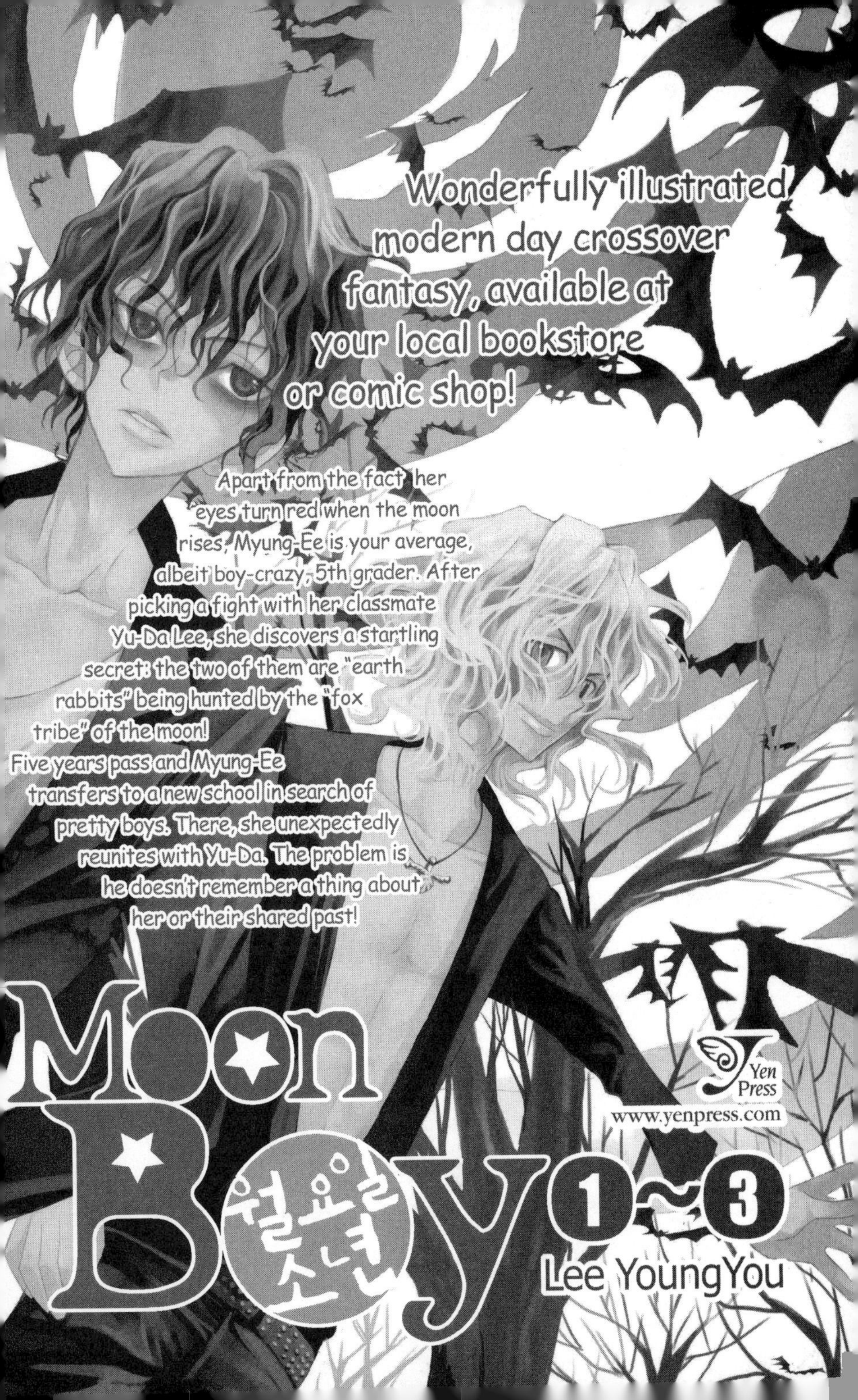
Wonderfully illustrated modern day crossover fantasy, available at your local bookstore or comic shop!
Apart from the fact her eyes turn red when the moon rises, Myung-Ee is your average, albeit boy-crazy, 5th grader. After picking a fight with her classmate Yu-Da Lee, she discovers a startling secret: the two of them are "earth rabbits" being hunted by the "fox tribe" of the moon! Five years pass and Myung-Ee transfers to a new school in search of pretty boys. There, she unexpectedly reunites with Yu-Da. The problem is he doesn't remember a thing about her or their shared past!
Moon Boy 1~3
월요일 소년
Lee YoungYou
Yen Press
www.yenpress.com

What will happen when a tomboy meets a bishonen?

Tomboy Mi-ha is an extremely active and competitive girl who hates to lose. She's such a tomboy that boys fear her—exactly the way her evil brother wanted and trained her to be. It took him six long years to transform her into this pseudo-military style girl in order to protect her from anyone else.

Bishonen Seung-suh is a new transfer student who's got the looks, the charm, and the desire to sweep her off her feet. Will this male beauty be able to tame the beast? Will the evil brother of the beast let them be together and live happily ever after? Bring it on!

Available at bookstores near you!

Bring it on! 1~5 FINAL

Baek HyeKyung

Yen Press
www.yenpress.com

Available at bookstores near you!

CHOCOLAT
1~5
Shin JiSang · Geo

Kum-ji was a little late getting under the spell of the chart-topping band, DDL. Unable to join the DDL fan club, she almost gives up on meeting her idols, until she develops a cunning plan–to become a member of a rival fan club for the brand-new boy band Yo-I. This way she can act as Yo-I's fan club member and also be near Yo-I,

How far would you go to meet your favorite boy band?

who always seem to be in the same shows as DDL. Perfect plan...except being a fanatic is a lot more complicated than she expects. Especially when you're actually a fan of someone else. This full-blown love comedy about a fan club will make you laugh, cry, and laugh some more.

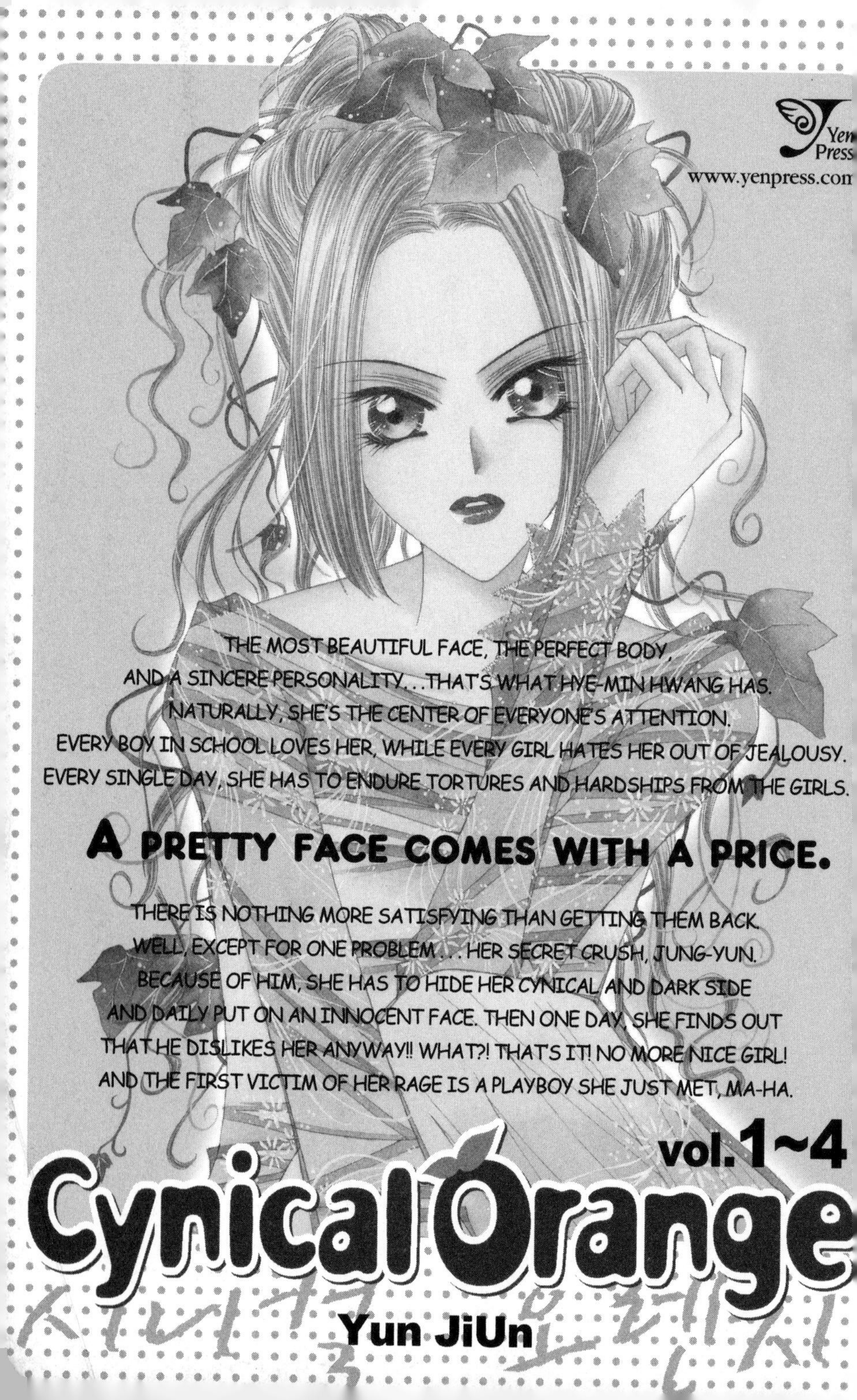
Yen Press
www.yenpress.com
THE MOST BEAUTIFUL FACE, THE PERFECT BODY,
AND A SINCERE PERSONALITY. . .THAT'S WHAT HYE-MIN HWANG HAS.
NATURALLY, SHE'S THE CENTER OF EVERYONE'S ATTENTION.
EVERY BOY IN SCHOOL LOVES HER, WHILE EVERY GIRL HATES HER OUT OF JEALOUSY.
EVERY SINGLE DAY, SHE HAS TO ENDURE TORTURES AND HARDSHIPS FROM THE GIRLS.
A PRETTY FACE COMES WITH A PRICE.
THERE IS NOTHING MORE SATISFYING THAN GETTING THEM BACK.
WELL, EXCEPT FOR ONE PROBLEM . . . HER SECRET CRUSH, JUNG-YUN.
BECAUSE OF HIM, SHE HAS TO HIDE HER CYNICAL AND DARK SIDE
AND DAILY PUT ON AN INNOCENT FACE. THEN ONE DAY, SHE FINDS OUT
THAT HE DISLIKES HER ANYWAY!! WHAT?! THAT'S IT! NO MORE NICE GIRL!
AND THE FIRST VICTIM OF HER RAGE IS A PLAYBOY SHE JUST MET, MA-HA.
vol. 1~4
Cynical Orange
Yun JiUn

Sometimes, just being a teenager is hard enough.

Da-Eh, an aspiring manhwa artist who lives with her father and her little brother, comes across Sun-Nam, a softie whose ultimate goal is simply to become a "Tough guy." Whenever these two meet, trouble follows. Meanwhile, Ta-Jun, the hottest guy in town, finds himself drawn to the one girl that his killer smile does not work on–Da-Eh. With their complicated family history hanging on their shoulders, watch how these three teenagers find their way out into the world!

HISSING

앙상

1~4

Available at bookstores near you!

Kang EunYoung

Totally new Arabian nights, where Shahrazad is a guy!

Everyone knows the story of Shahrazad and her wonderful tales from the Arabian Nights. For one thousand and one nights, the stories that she created entertained the mad Sultan and eventually saved her life. In this version, Shahrazad is a guy who wanted to save his sister from the mad Sultan by disguising himself as a woman. When he puts his life on the line, what kind of strange and unique stories would he tell? This new twist on one of the greatest classical tales might just keep you awake for another ONE THOUSAND AND ONE NIGHTS.

Available at bookstores near you!

One thousand and one nights 1~4

Han SeungHee · Jeon JinSeok

The Antique Gift Shop 1~4

Lee Eun

Available at bookstores near you!

Yen Press

www.yenpress.com

CAN YOU FEEL THE SOULS OF THE ANTIQUES? DO YOU BELIEVE?

Did you know that an antique possesses a soul of its own?
The Antique Gift Shop specializes in such items that charm and captivate the buyers they are destined to belong to. Guided by a mysterious and charismatic shopkeeper, the enchanted relics lead their new owners on a journey into an alternate cosmic universe to their true destinies.
Eerily bittersweet and dolefully melancholy, The Antique Gift Shop opens up a portal to a world where torn lovers unite, broken friendships are mended, and regrets are resolved. Can you feel the power of the antiques?

Angel Diary vol. 5

Story by YunHee Lee
Art by Kara

Translation: HyeYoung Im
English Adaptation: J. Torres
Lettering: Terri Delgado · Marshall Dillon

ANGEL DIARY, Vol. 5 © 2003 Kara · YunHee Lee. All rights reserved. First published in Korea in 2003 by Sigongsa Co., Ltd.

Yen Press
Hachette Book Group USA
237 Park Avenue, New York, NY 10017

Visit our Web sites at www.HachetteBookGroupUSA.com and www.YenPress.com.

Yen Press is an imprint of Hachette Book Group USA, Inc. The Yen Press name and logo are trademarks of Hachette Book Group USA, Inc.

First English Printing: December 2006
First Yen Press Edition: July 2008

ISBN-10: 89-527-4611-2
ISBN-13: 978-89-527-4611-5

10 9 8 7 6 5 4 3 2

BVG

Printed in the United States of America